Educational Theory and Practice in St. Augustine

Educational Theory and Practice in St. Augustine

George Howie M.A. M.Ed. Ph.D.

LONDON
Routledge & Kegan Paul

First published in 1969
by Routledge & Kegan Paul Ltd
Broadway House, 68-74 Carter Lane
London, E.C.4

Printed in Great Britain
by C. Tinling and Co Ltd
Liverpool, London and Prescot

SBN 7100 6046 7

Contents

Preface

This study of the educational thought and practice of St. Augustine is inspired by the belief that, in spite of the complex and unique problems of education in our age of technological advance and nuclear menace, the essential features of human life are the same today as they were yesterday. If this is so, the most penetrating thought on the aims and methods of education, irrespective of its age, should shed light on the problems with which we have to grapple today.

The author shares Aristotle's view that education is a practical art, the purpose of which is to enrich human life by exploiting the resources of wisdom and sensitivity which are latent in everyone. In fact St. Augustine stimulates us to look at education from both the idealistic and the practical, or pragmatic, standpoints. From the one we study the general principles gathered by St. Augustine from his long experience of self-education and from his intellectual search into the domain of spiritual reality. From the other we find that the educational principles, declared by St. Augustine and verified in his own experience, will work for us, as they did for him. Although we live in a very different world, it is still inhabited by people of the same essential nature as those who walked the busy streets of the Carthage, Rome and Milan of his time.

This book is a study of the art of teaching with reference to the thinking of one who was deeply interested in education as a fundamental human activity. What St. Augustine has to say about teaching and learning, springing as it does from his personal experience, should have something of value to say to our teachers of today and all who are interested in revitalising education so that it can more effectively lead man to what St. Augustine calls 'the happy life'.

The debt owed to St. Augustine as a formative spirit in the development of educational thought has received too little recognition by modern educational theorists. But certain significant strands of theory, e.g. perennialism and essentialism, are clearly in the tradition of St. Augustine and express his ideals. He is of course the leader of those who see absolute truth as the proper goal of the human understanding and oppose the relativist philosophies which seem to gather momentum in the twentieth century. Like ourselves, St. Augustine lived in an age of human crisis darkened by storms of barbarism. Yet his outlook, founded on supreme confidence in man's capacity to understand himself and his divine destiny, is characteristically optimistic. With his trust in wisdom as the highest value and in the human intelligence as an educative instrument of great power, St. Augustine provides a challenge to our age of doubt and confusion.

The author desires to record with gratitude his debt to the personal inspiration and writings of the late Dr. S. J. Curtis, who as Senior Lecturer and later Reader in Education at the University of Leeds first attracted the author's attention to St. Augustine and whose advice was of great help in the writing of this book. Thanks are also due to the author's wife and family for the forbearance they showed during the years of preparation and the practical help they gave at various stages of the project.

GEORGE HOWIE

University of Sydney
March, 1968

Augustine	*Do you regard understanding as anything other than a good thing?*
Evodius	*I regard it as such a good thing that I cannot see that man can possess anything more excellent. I could never admit that it is bad to understand anything.*
Augustine	*Then if understanding is entirely good and is the necessary result of learning, everyone who learns is doing a good thing—So do not look for an evil teacher. If a man is evil, then he is not a teacher. If he is a teacher, then he is not evil.*

The Free Will i, 3.

1 The Self-Education of the Teacher

Thou dost rouse us up to find our delight in praising Thee because Thou has made us for Thyself and our hearts are restless until they find their rest in Thee.

Confessions i, 1.

The life and work of St. Augustine form the last and most distinguished chapter in the tale of Roman North Africa's outstanding contribution to Latin thought and letters. His thought and his whole life bring a fitting climax to a scene which was soon to be darkened by the gathering clouds of the barbarian invasion destined to end the seemingly indestructible Empire. At the time of Augustine's birth the gathering storm cloud passed almost unheeded by those who were engrossed in the busy hum of the Empire's life. Seventy years later as he lay dying, Alaric had taken by storm and sacked the capital city of Rome, and the Vandals were beating on the walls of Augustine's episcopal seat of Hippo.

Aurelius Augustine was born in A.D. 354 on the Ides of November in the small town of Tagaste in the Roman province of Numidia Proconsularis. In the streets of the town could be seen the characteristic physical traits of the native Africans, but mingled with these were clear indications of the races who had visited the region, either as friends or foes, in the course of the centuries—Phoenician, Greek, Jew and Roman. The virile African strain had easily absorbed them all, so that, as is still the case today, the area remained a distinctively African scene with only indistinct traces of other racial elements which had been drawn into its life and culture. The Africans, while for a time maintaining their own separate identity, had come to merge their native gods with those of the Roman pantheon. Christianity had quickly advanced among those whose first allegiance was to Latin culture; the native Africans themselves were scarcely affected by it and retained their devotion to their own and Punic paganism.

The family into which Augustine was born belonged to the middle class. The mother, Monica or Monnica, was a devoted Christian; the father, Patricius, was an unregenerate pagan both in faith and morals until his later years when he was somewhat uncertainly won over by the persistence of his wife. He held the office of *decurio* of Tagaste under the Roman administration, a title given to members of the senates of the municipalities and colonies. He also appears to have been a landowner in a small way;[1] if this is true, then in spite of his name he may have been a native Numidian, the settling of Roman veterans in North Africa having ceased two centuries before. From the pages of the *Confessions* of his son he stands out as endowed with a rough kindliness of character accompanied by a tendency to violent outbursts of anger. Yet Augustine speaks of him with some respect, and particularly commends him for the efforts he made to open the pathway of higher education for his son. Although only a 'poor freeman' he succeeded in sending Augustine to the School of Rhetoric in Carthage. 'Beyond his means', says Augustine, 'he furnished me with everything necessary for a long journey for the sake of my studies. Many citizens far more wealthy did not do such a thing for their children.'[2]

But St. Augustine's greatest debt was to his mother, whose force of character and Christian example were dynamic influences in his life. It is probable that she herself was of Libyan extraction, her name being derived from the Libyan deity, Mon, who was worshipped in the nearby town of Thibilis. She emerges in St. Augustine's *Confessions* as one who, like her son, had reached the serenity of faith only after a long course of spiritual travail. Compensating for the neglect of the father, she showed great concern for the spiritual instruction of her son: 'My tender young heart', says Augustine, 'had drunk in the name of Christ even with my mother's milk and held it deeply within me.'[3]

In the tradition of Roman education Monica taught her children at home, until they were of an age to attend the

[1] *Letter* 126, 7.
[2] *Confessions* ii, 3, 5.
[3] *ibid.* iii, 4, 8.

elementary school. But Augustine's recollections of his school-days were largely unhappy. He saw little point in his studies with the result that he found it difficult to concentrate and was frequently punished. In spite of this, however, he remarks on his natural delight in play. Looking back upon the frolics of childhood, he sees the spontaneous play activities of children as being comparable to the more serious business of adults:

> The trifling pursuits of grown-ups are called business, while those of children, which are of the same quality, are punished by them.[1]

STUDENT OF GRAMMAR AND RHETORIC

His elementary education completed, Augustine was sent to the grammar school at Madaura, twenty miles south of Tagaste, where he began the study of Latin and Greek literature. Here his studies were more congenial in spite of the fact that the discipline was only a little less rigorous than in the elementary school. He bears witness to his love of the poets, and in particular of Vergil. Episodes like the tragic love of Aeneas and Dido fascinated him, and in later years he tried to persuade himself of the vanity of such interests. Greek brought him less pleasure; he pays tribute to the genius of Homer, but the experience of reading him was spoiled by the hard and distasteful labour of learning a new language. The result was that he never fully succeeded in mastering Greek, and for this he blames the method by which the language was taught. The teaching failed to exploit the child's free curiosity, with the inevitable result that the lessons were characterised by 'a terrible coercion'.[2] Augustine tells us that he practised the usual stereotyped rhetorical exercises on pagan themes, all 'smoke and wind'. Undue importance was attached by the 'grammaticus' (teacher of grammar) to grammatical and syntactical accuracy and the

[1] *ibid.* i, 9, 15.

[2] *ibid.* i, 14, 23. In many places in his writings Augustine refers to and discusses Greek texts, but they were probably consulted in translation. In *The Trinity* iii, 1 and *Against the Letter of Petilian* ii, 38, he openly admits his poor knowledge of Greek; it is a striking example of the lasting effects of bad teaching in the impressionable years of childhood.

technique of making 'an eloquent and neat oration' without regard to the moral implications of the theme or the value of the conclusions reached. To this lack of concern for the moral outcomes of instruction Augustine attributes a further deterioration in his character. He reports that he told lies to his teachers, stole even from his father and was guilty of the sin of gluttony.[1]

In other respects residence in Madaura was not calculated to advance the moral and spiritual education of a young man inexperienced in the ways of the world and of a passionate temperament. Madaura's most famous son had been the pagan rhetorician, Lucius Apuleius Afer, whose fame had rested chiefly on a work of satire called *Metamorphoses*. But he had also been known as 'the Platonic philosopher' because of his successful efforts in bolstering up the practice of paganism with the philosophy of Plato.[2] Although there were Christians in Madaura, they were outnumbered by the pagans, whose worship of the Phoenician gods, such as Mars, whose naked statue adorned the forum of the city, impressed the young man from Tagaste. The pagan atmosphere of the town reached its crescendo in the annual Day of the Bacchanals, when leading citizens played their part in scenes of unrestrained licence.[3] Yet in its quieter moments Madaura was a centre of cultivated paganism, in which it was possible for Augustine to absorb the best of the Latin spirit. If residence there did not strengthen his Christian belief, at least it gave him experience of both the best and the worst expressions of pagan culture, criteria against which he could test both the Christian claims and the criticisms levelled against them.

The next episode in Augustine's life was destructive but fortunately brief. At the beginning of his sixteenth year he returned to Tagaste, where he lived in idleness for a year, while his father gathered the funds necessary to send his son to the School of Rhetoric at Carthage. In the *Confessions* he bemoans

[1] *Confessions* i, 19, 30.

[2] Afer had flourished in the middle of the Second Century A.D. His reputation as a Platonic philosopher rested on two works, the one *Concerning the God of Socrates* and the other *Concerning Plato and his Dogma*. See J. E. Sandys, *History of Classical Scholarship* (Cambridge, 1903) vol. i, pp. 310–11.

[3] P. Alfaric, *L'Évolution intellectuelle de St. Augustin*, vol. 1. Also V. J. Bourke, *Augustine's Quest for Wisdom*, p. 71.

the delinquent tendencies of this wasted year. He portrays himself as roaming the streets of Tagaste with his friends. The adolescent need to live up to the expectations of his fellows led him to the commission of petty crimes. It was at this period that he committed a sin, which seems comparatively insignificant but which haunted him all his life because of the motive, or rather lack of motive, which produced it. Late one night with some of his comrades he went to an orchard with the intention of robbing a pear tree. Having helped themselves lavishly to the fruit, they carried it off, but, not being really hungry, they threw most of it to the hogs. The robbery had been wantonly committed. It had not been done even to gratify hunger but merely 'through a hatred of righteousness and an excess of iniquity'.[1] The motive was not simply the enjoyment of the fruit but something more insidious, the enjoyment of the crime itself; it was an example of the moral degradation which consists in the love of destruction for the sake of destruction. But the strength of the attack of conscience which followed shows the true sensitivity of Augustine's nature. The effect of the experience was one which remained vividly in his mind in the ensuing years and played its part in directing the long, difficult course of his spiritual wanderings.

At the age of seventeen the young Augustine arrived in Carthage to undertake the second stage of his education. It was now clear that his destiny was to subject him to still more difficult trials of strength. The city appeared to him as 'a cauldron full of abominable loves', which 'crackled' around him.[2] It was a city in which Christianity was then strongly entrenched. But the Christians were too occupied with theological differences among themselves, and particularly with the controversy between the Catholic and Donatist parties, to concern themselves with the pagan masses and the blatant idolatry which surrounded them. Magicians and fortune-tellers plied their profitable trades at every street corner.[3] It was a city given over to the pleasures of the amphitheatre and to the worst excesses of the stage, a city engrossed with 'shams and shadows'. Among the spectacles, which the streets had to offer, were the

[1] *Confessions* ii, 4, 9.
[2] *ibid.* iii, 1, 1.
[3] *ibid.* iv, 3, 4.

lewd ceremonies in honour of the pagan gods and goddesses, dances of prostitutes around the statues of the Goddess of Heaven and processions in honour of the oriental Cybele, the mother of the Gods.[1]

Within the rhetoric school, in which he was established, the frank and amiable nature of Augustine made him popular among his fellow students but, as at Tagaste, this served to increase the temptations which crowded upon him. With true insight into the adolescent mind he sees that it was simply the desire to find an object to which he could attach his love which caused him to indulge in so many vain and unprofitable searchings. But always love passed into lust and 'defiled the pure springs of friendship with the filth of uncleanness'.[2] In whatever light he views himself from the later standpoint of the *Confessions*, Augustine was clearly a youth of basically good intentions, delighting in the companionship of friends and with considerable intellectual gifts. He distinguished himself in the 'windy exercises' of the rhetoric school. Of the books set for study one in particular laid hold upon his mind, the *Hortensius* of Cicero,[3] in which the great orator exhorted his friend Hortensius to pursue the life of philosophy as being a superior ideal to that which makes rhetoric the highest exercise of the faculties of man. In this book Augustine at last found one which engrossed him, not primarily for its beauty of style, but for its intellectual content. Its intellectual appeal lay in the fact that the book did not try to attach the reader to any one school of thought but simply stressed the value in human life of free but disciplined thought.[4] Its aim was not to communicate a philosophy but to commend the exercise of philosophising as an indispensable adjunct to the good life. This encounter of St. Augustine with Cicero marks the first clear advance in his spiritual progress which eventually brought him to total commitment to Christ. As to his Christian observances at the time, Augustine makes it clear that he had not severed his connection

[1] *City of God* ii, 4.

[2] *Confessions* iii, 1, 1.

[3] *ibid.* iii, 4, 7. Also *Soliloquies* i, 17 and *The Happy Life* 4.

[4] *Confessions* iii, 4, 8: I was delighted by the *Hortensius*, because its words stimulated me not to love, seek and embrace this sect or that but merely to follow wisdom itself, whatever that might be.

with the Church but that he performed his duties in a formal and perfunctory way.

THE MANICHAEAN PERIOD

It was in the second year of his residence at Carthage that Augustine took a mistress, to whom, as he tells us, he was faithful for twelve years and who bore him his son, Adeodatus.[1] In the same year he undertook another commitment of considerable importance in the chronicle of his spiritual development. Much to his mother's grief he became an auditor in the sect of the Manichaeans of which he was to remain an adherent for nine years.

The sect was named after the prophet, Mani, who was said to have been born at Ecbatana in the second decade of the third century A.D. and to have attempted to reconcile the Mithraic religion of the East with the doctrines of Christianity.[2] From the earlier half of the fourth century, the teachings of his followers began to exercise an important influence throughout the Roman Empire and in the latter half of the century constituted a distinct threat to the progress of Christianity. Their scriptures consisted of five writings of Mani headed by the *Epistola Fundamenti*, which dealt with the origin, present condition and future destiny of the universe.

Central to the Manichaean belief was the dualism (fundamental to Mithraism) of the two contrary and warring principles of good and evil. The Manichaeans were deeply concerned with the problem of evil in human life, and they found the key to the solution of the problem in a perpetual state of more or less open warfare waged in the universe as a whole and in the individual human soul between the opposing forces of the Princes of Darkness and of Light. Good, personified as the Father of Light, was conceived as quasi-spiritual in its nature; evil, in the person of the Prince of Darkness, as grossly material. The curious intermingling of the spiritual and the material in the

[1] A.D. 372. *Confessions* iv, 2, 2.

[2] For Manichaeism see E. N. Pickman, *The Mind of Latin Christendom*, vol. 1, pp. 63–6; V. J. Bourke, *op. cit.*, pp. 17–23; J. J. O'Meara, *The Young Augustine*, pp. 61–79 and in particular P. Alfaric, *op. cit.*, pp. 79–158 and 215–25.

composition of man was attributed by the Manichaeans to a ruse on the part of the Father whereby he sought to bait the Devil with part of his own (the Father's) substance incorporated in a creature whose nature was essentially material. But even in their conception of spiritual substance or 'light', the Manichaeans did not demonstrate their ability to think in wholly non-material terms. The atmosphere and dwelling place of the Father of Light was the most ethereal and subtle matter that can be imagined, but still matter. The Kingdom of Light was spoken of as being contiguous with the Kingdom of Darkness in a clearly physical sense.[1] The Manichaean inability to break with purely material concepts clearly emerges in Augustine's exposition of his modes of thought as an adherent of the sect:

> When I wanted to think of God, I could not think of Him in any other way than in terms of material elements. . . . I thought that evil also was a substance of a similar kind, having its own foul and misshapen mass, whether dense, which the Manichees called earth, or fine and subtle, like the material of air.[2]

This materialistic outlook, characteristic of Manichaeism, constituted a stumbling block in the way of Augustine's progress towards spiritual understanding. Furthermore, the dualistic theology and cosmogony reduced both God's and Man's personal responsibility for the state of the universe and for the consequences of divine and human action. On the one hand evil now no longer must be laid at the door of God alone. Rather it must be regarded as issuing from the principle of evil, which was in bitter opposition to God, and from the necessary and continual warfare of things. Matter and the demons were undoubtedly the source of all evil as they were the creators of matter. Thus man in his purely physical aspect is a creation of the Devil; he is an amalgam of light and darkness, of subtle spirit and gross matter, dramatically portraying within himself the conflict of two opposing principles which are within him and yet not of him. They are in fact powers beyond his control,

[1] *Against the Letter of the Manichaean*, 19. Alfaric, *op. cit.*, pp. 78–9.
[2] *Confessions* v, 10, 20: 'I conceived of two masses, mutually antagonistic, both infinite, but the evil was smaller and the good larger.'

and the alternations of victory in this unending strife issue in overt action for which man himself cannot be held wholly responsible. It was a doctrine of human non-responsibility, convenient as an explanation of moral lapse and very tempting to the neophyte Augustine:

> I was of the opinion that it is not we who sin, but that it is some other nature within us which sins. So it pleased my pride to be exempt from blame, and, when I committed some crime, not to admit that it was I who had done it. . . . I loved to excuse myself and to accuse something else which was with me but which was not myself.[1]

It is clear that the Manichaean concern with the outcome of the ceaseless struggle for the domination of the universe and of man harmonised with Augustine's psychological state at a period when he was tormented by the prickings of his own passionate nature and at the same time deeply concerned to discover the means to a victory of the good over the evil in the universe as a whole, as well as in his own personal life. On the one hand, the explanation of evil in terms of the real existence of an anti-Christ explained the existence of sin, but did not render the struggle of good and evil any less oppressive or hold out clear promise of an ultimate victory of the good.[2] On the other hand, the notion of human non-responsibility, founded on the conception of two equally sovereign and warring powers in control of the universe, could not satisfy one whose temperament, nurtured from childhood in monotheism, required an explanation in terms of order rather than of conflict and chaos. The Manichaean way could offer no more than an uneasy truce in his spiritual conflict.

THE SEARCH FOR DIRECTION

In the year A.D. 375 Augustine had temporarily returned to Tagaste and to a mother who refused him admission to her home in disapproval of his Manichaean association. For a few

[1] *ibid.* v, 10, 18.

[2] The dualistic principle undoubtedly made its mark on Augustine's thought, e.g. the concept of the two cities in *The City of God* and his support of the Platonic notion of the two realms of existence, material and spiritual.

months he acted as a teacher of grammar, but returned to Carthage in the following year. The death of a friend, whom Augustine had introduced to Manichaeism but who had been later baptised into the Christian church, is the reason Augustine gives for his decision to leave Tagaste.[1] But we may interpret his inability to settle down in the vocation of grammar teacher as a conflict of two opposing forces working within him. On the one hand the retreat to Tagaste was an attempt to escape from the implications of the Manichaean faith, which were becoming increasingly oppressive to him and to recapture, if he could, the simple faith of his mother. On the other he was subject to the temptations of wordly pleasure and ambition; he tells us[2] that he was drawn back to Carthage by the ambition to use the rhetorical skill he had developed both as an orator and teacher in the great North African city. He returned 'for the sake of its greater professional rewards and opportunities'. In Carthage then from his twentieth to his twenty-ninth year he plied the orator's trade, selling his skill to the highest bidder.[3] He represents himself in the *Confessions* as being dead to all considerations save those of material success and worldly ambition. Yet the content of his first book, which he wrote towards the end of this period, shows that he had by no means abandoned the spiritual and intellectual quest for truth. This treatise no longer survives; it was called *Concerning the Beautiful and the Fitting* (*De pulchro et apto*), and was dedicated to the Roman orator, Hierius, whom Augustine admired but knew only by repute.[4] In this work, as he tells us, his search for truth and beauty was still restricted to physical forms. Nevertheless, he could not entirely repress the haunting suspicion that truth lies in the area of spiritual existence:

> The very force of truth was assaulting my eyes; and yet I was turning my throbbing mind away from what was immaterial to lines and colours and swelling masses; because I could not see these things in my mind, I was entertaining the thought that I could not see my mind.[5]

[1] *Confessions* iv, 4–9.
[2] *Against the Academics* ii, 3.
[3] *Confessions* iv, 2, 2.
[4] *ibid.* iv, 14, 21.
[5] *ibid.* iv, 15, 24.

As the *Hortensius* of Cicero had already exercised a formative influence on Augustine's mind, so at the beginning of his period of rhetoric teaching in Carthage another book gave a new direction to his thought, namely the *Categories* of Aristotle.[1] His quick intelligence enabled him to master the content of this work as well as to extend his reading in the liberal arts, particularly in rhetoric, logic, geometry, music and arithmetic. The effect of this reading was progressively to wean him from the Manichaean faith; but having as yet no stronger faith to lean upon, he was still drifting without a rudder on the tempestuous seas of his own unco-ordinated learning. The feeling of aimlessness was not allayed by the arrival in Carthage of the celebrated Manichaean Bishop Faustus. Augustine lost no time in searching him out and plying him with questions. But the answers, fluently and lucidly delivered as they were, failed to satisfy. Augustine found Faustus charming, eloquent and witty but superficial in his learning and lacking conviction. This much Augustine was prepared to grant him—that he was 'not altogether ignorant of his own ignorance'.[2] In all, the visit of Faustus served merely to hasten Augustine's final defection from the sect of which Faustus was the acknowledged leader, and to strengthen his conviction that rhetoric without intellectual content was simply windy nonsense.

At the end of the year A.D. 383 Augustine set sail from Carthage to Rome. He was once more seeking an escape from a situation of tension and disillusionment. But again his spiritual hunger would not allow him to rest, but drove him on to commit himself more thoroughly to the vortex of conflicting philosophies. Once more he rationalised his departure from Carthage: he was depressed and frustrated by the unruly, ill-disciplined conduct of the students; he would move to Rome, where he was assured that students were well behaved. At the same time he revealed his mental conflict by deceiving his mother as to his intentions and abandoning her in Carthage, where she had joined him. In Rome he lived with some Manichaean friends

[1] *ibid.* iv, 16, 28.

[2] *ibid.* v, 7, 12: As an example of Faustus' superficiality Augustine in his treatise *Against Faustus the Manichaean* notes that on the one hand Faustus asserted that everything was made of matter, while at the same time he was quite unable to say what matter was.

and still found some comfort in the doctrine that sin was due not to man's own waywardness but to 'another nature in us'. Yet his mind continually returned to the Catholic faith, although he could not find anyone completely able to refute the arguments of the Manichaeans. So he stayed uneasily with Mani in default of a surer resting place for his faith, although he tells us that his defence of Manichaeism was now less spirited than it used to be.[1]

CRISIS IN MILAN

The students of the rhetoric school in Rome were less unruly than at Carthage, but this was counterbalanced by their unfortunate habit of decamping when the time came to pay their tuition fees to their teachers. This is one of the reasons Augustine gives for his next move from Rome to Milan, which occurred after only one year's residence at Rome. But now there was a more compelling reason for a move, which was once again both an escape and a further involvement. Augustine had applied for the vacant post of Professor of Rhetoric at Milan, for which Symmachus, the Roman prefect, had been asked to find a suitable candidate. Augustine had the support of several influential Manichaean friends and, having submitted himself to the test of a public oration delivered before Symmachus himself, he obtained the post which advanced him at one leap to the pinnacle of his profession and marked the culmination of the rhetorician's worldly ambition.[2]

In Milan Augustine approached his day of destiny; the narrative in the *Confessions* becomes more turbulent as he makes his last, frantic attempts to beat off the certainty, which was to possess him. He reported to his mother that he was no longer a Manichaean, although not yet a Christian.[3] He listened

[1] *Confessions* v, 10, 19: Nec eam defendebam pristina animositate.

[2] P. Courcelle, *Recherches sur les Confessions de St. Augustin*, p. 79, examining the implications of Augustine's appointment in Milan in the autumn of A.D. 384 notes that this was the year of reaction against the pro-Catholic policy of the Emperor Gratian, who had been killed in battle the preceding year. Symmachus exerted a prominent influence in the pagan party, and, as Courcelle points out, Augustine was not yet a Catholic.

[3] *Confessions* vi, 1, 1.

to the sermons of the famous Ambrose, Bishop of Milan, and declared that Ambrose was indeed a 'happy man', not only because of his eloquence but because he was held in such universal esteem.[1] The *Confessions* provide a portrait of the great Bishop, revealing the close attention with which Augustine must have observed him. We see Ambrose engrossed in his private reading: 'When he read, his eyes scanned the page, but his heart explored the sense'. In the first place Augustine was impressed by Ambrose's eloquence, but soon the content of the sermons came to lay hold on his mind, and, by comparison with Faustus, he found Ambrose 'more learned but less sparkling'.[2] Augustine tells us that he longed to put questions to Ambrose, but was prevented by reason of the crowd around him. When briefly presented to Ambrose, the Bishop greeted him 'in the manner of a father'. The influence of Ambrose on Augustine's struggling faith was, therefore, rather through his sermons than directly through personal conversation.[3]

Augustine represents his condition at this time as one of scepticism in the manner of the New Academy. He was still bending his mind to see if he could 'convict the Manichaeans of falsehood'.[4] His continuing doubts as to the validity of the Christian revelation still flowed from his inability to conceive of a spiritual substance. However, as a temporary measure he determined to become a catechumen in the Catholic Church, a course his mother had persistently recommended to him.

Around him in Milan Augustine gathered a group of relatives, friends and former pupils from Carthage. His mother's arrival was followed by that of his mistress and their son, Adeodatus;[5] there was also Alypius, a native of Tagaste, who had been a pupil of Augustine both at Tagaste and Carthage and, having come to Milan to practise as a lawyer, had quickly become known for his resistance to bribery.[6] Nebridius and Evodius, also North Africans, were added to the company, which con-

[1] *ibid.* v, 13, 23.

[2] *ibid.* v, 13, 23.

[3] See P. Alfaric, *op. cit.*, pp. 370–1 for an assessment of the extent of the influence of Ambrose on Augustine.

[4] *Confessions* vi, 14, 25.

[5] Monica probably arrived in Milan in the spring of A.D. 385. P. Courcelle, *op. cit.*, p. 87.

[6] *Confessions* vi, 10, 16.

tained Augustine's younger brother, Navigius, two cousins, Lastidianus and Rusticus, and two young pupils, Licentius and Trygetius.

Meanwhile, Monica, feeling that the life of celibacy must always be an impossible burden to her son, arranged that he should marry into a good family, whose daughter at the time was two years below the legal age for marriage.[1] In preparation for this event, Augustine must abandon his mistress, and there is no reason to doubt the sincerity of his grief when he reports: 'She was torn from my side as an obstacle to my marriage; my heart, which clung to her, was torn and bleeding'.[2] Thus, leaving their son in his father's care, the anonymous woman, with whom Augustine had lived in virtual marriage for twelve years, returned to Africa with a vow of continence, which Augustine himself could not match; he declared in the *Confessions* that he was unable 'to imitate a mere woman' and took another mistress.[3]

The *Confessions* speak with dramatic force of St. Augustine's spiritual travail at this time. The reading of the *Hortensius*, while recommending the study of philosophy, had led to nothing more than the sceptical conclusion that truth may be forever impossible to find. His study of the works of the philosophers of the New Academy, still powerfully influenced by the scepticism of Carneades (214–129 B.C.) must have begun when St. Augustine was in Rome:

> The thought sprung up within me that those philosophers, called the Academics, were more prudent than all the rest, because they were of the opinion that we must entertain doubts about everything and had laid down that no truth can be grasped by man.[4]

Of course such a conclusion could be of only passing interest to one whose temper could not long rest on the shifting sands of scepticism. Nevertheless, the strength of the impression made upon Augustine by the Academics, made it necessary for him to refute their arguments by marshalling in writing the contrary

[1] The legal age was only twelve years. Gibbs and Montgomery, *Confessions of St. Augustine*, p. 165, n. 5.

[2] *Confessions* vi, 15, 25.

[3] *ibid.*

[4] *ibid.* v, 10, 19.

ones. St. Augustine did this in his first surviving work, the dialogue *Against the Academics*, written in A.D. 386, the period between his conversion and baptism.[1]

But the writing of *Against the Academics* was preceded by two important landmarks in Augustine's intellectual progress, namely his attachment to the philosophy of Plato and his final commitment to Christ. These events, which marked the most rapid and formative period of his spiritual growth, occurred in little more than eighteen months.

In the *Confessions* Augustine remarks that he 'read certain books of the Platonists, translated from Greek into Latin'.[2] It is likely that by this he meant not the works of Plato himself but the writings of those who followed the path of Plato, such as Plotinus, Iamblichus, Porphyry and Apuleius of Madaura.[3] There are those who find in this last year of spiritual searching two separate conversions, the first to Platonism and the second to Christianity. While some hold that only the second was the true and significant conversion, others, such as Courcelle,[4] see the whole movement of this critical year as a conversion to what may best be described as Christian Platonism. There is some support for this view in the distinctly Platonic tone of the dialogues of Cassiciacum written in the period immediately following the spiritual climax in the garden at Milan. Undoubtedly Plato—'almost a Christian', as Augustine calls him—filled in certain gaps, which the Scriptures could not fill. But a reading of the turbulent narrative of the *Confessions* yields the impression of one continuous, irresistible movement from the conflicting currents and whirlpools of doubt to more settled waters. In this precipitate movement of St. Augustine's mind a multitude of impressions, simultaneously received, interacted with one another and so played their part in the final con-

[1] *Reviews* i, 1.

[2] *Confessions* vii, 9, 13: quosdam Platonicorum libros ex graeca lingua in latinum versos.

[3] Augustine lists these in *The City of God* viii, 12.

[4] P. Courcelle, *op. cit.*, p. 157 argues not very convincingly that Augustine derived his Christian Platonism from the sermons of Ambrose. J. J. O'Meara, *op. cit.*, pp. 113–22 and E. Gilson, *La Philosophie au Moyen Age*, p. 112, do not see Ambrose as the exponent of a philosophical system. Ambrose's sources were the Jew Philo of Alexandria and the Christian Origen rather than the pagan philosophers.

summation. Therefore, it is better to refrain from making any clear distinction into two 'conversions' while at the same time seeing St. Augustine's introduction to Platonism as a critical juncture, and an indispensable prerequisite to his final commitment to Christ. Undoubtedly Augustine brought to the reading of the Platonic books a mind already orientated towards Christianity. As Boyer puts it:

> He was influenced in his reading by his Christian beliefs. In Plotinus he was searching for an understanding of the assertions of Ambrose.[1]

The insights of Platonism into the nature of immaterial reality needed to be complemented by the Christian revelation; on the other hand, Christian revelation must be subjected to the analysis and clarification of philosophy before it could be fully understood. Plato and Christ must, therefore, interact in the service of truth, and this dynamic fusion was to form the groundwork of Augustine's teaching commitment. Thanks to Ambrose on the one hand and the writings of the Platonists on the other, St. Augustine was able to advance from the negative attitude of bewildered scepticism to a real sense of the possibility of truth and then to a discovery of the direction in which truth lies.

Ambrose had encouraged him to a critical scrutiny of Christian doctrine, for example by suggesting figurative and more acceptable explanations of Old Testament texts, which Augustine could not accept in the literal sense. Ambrose's precept, 'the letter killeth but the spirit giveth life'[2] was to become a very important stimulus to his thinking and teaching. On the other hand, the Platonists removed one of the major metaphysical obstacles from his path, namely the difficulty of conceiving immaterial reality. They taught him with conviction that the only true reality was in fact immaterial, whereas the data of sense perception were little more than distracting.

In this critical effort of thought and careful, laborious testing of suggested answers to critical problems, we have the making of the teacher, defined in terms not of one who merely transmits

[1] C. Boyer, *Christianisme et néo-Platonisme dans la formation de St. Augustin*, p. 98.

[2] *Confessions* vi, 4, 6: Littera occidit, spiritus autem vivificat.

what he has received from others but who communicates to his students the fruits of his own living thought.

In his final struggle with the contending forces within him Augustine turned to the priest, Simplicianus, who had baptised Ambrose himself. Simplicianus was glad to hear that Augustine had fallen under the influence of Platonism, and told him of the famous Roman orator, Victorinus, who had given up his worldly honours at the call of Christ when Julian the Apostate had issued his decree forbidding Christians to be teachers. Augustine longed to imitate him, but the Manichaean warfare of good and evil was continuing to rage within him. While inwardly assenting to the truth, he yet pleaded for time to enjoy secular satisfactions a little longer. The introspective power displayed in the *Confessions* is penetrating:

> I had nothing to say when Thou didst say to me, 'Awake, thou that sleepest' . . . except the lazy and indolent words, 'Soon, soon; let me alone a little while'. But 'soon' had no limit and 'allow me a little time' was extending to infinity.[1]

So he recognised that it was not a question of good and evil competing within him for the victory but simply the effect of a weak and divided will:

> I wanted it, and yet did not want it. I was neither all for it nor all against it. Thus I was struggling with myself.[2]

In a frenzy of self-accusation Augustine sought refuge in a garden adjacent to the lodgings he shared with his friend, Alypius. The narrative continues with considerable psychological insight:

> The sound of my voice was strange; my face, cheeks, eyes, colour, and the manner of my speech gave a clearer indication of my mind than the words I uttered. . . . I was sick and in torture, accusing myself far more bitterly than I had been accustomed to do, twisting and turning in my chain until it should be completely broken, that chain by which I was now so slightly held. . . . I continued to say within myself, 'Come, let it be done now; let it be done now,' and with the very words I was already moving towards a resolve. Now I was

[1] *Confessions* viii, 5, 12.
[2] *ibid.* viii, 10, 22.

almost making it, and yet not quite, nor yet was I slipping back into my former state, but was standing hard-by and drawing my breath. And now I was trying again and was still a little nearer still and yet still a little nearer. And now I was all but touching and grasping it; and yet I was not there, nor was I actually touching and grasping it, still hesitating as I was, to become dead to death and to become alive to life.[1]

But the decision could not be indefinitely repelled. As he flung himself in tears to the ground, the voice of a child from a neighbouring house chanting the refrain *tolle, lege* ('take up and read') sent him feverishly to open the Scriptures, where he read *Romans* xiii, 13–14:

> Not in rioting and drunkenness, not in chambering and wantonness, not in strife and envying; but put ye on the Lord Jesus Christ and make not provision for the flesh to fulfil the lusts thereof.

He closed the book, not needing to read more:

> As though my heart were flooded with a light of peace, all the shadows of doubt melted away.[2]

SEMINAR AT CASSICIACUM

The scene in the garden took place at the beginning of August, A.D. 386. Immediately Augustine decided to resign his chair of rhetoric—'to snatch the service of my tongue from the speech market'.[3] Milan must appoint some other 'seller of words' for their scholars. For this Augustine gave two reasons, first that he was now in the service of God, and secondly that he was suffering from chest pains, which rendered him no longer fit for the strain of public speaking.[4] Thus the popular but dissatisfied

[1] *ibid.* viii, 8, 19 and 11, 25.

[2] *Confessions* viii, 12, 29. P. Courcelle, *op. cit.*, pp. 190–1 suggests various interpretations of *tolle, lege*; for example, that it was the voice of a schoolchild repeating the paradigms of the third conjugation; that it was a cry uttered by children playing at boats—'Lift up (the anchor) and gather up (the rope)', etc. But he concludes that the voice may in fact have had no physical reality, being merely the dramatic projection of Augustine's thinking at the moment of most acute crisis.

[3] *Confessions* ix, 2, 2.

[4] *ibid.* ix, 5, 13.

orator became the Christian teacher, who had exchanged teaching as a means of livelihood and self-glorification for teaching as a vocation. It is significant that in the months between St. Augustine's conversion in the autumn of A.D. 386 and his baptism in the following season of Lent, he showed the reality of this new vocation in a teaching situation of unique interest.

His friend Verecundus, a grammar teacher and pagan, offered St. Augustine the use of his country house at Cassiciacum, near Milan.[1] As soon as he had resigned his post, Augustine went there accompanied by his mother and son, his brother Navigius, his cousins Lastidianus and Rusticus, his pupils Licentius and Trygetius and his friend Alypius.

The purpose of the retreat was to reach a clearer understanding of what had already been accepted by faith:

> I was impatiently desirous of grasping the truth, not merely by believing but also by understanding it.[2]

The six months spent at Cassiciacum were, therefore, largely devoted to free and uninhibited discussions of the implications of the Christian commitment. It was the kind of free learning situation, which appealed to Augustine himself, who appears to have had rather poor success in lecturing to large classes in Rome and Carthage, where the students had a more narrowly vocational and mercenary attitude to education. The seminar discussions at Cassiciacum issued in a number of dialogues written in the Socratic manner. These purport to be verbatim accounts of what was actually said as taken down by a secretary, whom Augustine employed for the purpose, although they must have been edited by Augustine for the purpose of publication. They are philosophical rather than religious in spirit, and in the *Confessions* Augustine refers to them somewhat disparagingly as being deficient in seriousness and still breathing the pride of the rhetoric schools. The first of these dialogues is *Against the Academics*, followed by *The Happy Life*, the two books on *The Principle of Order* (*De ordine*), the *Soliloquies*, and finally *The Immortality of the Soul*, which is a continuation of the *Soliloquies*.

[1] Probably the site of the modern Casciago in Lombardy.

[2] *Against the Academics* iii, 20.

The philosophical instrument used in the dialogues is the Neoplatonic philosophy, and the purpose is to analyse Platonist concepts with a view to finding to what extent they agreed with and supported the doctrines of Christianity. The special interest of the dialogues lies in the fact that they show us at first hand the elaboration of that synthesis of Platonism and Christianity, of philosophy and religious faith, which is the greatest contribution made by Augustine to the history of thought.

The Cassiciacum dialogues explore the approaches to truth and clear the ground, rather than reach final conclusions. The serenity of the Milanese countryside, which breaks through at more than one point in the dialogues, admirably matches the mood of the teacher and his students and is in marked contrast with his earlier spiritual turmoil. Inconclusive enquiry now no longer breeds despair, since it is fortified by a guarantee that final truth exists and can be discovered. *Against the Academics* for instance ends on such a note of confidence:

> Just how human wisdom is constituted I cannot see as yet. But since I am only in my thirty-third year I don't see why I should despair of finding it in the end. I intend to continue my search, holding in contempt all those other things which mortals consider good. These discussions are enough to convince me that the sceptical position of the Academics cannot impede this search. Without question there are two things which bring us to learn, authority and reason. I am certain that I shall never depart from the authority of Christ, for I find none stronger. And the search must continue by the most subtle reasoning; for it is now my conviction that what I want most is to grasp the truth, not by faith alone but also by understanding. In the meantime I shall put my trust in those teachings of the Platonists, which are not opposed to our sacred writings.[1]

At the beginning of Lent, A.D. 387, Augustine and his friends returned to Milan, where he enrolled among the candidates for baptism and was instructed in the doctrines and practices of the Church. At Easter he was baptised along with Alypius and Adeodatus.

[1] *Against the Academics* iii, 20.

RETURN TO AFRICA

After his baptism Milan had little to offer Augustine, and there were compelling reasons why he should return to his homeland. The North African Church required a more educated priesthood, and he was convinced that the first service he must render to his native land must be to establish seminaries for the instruction of the future leaders of its Church. However, as Augustine and his company were preparing to take ship for Africa, Monica fell ill and died, an event which moved Augustine deeply.[1] At her funeral he wept for a mother 'who for many years had shed tears for me'. But there was the solace of the new faith in the immortality of the soul, and his life's work was before him.

The death of Monica delayed the departure for Africa for over a year, and during this period Augustine composed three other dialogues: *The Greatness of the Soul*, *On Music* and *The Free Will*. The first explores the concept of the spiritual nature of the soul, and all three are rich in psychological interest. *The Free Will* reinforces the message of the *Soliloquies*, namely that, if the human will is to be directed towards a knowledge of God, man must first be able to master himself. He must, therefore, know what he himself really is.

In the autumn of A.D. 388 Augustine crossed to Africa, and in the following year suffered another serious bereavement in the death of his son, Adeodatus. Possibly by way of tribute to his memory, Augustine wrote the dialogue called *The Teacher*, in which the participants are Augustine himself and Adeodatus. Augustine tells us that all the words he put into the mouth of Adeodatus in the dialogue were authentic, and that the actual discussion had taken place in Adeodatus' sixteenth year. The strength and independence of mind demonstrated by Adeodatus in the dialogue supports Augustine's appraisal of Adeodatus' ability at the age of fifteen years—'In intelligence he was superior to many grave and learned men'.[2]

On his arrival in Africa Augustine made straight for his native Tagaste, where he remained for the next three years. The seclusion of these years was more apparent than real. Through

[1] *Confessions* ix, 8, 17.
[2] *ibid.* ix, 6, 14.

correspondence he kept in close contact with friends in other places. Examples of his letters of this period illustrate his delight in informed controversy, the warmth of his personality and the respect in which he was held by both Christians and pagans. Nine of the letters are to or from his friend and former pupil, Nebridius. In these he discusses difficult psychological and philosophical problems, such as the possibility of thought unsupported by physical images.[1] Nebridius declares that Augustine's letters bring to his ears 'the voice of Christ and the teaching of Plato and Plotinus'; they are eloquent and penetrated by wisdom.[2] There is a letter from Maximus, a teacher of grammar at Madaura and Augustine's reply to it.[3] Confident in his superiority to the average pagan, Maximus addresses a semi-serious question to Augustine regarding the nature of the Christian God. Augustine replies in the pungent style of the trained controversialist. 'Are we engaged in a serious debate with each other?' Augustine begins by asking, 'Or is it your desire that we merely amuse ourselves?' Maximus has shown himself 'more witty than weighty', and gets the sort of reply which his attitude deserves. In the remaining letters Augustine gives straightforward advice to more serious and less sophisticated enquirers. Each question is treated with the care and attention to detail of the devoted teacher; to serious enquiries he returns serious and exhaustive answers.

ORDINATION: THE DONATIST HERESY

At this stage Augustine seems to have had no ambition for advancement in the Church, his desire being to remain a simple scholar and teacher of the faith. His friend and biographer, Possidius, remarks that he deliberately kept away from places where there was a vacant see, in case he should be asked to fill it. However, at the beginning of A.D. 391 he paid a visit to the busy seaport of Hippo, to which a minor official of the imperial government who was interested in the monastic life had invited him.[4] Augustine had accepted the invitation with few fore-

[1] *Letters* 6, 7 and 8.

[2] *Letter* 6 from Nebridius to Augustine.

[3] *Letters* 16 and 17.

[4] Possidius, *Life of Bishop Augustine*, 3–4. Sermon 355, 2. Hippo was situated 150 miles due west of Carthage on the coast of the

bodings, since the see was occupied by Bishop Valerius. But Valerius was a Greek, unable to speak fluently in Latin and having no knowledge of the Punic language. Furthermore he was advanced in years, and looking for a priest to assist him in the work of preaching. The people of Hippo were acquainted with Augustine's qualities. Thus, while he was standing in the church blissfully unaware of the developing situation, he was seized and forcibly led up to the Bishop, who was requested to ordain him. In spite of his tears, which were wrongly put down to the fact that he was being made a presbyter and not a bishop coadjutor, he was duly ordained on the spot. Possidius gives an interesting description of the scene.[1]

The church at Hippo, when Augustine began to minister there, was in a depressed and divided state. The people of Hippo were by no means entirely Catholic. In addition to a large pagan element, various heresies and schisms were prominent in the scene, the Donatist faction being particularly strong. Against such an array of conflicting and opposing forces the aged Bishop Valerius could do little to strengthen the morale of his flock. Possidius represents him as stating that 'it was providential that a man such as Augustine had been given to him to build up the Church by the word of God and by his invigorating teaching'.[2] In a letter Augustine reveals his feelings of inadequacy for the teaching function he would have to perform in preaching and giving catechetical instruction to those preparing for baptism.[3]

Soon after he took up residence at Hippo, Augustine organised a monastic community within the precincts of the church.[4] The function of this community was primarily educative, to train a more educated priesthood. Already at Tagaste, three years before, Augustine had established a similar community devoted, as Possidius says, 'to fastings, discussions and good works'.[5]

[1] Possidius, 5. *Letter* 21, 2 to Valerius.
[2] Possidius, *loc. cit.*
[3] *Letter* 21.
[4] Possidius, *op. cit.*, 5. *Sermon* 355, 2.
[5] Possidius, *op. cit.*, 3.

---

province of Numidia about two miles from the modern Bone. The population at the time has been estimated as about 30,000 people. Bourke, *op. cit.*, p. 124.

And again, after his consecration as Bishop of Hippo, he set up within the Bishop's palace three similar communities, one consisting of priests and minor clerics and two consisting of laymen, modelled on the communities, which he had heard of and perhaps visited at Rome and Milan.[1] The purpose of all these communities was not to separate their members from the affairs of the world but to prepare them for more intelligent Christian participation in its life. They were in fact designed to become competent Christian teachers, who in their encounters with both believers and unbelievers would know what to teach and how to teach it. Bourke describes the first community at Hippo as 'one of the first theological seminaries',[2] and one which made the greatest contribution to the success of the Church in North Africa in the fifth century. Possidius mentions the names of several of its members, who later became bishops of African sees, for example Alypius, who became Bishop of Tagaste and later Primate of Numidia, and Possidius himself, who became Bishop of Calama.

The priority given to the establishment of such communities expresses St. Augustine's conviction as to the value of education for the Christian as well as for the pagan. This interest in the training of the Christian teacher, both lay or cleric, remained strong throughout Augustine's life. The Christian teacher must be liberally educated, and his knowledge must be won, as Augustine's own knowledge had been, at the cost of the laborious personal effort of thought. It is to this conviction that we owe the two books of St. Augustine *On Christian Education* and *On the Instruction of the Uninstructed.* In the period with which we are dealing, we have glimpses in Possidius of Augustine as priest, and later as bishop, practising the work of Christian teaching both formally and informally, by conversation as well as by sermons, letters and books. At Tagaste 'through discussions and the writing of books he continued to teach not only people who were present with him but those who were absent too'. At Hippo 'he went on teaching and preaching both privately and publicly in his house and in his church'.[3] In the incessant controversy with the heretical sects, which

[1] Possidius, *op. cit.*, 25. *Sermon* 355, 1 and *Sermon* 356.
[2] Bourke, *op. cit.*, p. 126.
[3] Possidius, *op. cit.*, 7.

troubled the North African Church during Augustine's priesthood and episcopy, the need for both laymen and priests sufficiently well instructed in the grounds of their faith and broadly educated in the liberal disciplines of the classical encyclopedia was to be repeatedly demonstrated.

In this period Augustine wrote a number of treatises, designed to refute the heresies of the Manichaeans. But the strongest faction with which Augustine clashed during these years was the party of the Donatists.[1] Starting as a movement of protest against any form of compromise with the secular state and maintaining that anyone who made such a compromise was putting Caesar before God, the Donatists became increasingly militant and unyielding as the state intervened to deal with them. In the eyes of the Donatists, the Catholics had betrayed their faith, and thus had forfeited their right to be considered the true Church. It was the Church of the 'traitors'.[2] Donatism in the time of Augustine had in fact become almost a national African movement, appealing to the forces of social discontent. The Donatists, steeled by the effects of persecution, were firmly insistent on following a literal and sometimes fanatical interpretation of scriptural texts; appearing in the guise of defenders of the poor and oppressed, they forced landlords to enfranchise their slaves and to free their debtors. Dawson says of them:

> In fact we have in Donatism a typical example of the results of an exclusive insistence on the apocalyptic and anti-secular aspects of Christianity, a tendency which was destined to reappear at a later period in the excesses of the Taborites, the Anabaptists, and some of the Puritan sects.[3]

In the year A.D. 396 Augustine was consecrated coadjutor Bishop to Bishop Valerius, and within a year the death of

[1] For the Donatists see L. Duchesne, *The Early History of the Christian Church*, vol. 2, pp. 79–97. Christopher Dawson in *Monument to St. Augustine*, pp. 55–7. R. W. Battenhouse, *A Companion to the Study of St. Augustine*, pp. 43–7.

[2] *Traditores*, the term originally applied to those members of the clergy, who handed over the sacred books to the persecutors of the Church in the time of Diocletian. In the Donatist view the Catholic clergy from that time could no longer validly administer the sacraments. Bourke, *op. cit.*, pp. 133–4.

[3] Christopher Dawson, *op. cit.*, p. 55.

Valerius laid the whole responsibility for the welfare of the Church in the see of Hippo on his shoulders. During the years of his episcopate the volume of works which came from his pen is incredibly great, when considered in the light of his many other duties, some of which involved long journeyings to distant parts of his see. The variety of his writings, in the form of exegetical works, doctrinal treatises and controversial works in refutation of heresies and schisms, is impressive. But this is to leave out of account some of the major contributions to Christian thought and letters which form his chief claim to fame, for example the *Confessions*, *The Trinity*, *The City of God*, achievements more to be expected from the secluded scholar than the pastor and administrator of an important see in a period of reconstruction and strife. Burdensome although his administrative duties undoubtedly were, there is no doubt about the pleasure Augustine felt in his teaching function. From many allusions in his writings we know how he warmed to the company of his fellow men and how easy and stimulating were his personal relations. These qualities of human sympathy and intuitive understanding, when added to the intellectual zest and considerable powers of exposition, are the qualities of one to whom teaching is both a vocation and a means of creative expression. The importance of close personal contact and the free expression of thought characteristic of the Cassiciacum dialogues is carried over into the controversies with those who expressed unorthodox views. For example, he reminds the Donatist Bishop of Hippo, Proculeianus, of his promise to debate their differences either in public or by means of letters and private conversation. He wishes for an 'amiable investigation' of a matter of such urgent moment as a divided Church. 'What have we to do,' he asks, 'with the dissension of a past generation?' Time has healed many wounds on both sides. There is therefore the possibility of a reconciliation, and this is the supreme task, to which men of goodwill on both sides must dedicate themselves.[1] Proculeianus, however, overawed by Augustine's reputation, refused to meet him, admitting openly that he was no match for Augustine in learning, a decision which considerably distressed Augustine.[2]

[1] *Letter* 33.
[2] *Letter* 24, 5–6.

The Donatist schism continued in a spirit of bitterness until it was suppressed by an imperial edict of A.D. 412. However, it was quickly succeeded by a new heresy of equally formidable strength.

The Pelagians took their name from the monk, Pelagius, who after making a reputation in Italy and Sicily had arrived in Carthage in A.D. 410.[1] Their heresy was not a new one; its roots have been traced back to the teachings of Origen, and further back still to the Stoics. In brief, the Pelagians were concerned to minimise the need for divine grace as a prerequisite of human salvation by denying the reality of original sin and magnifying the natural capacity of the human will to achieve the good life. In arguing his case, Pelagius, a man of meagre education but of considerable natural ability, had made skilful use of texts from Augustine's treatise, *The Free Will*, and it became increasingly evident that a well-reasoned and authoritative statement of the Catholic case must be published. Augustine himself provided this in a number of treatises; furthermore his sermons and letters of the period are full of assertions as to the necessity of divine grace for salvation; grace comes to man, not by his either desiring or meriting it, but as a free gift from God.[2] The Pelagian heresy was eventually condemned by Pope Zosimus after a conference of bishops at Carthage in A.D. 418, this being achieved largely as a result of Augustine's skill in debate.

TALE OF TWO CITIES

But the crises of the times were not all to be alleviated by bloodless battles of words. It was in the reign of Arcadius and Honorius, the two sons of Theodosius, that the Rhine–Danube frontier was first seriously breached. This was followed in rapid succession by Alaric's invasion of Greece, the destruction of Corinth and the invasion of Italy in A.D. 401. After three sieges and attempts at appeasement by a weak senate, the city of Rome was taken and sacked in A.D. 410. The occupation of Rome,

[1] For Pelagianism see Bourke, *op. cit.*, ch. 10; Duchesne, *op. cit.*, vol. 3, chs. 6–8. Augustine refers to Pelagius as 'Brito', *Letter* 186, indicating either a British or French (Breton) origin. Duchesne, *op. cit.*, vol. 3, p. 45 calls him 'a native of Britain'.

[2] e.g. *Sermon* 131, 6.

which lasted only six days, was merely the prelude to the invasion of Sicily and the continent of Africa.

The effect of the sack of Rome on the mind of Augustine was tremendous, and he reacted in a characteristically positive way:

> As a result of the invasion of the Gothic forces under their king Alaric, and owing to the impetus of this great disaster, Rome fell. The devotees of the many false gods, i.e. those whom we usually call 'pagans', tried to blame this overthrow on the Christian religion, and began to blaspheme the true God even more harshly and bitterly than they had been accustomed to do.[1]

Indirectly as well as directly, by fostering moral anarchy as well as by inflicting physical destruction, the barbarian invasions were undermining the faith. 'And so', Augustine continues, 'burning with enthusiasm for the house of God, I set about the writing of the books of *The City of God* in order to combat the blasphemies and errors.' With these words Augustine introduces his retrospective appraisal of one of his major contributions to Christian letters, a work begun in A.D. 413, three years after the sack of Rome and not completed until A.D. 426, four years before his death.

The City of God is an expansive work; the extent of the canvas on which it is painted and the wealth of detail incorporated within the whole may render the overall unity of the plan difficult to perceive. It is the confused and thronged arena of human life which Augustine is depicting, a scene in which two cities, an earthly and a heavenly one, are intermingled, while those who come and go upon the scene are citizens of both and suffer from the strains and complications of a double allegiance. There is a division or alternation of loyalties, a persistent inability to reconcile them and clearly to determine priorities when the temporal comforts of the earthly city conflict with the duties of the heavenly citizenship. All this makes a turbulent and complicated scene; but repeatedly we are recalled from absorption in the detail to the urgent lesson which man must learn and which the course of events on the earthly scene is pressing to its inevitable conclusion: Earthly cities have not come into exist-

[1] *Reviews* ii, 43.

ence by chance but by the will of the one God, by whose pleasure they continue to exist. Human prosperity is not to be had by sacrificing to the multitude of deities and demons, which clamour for worship in the streets and market places of the earthly city, but by revering the one true God, at whose command earthly empires rise and fall. If through the calamity which has overtaken the 'eternal' city of Rome, man is brought to remember this fact and to temper his conduct to a wisdom higher than that of the huckster or the military commander, he may yet win through to safety. Everything depends upon the possession of that strength of character, which is the outward expression of spiritual understanding.

The City of God falls into two parts: in the first ten books Augustine reviews objectively the history of Rome, showing the futility of supposing that to place one's faith in pagan gods or in purely human judgement is to secure the safety of the state; in the last twelve books he extends the plan of the work as he had originally conceived it and goes on to formulate a philosophy for the Christian society. Man must never fail to recognise that he is a member of two communities. The first of these is the community of those who love God and whose conduct is wholly motivated by this love; on the other hand there is the community of those who place their faith in material possessions and who find their springs of action in love of these. On earth the two cities are intimately mixed together:

> The temporal careers of these two cities are mixed together from beginning to end—both alike enjoy temporal goods or suffer temporal ills but differ in faith, in hope, in love, until they be separated by the final judgement and each receive its end.[1]

In essence, therefore, *The City of God* describes a moral conflict rather than propounds a political programme. There is a continuing and often violent clash of loyalties within the human soul, a fact of which Augustine had himself been constantly and painfully aware in his own experience. It is the purpose of the work to point to the heavenly city and its King as the source of, and authority for, the moral values by which man should regulate his conduct on earth.

[1] *The City of God* xviii, 54.

TEACHER OF THE FAITH

Returning to the time of Augustine's consecration as Bishop of Hippo, we shall briefly review those of his writings which are of the greatest relevance to his views on education. In A.D. 397 Simplicianus, Augustine's spiritual mentor at Milan, who had succeeded Ambrose in the see of Milan in that year, sent Augustine a number of questions on doctrinal matters. Augustine's answers are known as the treatise *Concerning Seven Various Questions in Reply to Simplicianus*. They were accompanied by a letter in which Augustine acknowledges with gratitude both the 'fatherly affection' which he has enjoyed from Simplicianus and the latter's acknowledgement of his scholarship and authority.[1]

Probably in the same year Augustine began two of his major works, *Christian Education* and the *Confessions*. Of the four books of the former, only the first two and a part of the third were written in A.D. 397; the work was completed much later, i.e. in the years A.D. 426–7.[2] The purpose of *Christian Education* is to provide a manual of instructions to the Christian teacher, whether layman or cleric. The first three books deal with the rules for the interpretation of Scripture and the fourth with the techniques for imparting such knowledge once it has been gained. It is a work of considerable pedagogical importance, and was to remain the classic text book for the Christian educator for centuries.

The *Confessions* are the most widely known and best loved of Augustine's writings. Cast in the form of a prayer to God or of a meditation in the close presence of a listening God, they are unique in the world's literature as a record of personal religious experience and an exposure of the inmost recesses of the human psyche at grips with the conflicting demands and tensions of life. The intimate and acutely introspective analysis of the author's progress from anxiety and doubt to the serenity of knowledge is carried on in a full consciousness of the soul's affinity with a power, which is beyond itself and by which it was made. In the first ten books, St. Augustine reviews the course of his life's experience from his birth to the death of his mother in A.D. 387. All the elements making up the tissue of that life,

[1] *Letter* 37.

[2] *Reviews* ii, 4.

which had seemed to lack any common purpose or inner unity, now in retrospect and in the light of spiritual understanding are seen to have worked together for good. Thus the unity of the *Confessions* does not so much derive from the unity of the author's life, a life which had not yet run its full course when the work was written, as from the will of the one God, the unchanging and loving reason of things. This explains why Augustine makes no attempt to form a comprehensive catalogue of all that happened in the first thirty-three years of his life. He merely selects items which display with particular clarity the will and purpose of the divine overseer, and which give penetrating insights into the mysterious ways in which that will manifests its purposeful activity. The *Confessions*, like *The Pilgrim's Progress*, is the story of the individual soul's unremitting search for God: 'Our hearts are restless until they find their rest in Thee'.[1] The turning points along the road of exploration and quest are not necessarily those which seem most critical or catastrophic at the time they are experienced. They are not infrequently those of seemingly minor importance and little external significance, but which because of the light they shed on some unresolved inner conflict of the soul have a profoundly moving and dramatic effect. So it was with the well-known episode of the stealing of the pears, which provided in a flash of intuition the key to the seeming inevitability of sin combined with the possibility of victory in the struggle against evil. Viewed in this way, the episodes, which feature most prominently in the *Confessions*, are not, in a sense, those which are unusual and bizarre. They are rather the experiences which are common in the life of every man and of universal import. M. C. D'Arcy sums up the point in this way:

> He (Augustine) has the same power as Pascal and at times Newman of making what is intensely personal pass into the universal so that the reader seems to be following his own story. To use the language of his system, his own experience evokes in the memory of others an echo which is recognised to be true.[2]

Thus the method of the *Confessions* is the method of recollec-

[1] *Confessions* i, 1.
[2] In *Monument to St. Augustine*, p. 156.

tion guided by faith and reinforced by reflective thought. The purpose is to show, through the significant experiences of Augustine's own life and growth, the characteristic ways in which God breaks through into every man's life. Therefore, Augustine recalls and reinterprets for himself and his readers the events which in retrospect appear to him to be of the greatest significance in that long course of self-education which led him from doubt and disillusion to final certainty. Those who find fault with the *Confessions* on account of their lack of completeness or objectivity should remember these facts. 'It is more important for us to know', says Burnaby, 'how the Bishop of Hippo understood his own intellectual and religious development than to be sure whether his understanding exactly corresponded to the facts.'[1]

In the course of the four years during which he was writing the *Confessions* Augustine also wrote the work *Concerning the Instruction of the Uninstructed.* Written in response to a request from Deogratias,[2] a deacon of Carthage, it is a handbook of method for the Christian teacher in his task of instructing candidates for baptism and all who seek knowledge of the Christian faith. In *Christian Education* Augustine had dealt at length with the means whereby the Christian teacher may improve his own scholarship. In *The Instruction of the Uninstructed* he takes the teacher's scholarship for granted and concentrates on the pedagogical principles governing the successful presentation of subject matter to the learner. If the Christian teacher is unmethodical and dull, he will at once be unfavourably compared with the skilled secular teacher, and for the Christian cause this could be a great disaster.

About the year A.D. 399, Augustine began the fifteen books of his important work *On the Trinity*, which forms a valuable contribution to a controversy which had raged fiercely and which had by no means been resolved by the Council of Nicaea's assertion of the 'consubstantiality' of the Son with the Father as a dogma and test of orthodoxy for those seeking office in the

[1] J. Burnaby, *Amor Dei: A Study of the Religion of St. Augustine*, p. 29.

[2] Probably the Deogratias who was the recipient of a letter from Augustine *c.* A.D. 406 (*Letter* 102). Migne, P. L., vol. 40, p. 309, n.(b). Bourke, *op. cit.*, p. 155.

Church.[1] As in the *Confessions*, *The Trinity* provides a rich source of psychological and educational interest through Augustine's application of the principle of introspective self-examination.[2] *The Trinity* explores the implications of the notion that man is made in the image of God. This must mean that the nature of the divine Trinity must be reflected in the inner depths of the human soul. Therefore, if man is to understand what he really is, he must look within; furthermore it is only by coming to know himself that he can reach an understanding of the nature of God. The way to an understanding of the divine begins with a knowledge of the self.

Simultaneously with the composition of *The Trinity* St. Augustine was writing his definitive treatment of a theme which had held a continuing interest for him,[3] *The Literal Interpretation of Genesis*. In this work St. Augustine explores the meaning of *Genesis* 'not according to allegorical interpretations but according to the exact sense of what is described'. He sees *Genesis* as unfolding a true account of events which actually occurred, there being no concealed meaning different from what the words suggest. For example, the statement 'And the earth was without form and void' makes it quite clear that God's will in the creation was not restricted by any pre-existing materials available for his task. He actually created the universe from nothing.[4] But, although *Genesis* speaks only the truth, there are two levels of truth to be penetrated by the discerning reader—a material and a spiritual level, corresponding to the two aspects of the created universe. Thus, when God said, 'Let us make man in our image,' he intended this to be interpreted in association with the words which follow—'and let him have dominion

[1] E. N. Pickman, *The Mind of Latin Christendom*, vol. I, p. 534; J. Burnaby in introduction to '*The Trinity*' in *Augustine, Later Works*, p. 18. For the creed of Nicaea see Duchesne, *op. cit.* ii, p. 118.

[2] The method is described in *Confessions* vii, 10, 16: Being urged to return to myself, I entered into my inmost being, with Thee as my guide; and I was able to do so because Thou art my helper.

[3] St. Augustine had previously dealt with the theme in *On Genesis against the Manichaeans*. Later he wrote an uncompleted work *On the Literal Interpretation of Genesis* directed against the Donatist heresy. The theme is central to the last three books of the *Confessions*.

[4] *The Literal Interpretation of Genesis* i, 29: Unformed matter is not prior to things possessing form, because both were created at one and the same time.

over the fish of the sea,' etc.[1] Man is made in the image of God in respect of those attributes by which he is superior to the animals and which he shares with God, in particular his power of rational understanding (*intellectus*). To interpret the statement as indicating a merely physical resemblance is to ignore the spiritual nature of the Creator, and to gain an incomplete understanding of the words.[2]

As divine will was the cause of the creation of the universe, so human will was the cause of the first significant event of recorded history, the fall of man, which has been a dynamic element in all subsequent history. The book of *Genesis* provides an account of the origin of evil, the central explosive fact in the situation being the will of man. Thus St. Augustine focuses attention on the will, which occupies a prominent place in his educational theory. In his exploration of the meaning of *Genesis*, St. Augustine elaborates some of his most noteworthy cosmological and psychological theories, for example the notion of the 'seminal seeds' (*rationes seminales*) and the doctrine of the 'eternal Reasons' (*rationes aeternae*) by which he adapts the Platonic theory of ideas to Christian revelation. In exploring the nature of the soul and its relationship with the body, St. Augustine rejects Tertullian's materialistic view[3] and the Pythagorean doctrine of the transmigration of souls.[4] In scrutinising the two most popular explanations of the origin of souls, the *traducianist* and the *creationist*, St. Augustine can find no strong Scriptural support for either. On the whole he favours the traducianist explanation, inasmuch as it harmonises with the observed facts of heredity and supports the notion of the seminal seeds.[5]

THE END AND THE BEGINNING

The Literal Interpretation of Genesis, written between A.D. 401 and 414, is the last of the writings of St. Augustine which are

[1] *Genesis* i, 26.
[2] *The Literal Interpretation of Genesis* iii, 30.
[3] *ibid.* vii, 4; x, 25–6.
[4] *ibid.* vii, 14.
[5] On the seminal seeds see *ibid.* ix, 17–18, and *infra*, ch. 4, pp. 12–13. On the traducianist and creationist theories of the origin of souls see *infra*, pp. 113–14.

important for his theory of education. In the remaining years of his life he continued to pour forth letters in reply to questions posed by friends and fellow bishops and to write in defence of the Church against heresy and schisms. The integrity and seriousness with which he played the role of teacher may be illustrated by the following episode which he relates in *On Christian Education* and which occurred on a visit he made on Church business to Caesarea in Mauretania in the summer of A.D. 418.[1] His visit coincided with the celebration of an annual free-for-all fight in the streets of the town. It was known as the *caterva* (mob) and was invariably accompanied by bloodshed. Filled with distaste for the scenes he had witnessed, St. Augustine preached a powerful sermon against the practice, with the result that the custom seems to have been abandoned.[2] He reports that the people had loudly applauded him at a climax in the sermon. But with his accurate psychological insight he did not stop there, as he might have done in the days of his secular oratory. The applause showed that the people were delighted with the power of his eloquence but not necessarily moved to repentance. Therefore, he continued to speak until he had reduced his audience to tears. Augustine uses the event to show that the function of the teacher is not merely to delight his audience but to persuade and change them. The episode shows the characteristically energetic way in which Augustine applied himself to his pastoral duties.

On his return from Caesarea St. Augustine had to reply to an attack on his views on the origin of the soul, made in two books by Vincentius Victor.[3] The reply was published in A.D. 419 under the title of *The Soul and its Origin*. Here Augustine defended himself against the charge of unorthodoxy, but did not seek to disguise the fact that he was still torn between the traducianist and creationist explanations of the origin of the soul. In this treatise—and also in a letter of A.D. 415 to Jerome—he carefully scrutinised the claims of the rival views, but, as he remarks in his *Reviews*, 'I did not give any answer of my own to

[1] *Letter* 190, 1 of A.D. 418 to Optatus.

[2] *Christian Education* iv, 53 reports the event and its consequences: It is now 8 years or more since anything of the sort was attempted there.

[3] *Reviews* ii, 56.

the question I proposed'.[1] The problem remained a puzzling enigma.

Augustine's last years were to be troubled by sporadic outbursts of Manichaeism, Donatism and Pelagianism. Possidius tells us that in A.D. 421 Augustine assisted in the investigation of Manichaean excesses at Carthage,[2] and in the same year he was engaged in controversy with Julian of Eclanum, a defender of Pelagianism, who had gone to the absurd lengths of claiming that Augustine had introduced Manichaean elements into Catholic doctrine.[3] The Epiphany of A.D. 426 Augustine travelled to Milevis to clear up a misunderstanding over the succession of the late Bishop Severus.[4] In the same year he named his own successor and in the course of an address to his people, which he reports in a letter, he expressed the hope that his successor might be allowed to take over some of his work so that he might have more leisure for study.[5] Two of his actions in his last four years are typical of the satisfying unity of his life and indicative of his vital interest in education. He found time to complete his work *On Christian Education*, the greater part of which had been written twenty-nine years before; and he painstakingly compiled a catalogue of all his writings, chronologically arranged in the form of critical reviews under the title of *Retractationes* (*Reviews*). He noted the date and circumstances of composition, summarised the argument of each work and offered a critical reassessment of points on which his views had changed since they were first published. In a letter to the Roman tribune, Marcellinus, written some years before, Augustine made clear the purpose he had in mind:

> A man who wishes others to be led into error so that his own mistake may be covered up is guilty of a perverse love of self. How much better and more useful it is that others should not go astray as he himself went astray—If God grants my wish, namely that I should compile and point out in one treatise, specially designed for the purpose, everything which properly

[1] *Letter* 166. *Reviews* ii, 45.

[2] Possidius, *op. cit.*, 16.

[3] The arguments employed are set out in Augustine's *Against Julian, a Defender of the Pelagian Heresy*, written in A.D. 421.

[4] *Letter* 213, 1.

[5] *Letter* 213 of A.D. 426.

displeases me in my books, then men will see that I am not an uncritical receiver of my own opinions.[1]

Meanwhile events in the larger world were moving rapidly towards catastrophe. Barbarian penetration of the heart of the Empire and civil strife due to disagreement between the two Roman commanders in North Africa, Aetius and Boniface, contributed to weakness in the face of the barbarian onslaught. A conspiracy on the part of Aetius to have Boniface removed from his command caused Boniface to raise the standard of revolt and actually to implore the help of a Vandal army from Spain under Geneseric. Of the ruthlessness of the Vandal hordes which plundered the wealth of the province Possidius gives a vivid account.[2] In a letter addressed to Boniface Augustine protested at the inactivity of the Roman troops in the face of so great a threat and all but accused him of treason.[3]

In the midst of these mortal dangers Augustine continued to provide spiritual guidance and help wherever it was needed. In a letter of A.D. 428 or 429 he advised Honoratus, Bishop of Thiaba in Mauretania, that bishops must stay with their flocks in the face of the invader as long as they were needed: to flee in the hour of danger would be to deprive Christ's people of that nourishment by which alone their spiritual life can be sustained; the priest, who so acts would be 'a hireling who seeth the wolf coming and fleeth because he careth not for his sheep'.[4]

The disastrous course of events had been accelerated by the double-dealing of Boniface and the self-seeking machinations of Aetius. At a conference in Carthage Boniface agreed to turn the Roman armies under his command against Geneseric. At a battle early in A.D. 430 Boniface was defeated and sought refuge within the walls of Hippo, to which the Vandals promptly laid siege.[5]

Meanwhile within the besieged city the Bishop's life was drawing to a close. Stricken by a fever, he lay surrounded by his fellow clerics, among them Possidius himself, who was thus able to give a poignant eye-witness account of the last scene. He tells us that Augustine's last days were spent in continuous prayer for the deliverance of his people from the barbarian

[1] *Letter* 224 of A.D. 412.
[2] Possidius, *op. cit.*, 28.
[3] *Letter* 220.
[4] *Letter* 228.
[5] Possidius, *op. cit.*, 28.

enemy. He died probably on 28th August in the third month of the siege and in the 76th year of his life 'while we stood by him, watching him and praying with him'.[1]

The siege dragged on for fourteen months, and the power of the Vandals was to increase until the death of Geneseric in A.D. 477. The Vandal kingdom included all Roman North Africa with the Balearic islands, Corsica, Sardinia, and the fortress of Lilybaeum in Sicily. It was the apparent triumph of the temporal over the eternal city in the world of men and likely to be the end of the North African Church. But, as Augustine himself well knew, in the changing world of time and space appearances are illusory: the subtle power of the human spirit, nourished by education, is not wholly at the mercy of physical arms; the light kindled by the persuasive influence of the humane teacher may be temporarily obscured but is difficult, if not impossible, to quench. The influences of earthly conquerors is short-lived in comparison with those whose conquests are in the realm of ideas and whose first allegiance is to 'that other city, that heavenly city, a stranger and a pilgrim on earth, which makes no false gods but which herself is made by the true God'.[2]

St. Augustine's influence as a teacher was to live on over the centuries of physical defeat to play its part in building a new Europe, in which man would continue on the path of his self-education with renewed confidence. This influence stemmed from the ideas he originated but also from the strength and humanity of his personality as expressed in his relationships with people. Possidius recognised this ultimate source of a teacher's influence when in the concluding words of his biography of St. Augustine he said:

> People who read what he has written on divine matters can gain great advantage. But I think that the people who got most from him were those who also heard and saw him in person as he talked in his church, and especially those who had some experience of his conversation.[3]

[1] Possidius, *op. cit.*, 31. For the evidence as to the exact date of his death see the Benedictine Life of St. Augustine, Migne, *Patrilogia Latina* vol. 32, pp. 576–7.

[2] *The City of God* xviii, 54.

[3] Possidius, *op. cit.*, 31.

2 Fundamentals of St. Augustine's Thought

We should not imagine that it is essential to our happiness that we should know the causes of the great convulsions of the physical world, causes which lie concealed in the deepest recesses of nature—but we ought to know the causes of good and evil, as far as it is granted to men in this life to know them, so that we may avoid the errors and troubles, of which this life is so full. Enchiridion 16, 5.

In so far as concerns the nature of man, there is nothing in him better than mind and reason. But the man who wishes to enjoy the happy life should not live according to man when he ought to live according to God so that he may attain happiness. If he is to attain such happiness, the mind must not be content with itself but must give allegiance to God.
Reviews i, 2.

St. Augustine's self-education, as portrayed in his *Confessions*, is a dynamic movement of the soul from bewilderment and doubt to understanding and faith. A study of the *Confessions* shows that education, liberally interpreted, is vastly more subtle, intimate and purposeful than schooling in the narrow formal sense—'the hateful sing-song of the schools',[1] as Augustine describes his own experience of school education. His understanding of the meaning and purpose of life was reached only after an intensively personal and poignant search for the answers to basic problems. Although he practised as an instructor before he had reached conviction, it was only after his conversion that he began to educate. The practice of education, seen as a total, all-embracing function of the life of man, can be accomplished only on the basis of commitment to a philosophy of life. In this and the following chapters we shall briefly examine some aspects of that total view of life and of man, which enabled St. Augustine to fuse content and method into one unified and

[1] *Confessions* i, 13, 22.

meaningful whole, and so to deserve the title of Teacher of the Faith.

THE SUPERNATURAL BASIS

St. Augustine's philosophy is founded on a conviction of the supernatural destiny of man, who finds his completion in a realm of existence unbounded by space and time; that is in the unchanging life of the spirit, for which all earthly existence is preparatory.[1] Behind the apparently solid world of material objects (*corpora*) is the immaterial world, open to the human understanding in some such way as the physical world is exposed to sense perception. The spiritual area is characterised by its permanence, in contrast to the situation of change and decay in which the physical environment is continually and necessarily involved.[2] Since spirit is prior to matter, it is the cause of all physical existence; the first principles or 'eternal reasons of things' (*aeternae rationes rerum*), by which the movements of physical nature are controlled and directed, are to be found in the area of spiritual existence. The apparently conflicting phenomena of the natural universe are resolved into order and unity when man comes to understand those immaterial principles which are the source of all reason and intelligence. The supreme 'reason' (*ratio, logos*) is God, by whom everything was created, and whose will it is that man should be formed in His image, and in the end be gathered back into His being: 'Thou has made us for thyself, and our hearts are restless until they find their rest in Thee'.

If man's experience and vision are limited to the changing, restless phenomena of physical existence, he cannot feel securely at home in the universe, but must be continually frustrated in his hopes and plans. Without an understanding of immaterial,

[1] e.g. *Christian Education* i, 42: The soul has its own true and sure resting place in eternity.

[2] Augustine's criteria of real existence are set out in *The Practices of the Manichaeans* i, 1: 'That is fully real which is always exactly the same, which is in every way like itself, which cannot in any part be corrupted or changed, which is not subject to time, which cannot be any different now from what it has been. This is what is meant by existence in its truest sense.' The definition of course owes much to Platonism.

eternal truth he must, therefore, be disappointed in his search for happiness (*beatitudo*) which, by universal consensus, is the goal of all human endeavour.[1]

The difficulty in attaining happiness and security lies in human weakness and a disinclination to renounce more immediately attainable and superficially attractive objectives for the sake of the more demanding effort and self-sacrifice which lead to more solid satisfactions. Augustine does not hold that man must entirely renounce the pleasures of the senses; but he must succeed in emancipating himself from the dominance of sense impression. He must arouse himself from transient sensual pleasure to the supremely purposeful and satisfying activity of pure thought; until he does this, he must inevitably fail to realise the happy life.

Augustine holds, therefore, that a true understanding of the nature of the happy life for man is an essential prerequisite to the understanding of education. Human happiness consists in intellectual activity, that is in the pursuit of knowledge. As soon as a man commits himself to this life of the intellect, he knows that he has found the key to the happy life. Therefore, as St. Augustine puts it, 'No man knows the happy life and is unhappy'.[2] The purpose of education is to assist the learner to develop a love of intellectual enquiry, through which man progressively enlarges his understanding of real existence, introducing order into the apparent chaos of human experience, and seeing the flux of the temporal world against a secure background of unchanging truth.

This activity of learning, which consists in the direction of the human intelligence towards its own proper ends, was demonstrated in the experiences of group learning recorded in St. Augustine's Cassiciacum dialogues. It is logical that the first three of these dialogues should be devoted to probing the conditions of the happy life, namely *Against the Academics*, *The Happy Life*, and *The Principle of Order* (*De ordine*).

In the first book of *Against the Academics*, Augustine pursues

[1] e.g. *The Trinity* xiii, 25: It is a characteristic of all men that they want to be happy. Also in *The Practices of the Catholic Church* 3, 4: We certainly all want to live happily—there is nobody belonging to the human race who would disagree with this opinion.

[2] *83 Various Questions* 35.

the question of whether the happy life is adequately defined in terms of 'enquiry into truth' (*veritatis inquisitio*).[1] In terms reminiscent of both the Platonic and Aristotelian schools, it is argued that man cannot be happy, unless he lives 'in accordance with that which is best in man'; this best thing is 'mind' or 'reason'. Cicero, as Augustine claims, had sufficiently appreciated the fact that the happy man is one who 'searches' for the truth. But with the tincture of scepticism to be expected in a thinker who has not received the Christian revelation, Cicero necessarily concluded that man cannot carry out this search with success. However, Augustine establishes the conclusion, which he considers irresistible for the Christian believer, that human happiness consists in a progressively more complete realisation of the ultimate end of education, which is a knowledge of the spiritual and the divine.

The happy life is, therefore, defined in terms of both the process and the aim. The aim is to know God, and the process is intellectual enquiry designed to elaborate an ever more complete picture of reality as it actually is.[2] Both the process itself, which is carried on within this temporal existence, and the aim, whose final completion lies beyond this mortal life, are productive of happiness in themselves. In regard to both, the learner must be selective, as Augustine sees it. He must not seek to learn anything and everything, but must discipline his intellect to tread the path of wisdom, which leads to an understanding of principles of ever-widening generality. The discipline is philosophy, and the end is wisdom.

In *The Happy Life* Augustine pursues the theme, seeing life as a voyage full of hazards and temptations designed to divert man from reaching his true resting place. If happiness is the fulfilment of life, and so of education, unhappiness is a falling short of the true measure which makes up the value of human life. A rich man who places supreme value in his material possessions is necessarily insecure and unhappy because he does not possess what is permanent and of unchanging value, namely an understanding of eternal truth. It is this which renders man independent of the inevitable chances and changes of the

[1] *Against the Academics* i, 2–4.

[2] *The Free Will* ii, 52: The essence of the happy life consists in a disposition of the soul cleaving to the unchanging good.

voyage of life.[1] The secret of human happiness lies, therefore, in accurately assessing one's real needs:

> In my opinion the man who does not possess what he loves, whatever it is, cannot be called happy; nor can the man who possesses what he loves, if it is harmful; nor the man who does not love what he does possess, even if it is the best thing for him. For the man who desires what he cannot get is tortured. And the man who has got what ought not to be desired is deceived. And the man who does not desire what ought to be possessed is sick—None of these is happy.[2]

The theme runs throughout St. Augustine's teaching and is expressed in various forms in words which have echoed down the centuries. 'What else is the happy life, unless it consists in an intellectual grasp of what is eternal?', he asks.[3] And again, 'The happy life certainly consists in the joy which comes from truth'.[4] Therefore, 'That man is happy who possesses Thee, O God'.[5] God is 'the highest good' (*summum bonum*), because He is the context in which all existence is illuminated and becomes meaningful. He alone is, therefore, the source of all knowledge—'the truth and light of the rational soul'.[6]

If happiness is defined in terms of wisdom, i.e. the knowledge of eternal reality, man may be faced by the question, 'Is knowledge possible?'. As we have already noted, St. Augustine's own intellectual evolution is marked by the conviction that a knowledge of reality is possible for man. Truth exists, and through the discipline of education it can be grasped by the rational intelligence of man. All man's efforts of learning are in fact motivated by this faith. Of particular interest to Augustine's

[1] In *The Free Will* ii, 26, Augustine says: Everybody is happy who attains the chief good—just as it is universally agreed that we wish to be happy, it is similarly agreed that we wish to be wise, because nobody is happy without wisdom. Nobody is happy except by the possession of the chief good which is seen and possessed in the truth which we call wisdom.

[2] *The Practices of the Catholic Church* i, 4.

[3] *83 Various Questions* 35, 1: Quid est aliud beate vivere nisi aeternum aliquid cognoscendo habere.

[4] *Confessions* x, 23.

[5] *The Happy Life* 11.

[6] *Letter* 137, 17.

thought in this connection is *Against the Academics*, in which he works out the arguments against the sceptical position in regard to the possibility of knowledge. In the first place his confidence is founded on the universality of the human desire for happiness and on the conviction that happiness, the highest good, consists in knowing.[1] So the philosophers of the New Academy are seen as wallowing in a slough of despond; they desire truth, but at the same time they lack the faith that it exists or can be discovered. This amounts to a denial of knowledge as the supreme good for man; something non-existent or non-attainable could not be properly described as man's chief good. 'All the attitudes of the Academics', says Augustine, 'are therefore vitiated by the attitude with which they begin their search.'[2] Man's behaviour is marked by a continual drive towards knowledge; no such phenomenon would manifest itself, if the possibility of attaining knowledge were continually frustrated in his experience.

To this sort of argument the Academics reply that they have an end in view; they are aiming not at truth but at the probable, which they say is sufficient for all practical purposes. But to Augustine this is blatant self-deception. The probable is a meaningless concept in the absence of unvarying standards (*modi*) by which the probable can be measured. The probable is what is 'like' the truth, and, without an exemplar, there can be no copy or likeness. It would, therefore, be absurd to contend, as did Carneades, that we can know the probable without first knowing the truth itself.[3] If man confines his search to the probable, his intellectual progress may be temporarily stimulated but, he must inevitably fall into disillusionment and despair. The discipline of philosophy is a witness to man's inner conviction as to the possibility of knowledge; in his moments of reflection he knows that truth must be accessible to him when he

[1] *The Free Will* ii, 26: Before we ever become happy, the notion of happiness is impressed on our minds. It is in virtue of this notion that we say in faith and without hesitation that we want to be happy. Also *The Trinity* xiii, 6.

[2] *The Happy Life* 14.

[3] Carneades (214–129 B.C.) was a prominent member of the New Academy who developed the sceptical tendency of the school through his trenchant criticism of the dogmatic stoicism of such as Chrysippus. *Against the Academics* iii, 40–1.

has developed an adequate sense of direction. The quality of this proper human optimism is expressed in the concluding words of *Against the Academics*:

> I do not see as yet exactly how human wisdom is constituted. But since I am only in my thirty-third year I don't think I should despair of attaining it in the end.[1]

Augustine holds that human insecurity and unhappiness derive from the non-possession of unvarying standards by which to distinguish between truth and falsehood; therefore he defines wisdom as 'a standard of the soul (*modus animi*) by which the soul measures itself so that it neither runs away into excess nor restricts itself to something less than its full measure'.[2] Reason clearly points to the existence of absolute standards of truth built into the nature of the universe. But these 'eternal reasons' must themselves have been created in the beginning; their existence as realities are, therefore, founded on the conception of a 'supreme standard' (*summus modus*), which has itself not been created. In Augustine's view the great achievement of Christian revelation has been its clear demonstration of the existence of a supreme Creator, who has established His Creation on the basis of laws, which only He Himself could initiate, since He alone existed in the beginning. Therefore, in the last resort the reality of a God, who has communicated part of Himself to the universe and to man, is the only supposition upon which the possibility of human happiness can be supported:

> Whoever comes to the supreme standard by the pathway of truth is happy. To possess God with the soul and to enjoy Him—these are one and the same thing.[3]

Thus the evidence for the existence of a Supreme Being rests on the recognition of a rule of law and order running through the whole of the universe. It is the purpose of the dialogue *The Principle of Order* to show how absolute and unvarying this rule is. Even a casual acquaintance with the physical world shows that its phenomena are often predictable. The reason why events seem to happen accidentally is that we fail to penetrate

[1] *ibid.* iii, 43.
[2] *The Happy Life* 33.
[3] *ibid.* 44.

sufficiently deeply into the complicated nexus of cause and effect. For example, the apparently casual falling of leaves and the direction of their fall may appear as examples of uncaused movements. But the truth is otherwise, if the matter is closely investigated. Such movements are governed by a complex of factors, for example the strength of the wind, the position of the trees and of the branches from which they fall and the weight of the leaves themselves, as well as 'by other innumerable and more obscure causes'. Some of these causes may entirely elude our senses; nevertheless they exist.[1] There is, therefore, in Augustine's philosophy no such thing as pure chance:

> 'Is there anything', I ask you, 'which in your opinion runs contrary to the principle of order?' 'Nothing,' he said, 'For how can anything run contrary to a principle which fills and occupies the whole universe? What contradicts the principle of order must necessarily be outside the principle. We must, therefore, conclude that nothing runs contrary to the principle of order.'[2]

Thus the principle of order in the physical world is in itself a sufficiently persuasive demonstration of the reality of God. The existence of physical nature postulates an immaterial originating first principle. But this is not to say that the changing material world can yield a knowledge of God. In order to understand what man can understand of the nature of God requires, as we have already shown, an effort of the pure intelligence. The physical world with its wealth of varied phenomena suggests the existence of God by analogies, but cannot by itself lead the enquiring student to a knowledge of the supreme reality. Having been stimulated and guided in his first steps, the learner must make his own effort of learning without extraneous help, if he is to attain the goal of the intellectual understanding of eternal truth. He does this by putting to its proper use the divine element within him, i.e. his rational intelligence, which is given him for the purpose of determining a value system:

> The Creator has given us a mind and natural reason, which tell us that living things are to be preferred to things that are not alive, immortal things to things that are mortal, what is

[1] *The Principle of Order* i, 11.
[2] *ibid.* i, 15.

powerful to what is impotent, good to evil, the incorruptible to the corruptible, the unchanging to the changing, the invisible to the visible, the immaterial to the material, what is happy to what is miserable.

Therefore, to live well is 'simply to love God with all the heart and with all the soul and with all the mind'.[1] To Augustine this statement represents both the aim and the method of education, regarded as the drawing out of the latent potentialities of man so that he more fully realises the divine within him.

St. Augustine's own wide-ranging studies in philosophy led him to examine the contributions of the various philosophical schools, such as the Epicureans and the Stoics. Their attempts to find the explanation of the universe in terms of material first principles, such as fire, air or water, were all unconvincing. It was finally in the school of Platonism that he found a real advance in man's understanding of the nature of things. The Platonists had been able to break out of the shackles of sense perception and identify a spiritual superstructure transcending the physical universe. In his assessment of the worth of Plato himself, Augustine uses the expression 'almost a Christian' (*paene Christianus*), and justifies this by showing that Plato placed his faith 'in wisdom which is not human but divine and entirely unchanging, and in truth which is always consistent with itself'.[2] In the followers of Plato Augustine found a unanimous conviction that God is 'the cause of all existence, the ultimate reason for understanding and the objective, in reference to which the whole of life is to be regulated'.[3]

The full extent of St. Augustine's debt to Plato will emerge as we study his theory of learning in closer detail. In the meantime let us note that it was from Platonism that Augustine understood both the aim and the method of education: the aim is a knowledge of the ultimate, transcendent cause of all existence, which Plato called 'the idea of the good'; the method is the Socratic method of question and answer, which must begin with self-examination, for it is within the soul and not in the external physical environment that dependable knowledge is to be found.

[1] *The Practices of the Catholic Church* i, 46.

[2] *Letter* 118, 20.

[3] *The City of God* viii, 4.

Hence Augustine defines the whole subject matter of philosophy as 'God and my Soul'. It is through his spiritual essence that man is connected to God and able to comprehend the nature of immaterial reality; therefore, the first step in man's progress towards an understanding of reality is that he should painstakingly explore and accurately define his own nature. The sequence of events in true education is made clear in the interchange between Reason and Augustine, which takes place near the beginning of the *Soliloquies*, themselves a first-hand demonstration of the inward approach to understanding:

> *Reason:* What then do you want to know?
> *Augustine:* Everything I have prayed for.
> *Reason:* Sum this up in brief.
> *Augustine:* I want to know God and my soul.
> *Reason:* Nothing more?
> *Augustine:* Absolutely nothing.[1]

In order to understand the unchanging reality, which lies behind the world of change, man must turn his thought away from physical phenomena, reflected in sense perception, and indulge in a process of inner research unaided by sense data. 'Truth has its dwelling', as Augustine says in *True Religion*, 'in the innermost part of man',[2] that is in the immortal soul whose capacity is unlimited. To turn the eye of the mind inwards is not to restrict and enclose thought, but rather to expand immeasurably its range and scope. It is the way to an understanding of the divine:

> Descend into yourself; go to the secret chamber of your mind. If you stay far from your own self, how can you draw near to God? For it was not in the body but in the mind that man was made in the likeness of God. In His own likeness let us seek God; in His own image recognise the Creator.[3]

Similarly in the *Confessions*, which resemble the *Soliloquies* in their exploration of the self, Augustine attributes the successful

[1] *Soliloquies* i, 7. See also *The Principle of Order* ii, 47, where the purpose of philosophy is defined in terms of 'a double question', i.e. about the soul and about God.

[2] *True Religion* 72.

[3] *Tracts on St. John's Gospel* xxiii, 10.

outcome of his own self-education to his eventual recognition of he principle of interiority derived both from the Scriptures and the Platonic writings:

> All this suggested to me that I should turn back to myself. So I entered into the depths of my being under Thy guidance, and I was able to do it because Thou didst help me. I entered, and with the eye of the soul, such as it was, I saw above the eye of my soul and above my mind the unchangeable light.[1]

FAITH BEFORE UNDERSTANDING

As Augustine's own experience bore in upon him the need to look within for the answers to the fundamental problems, so also experience taught him a second principle of method, namely that faith must come before understanding: 'Believe in order that you may understand' (*crede ut intelligas*).[2] The process of learning can begin only when there is present in the mind of the learner a conviction as to the real existence of what he seeks. On that condition knowledge comes as 'the reward of faith':

> The reward of faith is to see what we believed before we saw it.[3]

The thesis was suggested to Augustine by the Scriptures. There is the statement of Isaiah—'unless ye first believe, ye shall not understand'—and the command of Christ—'Seek and ye shall find', implying a persistent search, motivated by belief in the real existence and absolute value of what is sought.[4] The principle is stated in different forms in many places in Augustine's writings. For example in the *Tracts on St. John's Gospel*:

> Do not seek to understand in order that you may believe, but

[1] *Confessions* vii, 10, 16. The advice 'Return to thyself,' may be traced back through Plotinus' phrase, ' '*αναγε ἐπὶ σαυτόν*' in *Enneads* i, 9, and his statement of the divine command that men should 'know themselves' in *Enneads* iv, 1, to Plato's 'Know thyself'.

[2] For a closer analysis of Augustine's views see E. Gilson, *Introduction à la philosophie de St. Augustin*, pp. 39–47. For the relation of faith and knowledge in the Alexandrian fathers see C. B. Bigg, *The Christian Platonists of Alexandria*, p. 114.

[3] *Expositions of the Psalms* 109, 8.

[4] *Isaiah* vii, 9. *Matthew* vii, 7.

believe in order that you may understand, since, unless you believe, you will not understand.[1]

The recommendation that belief must come before understanding seems to strike at the roots of the scientific realism characteristic of modern thought and the progressive approach to education. The scientific method stresses the value of suspension of judgement and caution in regard to belief, except in the face of very demanding evidence. In the pragmatic philosophy truth is always to be regarded as hypothetical and subject to revision in the light of further experience. However, St. Augustine is concerned with the discovery of absolute truth and not with scientific enquiry into physical nature. Scientific knowledge comes through sense experience, but truth is reached by intellectual research, motivated by a conviction that there is something to be known which transcends the senses. In this area 'we must believe before we can understand, and we must take care that our faith is not a pretence'.[2]

The principle of faith before understanding does certainly elevate the part played by faith and authority in the education, while not minimising the importance of reason. It allots to reason a purely instrumental function, a means to an end, which is not the creation of truth but the demonstration of what is above, and prior to, the human reason. It denies to reason the power of penetrating to truth by its own unaided efforts, but does not restrict the power of reason to give strong support to what is already believed.[3] Indeed, as the Cassiciacum dialogues show, the effort of rational thought is necessary for the consolidation of what is first taken on trust. In other words, faith ought not to remain blind, but must be followed up by the enquiry of reason. In this Augustine follows the thought of the liberally minded Clement of Alexandria who defines faith as 'so to speak a comprehensive account of essentials', while knowledge, properly so called, is 'the strong and sure demonstration of what is

[1] *Tracts on St. John's Gospel* xxix, 6. For further references to the principle in Augustine see *Sermon* 43, 7; *The Free Will* ii, 5; *Against the Academics* ii, 9, etc.

[2] *The Trinity* viii, 8.

[3] *Expositions of the Psalms* 118. Also *Sermon* 18, 3: Our understanding contributes to the comprehension of what it believes.

received by faith'.[1] For man with his rational mind, understanding is the desirable and proper consequence of belief:

> Faith opens up the approach to understanding; unbelief closes it.[2]

The proper function of reason is to ask questions about everything, including questions about the world which transcends the senses and about God Himself. If such questions are motivated by an existing belief, they will not be flippant but seriously directed to the purpose of learning and will serve to consolidate and not to weaken faith. For example, in a letter to Consentius, who had asked Augustine to answer some questions on the perplexing problem of the Trinity, Augustine advises him in a memorable phrase, which crystallises his own educational faith, to 'fall deeply in love with understanding' (*intellectum valde ama*). Augustine goes on to justify the recommendation:

> Banish the thought that God hates that faculty (i.e. reason), by which He made us superior to all other living creatures; or that we should so believe that we neither accept nor search for rational understanding.[3]

The point is then made that the principle of faith before understanding is in itself one which must be capable of being rationally demonstrated. If it were not so, then we ought to discard it as false.

At this point we should, however, note that St. Augustine does not assert that faith comes without any preliminary thought. We do not suddenly believe in what has not been already in our thoughts. Thus, whereas the main function of thought is to clarify the content of faith, it has also the function of bringing that faith into being. St. Augustine makes the point for example in the following passage:

> Who does not see that thought precedes belief? No one would believe anything, unless he first thought that it ought to be believed. However brief a moment it may be, some kind of thought precedes the will to believe and, however rapidly the latter follows, so as to seem most closely joined with it,

[1] Clement, *Stromata* ii, 2

[2] *Letter* 137, 15.

[3] *Letter* 120, 1, 3.

yet it is necessarily the case that everything which is believed is believed after thought has preceded—Not everyone who thinks believes, but everyone who believes thinks. Thought goes along with belief and belief with thought.[1]

Education is therefore a process in which thought and belief, reason and faith, work together towards the goal of understanding. But the essential point which Augustine makes is that learning cannot be carried forward on the basis of scepticism as to the possibility of a successful outcome. A sense of purpose and direction is necessary for the successful outcome of learning.

That faith must of necessity precede understanding is rationally demonstrated by Augustine by observation of the well-known facts of human behaviour. He sees that the young child begins by accepting his beliefs on trust from parents and teachers, and acts confidently on such beliefs accepted on authority. Later he should want to understand the reasons for what he has already accepted on faith. This is when he must in fact 'fall in love with understanding', and to cultivate and properly direct this love is the highest task of the teacher. But it is not only the child who obviously acts on faith rather than on reason. In the conduct of the practical business of life, adults too must take many of their beliefs on trust, since there is no time to develop a rational understanding of everything they need to employ in the business of their daily lives. Again, in relation to the understanding of ultimate reality, it is obvious that man makes his first contact with the word of God through the Scriptures or from the words of a teacher. He begins by repeating with little understanding what the teacher says, and by the initial whole-hearted acceptance of the authority of the teacher, particularly of the divine teacher who speaks through the Scriptures, the soul is purified and so made fit 'to reach the vision which passes not away but abideth'.

There are, therefore, two pathways to truth, authority and reason. Of these Augustine holds that authority comes first in temporal sequence and, for the uneducated majority, may remain the only guide.[2] But for as many as are capable of

[1] *On the Predestination of Saints* 2, 5.

[2] *The Principle of Order* ii, 26: There are two factors which must necessarily bring us to learn, namely authority and reason—Authority is first in time but in reality reason is first.

intellectual effort, reason is the more trustworthy guide by which man is led to the full enjoyment of the rewards of faith.

In his own teaching Augustine followed this principle. For example, it may be observed in operation in the overall plan of his great work, *The Trinity*, which begins by setting out in unambiguous terms the relevant information which the Scriptures provide and in the second half goes on to develop a more complete understanding of what up to this point has been uncritically accepted on faith:

> It is now our purpose to address ourselves to the same theme as before, but by a more inward method of approach, still observing the same rule that the truth which has not yet become luminous to the understanding, will still not escape the firm grasp of faith.[1]

One further important limitation of the principle that faith must precede understanding should be made clear. Augustine declares that the method is applicable only with reference to the understanding of 'divine matters':

> There are some things, which we do not believe unless we understand them, and there are other things which we do not understand unless we believe them.[2]

Here he is making a distinction between scientific knowledge and the knowledge of spiritual reality. Whereas a scientific or sceptical method involving cautious suspension of belief until the evidence warrants confident assertion is appropriate to the investigation of the physical world, the method for the investigation of spiritual reality requires a preliminary acceptance by faith. In either case learning must be preceded by the desire to learn—by the ardent love of understanding—but in the latter case this love must be more specifically directed and more clearly and positively motivated. Seen in this light, this aspect of Augustine's methodology states an important pedagogical truth which we must now follow up by an examination of his concept of love as the motive power of learning.

[1] *The Trinity* viii, 1.

[2] *Expositions of the Psalms* 118. Also *Sermon* 18, 3.

THE SIGNIFICANCE OF LOVE

Augustine sees faith as the context in which the desire to learn is conceived and love as the dynamic element which moves the will to reach out after the knowledge which it desires to possess. In Gilson's words love is 'the inmost mover of the will' (*le moteur intime de la volonté*).[1] The notion is expressed in Augustine by the use of the Latin words *amor*, *caritas* or *dilectio*. In *Christian Education*, love is called 'a movement of the mind directed to the enjoyment of God for His own sake and the enjoyment of oneself and one's neighbour for God's sake'. 'Love' is clearly distinguished from 'lust' (*cupiditas*), which is in the same place defined as 'a movement of the mind directed to the enjoyment of oneself and one's neighbour and any other physical object for their own sake and not for the sake of God'.[2]

Love is generated by faith. Because faith is 'seeing through a glass darkly', implying only a partial and incomplete possession of the desired object, the movement of learning is therefore the desire to complete knowledge by filling in the missing details. In the first place, love is stirred into the activity of learning by partial knowledge; as Augustine puts it, 'No one loves what is unknown' (*nemo amat incognita*); in the second place, the purpose of learning is to complete one's knowledge of something which is already known in part. Augustine holds that there is no such thing as learning something entirely new; it is always a matter of building on some existing and incomplete knowledge. Curiosity is, therefore, defined as 'fashioning in the mind an imaginary form, by which the mind is stimulated to love'. This imaginary form is not created out of nothing, but out of the materials of existing experience:

> The learner fashions such a form out of what he already knows—if he loves this, this love will take its start from what he has already learned.[3]

The thought appears again in the following sentence from the same place in *The Trinity*:

[1] E. Gilson, *op. cit.*, p. 174.

[2] *Christian Education* iii, 16. In *The City of God* xiv, 2, however, Augustine talks of 'good love' and 'bad love' (*bonus amor*, *malus amor*). Elsewhere the term *amor* is used to imply the altruistic love of that which ought to be loved.

[3] *The Trinity* x, 3.

The whole love of the desiring mind, that is of the mind desiring to know what it does not know, is not the love of what it does not know but rather of what it does know, on account of which it wishes to know what it does not know.

Learning moves from the known to the unknown. For example, it is through some momentary and partial glimpse of the spiritual element within us that we are led to desire to know about our soul. Examination of the nature of the soul raises questions regarding the nature of God Himself; thus our thought progresses from simpler to more difficult questions, and each step as it is taken, opens out more enticing and attractive prospects.

The love of knowledge is, therefore, deeply implanted in the human soul; but, if learning is to occur, that love must be specifically directed: 'There is no such thing as love which loves nothing'.[1] Furthermore, on the assumption that education properly understood is directed to the understanding of goodness and truth, love, as distinct from its opposite, lust, is a movement directed towards the possession of some worthy object. Only when life is so directed can it lead to happiness, the good for man:

It is not the man who possesses what he loves who is really happy but the man who loves what ought to be loved.[2]

What really counts in human education is, therefore, the precise object of a man's loves and hates—'What is loved, this is the important matter' (*interest quid ametur*).[3]

Using the analogy of physical objects, Augustine shows that the human soul has its own proper direction, which is towards God. Nevertheless, the freedom of the will means that, unlike the objects of the physical universe, man can misdirect his love towards unworthy objects. Man's love is to his soul as weight is to physical objects:

Weight does not carry objects only in a downward direction, but always towards their own proper places. Fire moves upwards; a stone downwards. They are all moved by their

[1] *ibid.* viii, 12.
[2] *Expositions of the Psalms* 26, 7. Also *The Trinity* xiii, 9.
[3] *On the Excellence of Widowhood* 26.

> weights and make for their own proper places. Oil poured under water is carried to the surface of the water. Water poured over oil sinks below the oil. They are all moved by their weights and make for their own proper places. Things out of their place are disturbed; restored to order, they are at rest. My love is my weight. It is by this that I am carried wherever I am carried.[1]

Augustine's theory leads to the conclusion, which receives strong support from the experiences of teachers, that learning, in the liberal sense of an enrichment of the understanding, cannot be coerced, but can occur only in an atmosphere of free choice, in which the movements of the mind are directed by a genuine interest in the thing to be known. Therefore, it is the teacher's first concern to engage the enthusiasm of the learner in the task in hand, and through the presentation of desirable objectives, to arouse the learner's will to learn. This inner volition can be stirred into action only from within by the stimulus of the desire to possess and enjoy something for oneself:

> Will is a movement of the mind compelled by nobody and directed to the possession of something.[2]

The doctrine of the freedom of the will is central to Augustine's view of man and his education. A stone unquestioningly obeys the law of its own nature, which is that it should move only by the application of external force; it cannot be held responsible for its behaviour, which is not self-activated. In man, however, behaviour is under the control of the will, and he is, therefore, fully responsible for his acts. To St. Augustine the

[1] *Confessions* xiii, 9, 10: *Pondus meum amor meus; eo feror quocunque feror*. Also *Letter* 157, 9: My mind is carried along by love as if by a weight. Also *The City of God* xi, 28: Just as a physical object is carried along by its weight, so my mind is carried along by love wherever it is carried. Augustine is following the concepts of the Aristotelian physics, e.g. Aristotle, *Physics* iii, 5, 205a: Every physical object naturally rests somewhere, and for each there is a special place which is the same for both the part and the whole.

[2] *Against the Manichaean Conception of Two Souls* 14. Also *Tracts on St. John's Gospel* xxvi, 3: If a man is dragged, he comes unwillingly. If he comes unwillingly, he does not believe; if he does not believe, he does not come.

freedom of the will is a reality about which there can be no dispute:

> There is nothing I realise more strongly within myself than that I have a will and that it is my will which prompts me to enjoy this thing or that. What could I call mine, if the will by which I make my choices is not mine?[1]

The denial of the efficacy of human volition was one of the main obstacles which prevented Augustine's wholehearted acceptance of the doctrine of the Manichaeans. When in Christianity he found solid support for the freedom of the human will, it played a highly important part in his thought about human nature and education. Starting from his conviction that nothing happens without a cause, he finds the efficient causes of all the movements, both of the natural world and of the soul, in the operation of wills. Augustine notes that causes are popularly classified as fortuitous, natural and voluntary; but on analysis he discovers that the distinction is unreal. There is in fact no such thing as a fortuituous cause. Natural causes are to be traced back to the will of the Creator; they are, therefore, 'voluntary'. Augustine's thought leaves no room for the conception of 'luck'. He holds that it is in default of an accurate knowledge of God that pagans resort to attributing events, which they cannot explain, to luck. But in fact they reveal an underlying and instinctive perception of the real state of affairs when, with seeming inconsistency, they talk of fortune 'willing it' that this event or that should occur.[2] Those who have received the Christian illumination look to God as the source of every occurrence. Where, due to the intricate and complex connections of events, they cannot trace out the connection to the divine will, their faith in the universality of the divine providence enables them to believe that the divine will is causally involved. Augustine's assertion that in God 'resides the power which acts on the wills of all created spirits'[3] may suggest, as it does to Cochrane, that 'at this point the question arises whether the Christian logos does not rescue man from the

[1] *The Free Will* iii, 3.

[2] *Reviews* i, 2.

[3] *The City of God* v, 4. C. N. Cochrane, *Christianity and Classical Culture*, p. 481.

tyranny of nature only to make him the puppet of God'. Here certainly Augustine is involved in an insoluble dilemma; he is convinced both of the freedom of the human will and of the reality of divine foreknowledge as an essential attribute of God's omnipotence:

> To confess that God exists and at the same time to deny that He has foreknowledge of future things is the most manifest folly.[1]

In *The City of God* Augustine challenges the stoic conception of an impersonal, irrevocable fate governing events, as expressed for example by Cicero in his *Concerning Divination.*[2] To Cicero it seemed that, if he granted the possibility of foreknowledge of events, he could not deny the domination of events by fate; and there would be the end of human responsibility and the possibility of education in its fullest sense. Being unable to endure this conclusion, Cicero denied the notion of divine foreknowledge. Augustine shows that by this conclusion Cicero was not in fact denying the existence of God, although he was taking away what to the Christian must be one of God's essential attributes, namely omniscience.

The problem of reconciling divine foreknowledge with human responsibility and the integrity of the human will is a difficult one.[3] On the one hand, Augustine could not give assent to the Manichaean denial of responsibility to man; on the other hand he could not in any degree diminish the omniscience of God. Augustine wrestles with the apparent contradiction involved in the two statements that 'we do not sin by necessity', and on the other hand that 'God has foreknowledge of all that is to be'. He strives to refute the view that God has resorted to a pious fraud in giving man the illusion of free will, while denying him the reality. How can man be regarded as in any real sense the architect of his own destiny, if God knows from the beginning of time exactly what he will choose to do at every moment of

[1] *The City of God* v, 4: '*Qui non est praescius omnium futurorum non est utique Deus*'.

[2] Cicero, *De Divinatione* ii.

[3] The most important texts on this problem are *The City of God* v, 9–11 and xi, 21; *The Free Will* iii, 2–4. For discussions of the adequacy of Augustine's arguments see C. N. Cochrane, *loc. cit.* and E. N. Pickman, *The Mind of Latin Christendom*, vol. 1, p. 398 ff.

apparent choice?[1] Augustine's dilemma arises from the fact that he believes in human freedom and also in divine omniscience, and according to his usual method his thought is directed to the task of understanding what he already accepts by faith.

In brief, Augustine's argument leads him to deny that to have foreknowledge of what will happen is the same thing as to exercise a compulsive force upon the course of events. The difficulty lies in the human tendency to see the mind of God as operating like the human mind but on a larger scale, that is to see God as physically limited as we are. He is in fact not confined within a framework of past, present and future:

> He does not look forward to the future as we do, nor to what is present nor back upon what is past; but in a manner quite different and profoundly remote from our way of thinking. He does not pass from this to that by a transition of thought but sees everything with absolutely unchangeableness—variations of time, past, present and future, although they alter our knowledge, do not affect His . . . so He knows all times with a knowledge which time cannot measure.[2]

This sums up the trend of Augustine's argument on free will and predestination, an argument based on a reiteration of the infinite nature of God as contrasted with the finite nature of man. It is almost as far as Augustine goes in supplying the key to the dilemma. The endowment of man with freedom of will was an essential element in God's plan of creation. Man has the power of self-determination, and the fact that God knows in advance how he will act is not to say that that freedom is illusory. Using the analogy of memory, Augustine points out that, as human beings exercise no compulsive influence on past events through their possession of retrospective knowledge, so 'God by His foreknowledge does not use compulsion in the case of future events'.[3] Looking again at the limited framework of human knowledge, we see that it is often possible to predict accurately what a man will do in the future; thus in a partial

[1] *The Free Will* iii, 9 Evodius puts the dilemma in this way: 'I should like to know with what justice God punishes sins which must necessarily be committed; or how they are not necessarily committed when He knows that they will be committed'.

[2] *The City of God* xi, 21.

[3] *The Free Will* iii, 11.

degree we do in fact enjoy the prescient characteristic of God. But to say that we know how a man will act is not the same thing as intervening to coerce him. 'Sin is therefore committed voluntarily', Augustine repeats, 'and not by any compulsion from God's foreknowledge—my power of willing is not taken from me by God's foreknowledge'.[1]

The dilemma arises from St. Augustine's inability to conceive of God as still engaged in working out the plan of His creation and inviting man to be an intelligent co-partner with Himself in an on-going evolutionary movement. In this respect the modern pragmatists, such as William James, regard the philosophy of supernatural idealism as lacking a realistic challenge to educational effort in a fully creative sense.[2] While this may be said, there is nevertheless the challenge presented by Augustine's consistent emphasis on human self-responsibility. Man has the freedom to sin, and, if this is a flaw in God's creative purpose, it must be freely admitted. Yet this same freedom, directed by intelligence and warmed by love, can be widely and liberally applied by the Christian in the secular society for the benefit of his fellow man. Above all, the terrible responsibility of free will lays on the individual person the full responsibility for furthering his own education, which becomes a matter of personal, disciplined involvement and research rather than of involuntary indoctrination by a higher authority. As Augustine says to Valentinus, abbot of Adrumetum, and to his monks, among whom a difference of opinion had arisen on the question of the free grace and justice of God: 'Pray that you may devoutly believe in order that you may wisely understand, for indeed our free will exists for this very end that we should wisely understand'.[3] Both for the modern scientific realist and the classical

[1] *ibid.* iii, 11 and iii, 8.

[2] For a vigorous statement of the evolutionary approach, see Wm. James, *Pragmatism*, (Longmans Green, N.Y., 1907), pp. 290–1: 'Suppose that the world's author put the case to you before creation saying, "I am going to make a world not certain to be saved, a world the perfection of which shall be conditional merely, the condition being that each several agent does its own level best. I offer you the chance of taking part in such a world. Its safety, you see, is unwarranted. It is a social scheme of cooperative work genuinely to be done. Will you join the procession? Will you trust yourself and trust the other agents enough to face the risk?" '

[3] *Letter* 214, 7.

idealist the doctrine of human freedom implies that every man must be his own teacher, and we shall later see that this is fundamental to St. Augustine's theory of teaching and learning. Through education, which must in the end be crowned by the conferment of divine grace, the free gift of God, man rises to a higher level of freedom. Man always possesses the ability not to sin, if he so chooses; by the conferment of grace he advances to the more perfect freedom which consists in the inability to sin. Augustine is sure that, by the coming of grace, there is no reduction of human freedom; by this gift the will is not made void, but is rather established in a greater measure of freedom.[1]

CONCLUSION

This chapter has been designed to bring into relief the basic elements of Augustine's thought, which determined his views on the nature and purpose of education. To advance further would be to explore questions more properly located in the area of pure theology and belong to Augustine's later thinking. Indeed it is by the optimistic and humane thought of his formative years rather than by the more rigorous theological doctrines of his later years, elaborated as they were in and through conflict with heretical sects within the church, that Augustine makes his most enduring contribution to the understanding of education. The doctrines of original sin, free grace and predestination, make their appearance in St. Augustine's thought in their definitive form in the treatises he directed against the Pelagians, beginning in the year A.D. 411 when he was 57 years of age. Rigorous as they may at first seem, Augustine never entirely allows his eye to wander from the realities of the human situation. Even the doctrine of the unavoidability of damnation, if it is so foreordained, is tempered by the suggestion that the degrees of punishment will be adapted to the circumstances of cases.[2]

[1] *Concerning the Grace of Christ and Original Sin* 14: 'That man who knows what he ought to do but does not do it has not yet been taught by God according to grace but according to the law, not according to the spirit but according to the letter'. E. N. Pickman, *op. cit.*, p. 393.

[2] *Enchiridion*, 93: 'The gentlest punishment of all will fall upon those who have added nothing to the original sin which they brought with them into the world. And, in the case of those who have added to it, their damnation will be more endurable in proportion as their iniquity was less.' Also *On Grace and Free Will* 5.

Similarly, with regard to the emphasis he places on human responsibility, Augustine does not overlook the obvious fact that, owing to some inherited taint or secret compulsive force, there are men who seem unable to escape from the necessity to sin. 'This discovery', as Pickman remarks, 'is no more original in Augustine than it is in modern criminology; the recognition of inherited sin indeed is common to primitive people'.[1] So too there are those so favoured in their original endowment that goodness is no effort. In neither case does it seem entirely in accordance with justice that the former should be punished and the latter rewarded. But just as the state punishes those who sin due to the overwhelming pressure of unfavourable circumstances, so does God; such observations are in Augustine's view in accord with the facts of common experience. And, if we ask why it is that, since God desires man to pursue goodness and be saved, he does not bestow his free grace upon all without exception, Augustine answers that this would be to deprive man of an important stimulant to effort. The awareness of the possibility of grace is a mighty encouragement to the continual effort of the human will, an effort which Augustine holds must always be necessary to the attainment of wisdom and happiness in this life. Thus in his basic philosophy Augustine brings some of the conflicting facts of human nature to the attention of educators. While he points to the reality of the perpetual warfare against sin, which man must face, he at the same time lays emphasis on the powerful strength of man's voluntarily conceived purposes, when through the activity of reason he comes to see unity and consistency running through the whole of existence. Man achieves this insight when he learns to refer the temporal and changing to an unchanging and infinitely extended spiritual context. The progressive elaboration of this frame of reference sums up for St. Augustine the whole work of education, which begins and ends with the faith that God exists and is man's highest and most enduring good.

[1] E. N. Pickman, *op. cit.*, p. 403.

3 Psychological Aspects

Consider then how deficient is our knowledge of our own nature. Our ignorance covers not only what we have been but what we now are and includes not only what relates to our bodies but also what relates to our inner selves. The Soul and its Origin iv, 12.

Man has been created in the image of God not in respect of his physical form but in respect of his rational mind. This fact is proclaimed not only by true reason but also by the authority of the Apostle himself.
The Trinity xii, 12.

The successful practice of teaching is founded on an accurate understanding of the psychology of the learner. References we have already made to the writings of St. Augustine, in particular the *Confessions* and *Soliloquies*, show that the study of the human psyche was of absorbing interest to him. He expressed the conviction that this study must begin with an examination of the self; unless the teacher reaches an unprejudiced understanding of himself, he cannot further his own education, much less educate others. The knowledge of the soul is in fact the first step in the search for truth: 'Philosophy has a double question to ask, first about the soul and then about God'.[1]

THE NATURE OF MAN

St. Augustine's psychology is built on Christian insight, supplemented by accurate observation and self-analysis. The article of faith upon which he elaborates his whole account of human psychology is that spiritual existence transcends and thus controls physical existence. Therefore, he defines man as 'A rational soul using a mortal and earthly body'.[2] Following the principle

[1] *The Principle of Order* ii, 18.

[2] *The Practices of the Catholic Church* i, 52: *Anima rationalis est mortali et terreno utens corpore*. E. Gilson, *Introduction to the Study of St. Augustine*, p. 58 traces the origin of the definition in Plotinus, *Enneads* vi, 5 and in Plato, *Alcibiades* 129e.

that faith leads to understanding, Augustine strives to elucidate the far-reaching implications of this definition. He believes that man in this mortal life is a union of the spiritual and permanent on the one hand and the material and transient on the other; observation of man persuades him that this union of body and soul is close and intimate, and that this fact is as relevant to man's educational progress as is the fact of his dual nature.[1] He sees that the contrary tendencies and divided loyalties which appear in human behaviour arise from this close union of two separate and distinct substances. Hence an important function of education lies in the recognition and reconciliation of these two contrary natures, a lesson which is constantly impressed on the reader of the *Confessions*. The need for this reconciliation is, as we have seen, central to the argument of *The City of God*.

St. Augustine does not underestimate the importance and urgency of man's physical needs, and the extent to which at times they must draw man away from the higher satisfactions associated with his spiritual part. He is, therefore, concerned to discover as much as possible about the nature of this union of soul and body, which is man. But this again is by its very nature a difficult problem, which in *The City of God* he admits may be beyond the understanding of man:

> . . . the mode of union, by which bodies and souls are bound together and become living beings, is thoroughly marvellous and beyond the comprehension of man, although it is this very union which is man.[2]

In an earlier writing St. Augustine had attempted to communicate the subtlety of the body–soul relationship by analogies drawn from physical nature. He recalls Plato's metaphor of the two-horsed chariot and horseman, three elements bound together and moving in close unison under the direction of the horseman. In the same place he likens man to a lamp; in its most significant aspect a lamp is an intangible flame, but from

[1] e.g. *Tracts on St. John's Gospel* xix, 15: *Anima habens corpus non facit duas personas sed unum hominem*. As Gilson notes, *op. cit.* p. 58 n. 2, Augustine inherits the Platonic definition of man but his Christianity leads him to lay greater emphasis on the unity of soul and body.

[2] *The City of God* xxi, 1.

another standpoint it is a physical object, with which the living flame is indissolubly connected.[1]

However this may be, the important fact, nurtured by faith and sustained by observation and thought, is that soul is superior to body. The soul 'gives life to the body',[2] which is to say that it controls and directs every aspect of the organism's behaviour. It maintains the unity of the body, presides over physical growth and reproduction and regulates the distribution of the body's nutriment. 'Augustine sees the life process of human beings', says Cochrane, 'in terms of a body–soul complex, in which the body fulfils the requirements of an organ or instrument to the soul, and this he applies no less to the elementary vital functions than to the highest manifestations of conscious and deliberate activity.'[3]

The spiritual conception of the soul implies that the soul is not subject to change and decay, as material objects are, and that it is *simple*, i.e. indivisible or uncompounded.[4] Since these qualities are entirely remote from information presented in sense experience, they are difficult to comprehend. This is the reason why, as St. Augustine found in his own experience, it is hard to understand the nature of the soul. The difficulty is increased by the tendency of ordinary speech to work within a conceptual framework appropriate to the analysis of physical nature. Thus the statement of Genesis that 'The Lord God formed man of the dust of the ground and breathed into his nostrils the breath of life; and man became a living soul' is merely, as it were, a visual aid to the understanding of what really happened. The 'breath' of God was not in fact the physical air which we all breathe, but an immaterial substance, quite different from air. It is this substance, bearing a merely superficial likeness to 'breath', which gives life to inanimate matter.[5] The essential difference is that all physical elements, however tenuous or small, are capable of being divided into parts, whereas what is immaterial is indivisible and therefore not subject to change, decay and death. In his treatise *On the Soul and its Origin*,

[1] *The Practices of the Catholic Church* i, 6.
[2] *The Christian Struggle* 22.
[3] C. N. Cochrane, *Christianity and Classical Culture*, p. 444.
[4] *The Size of the Soul* 2.
[5] *The Literal Interpretation of Genesis* vii, 19.

Augustine defines a physical object (*corpus*) as being 'composed of larger and smaller parts, which occupy larger and smaller areas'.[1] All physical objects are, therefore, compound in nature and occupy space. By contrast the soul is 'simple' and has no local habitation; it is all that physical nature is not.

In the dialogue, *The Creatness of the Soul* (*De Quantitate Animae*) Augustine and Evodius probe into the nature of the difference between soul and body. The dialogue poses the question, 'How big is the soul?' (*Quanta est anima?*). The form of this question suggests that the soul has bulk, as physical things do, but the conclusion of the dialogue is that the soul has no 'size' in this sense. The question is, nevertheless, a proper question to ask about the soul, but one that must be understood in another frame of reference. We are asking, 'What are the soul's powers?' or 'How great is the soul's capacity?'. In fact we want to know, 'What is the soul able to do?'.[2]

The argument in *The Greatness of the Soul* leads to the conclusion that through its non-participation in the physical properties, which in the popular view are the criteria of real existence, the soul is raised to a distinctly higher level of existence, from which it dominates and controls all physical movement. Thus the soul 'uses' the body. A good deal of time in the dialogue is devoted to demonstrating that the soul is not located somewhere inside the body, as is commonly supposed.[3] If it were confined in this sense, as an object is contained within a box or a sack, it would be difficult to account for the fact that feeling is located throughout the whole body and not in any one part. Another fact, which impresses the disputants, is the unlimited capacity of the soul to store impressions,[4] and this is accepted as the strongest support to the presumption of the 'different', i.e. non-material nature of the soul.

[1] *The Soul and its Origin* iv, 17.

[2] *The Greatness of the Soul* 4.

[3] As Aristotle located the soul in the heart and Galen in the brain. Plotinus, *Enneads* iv, 3, 20, may no doubt have inspired Augustine's thinking: 'Neither the soul nor any part of it may be considered to be within the body as in a space; space is a container, a container of body. It is the home of such things as consist of isolated parts.'

[4] See also *Co fession*

Added to the argument based on the unlimited capacity of the soul is the argument based on the soul's capacity to 'see' what is immaterial. On the higher level of the soul's understanding there is its capacity to grasp absolute truth. But the argument in *The Greatness of the Soul* starts on a lower level: in the world of material existence there is no such thing as length without breadth, but the mind can contemplate 'length pure and simple'.[1] Similarly, a point (punctum), defined as 'the starting point or termination of a line', has in itself no physical proportions. Nevertheless, the soul can see the point in all its purity, i.e. in its true immaterial nature. All this is sufficient proof that the soul has the power 'to discern immaterial realities' (incorporea cernere), which it can do only on the assumption that its own nature is also immaterial.

Care is taken to show that by immaterial nature is meant something quite different from the nature of even the most tenuous physical substances, such as air. At the same time, St. Augustine introduces one phenomenon, which causes him some difficulty: 'We used to be amazed when we were boys', he tells Evodius, 'at the way the tails of lizards would continue to wriggle when we had cut them off from the rest of the body'.[2] All physical substances are divisible; by contrast all immaterial substances, such as the soul, are indivisible. How then is the continuing movement of the severed tail of the lizard to be explained, except on the assumption that the soul also has been divided by the knife? If the soul can be divided, it is made of parts, i.e. material. This is an inconvenient fact for one who believes that the soul is immaterial, and it is one for which Augustine can find no adequate explanation.[3] The fact of the continuing life in the divided worm may be a fact about the body and not about the soul at all; on the other hand it may be accounted for by the assumption that the soul is 'both one and

[1] *The Greatness of the Soul* 10.

[2] *ibid.* 62.

[3] *ibid.* 63. Aristotle in *De Anima* i, 5, mentions that 'certain plants and insects go on living for a time when divided into segments'. He concludes that the soul is divisible in the sense that it continues to exist *as a whole* in each of the divided segments. In the physical sense it is not divisible. The souls present in the divided parts of the plant or insect are 'homogeneous with one another and with the whole'.

many'.[1] Augustine and Evodius agree that they must wait for a reasonable explanation to turn up. In the meantime, the overwhelming weight of evidence is, in Augustine's view, on the side of the spiritual nature of the soul.

A further interesting line of argument pursued in *The Greatness of the Soul* concerns the apparently parallel and simultaneous growth of soul and body. However, it is established that there is no absolute correspondence between the size of the body and the power of the soul, which is mysteriously united to it. If such a correspondence existed, an elephant would be more intelligent than a man or an ass than a bee.[2] St. Augustine appeals to observation to show that there is little or no correlation between physical size and intellectual ability:

> There are many men whose limbs are slighter and shorter, and who show themselves more gifted intellectually (*prudentiores*) than others who are endowed with a great bulk of a body.[3]

Other facts are adduced, such as that the body ceases to grow before the powers of the soul are fully developed, and that in physical combat the result is not determined solely by the comparative measure of the physical strength of the opponents, but by psychological factors, such as strength of will and intelligence. In discussing this point, St. Augustine employs interesting analogies from the natural world, showing his mastery of the commonly accepted physical notions of his day. When, for example, two moving physical objects collide, the heavier will cause the lighter to deviate from its course: 'By nature's law lighter masses yield to heavier ones'.[4] But even here other factors affect the outcome. The comparative velocity of the two objects

[1] The influence of Plotinus is again obvious. His 'world soul' is indivisible but in breathing life into bodies it is multiplied into many souls, while retaining its fundamental unity and being undiminished: 'The soul is one and many, divided and yet unable to be divided', *Enneads* i, 2, 2.

[2] *The Greatness of the Soul* 24.

[3] *ibid.* 29.

[4] *ibid.* 37. Augustine also follows the erroneous view of his day to the effect that, if two stones of unequal weight are dropped from a height, 'the larger stone reaches the ground first', a theory which was not to be abandoned until Galileo dropped his stones from the leaning tower of Pisa at the end of the sixteenth century.

at the moment of impact is relevant. A heavier stone thrown up into the air and meeting a lighter stone thrown towards the ground will cause the lighter to be not only deflected from its course but even 'forced back skywards'. But if the lighter stone is hurled into the air with greater impetus than the heavier stone, it may well reduce the speed of the heavier stone and may even deflect it from its course. When this happens, it is possible to say that the lighter stone has imposed its 'will' upon the heavier stone through the stronger impetus of its flight.

It is made clear that these are mere analogies designed to show that, even in the physical world, phenomena are not always capable of simple explanation; the observer must look for more hidden causes. In a test of physical endurance, if the victory goes to the combatant who is less strong physically, this is because he has a soul of greater strength. Physical combat between men is more than a mere collision of inert masses. It is essentially a matching together of two souls 'using' bodies. Thus strength, comprehensively defined, is a combination of physical and spiritual elements: It is 'an impulse of the soul (nutus animae), and a mechanism of the nerves and the weight of the body'. The phychological analysis proceeds as follows:

> It is the will which gives the impulse; and the will is intensified by hope or courage, but retarded by fear and much more by despair. For in fear, provided that there is an element of hope, a greater degree of physical energy generally makes its appearance. . . . The soul's impulse uses the nerves like many thongs to move the weight of the body . . . the soul has its own reserves of strength from which greater courage and confidence are brought forth.[1]

Therefore, man reveals his true 'strength' or capacity in the precise use which the soul makes of the body.

Although a close examination of human behaviour does not support the notion of the parallel growth of soul and body, there is the obvious fact that the soul does in some sense 'grow' as man advances in growth from childhood to maturity. 'I am troubled,' says Evodius, 'by the fact that, as far as we can see it, the soul of a newly born child is totally unskilled and not endowed with reason.'[2]

[1] *ibid.* 38.   [2] *ibid.* 34.

In what sense then does the soul 'grow' or develop? In answering this question, Augustine selects an aspect of child development, which particularly interested him, namely the emergence of articulate speech in the young child.[1] Is this evidence of the 'growth' of his soul? It appears that the power of speech is not a natural or inevitable growth, but is developed by a process of imitation. Reared in a deaf and dumb society, the child would not learn to speak.[2] Speech is an art, which, like tight-rope walking and all other arts, is learned partly by unconscious imitation of examples and partly by deliberate instruction. In fact the development of speech is one example of the soul's capacity to learn, i.e. of 'its greater power to act when it is educated rather than uneducated'.[3] Thus, with reference to the soul, growth is to be measured only in terms of an increase of knowledge and skill:

> It is in a sense correct to say that the soul grows as it learns, and that it is reduced when it gives up learning, but only in a metaphorical sense.

The arguments outlined in the previous pages were designed to establish the fact that the soul shares no elements in common with the body and is the superior element in the composition of man. In establishing that the soul is separate from the body, Augustine makes it clear that it can carry on an activity of its own without any reliance on, or assistance from, the body. This is the life of enquiry leading to a progressively firmer grasp of absolute truth. In fact the soul has a dual function to perform: it must continually animate the body, i.e. direct the body's vital functions; at the same time it has its own private intellectual function, which it is capable of attending to simultaneously with the attention it must give to the body. The capacity for attending to two functions at once without any apparent reduction of concentration on the life of pure thought is taken by Augustine as further evidence of the soul's immaterial and therefore unlimited nature.

[1] *ibid.* 31.

[2] Augustine also cites the example of a young man of Milan known to himself who was born deaf and dumb. Because he could not hear the speech of other people, he could not imitate them and therefore never learned to speak.

[3] *ibid.* 33.

In *The Greatness of the Soul* the discussion leans heavily on evidence based on observation of the physical world, whereas elsewhere St. Augustine relies more strongly on first-hand knowledge of the soul gained through self-scrutiny. His approach to self-knowledge is thoroughly opposed to the scepticism characteristic of the Academics; it is evident to anyone who thoughtfully approaches the matter that the soul can know itself in a very direct manner—'by a sort of inward presence, real and not imaginary'.[1] Since, as we have already noted, self-knowledge is the starting point of all higher knowledge, it is important to know that we can accurately and comprehensively know ourselves:

> When the soul seeks itself, it knows that it is itself which it is seeking, because it is not possible for it to know anything, unless it knows itself.[2]

What then does the human soul know of itself when it examines itself? In Augustine's view there are basically three elements in this awareness: The soul knows that it exists, lives and possesses the power of intellectual understanding. It recognises that existence is shared with inanimate objects and life with the animals, but that the human soul alone is endowed with the capacity for intellectual understanding:

> Everyone is convinced that there can be no intellect without life and no life without existence. Therefore, the possessor of intellect exists and lives in his own special and distinctive manner; his mode of existence is quite different from the corpse, because the corpse does not live; his mode of life is different from that of souls which have no power of intellect.[3]

Augustine goes on to express the self-evident functions of the soul in an extended catalogue:

> Who can doubt that the soul lives, remembers, understands, wills, thinks, knows and judges?[4]

[1] *The Trinity* x, 16.
[2] *The Literal Interpretation of Genesis* vii, 28.
[3] *The Trinity* x, 13.
[4] *ibid.* 14. The thought is reminiscent of Descartes, *Meditation* ii: 'What am I? A thinking being. What is that? A being who doubts, understands, affirms, denies, wishes, refuses, imagines and feels.'

This is all that is immediately given about the nature of the human soul and, because it is all that is immediately given, it is all there is to know. All existing theories about the composition of the soul, such as that it is made of air or fire, are not founded on direct knowledge of the self by the self, and must therefore remain purely speculative and unconvincing. Augustine insists that, in seeking a knowledge of the self, we must be careful not to add any extraneous speculative element to what we immediately observe of our own nature.

To sum up Augustine's conclusions on the soul of man, it is immaterial, which is to say that it is mortal and unchanging; it has a lower and a higher function, the former being to rule the body and the latter to pursue the life of wisdom. Because the soul is spiritual, it has the power to enter into a relationship with the spiritual world, and this power is strengthened by education. St. Augustine emphasises, however, that man is in this life a soul and body joined in indissoluble union and has therefore strong attachments to the physical world. It is a thoroughly realistic view which, as Cochrane puts it, 'insists upon the continuity of experience and denies the existence of any real hiatus between the life of sense and that of thought'.[1] In St. Augustine's own words:

> From the soul and the body, which are the parts of man, we arrive at the totality which is man. Accordingly spiritual man and carnal man are not two things but one. Both are one and the same thing, namely man living according to the principle of his nature.[2]

Although St. Augustine's analysis of the soul, like Plato's and Aristotle's, discovers a number of faculties or functions, the essential unity of the soul is carefully preserved. Whatever the soul attends to, it attends to with its whole being; whatever it does or suffers, is done to, or suffered by, itself as a whole. This emphasis excludes education in terms of faculty training and raises it to the level of an art. The teacher's work becomes more demanding and comprehensive, since his influence is brought to bear on man one and indivisible—'a rational soul using a mortal and earthly body'.

[1] C. N. Cochrane, *op. cit.*, p. 445.

[2] *The City of God* xiv, 2.

THE MECHANISM OF SENSE PERCEPTION

In his account of sensation Augustine does not radically depart from the current theories of his day, and is considerably indebted to Empedocles and Aristotle in particular. He declares that in sensation the initiative always rests with the soul, which 'feels throughout the whole body' (*per totum corpus sentit; ubique in corpore sentit*). Furthermore sensation is brought about by the meeting of like with like, as Aristotle had said:

> The organ of hearing is physically united with air, and, because it is in air, the air inside is moved concurrently with the air outside.[1]

Perception of sound is due to the pulsation of the external air against the air contained within the ear. In Augustine's words, hearing occurs when the external air is set in motion and its pulsations impinge on 'that which is similar to air lying within the sense organ'.[2] Smell and taste are associated with the presence of water in the sense organs, which come in contact with 'watery exhalations' from the objects sensed. A sensation of taste results from the mingling of substances taken into the mouth with the saliva:

> Whatever produces taste in the mouth is first mingled with the moisture in the mouth, even if it seems to have been quite dry when it was received into the mouth.[3]

Similarly, the sensation of touch results from the contact of an 'earthy or muddy element' (*terrunum et quasi lutulentum*) with its like. Each sense is, therefore, associated with the meeting together of one or other of the four basic elements of physical matter. In sight the element is fire, manifesting itself, as Plotinus himself described it, as light shooting forth from the eyes and encountering the external light of the sun:

> Sight depends upon the linking of the light of vision with the light leading progressively to the illumined object—In vision the object is grasped there where it lies in the direct line of vision; it is there that we attack it; it is there that the per-

[1] Aristotle, *De Anima* 420a.
[2] *On Music* vi, 11.
[3] *ibid.* vi, 10.

ception is formed. The mind looks outward—it does not see by virtue of some mark made upon it, like the impress made by a ring on wax.[1]

Augustine agrees with Plotinus that the activity of sensation is a function of the soul, which projects itself outwards towards the object to be sensed. Contact of the eye with the object seen is made 'in the place where the object seen is present' and not at the eye itself. Sight reaches out to the object by projecting a ray of light outward from the eye. This ray, by which the eye makes contact with the object sensed, is the basis of sensation:

> Sight extends itself outward, and through the eyes shines far out in every direction to light up what we see. So it sees rather in the place where the object seen is located and not in the place from which it breaks through to see.[2]

We need not linger on the defects of such an explanation. Aristotle had criticised the Platonic view on the grounds that the theory does not explain why, if our eyes are like lanterns shooting forth rays of light, we cannot see in the dark. In more than one place Augustine, however, shows that he is not too well satisfied with the explanation in terms of emanations of light from the eyes alone, and lays more emphasis on the meeting of like with like. In *The Literal Interpretation of Genesis*, for example, he remarks that the light, which is in the eye of the viewer, is 'so weak that, unless we are helped by the external light, we see nothing'.[3] And so, while maintaining the out-going nature of the process, he suggests the unique nature of vision as compared with the other senses, in that it requires the cooperation of a physical element distinct from the actual object sensed; this element is the external light of the sun. In his analysis of the process of mental or spiritual vision, i.e. intellectual understanding, Augustine uses this analogy of physical

[1] Plotinus, *Enneads* iv, 5, 2. Compare Empedocles quoted in E. E. Spicer, *Aristotle's Conception of the Soul*, p. 96, n. 3: 'Just as a man' thinking to sally forth through a stormy night, gets him ready a lantern, fastening to it horn plates to keep out all manner of winds—but the light leaping out through them shines across the threshold with unfailing beams.'

[2] *The Greatness of the Soul* 43. Also *Letter* 137, 5; *On Music* vi, 21.

[3] *The Literal Interpretation of Genesis* i, 31.

vision to show that, if the mind is to 'see' truth, it requires the aid of a light external to itself, the illumination of God.

Explaining the transmission of sense impressions from the sense organs to the brain, Augustine represents the brain as connected to the sense organs by narrow pipes or tubes (*tenues fistulae*); these extend 'to the ears, to the nostrils, to the palate'. He also more cautiously reproduces the opinion that 'the sense of touch is directed by the brain through the marrow of the spine and through the marrow enclosed in the bones to which the spinal column is joined—from this marrow the very finest ducts which produce the sense of touch are diffused throughout all the limbs'.[1] Later in the same book, he holds that the brain possesses three ventricles (*ventriculi*): the first, located in the front of the brain, is concerned with sense perception; the second in the back portion of the brain controls movement; the third, situated between the first and second, is the seat of memory. From the observable fact that movement in response to sense stimuli does not occur simultaneously with the stimulus but always after some lapse of time, however small, St. Augustine concludes that memory must act as an intermediary between the anterior and posterior ventricles, and is therefore properly located between them.[2] Such conclusions correspond in some measure to those later reached by experiment on the localisation of function within the brain. Augustine is aware that damage to the brain by disease affects sense perception, muscular control or memory according to the area where the damage has occurred.

In his account of the nature of sense perception in *The Trinity*, Augustine closely follows Aristotle's classic definition of sense as 'what has the power of receiving into itself the sensible forms of things without the matter'.[3] He also uses the metaphor of the signet ring impressing its likeness on wax, the wax receiving the impression of the ring without receiving the substance of which the ring is made. In the act of sensation we receive the forms of objects in the mind, and therefore vision is 'sense informed by what it senses'. Here too the emphasis is thrown on the soul's initiative: the soul 'forms within itself'

[1] *The Literal Interpretation of Genesis* vii, 20.
[2] *ibid.* vii, 24.
[3] Aristotle, *De Anima* 424a.

(*format in se*) impressions of sensible things. Vision requires two conditions, the object sensed and the seeing person, of which the latter is the active element in the process.[1]

The will of the percipient brings the sense organ into contact with the object to be sensed, and the visible form of the object is then impressed on the sense. Augustine makes it clear that the form impressed on the sense is not the same as the visible form which belongs to the sensible object, any more than the form impressed by a ring on wax is the actual form of the ring. In the case of the ring and the wax, the distinction is clear when the ring is withdrawn from the wax, and the wax is seen to retain an impression or reproduction of its form. In sense perception, the two forms are certainly similar, and are presented in such close conjunction that we have no means of separating the two. But certain observable phenomena, such as the after image, defined in modern psychological parlance as the tendency of a response to outlast its image but by Augustine as 'the remains of the form which was impressed on the sense',[2] serve to confirm the separate nature of the two forms. When we look at a bright object and then close our eyes, we have the impression of bright colours variously intermingling and gradually losing their brightness. This represents the vanishing remains of the form impressed on the sense when the shining object was still present to it.

In summary Augustine distinguishes three elements in the act of sense perception:

1. The visible form (*species corporis quae videtur*).
2. The form impressed on the sense (*impressa eius imago sensui*).
3. The will, which brings the sense into contact with the sensible object (*voluntas animi quae rei sensibili sensum admovet*).

The importance of the will in the process of learning has already received some attention and will be further discussed later in this chapter.

Behind the five senses, which receive the discrete elements of sensation, Augustine postulates a synthetic faculty which inte-

[1] *The Trinity* xi, 3.

[2] *The Trinity* xi, 4.

grates these elements and passes judgement on them; he calls it the 'interior sense' (*sensus interior*). Augustine's account of the interior sense follows closely Aristotle's account of the 'common sense' whose function is three-fold:

1. To compare or distinguish between simultaneously presented data of the different senses.
2. To perceive the 'common sensibles', namely motion, rest, figure, magnitude, number and unity.
3. To enable us to observe the senses themselves, for example that we have five senses through which data are supplied to the mind.[1]

The interior sense is seen as an intermediary between the several senses and the reason. When we reach back from the senses to the interior sense, we have passed the bounds of the physical world. The senses are physical and belong to the body; the interior sense on the other hand is immaterial and belongs to the soul. The interior sense, however, differs from the reason in that its perceptions fall short of knowledge, which is the province of reason alone:

> Unless the information conveyed to us by the senses of the body goes beyond that sense (the interior sense), it cannot become knowledge.[2]

The conception of a faculty which is aware of the senses, has the power of analysing and synthesising the data of the several senses, and nevertheless is distinct from reason, seems artificial. To Augustine, however, the distinction is necessary, since he cannot allow the divine attribute of reason to the animals. St. Augustine recognises the undisputed fact that animals do possess powers of discrimination, and can learn from experience. This could be possible only by assuming their possession of a syn-

[1] Aristotle, *De Anima* 418a: 426b. J. Beare, *Greek Theories of Elementary Cognition*, pp. 276–83. E. Spicer, *op. cit.*, pp. 77–81.

[2] *The Free Will* ii, 9. The sequence is described in *Confessions* vii, 17, 23: 'By degrees I passed from material things to the soul, which perceives through the senses of the body and thence to the interior faculty (*vis interior*), to which the physical senses communicate external things—and thence to the reasoning faculty, to which is referred for the exercise of judgement upon it whatsoever is received from the physical senses.'

thetic, or judicial, faculty of a lower order, with the function of 'presiding over all the other senses'. Thus the animal shares with man the interior sense, with which it is enabled to sustain its physical existence and avoid danger.[1] But rational thought has a function extending far beyond the requirements of physical security to embrace the notions of value and duty. St. Augustine puts it that 'reason judges the physical senses, approving their integrity and demanding that they do their duty'. This evaluative function is a responsibility of an entirely higher order than is possible for the animals. The wise use of it is the characteristic mark of the rational intelligence of man.

SENSATION AND KNOWLEDGE

In thus passing inwards from sense perception to the interior sense and to the power of reason and judgement, we are passing from the simpler function of sensation to the more complex function of understanding (*intellectus*). The discussion of the function of the understanding in the more abstract sense will be discussed further in the next chapter. In the meantime we should look further at his views on the process whereby man comes to understand his physical environment through sense perception.

Following the argument in *The Greatness of the Soul* we find that a clear distinction is made between sensation and knowledge, which are 'quite different things'.[2] Augustine proposes as a tentative definition of sensation that 'it is the soul not being unaware of something happening to the body'.[3] This definition is critically scrutinised and eventually enlarged and reconstructed. The difficulty is that the soul's state of awareness, resulting from attention to some physical stimulus, is very often an awareness of more than is in fact communicated by the sense organs. We may, for instance, see only smoke, and yet by

[1] *The Free Will* ii, 8: 'The faculty by which the animal sees is different from that by which it either avoids or desires to possess what it sees. The former belongs to the eyes, the latter is within the soul itself.'

[2] *The Greatness of the Soul* 58: '*Aliud sensus, aliud scientia*'.

[3] *ibid.* 41: '*Sensum puto esse non latere animam quod patitur corpus*'. The negative formulation 'non latere' (does not escape the notice) serves to stress an act of the soul as the prerequisite of sensation.

inference become aware of the existence of fire.[1] Therefore, an adequate definition of sensation, as contrasted with knowledge, must be carefully restricted to the data the senses actually supply. To take another example used in the discussion, we are aware of the growth of our hair or our nails. These are things 'happening to the body', but we are not informed of them through any physical sensation but only by inference from repeated observation of ourselves and of other people. In effect, the critical scrutiny of the tentative definition of sensation serves to reinforce the distinction between sensation and knowledge, the latter being defined as 'a state of awareness through the operation of reason'.[2] In the end there emerges a reconstructed definition of sensation:

> Sensation is a physical experience which by itself (*per seipsam*) does not escape the notice of the soul.[3]

The expression '*per seipsam*' is used to isolate the pure sense datum from anything added to or inferred from it by the intelligence. The definition is carefully phrased to stress the primacy of the soul in the cognitive act. Where there is no attention on the part of the soul, any physical experience 'escapes the notice of the soul', which is to say that there is no sensation. Augustine consistently denies that the body can inform the soul of anything—'To feel is not a function of the body but of the soul acting through the body'.[4] There is no compromise with the hierarchical principle that the servant is entirely at the command of the master; the inferior cannot in any degree affect or inform the superior.[5]

In all this there are many echoes of the language of neo-Platonism and especially of Plotinus, who for instance says that

[1] *ibid.* 45.

[3] *ibid.* 58: '*Non esse scientiam si quid non latet sed si per rationem non latet*'.

[3] *ibid.* 59: '*Sensus est corporis passio per seipsam non latens animam*'.

[4] *The Literal Interpretation of Genesis* iii, 7: '*Sentire non est corporis sed animae per corpus*'.

[5] E. Gilson, *Introduction à l'Etude de St. Augustin*, p. 76: 'In the hierarchical universe which is his (St. Augustine's) all beings are necessarily superior or inferior to one another by the very fact that they are different. In his eyes it is a basic principle that the inferior cannot in any way act on the superior.'

'sensation is the perception of material objects by the soul using the body', and again that 'It is not the eye which sees, but the active power of the soul'.[1] In the same exposition Plotinus uses the expression 'μὴ λαθεῖν', which is exactly reproduced in St. Augustine's 'non latet' (does not escape the notice).

Clearly the view of man as consisting of two separate and distinct elements, spiritual and physical, the former being superior and therefore initiating all action, prevents Augustine reaching a satisfactory explanation of the body–soul problem; nevertheless, as we shall see later, his theory emphasises the self-activating and responsible nature of man, and this gives support, to a teaching method, which relies less on teacher dominance and more on the learner's personal interest and activity. Augustine is well aware of the difficulties involved in a thorough-going application of the principles of the soul's absolute non-dependence on the body. In the sixth book of the dialogue, *On Music*,[2] Augustine enters into an interesting analysis of a typical act of cognition in an attempt to show how the soul's independence can be maintained, while the undisputed facts of sense perception are properly accounted for. Without pursuing the argument in detail, we may summarise the conclusions to which it leads: Contrary to the popular view, which sees physical stimuli bombarding the body as being the cause of sensation and so of understanding, Augustine reverses the process. Sensation is 'not of the body but of the soul acting through the body'; therefore, the cause of sensation is to be found in the reaching out of the soul to take note of the body's condition in relation to its physical environment. Sensation does not consist in the physical contact of a sense organ with an object, but in a heightened state of awareness focusing on some particular physical condition requiring attention. Augustine closely examines the factors involved in listening to and recognising the rhythms of music, and concludes that neither the physical

[1] Plotinus, *Enneads* iv, 6, 3.

[2] The first five books of *On Music* form an undistinguished treatise of metric, in which lines of verse and metrical feet are exhaustively catalogued. In the sixth book the epistemological question is raised as to how we come to know and recognise these various rhythmical patterns.

environment nor the body can produce any effect on the soul. While the basic physical functions, which the soul sets in motion and maintains, continue unimpeded, the soul need pay only a minimum degree of attention to the welfare of the body. But when the body encounters some opposition to its functions, the soul becomes more attentive and ready to initiate some necessary corrective action—'in consequence of some difficulty the soul becomes more attentive with a view to action'.[1] Sensation is, therefore, a conscious manifestation of the duty of guardianship, which the soul continually exercises in respect of the body. Pleasure and pain are interpreted in this light, pleasure being the attention of the soul directed towards what assists its efforts in respect of the body, and pain the expression of the soul's disapproval of what impedes the body's vital functions. So elsewhere Augustine defines grief as 'nothing other than a feeling of intolerance in respect of some division or corruption of the body',[2] while anger is 'a tumultuous eagerness to get rid of something which is restricting our freedom of action'.[3] Feelings of hunger and thirst are similarly accounted for.

Augustine's view of sense perception may be summed up in the following statement from *On Music*:

> It seems to me that, when the soul feels in the body, it does not suffer anything impressed on it by the body but that it concentrates a greater degree of attention on the body's experiences. I consider that this heightened activity, whether it be easy on account of the fact that the body's experience is agreeable to it or difficult because it is disagreeable, does not escape the notice of the soul. This and this alone is what is meant by sensation.[4]

In Augustine's interpretation, experience is never a matter of interaction between soul and body, but always the action of a vital soul upon a body, which is essentially passive and has no independent life or purpose of its own.

[1] *On Music* vi, 9: '*anima fit attentior ex difficultate in actionem*'.

[2] *The Free Will* iii, 69.

[3] *Letter* 9, 4 to Nebridius. Similarly vomiting is the manifestation of the soul's reaction to the presence of a noxious substance in the stomach.

[4] *On Music* vi, 9.

THE POWERS OF THE SOUL: WILL

In the tenth book of *The Trinity* Augustine analyses the functions, or powers, of the human soul in an attempt to gain insight into the nature of the divine Three-in-One. His conviction that man was made 'in the image of God' makes it seem entirely reasonable that a study of man's soul should shed light on the divine nature. In fact Augustine's effort to gain a rational understanding of the content of faith is rewarded by the discovery of a number of psychological trinities within the soul.

We have already had occasion to note one of these trinities expressed in the statement that the soul 'understands, exists and lives'.[1] Another of particular significance for our study is the trinity of will, memory and intellect, all three of which are always simultaneously involved in thinking and learning.[2] Augustine employs the characteristic mental attitude of doubt or scepticism to demonstrate that the mind always functions with the complete and indissoluble unity of the Three-in-One.[3] When a man doubts, he is in fact recalling some previous experience, which seems to contradict, or at least to sit in an uneasy relationship with, some later experience; doubt is, therefore, the manifestation of thought grappling with some apparently insoluble problem. This is also to say that the doubter is exercising the power of intellectual understanding. Furthermore doubt is clear evidence that man has a 'will' to attain certainty (*certus esse vult*). Hence the state of doubt involves the simultaneous engagement of each element in the trinity of will, memory and intellect; all three are functionally interdependent. The argument for the essential unity of man is pressed home:

> I remember that I have memory, intellect and will. I understand that I have intellect, will and memory. I have the will to will, remember and use my intelligence.

and therefore

> Because all are mutually comprehended in their entirety by each, each taken in its entirety is equal to every other, and

[1] *The Trinity* x, 13.
[2] *ibid.* x, 18.
[3] *ibid.* x, 14.

each is at the same time equal to all taken together; and these three are one mind and one essence.[1]

It follows that in any attempt to evaluate the quality of a person, all three functions must always be brought together in a combined assessment:

> The merit of a boy's character depends on the tenacity and facility of his memory, the penetration of his intellect and the strength of his will.[2]

The will is of great importance in Augustine's psychology. It is the active, restless, energising principle of the soul; its function is to unite memory and understanding in the act of thought and to execute the judgements of reason. It is the executive power, which attends to the lowliest vital functions of the body, 'holds the body together and preserves it from decay', and through sense perception 'seeks and selects whatever suits the nature of the body and rejects and turns away from what does it harm'.[3] At the same time, it is the agent which reaches out in desire towards a knowledge of God, the 'highest good' and 'highest wisdom', whose will for the world is assisted by right decisions and appropriate action on the part of man. In the search for knowledge, therefore, and in putting into action the conclusions of knowledge, the will plays a dynamic part.

By divine decree the will of man is free; therefore, he is responsible for the direction of his will, whether it be towards ends that are in tune with the purposes of God or alternatively towards lower ends. 'If we will,' Augustine remarks, 'it is not someone else who wills concerning us; the movement of our soul is spontaneous; this privilege has been given to us by God.'[4] And again:

> Will is an uncoerced motion of the soul directed to the attainment of an object or the prevention of its loss.[5]

[1] *ibid.* x, 18.
[2] *ibid.* x, 17.
[3] *The Greatness of the Soul* 70–1.
[4] *83 Various Questions* viii.
[5] *Against the Manichaean Conception of Two Souls* 14: *Voluntas est animi motus, cogente nullo, ad aliquid vel non amittendum vel adipiscendum.*

Will is, therefore, always a personal response, and, where it is responsibly exercised by man, it is a response founded on reason. At the same time an act of willing is an expression of a man's desire or love (*amor*, *dilectio*). At times Augustine seems to use 'love' and 'will' synonymously, although he talks of love as 'a stronger will' (*valentior voluntas*).[1] The distinction seems to be of little significance, except that the terms '*amor*' or '*dilectio*' suggest more strongly than '*voluntas*' the personal individual response and man's yearning for the attainment of the specific objectives, which he deems necessary for his happiness and well-being. So Augustine classifies all the movements of the soul as 'wills' (*voluntates*), and refines the description of them in terms of love pursuing, possessing or rejecting. The four basic movements or 'perturbations' of the soul are desire (*cupiditas*), joy (*laetitia*), fear (*metus*) and sadness (*tristitia*). 'Desire' is love reaching out to grasp the beloved object; 'joy' is love possessing and enjoying the beloved object; 'fear' is love fleeing from what is obnoxious, and 'sadness' is love experiencing the obnoxious thing.[2]

The integrity, or consistency, of the will is measured by the extent to which it expresses 'right love'. Movements of the will directed by the passions are in themselves neither good nor bad, and can be judged only in relation to the ends towards which they are directed. Thus anger, 'a turbulent desire to remove what hinders freedom of action',[3] is justifiable or not, depending upon the nature of the end, towards which the removal of the obstacle is the means. We have already had occasion to note this point and the support for it which Augustine finds in physics, namely that 'every sensible object naturally rests somewhere and for each there is a special place'. The weight of a stone naturally carries it down to the earth, unless its movement is perverted by some external contrary influence.[4] Similarly the soul's love, when it is allowed to follow its natural course, moves in the direction of knowledge and towards the divine source of all knowledge. This conception of will in terms of a movement

[1] *The Trinity*, xv, 41.

[2] *The City of God* xiv, 2. Also *Confessions* x, 14, 22.

[3] *Letter* 9, 4.

[4] The relevant texts are *Letter* 157, 9; *Confessions* xiii, 10; *The City of God* xi, 28; *supra*, pp. 55–6.

of the soul towards some clearly defined objective is the basis of Augustine's conviction that learning must always be an activity, which is both spontaneous and purposeful. On all levels of understanding the learner must be carried forward by the free movement of learning, 'the desire for knowledge' (*sciendi cupiditas*). St. Augustine's own experience of schooling drove home the point that external constraint is fatal to learning:

> Free curiosity is a greater encouragement to learning than a frightening compulsion.[1]

From St. Augustine's views on cognition we gathered that sensation is essentially a matter of the soul becoming 'more attentive to the experiences of the body'. The act of attending forms another of the psychological trinities discovered by Augustine: there is the sensible object, the act of seeing and the attention of the mind (*attentio animi*).[2] The last mentioned represents the purposeful action of the will in connecting the physical object and the mind of the viewer. In the first place, the will brings the sense organs to bear on the sensible object; thereafter it brings the object into intimate union with 'the internal gaze of the soul' (*acies animi*). So efficiently does the will perform this work of liaison that the mental impression, which St. Augustine calls 'the inner phantasy'[3] can hardly be distinguished from the external object, on which it is modelled. In fact, when the object is removed from the sense, the impression stored up in the memory may rise in the mind so vividly as even to produce hallucinations:

> The memory presents such an exact likeness of the physical appearance that not even reason itself is permitted to judge whether an object is actually seen externally or only something of the kind thought internally. It sometimes happens that men, who are seduced or frightened by too much thinking about visible things, have suddenly burst into speech, as

[1] *Confessions* i, 14, 23.

[2] *The Trinity* xi, 2.

[3] *ibid.* xi, 7. By 'phantasy (*phantasia*) Augustine is referring to the impressions of sensible objects (*species corporum*) stored up in the memory. See also *On Music* vi, 32.

though they were actually participating in such actions or experiences.[1]

The analysis of the function of the will as '*coniunctrix*', linking the sense datum with the sense organs and with the mind in an act of thought, is elaborated in considerable detail in the eleventh book of *The Trinity* to reinforce the vital part which the will plays in learning. So far we have concentrated on the part played by the will in sense perception, defined as 'the vision of a person seeing' (*visio aspicientis*). However, the act of thought is represented by another trinity, in which again the will plays an important part; this is the trinity of memory, internal vision ('the vision of a person thinking', *visio cogitantis*) and the will, which unites both of these (*voluntas quae utrumque copulat*), so that they form a unity of three things. 'When these three are fused', says Augustine, 'we call it thought.' The internal vision of a person thinking, otherwise called 'the gaze of the soul' (*acies animi*), is the function of evaluation or judgement, which constitutes the act of knowing. All these unifying functions of the will are brought together in the following words from *The Trinity*:

> The will joins the sense organ to the sensible object; it joins the memory to the sense, and the gaze of the mind of a person thinking to the memory.[2]

The successive links forged by the will in an act of cognition may now be diagrammatically illustrated, using the terms employed by St. Augustine in the course of his exposition: (see diagram on next page)

The function of liaison is the positive function of the will, but the will has the complementary function of terminating the act of attention:

> It separates the physical senses from the sensible objects by a movement of the body either to prevent our perceiving a thing or so that we may cease to perceive it; as when we avert our eyes from what we are unwilling to see or shut them . . . so

[1] *The Trinity* xi, 7.

[2] *ibid.* xi, 15: '*Voluntas sicut adiungit sensum corpori, sic memoriam sensui, sic cogitantis aciem memoriae*'.

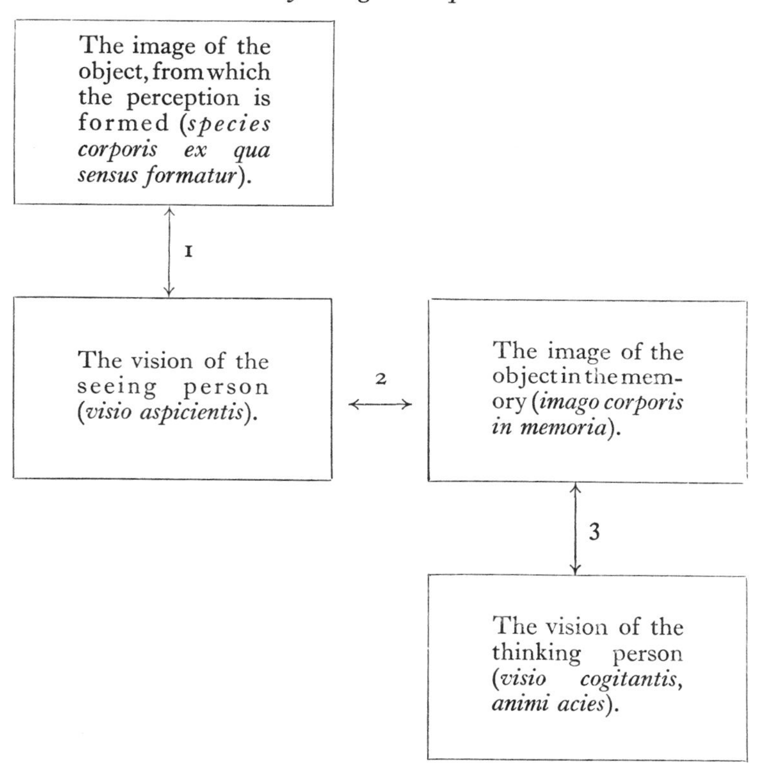

also we turn away from tastes either by shutting the mouth or by putting something out of the mouth.[1]

The withdrawal of attention also involves the breaking of the other links in the chain illustrated above. However, St. Augustine maintains that, so long as we are awake, we are necessarily attending to something. When concentration on one stream of sense impressions is withdrawn, the will immediately focuses attention on another stream. When this happens, the former sense impressions pass unheeded, i.e. they 'escape the notice of the soul' and are not imprinted on the memory.[2] As evidence of this Augustine notes the impossibility of recalling the meaning of what one has read or heard, unless attention has

[1] *loc. cit.*
[2] *loc. cit.*

been concentrated on the words. If we merely hear a person talking to us, but do not listen, we cannot repeat what he has said. 'It often happens,' St. Augustine remarks, 'that I read through a page of a book or letter, and neither know nor can repeat what I have read.'[1] In other words, learning depends upon the voluntary attention of the mind as a whole, i.e. of the memory and the understanding, activated by a purposeful movement of the will directed to some specific end.

MEMORY

The power of memory fascinated St. Augustine, and produces some of his most penetrating psychological analyses. The apparently infinite capacity of memory provides him with one of his strongest arguments in support of the spiritual nature of the soul. His delight in studying the phenomena of memory is exemplified in a passage from *The Soul and its Origin*, where he tells of an experiment he made on his friend, Simplicius, 'a man of excellent and truly amazing memory'. Augustine had asked Simplicius to repeat the last lines of each of the twelve books of Vergil's *Aeneid*, a feat which he easily accomplished. Simplicius further proved his capacity to repeat the penultimate lines of each successive book, to recite the lines in reverse order and to repeat his performance with some speeches of Cicero. On being congratulated by his audience, Simplicius said that up to that point he had not been aware of the full potentiality of his memory.[2] Augustine uses the anecdote to suggest that we have not yet done more than scratch the surface in our study of human psychology.

The extended passage in the tenth book of the *Confessions* is the most comprehensive and impressive exposition of the power of memory in Augustine's writings.[3] Throughout it there recurs like a refrain the awe he feels in its apparently infinite scope:

> Great is the power of memory, exceedingly great, my God, a spacious and infinite sanctuary within me. Who can penetrate its depths? Yet it is a function of my mind and a part of my

[1] *On Music* vi, 21.
[2] *The Soul and its Origin* iv, 9.
[3] *Confessions* x, 8, 12 to 26, 37.

> nature. . . . At this thought a great wonder rises within me; amazement seizes me.[1]

Since memory is a function of the spiritual soul, the content of memory enjoys a spiritual existence, in which there is neither past nor future, but only, as it were, an infinitely extended present. Thus the analysis of memory in the *Confessions* leads into an interesting discussion of the concept of time, designed to show that, in studying the operations of the mind, we must discard the ordinary conception of past, present and future.[2] In the framework of space and time, the past consists of what has been and no longer exists. The future is what will take place; therefore it too has no real existence. Only the present exists and is represented by an infinitely narrow point of consciousness in a continuing stream of impressions passing from the future into the past. In the area of sense impression, the present moment is fleeting and all else is non-existent. Thus Augustine argues that, if thinking depends on what is actually present in sensation at each passing moment, it could have no resources on which to draw; what is past is no longer available for scrutiny. The present 'flies with such speed from the future into the past that it is not extended one whit', says Augustine. It is, therefore, misleading to speak of the present time as being either short or long. The world is exposed to the viewer in a continual series of brief exposures, each of which is sustained only momentarily in sense impressions.

Thought is possible only on the condition that the resources of experience continue their existence so as to be continually available for mental inspection. In memory experience continues to exist 'in the present time', and can be scrutinised at will. Since mind, being immaterial, is not confined within the framework of space and time, the present time of the mind is not narrowed down to the series of successive fleeting exposures revealed to the senses, but is infinitely extended. This is the explanation of the mind's capacity to review very wide expanses of experience, and so derive meaning from the multiplicity of impressions presented consecutively to the senses.

Thus St. Augustine concludes that, as far as the activity of

[1] *ibid.* x, 8, 15.
[2] *ibid.* xi, 11, 18 to 28, 39.

the mind is concerned, we should not speak of past, present and future but rather of 'a present time of past events', 'a present time of present events', and 'a present time of future events'.[1]

The discussion of the nature of time arises from the attempt to understand the concept of eternity, which is the condition of spiritual existence. In the popular view, time is real and measurable, whereas eternity has a quality of vagueness and unreality. From a thoughtful examination of this assumption, however, Augustine concludes that the opposite is the case. The common opinion that something called 'time' actually exists, and can be measured by some objective measuring device, cannot be substantiated. For instance, the notion of present time melts into nothing when it is analysed:

> An hour passes by in fleeting particles. However much of it has flown away belongs to the past; whatever remains is in the future. If we think of an instant of time, which cannot be broken up even into the smallest particles of moments, that instant alone may be called the present. Nevertheless, this instant flies with such rapidity from the future into the past that it is not one whit extended. For, if it is extended, there is a division into past and future; the present has absolutely no extension.[2]

'What then', Augustine asks, 'do we really measure when we make a distinction between what is of longer or shorter duration?' We are said to be measuring time, but in fact time resolves itself into nothing more than 'a stretching out of the mind' over the content of memory.[3] Augustine examines and rejects the common view that time is measured by reference to the motion of physical objects, whether celestial or earthly, the objection being that physical objects cannot be assumed to be in perpetual motion. The potter's wheel is not in perpetual motion; nevertheless, we claim to be able to measure the duration of its

[1] *Confessions* xi, 20, 26. '*Tempora sunt tria, praesens de praeteritis, praesens de praesentibus, praesens de futuris.*'

[2] *ibid.* xi, 15, 20.

[3] *ibid.* xi, 26, 33. The '*distentio animi*' is, of course, a metaphor. No spatial extension is implied. Also *ibid.* xi, 37: 'The future is not a long time for it does not exist; the long future time is merely a long expectation of the future. Nor is the past a long time for it does not exist. A long past time is merely a long memory of the past.'

standing still as well as of its motion. 'Therefore', Augustine concludes, 'the motion of a physical object and that by which we measure how long the motion lasts are quite different things.'[1] We need a measure of motion itself, and this absolute standard, or criterion, of motion, like all other standards, must be found within the mind itself. This basic principle of St. Augustine's theory of knowledge is equally applicable to the measurement of time:

> It is within you, my mind, that I measure times—what I measure is the impression (*affectio*), which things in passing make within you and which stays on after they have gone away. I measure this impression, i.e. something which is still present with me, and not the things which produced the impression as they passed by.[2]

This analysis of time does not completely solve all the problems involved. In particular, there is a logical difficulty in talking of 'a present time of future things' as part of the furniture of memory; this certainly stretches the definition of memory beyond its usual limits. By 'a present time of future things' St. Augustine of course refers to an expectation of the future course of events based on the rational analysis of existing experience stored in the memory. The attempt to predict future events is seen as analogous to the attempt to infer what is likely to have happened in the past from existing experience stored in the memory. The difficulty is that two different meanings of 'memory' are involved in this argument; in the first place, memory is interpreted in terms of the content of past experience directly and immediately exposed to mental scrutiny; in the second place there is an extension of the meaning of the term to include the scrutiny itself and the inferences made therefrom.

We now turn to another important distinction made by Augustine in the course of his analysis of memory. When he reviews the content of memory, he finds three distinct categories:[3] first, impressions of the physical world, all of which are derived from sense perception; second, impressions of the

[1] *ibid.* xi, 24, 31.
[2] *ibid.* xi, 27, 36.
[3] *Confessions* x, 8, 13–14.

nature of the soul or self, its dispositions (*affectiones animi*) and its powers. In these two categories, Augustine is using 'memory' in the generally accepted sense, that is in relation to the accumulated experience of our world and of ourselves. In his third category of memory content, the term is extended beyond this limit to include the immaterial first principles, or eternal standards, to which all other impressions must be referred for evaluation.[1] The first two categories, drawn from sense experience and observation, consist of representations of things experienced; on the other hand, the third category consists of the actual realities and not of mere symbols or images of them. When these first principles are recalled from memory, their reality and unchanging truth are immediately recognised. Having been implanted in the memory by some means other than sense impression, they are 'brought out of their secret hiding places' by a purely intellectual activity, which does not rely on sense impressions but calls for an inward concentration of thought.

In his analysis of memory, Augustine offers some sensitive analyses and interpretations of the phenomena of remembering and forgetting. He talks for instance of 'the memory of forgetfulness', referring to the common experience of knowing that we know a person's name and yet cannot recall it. We are able to reject certain proferred names as not being the names we want; thus we 'remember' that we have forgotten the name, and this is what sustains our continuing search for the right name:

> Suppose that you have forgotten something, and your friends want to recall it to your memory. They will say, 'Is this it? Is that it?', mentioning various things of a similar kind. You do not recall what you are seeking, but you know that it is not one of the things they have mentioned. Now surely what has happened is not entire oblivion. The discernment, which refuses to accept a false suggestion, is itself a kind of memory.[2]

Augustine concludes that forgetfulness is not necessarily the utter blotting out of memories but merely a difficulty in recalling them. It is proper to say that we remember something as long as we remember that we once knew it:

[1] *ibid.* x, 9, 16; x, 13–20.
[2] *Soliloquies* ii, 34.

> We have not yet completely forgotten what we remember that we have forgotten.[1]

In regard to the relative difficulty or ease of recall, Augustine recognises that the recency of an impression is an important factor influencing recall and that impressions fade in a gradual manner:

> Impressions are gradually obliterated. They do not remain complete and whole for a long time.—We do not feel this progressive diminution—but we recognise that impressions begin to slip away from the very moment when they enter the memory. So we say, 'I have only a vague memory of this', when we try to recall something after the lapse of time but before it has completely disappeared.[2]

Yet Augustine is aware that this is not the sole explanation of forgetting. He understands that we can experience a kind of blockage, which prevents the recall of even a recent and strong impression. This is paralleled by the curious and familiar experience of involuntarily recalling a memory of the distant past at a time when our thoughts are occupied with something entirely different. In his analyses of forgetting in respect of recent impressions, Augustine seems to be feeling his way towards the notion of repression or unconscious voluntary forgetting. He puts it that, when we fail to recall such an impression, we are somehow 'not ourselves'. We are 'withdrawn from ourselves and denied to ourselves'. Correspondingly, when we succeed in recalling what we seek, we are 'brought back or restored to ourselves'.[3] There are occasions when we seek the solution of a problem and cannot find it; then suddenly, when we are not thinking about the problem at all, the solution unsought appears in the mind. Augustine does not suggest that the inexplicable forgetting of recent impressions is voluntary. But when we recall that in his conviction every event has a cause and also that all the movements of the mind are expressions of the will either desiring or rejecting some specific object, it would seem an easy extension of his thought to include the

[1] *Confessions* x, 19, 28.
[2] *On Music* vi, 6.
[3] *The Soul and its Origin* iv, 10.

notion of voluntary forgetting. But the psycho-analytic conceptions associated with this are alien to Augustine's time. The mysterious nature of this and other mental phenomena do, however, suggest to Augustine the extent of our ignorance of the nature of the mind and the need for further enquiry into it.

These are examples from a wealth of psychological insight revealed in many places throughout Augustine's writings. Our account of his views on memory may be concluded with one further example, which is of some importance in his educational theory and practice. This is the connection between memory and imagination. The question is dealt with particularly in an exchange of letters between Nebridius and Augustine.[1] Nebridius is of the opinion that there can be no memory without images. In reply Augustine makes the distinction which has already appeared in our discussion: When we remember physical things (e.g. Carthage), or the face of an absent friend, there is certainly no memory without an image; we cannot think of something we have not personally experienced, and to think of what we have experienced is to recall its image into the mind. On the other hand, in thinking of the eternal truths, we do not use images but look on them directly. Therefore it is wrong to say that everything we remember is a 'phantasy' (*phantasia*), by which Augustine means an image or, as it were, a pictorial reproduction of something experienced through the senses.

Nebridius' second difficulty is to account for the apparent fact that 'imagination perceives some things, which the senses never perceived'. This seems to suggest that we can think of things, which we have not actually experienced, i.e. that we can think without images, as for example when we imagine a black swan, or Medea with her team of winged dragons. Augustine answers that all such thoughts are in fact founded on sense experience, and bases his argument on the distinction between phantasies (*phantasiae*) and phantasms (*phantasmata*). Phantasies are the images of things experienced; a phantasm, on the other hand, is a construction of the imagination in the sense that, taken as a whole, it represents something which has never, or could never, come within the range of experience. Nevertheless, a phantasm is always composed of a number of separate sense impressions, each one of which we have actually experienced; imagination

[1] *Letters* 6 and 7 of A.D. 389.

fuses these together to form a novel image. We have experienced swans, and also separately the colour black. The imaginative power of the mind consists in its ability to create a composite picture, which taken as a whole has no reference to anything experienced in reality.[1]

Following up this argument, Augustine distinguishes three classes of mental images: There are the 'phantasies', that is 'images impressed by things experienced' (*sensibus rebus impressa*); second, there are images evolved by thought (*putatis rebus impressa*), that is the 'phantasms' or products of the imagination. Thirdly, there is a class of mental image grounded in the faculty of reason (*ratis rebus impressa*), as when the scientist reasons from what he has actually observed to conclusions about the universe, which reach far beyond the raw material of his experience. In dealing with mental images of this kind, Augustine warns of the danger of losing contact with reality and launching into pure phantasy. The distinction between what is actually grounded in sense experience and what is inferred must always be clearly in mind:

> It is a very serious kind of error to confuse phantasms with actual experience and to accept the former instead of the latter as true—There are people who pursue their phantasms in such a headlong manner that there is no other cause of false opinions than the confusion of phantasms with what is really known, i.e. experienced through the senses.[2]

In this analysis Augustine is evidently feeling his way towards the notion of wish fulfilment, by which images called up in the mind are accepted as true because there is a strong wish that they should be true. This is the way to such morbid psychological conditions as hallucinations. When the distinction between imagination and reality, that is between 'phantasm' and 'phantasy', becomes blurred, and imagination plays too dominant a part in human behaviour, the mind comes under the control of

[1] *On Music* vi, 32: 'It is one thing to discover a phantasy in the memory and quite another thing to form a phantasm from the memory.'

[2] *On Music* vi, 32. Also *Letter* 7, 4: 'It is harder for reason to resist false imaginings—it is not easy to preserve the exercise of reason free from this evil.'

'images of images'. It severs connection with reality, and is at the mercy of 'a seething welter of diverse and mutually contradictory movements following headlong one after the other'.[1]

CONCLUSION

Examples of Augustine's psychological insight could be considerably expanded, if space allowed. In the *Confessions* there are rich resources in the psychology of motivation, with particular reference to religious conversion. For example, he observes that the pleasure in virtuous action ought to arise solely from that fact that we are obeying the will of God; nevertheless the approval, or disapproval, of others is a powerful influence:

> The approval of others does increase my satisfaction, while on the other hand the disapproval of others has the effect of diminishing my satisfaction in well-doing—The things I think good in myself please me better when they please another person also. For in a sense I am not praised, unless my own opinion of myself is praised.[2]

Particularly perceptive are his occasional references to mob psychology and abnormal psychology, as for example the experience of Augustine's friend, Alypius, related in the *Confessions*. Unwilling to witness the cruelty associated with the gladiatorial games, Alypius had on one occasion been forcibly dragged by his fellow students to the Coliseum. 'You may drag my body to the place', he is reported to have said, 'but can you force me also to fasten my mind or eyes upon the spectacle?' The sequel is described:

> When they arrived, the place was boiling with the most savage delight. But he, closing the doors of his eyes forbade his mind to roam among such evils. Would that he had stopped his ears too! For at a certain accident in the fight a mighty shout from the whole people struck violently upon him, and, vanquished by curiosity and fancying himself steeled to despise and overcome anything he might see, he opened his eyes and was stricken with a deeper wound in his

[1] *On Music, loc. cit.*
[2] *Confessions* x, 37, 61.

> soul than the gladiator, whom he wanted to see, had received in his body—for as soon as he saw the blood, he therewith drew in ferocity. He did not turn away but fixed his gaze on the sight, and sucked in madness, although he was quite unaware of it. He delighted in the wickedness of the conflict and was made drunk by the pleasure of the bloody spectacle. No longer was he the man he was when he arrived at the place, but an associate of those who had taken him there—he looked, he shouted, he blazed with excitement and carried away with him a madness, which would goad him to return again.[1]

There is also the potent fascination of the gruesome in the analysis of the feelings of the crowd, who gather round to gaze on a mangled corpse lying in the street, although at the same time the sight repels and disgusts them—'They even fear that they may see it in their dreams—but nobody forced them to look at it'.[2]

In abnormal psychology, Augustine notes that the tendency to hallucinations is increased in sleep, illness or the state of ecstasy. In this condition reality and imagination become confused, and, as for example in delirium, there is a progressive withdrawal from the world of reality. First, the victim is aware of what is going on around him, but suffers momentary lapses into phantasy, talking for example, to an imaginary person, as though he were present with him.[3] As delirium increases, the victim becomes oblivious to the sights and sounds of his environment, and retreats into a world of his own private imagination. Augustine notes that visions, seen in dreams or ecstasy, are not always clearly distinguished from actual experience, even when the person returns to a normal state.[4] In accordance with his conviction that the body cannot affect the soul, Augustine attributes mental derangement to causes, which are purely psychological in origin. The mind is unable to direct its attention outwards, and is forced back upon itself, where it gives exclusive attention to images stored up within itself.[5] This

[1] *ibid.* vi, 8, 13.
[2] *ibid.* x, 35, 55.
[3] *The Literal Interpretation of Genesis* xii, 25.
[4] *ibid.* xii, 3.
[5] *ibid.* xii, 26.

over-concentration on inner vision may result in complete severance of contact with actual experience:

> When the origin of such visions lies in the body, it is not the body which produces the visions. The body has no power to produce any spiritual image. But, when the channels of sense, along which the movement of sense perception is directed, are either lulled by sleep or deranged or severed from the brain, then the soul, which can never cease from its own proper activity, produces likenesses of physical objects within itself. It does this because it is not permitted, or not fully permitted, to experience physical objects through the body.[1]

While St. Augustine's view of the body–soul relationship is dominated by certain assumptions common to the Platonic metaphysic, and is at some points at variance with experience, in general he gives a balanced account of human behaviour, and shows considerable insight into human motivation. His psychology suffers from the limitations of the knowledge of his time, and in particular from the absence of an experimental procedure. He lays a proper emphasis on volition, although in common with all thinkers of his time, he does not sufficiently stress the significance of instinct and emotion. Some of the basic psychological principles he educes are of considerable educational significance, and we shall find that they are consistently applied in St. Augustine's theory and practice of teaching. Chief among these are his emphases on the unity of the personality and the self-activity of the thinking self as the basis of all effective learning. In general, St. Augustine displays a psychological understanding, which is sufficient to form the basis of a consistent and effective theory of education.

[1] *The Literal Interpretation of Genesis* xii, 42. Also *The Trinity* xi, 7. In the latter passage the senses of the mentally deranged person are described as 'disturbed from their inner connection' (*ab interiore compage turbati*), which, as W. Montgomery remarks (*Aspects of Augustine's Life and Thought*, p. 144) is equivalent to our 'thrown out of gear'.

4 Intellect and the Quest for Truth

Evodius	*If this is what reason teaches, then I ask for nothing more.*
Augustine	*You are right in asking for nothing more than reason teaches.* The Greatness of the Soul, 7.

Everything we perceive through the senses is continually changing: the growth of the hair on our heads, the decline of our bodies into old age or their flowering into youth—all this is going on all the time, and never comes to a halt. Now we cannot learn about a thing that is continually changing. To learn about a thing is to grasp it as an object of knowledge, and it is impossible to grasp something which never stays the same. Therefore, we must not look for the purity of truth in the senses of the body. 83 Various Questions i, 9.

St. Augustine's intellectual progress from doubt to certainty reinforced his conviction that man cannot rest, until he achieves an understanding of absolute truth. Man's capacity for abstract thought gives promise of success in the quest for knowledge, provided that by self-discipline his will is consistently directed towards the higher values. Since man is equipped with a rational soul, he cannot enjoy the full measure of human satisfaction, unless the activity of self-education becomes the most significant preoccupation of his life.

St. Augustine's experience had also taught him that a successful outcome of the quest for truth can come about, only if at some point man passes from the lower to the higher level of education, from preoccupation with sense experience to an increasing intellectual concentration on the area of immaterial reality and absolute truth. 'True philosophy begins', as Gilson says, 'with the act of union with the supernatural order, which by grace frees the will from the flesh and by revelation frees thought from scepticism.'[1] Augustine's own tortured self-education shows that this transition from reliance on sense

[1] E. Gilson, *Introduction à l'Étude de St. Augustin*, p. 294.

knowledge to the pursuit of wisdom with the pure understanding is difficult to achieve, but nevertheless a necessary condition of advance. The nature of immaterial existence must be established on a basis acceptable to reason, and the bonds of connection between the supernatural order and the order of space and time must be clearly defined. Man must know not only that unchanging truth exists, but that he has the ability to grasp it; in other words, he must have a theory of knowledge. This chapter is concerned with exploring St. Augustine's account of the method of intellectual understanding, whereby man fulfils himself in his search for absolute truth.

THE PLATONIC FOUNDATIONS

St. Augustine's theory of knowledge is a synthesis of Platonism with Christian revelation. Augustine's need, like Plato's was to achieve certainty; both were convinced that this could not come through the study of the phenomena of physical existence, but only by the discovery of an area of existence, in which there is no coming into being or passing away. The conviction of the essentially uninformative nature of material existence distinguishes the Platonic–Augustinian method from the Aristotelian method, which moves inductively from particulars to general ideas.[1] In Aristotle's view, wisdom is the culmination of scientific observation; it is not to be attained by stopping up the senses and engaging in an activity of pure thought. By contrast, Platonism, while admitting that the objects and movements of the world of space and time, can stimulate the learner to ask questions about the nature of reality, denies that sense experience can in any sense lead the learner to an understanding of general principles. The search for unchanging reality must be pursued by a method which rigorously excludes sense data.

Therefore, Platonism and Augustinianism sharply distinguish between sense knowledge and purely intellectual understanding. The world of the intellect is infinitely superior; the 'ideas', or first principles, which are the objects of knowledge constituting the intelligible world, enjoy an absolute existence; they are prior to the world of material things, and are in fact the prin-

[1] For a thorough comparison of Platonic and Aristotelian epistemology see E. Gilson, *op. cit.*, pp. 112–13.

ciples which have brought into being and control all the phenomena of time and space. Thus the critical movement of learning is directed by a full acceptance of the superiority of the intelligible world, and by a rejection of the materialistic assumption that the world revealed in sense experience provides all the knowledge that man needs to have.

St. Augustine does not deny the reality or value of sense experience within its own proper limits. But again his own experience, as outlined in the *Confessions*, shows with what ease the world of sense can so dominate man's thinking that he forgets the true purpose for which his rational mind has been given him. The difficulty of the necessary reorientation of the soul derives from man's physical attributes:

> By the very condition that we are mortal and made of flesh, we more easily and familiarly handle what is open to sense perception than what is open to the intellect. This is because the former is outside us, while the latter is inside us; it is because the former is perceived by the physical senses, while the latter is understood by the mind.[1]

Augustine gives Plato and the Platonists full credit for clarifying the distinction between the world of sense perception and the world of intellectual understanding; he disclaims any genius of his own in discovering the 'ideas' or 'forms', which are the objects of intellectual knowledge:

> Plato realised that there are two worlds; the one is open to intellectual understanding and is the dwelling place of truth itself; the other is exposed to sense perception, and there is no denying that we experience it by sight and touch. He declared that of the two the former is true, while the latter merely resembles truth and is made in its image. Therefore, it is from the intelligible world, existing within the soul which knows itself, that truth is, as it were, polished and brightened; on the other hand, the sensible world can generate no knowledge but only opinion within the souls of the foolish.[2]

This is a doctrine for which Augustine finds strong support in the New Testament. The authority of Christ plainly supports

[1] *The Trinity* xi, 1.
[2] *Against the Academics* iii, 37. Also *Reviews* i, 2.

the distinction between physical and spiritual existence. In *The Principle of Order*, for instance, Augustine quotes Christ's words—'My kingdom is not of this world'—and interprets the words as distinguishing between the world of change and the world of unchanging truth.[1] Similarly when Christ prayed, 'Thy kingdom come',[2] he was looking forward to the final consummation when the sensible world with all its imperfections will pass away before the perfection of the kingdom of God, in which the half light of sense perception will give place to the supreme clarity of spiritual vision.

Thus Platonism and Christian revelation combined to support the superiority of the intelligible world over the world of sense perception. 'The understanding of the mind,' as Augustine says in a treatise against the Manichaeans, 'is far to be preferred to the sight of the eyes.' Physical experience has its own reality and lower value, but supplies only partial insights, which can mislead unless they are continually referred to criteria which are to be found 'in the mind and the understanding' (*in mente et intelligentia*).[3] The easy satisfaction offered by the senses can easily weaken the persistence and discipline characteristic of true educational effort and lead to the pursuit of trivial pleasure rather than lasting happiness (*beatitudo*).

In virtue of man's double nature the attention of the soul cannot be exclusively directed to the pursuit and enjoyment of absolute truth. In *The Trinity* Augustine sees two distinctive actions of the soul, namely 'action with regard to temporal things' and 'the contemplation of eternal things'.[4] The latter is the function of 'higher reason', the former of 'lower reason'. Since the soul is continually distracted from its higher work by more mundane business, it therefore falls short of the unchanging perfection, which belongs to spiritual reality. The soul is changeable in that it is 'capable of more or less'.[5] The point is made in *The City of God* by observing the different quality of thought and action in different people and in the same person at different times:

[1] *The Principle of Order* i, 32; *St. John* 18, 36.
[2] *St. Matthew* 6, 10.
[3] *Letter* i, 4.
[4] *The Trinity* xii, 4.
[5] *The City of God* viii, 6.

> The clever man judges better than the man who is slow; the man who is more skilled than he who is unskilled; and the man who is practised than the man who is unpractised. And the same person judges better after he has gained experience than he did before.[1]

From the imperfect nature of the mind, Augustine concludes that the mind cannot be its own source of authority in matters of truth. The first or ideal forms of reality are in the mind, but they do not belong to the mind or derive from it. They must have their origin in some existence which is itself unchangeable and which 'admits of no degrees of comparison'.[2] In directing its progress towards this source of knowledge, the soul must accurately estimate its powers and the limiting conditions under which it must work in this present life. In this full sense man must 'know himself', if he is to be able to live the life of truth and wisdom. The effectiveness of education on this ground is, therefore, to be measured by the extent to which the mind, by its own self-generating effort, pursues the absolute truths (*veritates*) of the intelligible world. These truths contrast at every point with the movements of physical existence:

> They have always had and always will have the same absolute being. And they are not fixed in space as physical substances are; but, as intelligible things in spiritual nature, they are as much present to the eye of the mind as things visible or tangible in space are to the senses of the body.[3]

SCIENCE AND WISDOM

Since man is involved in a dual existence during this life, there are two categories of things he must know: There is the knowledge which relates to his physical existence and well-being; on the other hand, there is the knowledge which enables him to live the happy life and at the same time to prepare himself for

[1] *loc. cit.*

[2] *loc. cit.*:'The first form (*prima species*) is not to be found in those things whose form is changeable.'

[3] *The Trinity* xii, 23. Also *The Practices of the Manichaeans* i, 1: 'That is most fully real which is always exactly the same, which is in every way like itself, which cannot in any part be corrupted or changed, which is not subject to time, which cannot be any different now from what it has been. This is what is meant by existence in its truest sense.'

the life of eternity. There is a knowledge of temporal things and a knowledge of eternal things, and to each there is a distinct and separate mode of knowing. Temporal things are known through the senses and can be known in no other way; on the other hand, eternal things can be known only 'by the eye of the mind' (*oculo mentis*).

This is the basis of Augustine's distinction between science (*scientia*) and wisdom (*sapientia*). As Marrou observes, Augustine uses the two terms in certain popularly accepted usages, but, as his thought develops, he comes to restrict them to the usage which sets them in opposition to each other.[1] In *The Greatness of the Soul*, for example, '*scientia*' is found in the common philosophical sense of knowledge grounded on reason, as opposed to faith (*fides*), by which is meant knowledge grounded on authority. 'To know' (*scire*) is one thing; 'to believe' (*credere*) is another.[2] Again, '*scientia*' is found as a synonym for '*disciplina*' (a subject of study), and sometimes, in its more general reference, to any kind of knowledge. Thus in the prologue to *The Trinity* Augustine refers to the high value men place on 'a knowledge of things in the earth and the heavens' (*scientia terrestrium caelestiumque rerum*), and goes on to say that 'a knowledge of God' (*scientia Dei*) is the supreme knowledge.[3] So also the term '*sapientia*' (wisdom) has its popularly accepted usages along with the increasing restriction of the term to the sense, which contrasts with '*scientia*' and indicates the highest reach of the human understanding and the ultimate aim of education. '*Sapientia*' is sometimes used as a synonym for '*philosophia*'; in *The City of God* it is applied to the 'cunning' of those who devote themselves exclusively to the affairs of the earthly city.[4] Closer to Augustine's distinctive use of the term, it is used to describe the attributes of God, who at the beginning of the *Soliloquies* is described as 'wisdom, in whom and from whom and through whom everything is true which is true'.[5]

[1] H. I. Marrou, *St. Augustin et la Fin de la Culture Antique*, pp. 561–9.

[2] *The Greatness of the Soul* 49.

[3] *The Trinity* iv, 1. Also *83 Various Questions* ii, 2.

[4] *The City of God* xiv, 28. It is in this sense that the serpent in the Garden of Eden is called 'wiser than all the beasts of the field'. *Genesis* 3, 1. *Sermon* 46, 28.

[5] *Soliloquies* i, 3.

Thus from the standpoint of man, wisdom is the enjoyment to the greatest possible extent of what is in the mind of God, that is of the divine Being. The content of the divine mind is truth; therefore wisdom is 'the contemplation of truth'.[1]

In their antithetical use, 'science' is the knowledge, which concerns practical action in relation to the needs of physical existence, while 'wisdom' refers to the understanding of absolute truth. Both practical action and pure understanding are founded on reason (*ratio*) and learning (*cognitio*, *intellectus*). Thus Augustine defines science as 'the rational learning of temporal things' (*temporalium rerum cognitio rationalis*) and wisdom as 'the intellectual learning of eternal things' (*aeternarum rerum cognitio intellectualis*).[2]

Scientific knowledge is founded on sense experience, a faculty which man shares with the animals. But in animals, sensation is not capable of being transmuted into knowledge; therefore, their behaviour is purely automatic, imitative, egocentric and lacking in real significance. The difference between animal and human behaviour is crystallised by Augustine in terms of the distinction between 'imitation' and 'art'.[3] Art implies knowledge, i.e. it is founded on rational thought; on the other hand, imitation is unthinking response to sensation. Thus in *On Music* Augustine notes that, when birds sing, they are not practising the art of music, but merely repeating sounds they have heard; animals merely 'move their bodies in accordance with the pleasure they get from sensation', but do not think.[4] In *The Trinity* Augustine observes that animals 'are able to perceive physical objects outside them, fix them in the memory and recall them'.[5] And again, he notes that swallows return to their nests after a year's absence, that dogs and goats recognise their masters and can find their way back home when lost.[6] Neverthe-

[1] *Concerning the Sermon on the Mount* i, 10.

[2] *The Trinity* xii, 25. Also *83 Various Questions* ii, 2: 'Wisdom concerns the understanding of eternal things, but science concerns those things we experience through the senses of the body.'

[3] e.g. *The Greatness of the Soul* 32; *On Music* i, 6–8; *The Immortality of the Soul* 5.

[4] *On Music* i, 8.

[5] *The Trinity* xii, 2.

[6] *On Music* i, 9. Augustine quotes Vergil, *Georgics* iii, 316: 'goats remember and return to their homes'.

less animal behaviour is limited to 'outer things', that is to what concerns the life of the body.

Human behaviour may be, and often is, purely imitative. In the dialogue *On Music*, Augustine distinguishes between the musician and the popular singer; the former understands the art of music, the latter arouses his audience through behaviour which is purely imitative.[1] The study of animal behaviour, which is unsophisticated and rudimentary, serves to mark clearly the limits beyond which man must go if he is to explore 'inner things', i.e. the things of the spirit, and to order his life according to the principles of unchanging truth. The distinction between inner and outer things is fundamental to Augustine's thought:

> The action by which we make good use of temporal things differs from the contemplation of eternal things—Whatever we do prudently, steadfastly, temperately and justly pertains to that science or discipline on which our behaviour depends in avoiding evil and desiring good.[2]

We have already remarked that in Augustine's view the higher enquiry into ultimate truth is not merely an extension or continuation of enquiry into the world of physical phenomena. The search for wisdom marks a new beginning in the education of man. In an illuminating passage from the *Soliloquies* Augustine stresses the inability of sense information to carry us forward on to the firmer ground of real understanding. He is talking of the futility of his own attempt to reach an understanding of geometrical first principles, while depending on sense data:

> In this business I employed the senses as one does a ship. My

[1] *ibid.* i, 6. Augustine refers to the popular idols of the day as 'theatrical labourers' (*theatrici operarii*). The whole passage forms a perceptive analysis of popular reaction to the current 'stars'—'the applause of the populace and all the rewards got on the stage belong to the class of things which are placed in the lap of fortune and which depend upon the judgement of the ignorant—there is nothing more fortuitous, nothing more exposed to chance or more in subjection to the domination and whims of the masses than these are'. The transient nature of such achievements is contrasted with the permanence of knowledge.

[2] *The Trinity* xii, 22–3.

senses carried me to the place where I wanted to go. But, when I dismissed them and, being as it were disembarked on land, began to revolve these ideas in my mind for a long time, my footsteps faltered. As I see it, one might sooner sail over dry land than understand geometry through the senses, even if they seem to be of some help in the first stages of learning.[1]

Augustine is here pointing to the inevitable dilemma which puzzles the thought of the idealist thinker and turns him towards the conception of a world of spiritual and unchanging reality. Sense data reveals contradictions, anomalies and imperfections. For example, the physical world presents only particular examples of circles, each one of them falling more or less short of perfect circularity.[2] In this way it raises the question, 'What is circularity pure and simple?', but it cannot furnish an answer. The idea of perfect circularity cannot be derived from physical approximations, however close; it can be understood only by pure thinking, that is by turning away from particular circles and consulting the ideal standard of circularity within the mind. By intellectually comprehending this standard, we can then proceed to evaluate all physical circles. Thus the conviction we have of our ability to evaluate particulars can be explained only on the assumption of a transcendent world of universals, the dwelling place of the perfect forms or archetypes of truth.

For St. Augustine truth is absolute and not relative, and he is at great pains to establish this truth on a solid foundation. His view of learning as a thoroughly private matter has already emerged in the course of our study; nevertheless, he points out that the objects of intellectual knowledge are not constructed by the individual mind or influenced by the individual learner's private experience or the constitution of his mind. By contrast with the objects of scientific knowledge, which are hypothetical, relative and impermanent, intellectual truth is one and the same for all who look upon it with the gaze of the mind. There are, therefore, many sciences, but only one wisdom.

In *The Free Will* Augustine examines the problems involved in establishing that wisdom is one thing and not many. How can it be shown that each individual thinker has the same conception

[1] *Soliloquies* i, 9.

[2] The most thorough treatment of the point with regard to geometrical principles is found in *The Greatness of the Soul* 10–21.

of the highest good for man? There are two main difficulties here: in the first place observation shows only too clearly that men have different values, and therefore, as it would seem, different conceptions of what constitutes the highest good—'It is clear that different men rejoice in different things, as if they were their chief good'. Secondly, every man's thoughts are in the last resort private to himself and cannot be directly inspected by another:

> There are as many minds as there are men; I cannot observe anything that goes on in your mind or you anything that goes on in my mind.[1]

Nevertheless, the unity and universality of intellectual knowledge is for Augustine a matter of faith. When faith explores the implications of this in its search for understanding, it finds overwhelming evidence of order in the universe to suggest that the whole of creation must derive from, and be dependent on, a supreme governing principle. The diversity of response and action, both in human behaviour and in the phenomena of the physical world, are undeniable facts of experience. But, using the Platonic analogy of the sun, Augustine shows how truth, coming from one and the same source, can give reality and meaning to a great variety of different things; the thinker soon becomes aware that behind the diversity of things there is an underlying unity:

> The things, which men see by the light of the sun, are many and various. But the light, in which each man sees what he enjoys looking at, is one. Thus, although there are many different good things from which man may choose according to his pleasure, nevertheless it may be that the light of wisdom, in which these things can be seen and possessed, is one light common to all wise men.[2]

The guiding principles, which Augustine also calls 'the rules and guiding lights of the virtues' are 'not only true but common to all men'.[3] If a man does not know them, it is because he has failed to practise the reflective thought, which leads to a clear

[1] *The Free Will* ii, 27.
[2] *ibid.* ii, 27.
[3] *ibid.* 28–9.

understanding of their truth and universality. Therefore, Augustine follows Plato in declaring that no man does wrong voluntarily but only through ignorance of the difference between right and wrong.[1] The bad man chooses the bad, imagining it to be the good. In doing so, he is guided by sense perception and not by intellectual understanding. When the good is grasped by the mental vision, it is immediately recognised as an entirely reliable criterion by which conduct may be directed and judged.

Augustine's distinction between science and wisdom leads to the conclusion that the philosopher, i.e. the lover of wisdom, is the man who most clearly realises the full potential of human development. Being able to take a comprehensive view of existence as a whole, both in its physical and spiritual aspects, he alone possesses real knowledge and therefore lives the good life. While other people pursue their own several private and conflicting interests, only the philosopher achieves a steady and consistent direction. The more a man involves himself in a multiplicity of unrelated temporal preoccupations, the less wise he is and the more removed from the truth which is the key to the happy life.

To sum up, Augustine interprets wisdom in terms of the search for and contemplation of absolute truth. Judgement does not take its start from the data of sense experience, but from a body of unchanging first principles perceived by intellectual vision. Thus, as Augustine puts it, 'we pass judgement not on truth (for that is self-evident to the thinker), but in accordance with truth'.[2] Scientific knowledge has its own importance and relevance to the temporal life of man. But, unless it is supplemented by wisdom, man's education is necessarily incomplete and defective. For the idealist thinker the goal of education is an activity which is purely intellectual.

THE ETERNAL REASONS

To the eternal standards or archetypes Augustine gives various names. The Platonic term 'ideas', rendered in Latin '*ideae*' is employed, but also 'forms' (*formae*), 'species' (*species*), 'reasons' (*rationes*) or 'eternal reasons of things' (*aeternae rationes rerum*),

[1] *Against the Academics* iii, 5: '*Nemo errat invitus*'.
[2] *The Free Will* ii, 34.

and 'rules' (*regulae*). The term 'reasons' (*rationes*) is most frequently used as most clearly suggesting Augustine's conception of principles, which exist originally in the mind of God and are the determinants of the order and meaning displayed in the world of created things.

In his *Reviews* Augustine quotes with approval Plato's definition of the intelligible realities as 'the eternal and unchangeable reason, according to which God made the world'.[1] As the design exists in the mind of the artist before it is reproduced in physical form, so the ideas exist in the mind of God. Augustine states this more emphatically and consistently than does Plato, who lacked the concept of a personal God whose reason is reproduced in the mind of man. Physical objects are the embodiments of the ideas of God reproduced in gross matter and therefore imperfect and changing. The archetypes or originals are perfect and eternal:

> The ideas are the original forms or reasons of things. They are fixed and unchangeable. Because they were not themselves formed, they are therefore eternal and always the same, being contained in the divine intelligence. Because they neither come into being nor decay, it is said that everything which comes into being and decays is formed in accordance with them.[2]

St. Augustine's view of the ideas as existing 'in the divine intelligence' forms a basis for the explanation of how man can get to know them. Because man's mind is created in the image of the divine reason, the thoughts of God are accessible to human understanding.[3] They can be seen, as Augustine puts it, 'by the interior and intelligible eye of the soul', but only by those souls, which keep that interior eye 'healthy, unblemished, serene and

[1] *Reviews* i, 2.

[2] *83 Various Questions* 46, 2. This Question is headed 'Concerning the Ideas' (*De Ideis*).

[3] *ibid.* 'The rational soul is superior to all the other things, which have been made by God, and is nearest to God. The more it cleaves to God in love, the more it is bathed by Him in an intelligible light and sees what is lit up by that light. It sees this not by means of the physical eyes, but through that very principle of its being, in which it excels all other things, that is through its intelligence. What it sees are those reasons (*rationes*), the sight of which renders it most happy.'

similar to the things it strives to see'. Thus the Christian notion of a personal God, directly accessible to man, is central to St. Augustine's theory of knowledge, and is his most significant reinforcement to the insights of Platonism. With some justice Aristotle had criticised Plato's epistemology on the ground that his 'ideas', or perfect archetypes, were too far removed from the actual world to be thought of as the causes of particular things in the phenomenal world. By postulating a divine, personal and loving administrator, St. Augustine removes some of the force of this objection, while continuing to maintain that the ideal forms have an existence separate from, and transcending, the world of space and time. By contrast, the Aristotelian view holds that the ideas are immanent in the physical world, a view which St. Augustine sees as seriously reducing the transcendent significance and essential superiority of the divine intelligence.

St. Augustine carefully analyses the conception of the separate existence of the eternal reasons. In all physical existence he distinguishes between the two forms, which belong to every material object. There is the externally impressed form, the form given by the craftsman; but, distinct from this, there is another internal form, which is 'the efficient cause of natural physical forms'.[1] This is the form which exists in the mind of God. The difference between the two forms lies in the fact that the craftsman impresses the form he conceives on pre-existing matter, while the internal forms were conceived by God before the creation of matter. They were in fact implanted at the beginning of time, and reveal their potential in the fullness of time. St. Augustine uses the analogy of planting, when he describes these seed-like principles of growth as 'the seminal reasons' (*rationes seminales*); they are the causes 'not only of all physical forms, but even of the very life of living creatures'.[2] Thus everything without exception was created in the beginning, although in the beginning the seminal reasons exist invisibly (*invisibiliter*), potentially (*potentialiter*) and in purely causes form (*causaliter*). Thus the course of history has been

[1] *The City of God* xii, 25.

[2] On the seminal reasons see *The Literal Interpretation of Genesis* iv, 51; v, 44–6; ix, 32. Also *The Trinity* iii, 13–19. V. J. Bourke, *Augustine's Quest for Wisdom*, pp. 225–7 and 231–4.

marked by the progressive unfolding of potentialities brought into being at the beginning of time:

> Just as everything, which in the course of time is to grow into a tree, exists invisibly in the seed from which it develops, so must the world itself be regarded. When God created everything at once, the world at once possessed everything which was made in it and along with it—All this existed as potentialities and causes, until in the course of time they grew into being in the form in which they are known to us now in the works which God is directing even up to the present time.[1]

Attempts have been made to see in this an anticipation of the notion of evolution in the creative sense. St. Augustine, however, specifically denies the suggestion of emergent novelty in the world, and by inference any notion of man as a genuinely creative participant with God in a continuing creative process. Equally he does not see God as exercising more than an administrative or supervisory function in the course of history since the period of the Creation ended:

> Each element of this physical world has its own limited power and quality, which determines what it can and cannot do and lays down what can develop from what. From these first principles of things everything which comes into being rises up and comes forth, each at its own proper time, and moves to its own proper end and falls into decline according to the rules of its own proper species. Thus a bean does not spring up from a wheat seed, nor wheat from a bean, a man from a beast or a beast from a man.[2]

Man cannot create new forms, although St. Augustine would

[1] *The Literal Interpretation of Genesis* v, 45. See also *The Trinity* iii, 16: 'All these things have been created originally and primordially in a kind of texture of the elements, but they come forth when the opportunity is offered to them.'

[2] *The Literal Interpretation of Genesis* ix, 32. Augustine's belief that God exercises merely a supervisory function in history is not to deprive Him of the power to alter the development of the seminal reasons, if He so wishes. God refrains from this tampering, because 'He is omnipotent, not with reckless power, but with the virtue of reason'. V. J. Bourke, *op. cit.*, pp. 231–4, lists the attempts to find a suggestion of creative evolution in Augustine's theory.

allow him ample opportunity for imaginative ingenuity and creative purpose of a secondary sort in searching out and developing the potentialities, which have been latent in the universe from the beginning of time. However, the lack of challenge to man, which the modern pragmatist, such as William James, sees as implicit in this doctrine, has some validity even allowing that in the discovery and utilisation of the seminal reasons man has undoubtedly a large scope for the operation of originality and resource.[1]

The notion of the seminal reasons links the spiritual world of the universals and the physical world of particulars. This connection is rendered more explicit by the continuing argument in *The Literal Interpretation of Genesis*, where Augustine postulates the existence of created things in three modes: first, they exist in the eternal reasons or archetypes in the mind of God; second, they exist in a latent form in the work of the six days of the creation; third, they exist in the actual physical manifestations which have developed, or will develop, in the period following the period of the creation.[2] Thus the seminal reasons are, as it were, the projections of the mind or thoughts of God in relation to His function as Creator of the world. They explain the development of apparently unformed matter into a great and ever increasing variety of physical forms.

With this explanation of the creation of material forms Augustine is satisfied. But he remains perplexed by the problem of the creation of souls, about which two theories in particular competed for his attention:[3] The creationist explanation saw God as creating each soul individually at the appointed time and despatching it 'to rule and give life to a body'. The traducianist explanation declared that all souls were propagated by the first soul, that is the soul of Adam, which God created in the six days of the Creation—'one soul was made, from which the souls of men, as they are born, are drawn'. On the whole Augustine favours the traducianist view on the authority of Genesis that

[1] See the quotation from Wm. James, *Pragmatism*, *supra*, p. 60.

[2] *The Literal Interpretation of Genesis* v, 28.

[3] The basic text surveying the various explanations of the origin of souls is *The Free Will* iii, 56–8. J. M. Colleran in his introduction to *The Greatness of the Soul* and *The Teacher* reviews Augustine's contribution to the problem. Also Gilson, *op. cit.*, p. 66 ff.

God ended His creative work on the sixth day, whereas the creationist view sees His creative work as continuing through subsequent ages. In addition the traducianist explanation of the origin of souls seemed to Augustine to fit certain observable facts of human behaviour, in particular the transmission of hereditary characteristics and the continuing existence through transmission from one generation to the next of the taint of the original sin of Adam. On the other hand, any theory other than the creationist theory postulates the pre-existence of the soul in respect of the body it inhabits. Augustine could find no scriptural support for this, and, as we shall see later in this chapter, this lack led him to seek and find a Christian theory of knowledge to replace Plato's doctrine of reminiscence, which also assumed the pre-existence of souls. The problem remained a mystery, and he was inclined to think that its solution is one which God has intentionally veiled from human sight.[1]

We shall now briefly review the important categories of first principles—'the eternal reasons of things', which St. Augustine regards as ultimate. These are a) the principles of dialectic (i.e. logical reasoning), b) the principles of number and c) the moral ideas.

Augustine's quarrel with the scepticism of the Academic philosophers was concerned in the first place to establish that the axioms of logic are grounded in eternal truth, and therefore are reliable starting points in the quest for knowledge. The effect of the argument conducted in the dialogue, *Against the Academics*, is to establish that the rules of logic have a divine authority and are therefore unassailable. The sceptic, Carneades, for instance had made a point of attacking the reliance placed by logicians on disjunctive propositions. He had charged that these gave only the appearance of knowledge without the reality. Augustine, however, sees them as positive and reliable starting points for further enquiry, because they narrow down the field of enquiry. For example, with reference to the controversies associated with the early Greek physicists, such as Democritus, Augustine sets out some of the disjunctive propositions, which are the starting points in physics:

[1] *The Soul and its Origin* iv, 16. In *Reviews* i, 3, written at the end of his life, Augustine admits that he has not solved the problem. See also *Against Julian* 2, 178, written even later than the *Reviews*.

> I know for certain that there is *either* one world *or* not one world. And, if there is not one world, there is *either* a finite *or* an infinite number. And again I know that our world has been organised as it is *either* by the natural operation of physical things *or* by some providence.[1]

It is precisely because the purpose of logic is to establish the laws of thought that it justifies its claim to be the fundamental study in the curriculum of the liberal arts. Logic is 'the truth, from which reason derives truth'.[2] Since all the liberal disciplines are concerned with truth, all of them must employ the principles of logical reasoning, if they are to encourage a respect for truth within their own fields and develop effective habits of thought in students. These principles are basic to all education, in that it is through the application of them that the learner can grasp the truths which are central to all the liberal studies.[3] The laws of logic, like all the eternal reasons, have been laid down by God, which is to say that they demonstrate the thought processes of God. Thus, if man is to reflect the image of God, as man was intended to do in the beginning, and to understand the divine purpose, he must come to know the principles of logical reasoning and conform to them.

The truths of mathematics share with the truths of logic a place of fundamental importance in Augustine's catalogue of the objects of knowledge open to the human intellect. Both are absolute and incontrovertible:

> If there are one and six worlds, that is to say that there are seven worlds and this is the case whatever my condition is (*quoquo modo affectus sum*). I confidently declare that this is so—that thrice times three make nine is necessarily true, even if the whole human race should be asleep and snoring.[4]

The emphasis Augustine lays on number derives from the influence of Plato and his successors. Pythagoras saw number as the principle of order in the physical world, the basis of all the predictable movements of cause and effect in the physical

[1] *Against the Academics* iii, 23. Also *ibid.* iii, 21: 'We know that a statement is true or false. Therefore, we do not know nothing.'

[2] *Soliloquies* ii, 21. See also *infra*, pp. 260–3.

[3] *loc. cit.*: 'Logic is the source of truth in all the disciplines.'

[4] *Against the Academics* iii, 25.

universe. In *The Principle of Order*, written immediately after *Against the Academics*, and again five years later in *The Free Will*, Augustine shows the arguments by which he himself arrived at this conviction. It is through the application of number that the Creator has constructed the shapes and forms of the universe and determined its movements. The delight we feel in the contemplation of beautiful shapes or in the experience of musical harmonies derives from the numerical relationships we find there:

> Whatever delights you in physical objects and entices you through the senses is governed by number—See the heaven, the earth and the sea; all that is bright in them or above them; everything that creeps or flies or swims; all have forms because they have number. Take away number and they will be nothing. From whom have they their being, if not from Him who has made number? They exist only in so far as they have number.[1]

Thus the successful reproduction of a form by a craftsman, artist or musician is possible only because he has come to know the unchanging laws of number. Craftsmen regulate their operations by numbers:

> They move their hands and tools, until what is fashioned in the outer world, being referred to the interior light of number, receives such perfection as is possible, and, being reported on by the senses, pleases the internal judge who beholds the transcendent numbers.[2]

Thus the study of the four liberal arts of music, arithmetic, geometry and astronomy, as St. Augustine sees it, becomes the study of numerical relationships; the common aim of all these arts is to develop an understanding of absolute number, the divinely ordained principle by which the universe is controlled.[3] Thus arithmetic, geometry and astronomy demonstrate 'the art

[1] *The Free Will* ii, 41.

[2] *ibid.* ii, 42.

[3] *The Principle of Order* ii, 42. With reference to all the forms and movements of the natural world, Augustine says in *On Music* i, 14: 'There are no undefined or undetermined intervals. Two movements are always in some numerical relationship to each other' (*habent ad se duo motus aliquem numerum*).

of measurement', while music is defined as 'the knowledge of modulation', i.e. of measurement (*scientia modulandi*).[1] The purpose of music as a liberal study is not the enjoyment of music or the ability to play on a musical instrument, but the intellectual understanding of the numerical relationships, which are the rational bases of harmonies and rhythms. The value of the study lies in the internal consistency or order, which it continually reveals to the student. This consistency leads him to reflect on abstract number as the basis of all rationality in the universe in all its manifestations.

In *The Free Will* St. Augustine sets down his arguments for the absolute truth of mathematical principles.[2] Prominent among these is the argument based on their public nature: in the perceptions we have of physical objects we are confirmed in the reality of the impressions we have when we observe that they are 'common and, as it were, public'.[3] So it is also with the principles of number. Although differences in natural ability enable one person to grasp them more speedily than another, once understood they are found to be exactly the same for everyone who knows them. There is also the argument based on the impossibility of finding mathematical principles exemplified in perfect form in the physical world, for example the idea of perfect circularity or of absolute unity, the latter of which is the basis of all other mathematical ideas. In the world of phenomena there are only suggestions of unity, since any physical object can be broken into parts; the smallest conceivable part, into which an object can be broken, is capable of further subdivision. Thus every object, however small, is both one and many, thus clearly demonstrating the essentially contradictory nature of sense data. It is only intelligible unity, i.e. the idea of unity existing in spiritual nature, which can teach us what unity itself is and so enable us to develop more refined mathematical concepts.[4]

The argument in *The Free Will* goes on to ask whether wisdom and number are the same thing, that is whether the laws of

[1] *On Music* i, 2. For a fuller discussion of the significance of music as a liberal art see *infra*, pp. 267–74.

[2] *The Free Will* ii, 19–24.

[3] *ibid.* ii, 19.

[4] *ibid.* ii, 22. On this point see Gilson, *op. cit.*, p. 123.

number constitute the whole of truth. It is concluded that number is only part of wisdom, or derived from wisdom, and this sustains the view that mathematical study is a true philosophical method. When a man ponders on mathematical truths, he is drawn to look inwards, to interiorise his thought; and, as we have noted, this is the necessary prerequisite to all intellectual understanding. Augustine is sure that the mathematical method gives a very clear demonstration of the transition from external phenomena to internal reality, from sense perception to pure thinking.

Finally, we should repeat that the standard of reference, by which Augustine judges beauty, is a numerical standard. Aesthetic pleasure derives from a perception of proportion and harmony, reflecting in natural things the thoughts of the Creator and in works of art the artist's grasp of these principles. Both the creation and the enjoyment of works of art reduces itself, therefore, to a knowledge of number, that is to an appreciation of the relationships of parts to wholes. The artist strives for the closest possible agreement between the numerical proportions expressed in his work and the standards laid up within him, which he has gazed upon by his power of interior vision. He will always be in some measure disappointed with his work because of the impossibility of conforming gross matter in a perfect degree to the unchanging principles of spiritual existence. So far as it goes, Augustine's theory of aesthetics is satisfactory. But in emphasising the intellectual element in aesthetic pleasure, he explains only one aspect of an experience, which is more complex than he realised. The notion of number lying at the foundation of artistic creation needs to be supplemented by other considerations, of which Augustine does not take account. An explanation of music purely in terms of 'the knowledge of modulation' justifies its place in a curriculum of intellectual education, but would not guarantee it a place in a curriculum of general education designed to awaken and enrich the emotions and sensitivity of man.

The remaining categories of intelligible realities in Augustine's theory consist of the basic moral directives and the ideas of the virtues. To turn one's attention to these is to approach nearer to the heart of wisdom itself. Augustine puts it that they are the brightest of the guiding lights of conduct and that they 'belong to wisdom itself'.[1] He goes on to declare that there is little need to catalogue these because everyone, who thinks, knows at once what they are and that they are 'true and unchangeable and open for the common contemplation of those who have the capacity to behold them, each with his own mind and reason'.

Moral relativism is, therefore, a dangerous although plausible absurdity, and amounts to a failure to think one's way through to the heart of reality. Most of the moral ideas most prominent in Augustine's thought have already been encountered in our discussion of his philosophy, for example that man should seek wisdom and live justly, that the eternal is superior to the temporal, that the inferior should be in total subjection to the superior and so on. We find the 'notion of happiness' (*notio beatitatis*), the 'notion of wisdom' (*notio sapientiae*) and the 'notion of the good' (*notio boni*), by which we are able to evaluate particular examples of goodness:

> Among all these good things we could not say that one was better than another, unless a notion of the good itself had been impressed upon us, whereby we approve one thing as good and prefer one thing to another.[2]

Human security and happiness depend upon man coming to understand these moral directives and conforming his actions to them. Therefore, Augustine holds that the knowledge of them represents a much higher level of human attainment than an acquaintance with physical things:

> The thought by which I understand justice, charity, faith, truth, goodness and so on is very far distant from that thought by which I think about well-known physical objects. You may say that the former thought is like a light by which—physical objects are clearly and faithfully displayed.[3]

DIVINE ILLUMINATION

Thus far our study of Augustine's theory of knowledge has established the grounds on which he asserts the reality of the

[1] *The Free Will* ii, 29.
[2] *The Trinity* vii, 4.
[3] *Against Faustus the Manichaean* 20, 7.

eternal reasons. We have shown his reasons for declaring that these objects of knowledge on the higher or philosophical level of education can be known by man. The human soul, endowed with an intellect and with the powers of willing and remembering, has an affinity with the divine mind, in which the first principles of things are established. Through his rational mind man is able to come into direct contact with the thoughts of God. Since the eternal reasons are in the mind of God, they are also in a sense in the mind of man, for the reason that man's mind is made in the image of God.

But we need further clarification of the question, 'How exactly does man come to know the ideas of God?'. Clearly these are not immediately self-evident without the labour of thought. It is also apparent that there are men who never come to know them at all. Is the activity of understanding absolute truths an activity of man or of God? Or is it a process of interaction between the two, a mutual activity, by virtue of which truth is, as it were, kindled into life within the mind of man?

Such questions led Augustine to formulate one of his most distinctive doctrines, the doctrine of divine illumination.[1] In so doing, he departs from the views of Plato and the Platonists, who explained the origin of knowledge in the human mind by the theory of reminiscence, i.e. that learning is remembering. In an existence previous to its attachment to the body, the soul has lived 'nearer the divine', where it has had the opportunity to see truth directly. On its union with the body it falls into a state of oblivion in respect of the ideas it has stored up within itself during its pre-existence. These ideas can, however, be recalled or rediscovered within the mind through the activity of reason, and in this way the soul can come into full repossession of its forgotten knowledge. By the concentrated effort of pure thought, freed from the distractions of sense, the soul can redirect its inner eye towards the world of intelligible reality. The doctrine is put in these words in Plato's *Phaedo*:

Knowledge is nothing other than remembering, and therefore

[1] On divine illumination in Augustine see F. Cayré, *Initiation à la Philosophie de St. Augustin*, pp. 209–43; E. Gilson, *op. cit.*, pp. 103–20; R. Allers, Illumination et Vérités Éternelles in *Communications, Congrès International Augustinien*, pp. 477–90.

> it must needs be that we learned at an earlier time what we now remember.[1]

But to the Christian thinker the pre-existence of the soul is not acceptable. God 'formed man of the dust of the ground and breathed into his nostrils the breath of life'.[2] This was the process whereby man was created a 'living soul'. Therefore the genesis of knowledge in the soul cannot antedate the creation of man, a conclusion which is equally necessary whether the traducianist or creationist explanation of the origin of souls is accepted. This is then one respect in which Plato, whom Augustine calls 'almost a Christian', falls short of the full enlightenment of Christian truth.

In his earlier writings Augustine uses language which is very close to the language of Plato. This has given rise to the question whether he did for some time after his conversion actually maintain the doctrine of reminiscence. For example in the *Soliloquies* he says:

> Doubtless, in learning the liberal arts, people draw them out from the oblivion, in which they have been overwhelmed or dig them out in some way or other.[3]

And again in *The Greatness of the Soul*:

> My view is that the soul has brought all of the liberal arts into this life along with itself, and what is called learning is in fact nothing other than remembering and recalling to mind.[4]

This is Plato pure and simple. However, it is certain that in his later years Augustine repudiated his youthful attachment to those elements of the Platonic theory, which are incompatible with Christian revelation. Thus in the *Reviews* he remarks with reference to the above passage from *The Greatness of the Soul* that the words are not to be taken as implying that 'the soul has enjoyed any existence prior to its union with the body, either here or in another body or in some other place, whether in a body or apart from a body'.[5] He goes on to repudiate the sug-

[1] Plato, *Phaedo* 73B. On the theory of reminiscence in Plato see *Meno* 81C–88B: *Phaedo* 72E–77B.

[2] *Genesis* 2, 7.

[3] *Soliloquies* ii, 35.

[4] *The Greatness of the Soul* 34.

[5] *Reviews* i, 2.

gestion that the slave boy in Plato's *Meno*, to whom Socrates taught a lesson in geometry purely by asking questions, was successful in his learning because he was stimulated to 'remember' certain geometrical principles. There is, says Augustine, a simpler explanation, namely that the soul, being by nature spiritual, is in tune with the ideas:

> The soul is by nature intelligible and is connected not only to intelligible things but also to what is unchanging. The soul is so constituted that, when it turns itself towards those things, to which it is connected, or towards itself, it gives true answers to the extent that it sees them.[1]

Similarly in the section of the *Reviews*, where he is criticising the passage from the *Soliloquies* just quoted, Augustine explains that learning in response to questions comes about because 'there is present in the learner a light of eternal reason, in which he sees those unchanging truths'.[2] Also in a passage from *The Trinity*, in which he again critically examines the theory of reminiscence as demonstrated by Socrates in the *Meno*, he concludes that the soul

> is so formed in its nature as to see those things which are joined to things intelligible and to see them in a sort of immaterial light of a unique kind.[3]

It has been suggested that, in rejecting Plato's doctrine of reminiscence, Augustine subscribed at least for a time to a doctrine of innate ideas.[4] Might it not be that in learning we do in a real sense remember the eternal verities, not because they were impressed on our souls in a pre-existence but because God impressed them there at the moment of the creation of our souls? The ideas then would be assumed to lie dormant in the soul until in maturity and with the effort of thought they are brought out into the light. In this way their origin and discovery

[1] *loc. cit.*

[2] *ibid.* i, 4.

[3] *The Trinity* xii, 24.

[4] e.g. F. Cayré, *op. cit.*, pp. 219–21 defines a theory of innate ideas based on supernatural foundations as one which 'attributes the formation of the first intelligible ideas to a divine action which would have placed them ready made in the soul at the moment of conception or of birth in such a way that all man has to do is to remember them'.

would be analogous to the way in which the seminal reasons make their appearance in the physical world. Discussion of this point has centred on a text in *Against the Academics* combined with the correction of this text, which Augustine makes in his *Reviews*.[1] In the former Augustine talks of the soul 'as it were returning to the place of its origin', when it seeks to grasp truth. In the *Reviews* he maintains that it would have been better if he had used the word 'going' instead of 'returning', on the grounds that the latter suggests too strongly the pre-existence of the soul. The notion of the soul as turning to the source of truth is held to imply the acceptance by Augustine of a doctrine of innate ideas. But the argument lacks the support of a sufficiently clear statement from Augustine, and the same conclusion emerges from similar interpretations of his description of the soul as 'naturally joined to' or 'connected with' the intelligibles. It is more reasonable to conclude with Cayré that in the formative period, in which these texts were written, Augustine was casting around for some explanation of the origin of knowledge acceptable to Christians and that he became attached to no particular explanation until about A.D. 389 he formulated the doctrine of divine illumination in *The Teacher*.

The origin of the notion of divine illumination can be traced to a remark in *Against the Academics*, where Alypius gives it as his opinion that 'it is only a god who can reveal the truth to man'. This statement is then seized upon by Augustine:

> I have never heard in the course of our discussion anything which has pleased me better, or which is more profound or true.[2]

Again in *The Happy Life*, his next dialogue, Augustine talks of 'this secret sun which pours its radiance upon our inner lights'. He goes on

> From it proceeds all the truths which we profess—this sun shows itself to us as being none other than God, a perfect being whom no imperfection diminishes.[3]

[1] *Against the Academics* ii, 22. *Reviews* i, 3.

[2] *Against the Academics* iii, 13.

[3] *The Happy Life* 35: '*Hoc interioribus luminibus iubar sol ille secretus infundit.*'

The meeting of the divine radiance with the 'inner lights' of the person who is striving to see recalls Augustine's explanation of physical vision in terms of a meeting of light emanating from two sources, i.e. from the sun and from the eyes.[1] He seems, therefore, to be pressing an analogy between outer sight and inner vision. In response to an actively enquiring mind, the 'secret sun', i.e. God, pours its radiance into the mind. There light meets light, and in this dynamic encounter truth is brightly illuminated.

This analogy, which occurs as a final thought in *The Happy Life*, is refined in the *Soliloquies*. Reason allows man 'to see God with his soul, as the sun is seen with the eye'. Reason is 'the power to look', but not everyone who looks actually sees, because seeing is disciplined and concentrated looking. Furthermore, if vision is to occur, the help of something analogous to the sun is needed. The objects of knowledge cannot be understood 'unless they are illumined by something else, which is, as it were, a sun'.[2]

It is interesting to note that, by this course of reasoning, which was carrying Augustine away from the Platonic account of the origin of knowledge, he continues to retain Plato's image of the sun. Thus, as the sun not only shines but more positively illuminates, so with God who is the source of our knowledge:

> He exists; He is known, and He causes other things to be known.[3]

The analogy is pursued at some length, while at the same time the fact that it is merely an analogy is stressed. God is 'as it were, another sun', and the doctrine of illumination is a simple metaphor. So the visible light (*lux visibilis*) is not to be confused with the invisible light (*lux invisibilis*), as the Manichaeans confused them. The invisible light is the light 'of that other sun, by whose truth human nature is irradiated',[4] a spiritual light of

[1] *supra*, pp. 73–4.

[2] *Soliloquies* i, 12–15.

[3] *ibid.* i, 15.

[4] *Expositions of the Psalms* 25, 3. Also *Soliloquies* i, 23 and *Confessions* vii, 10, 16: '(The light of God shining in the soul of man) is not the common light which all men may look upon; nor yet is it another greater light of the same kind—this light is none of these but different.'

a unique kind quite different from the physical light of the sun. And so we arrive at the formulation, already quoted from *The Literal Interpretation of Genesis*, and repeated in *The Trinity*, to the effect that the soul sees intelligible reality bathed 'in a sort of immaterial light of a unique kind' (*in quadam luce sui generis incorporea*).[1]

The dialogue, called *The Teacher* (*De Magistro*) will be examined more thoroughly in a later chapter. It is interesting both for the light it throws on the act of teaching and for its exposition in definitive form of the doctrine of divine illumination. The discussion of the nature of teaching leads to the conclusion that the real teacher of man is not the external teacher (*magister exterior*), but the internal teacher (*magister interior*). The external teacher, that is, as it were, the teacher in the classroom, has the function of stimulating the learner to learn. But the act of learning occurs only when the learner consults the teacher who 'dwells in the inner man':

> We listen to the truth, which presides over our minds within us, although of course we may be urged to listen by someone using words.[2]

The heart of the learning process is, therefore, a consultation of the interior master by the learner, and this consultation must be brought about by the effort of the learner's will. The essential element in learning is not the effort of the external teacher but a voluntary turning of thought towards the internal teacher and the illumination which this teacher provides. As we have already seen, it is only if this inner consultation is made that we can pass judgements on physical objects.

The doctrine of divine illumination in Augustine demonstrates most clearly the full extent of the Platonic–Christian synthesis, which is Augustine's most original contribution. His debt to Platonism is reflected, as we have seen, in the close approximation to Plato's language in his earlier writings. The neo-Platonists still further refined the conception of intellectual light and the sun which gives birth to meaning in the world of spiritual reality. Plotinus in particular gave definition to the idea of the divine originator of knowledge by stressing the

[1] *The Trinity* xii, 24.
[2] *The Teacher* 38.

indivisible and unchanging nature of the One. According to him, the existence of the multiplicity of particular things came about by the One diffusing itself abroad as the sun diffuses light.[1] The first emanation of the One is Nous or Mind. Man grasps the ideas through the instrumentality of his reason aided by the illumination of the Nous. Thus he prepares himself for union with the divine itself.

The Plotinian One became by easy transition the Augustinian God, while the Nous became the Word of God, the second person of the *Trinity* and the 'internal teacher', who is the cause of knowledge arising in the mind of man. Augustine followed Plotinus in placing the ideas in the mind of God. He followed Plotinus too in insisting on moral purity as the prerequisite of illumination. Plotinus' 'Let a man first purify himself and then observe' is close to 'Blessed are the pure in heart, for they shall see God':

> That light, which is God, no man sees except those about whom it has been said, 'Blessed are the pure in heart, for they shall see God'.[2]

Turning from Plato to Christ, Augustine found ample scriptural support for the notion of the divine Logos diffusing itself into the minds of men for their instruction, and at a moment in history incarnated. There is the analogy of light, for example, in St. John:

> In the beginning was the Word and the Word was with God and the Word was God—in Him was life and the life was the light of man. And the light shineth in darkness—That was the true light which lighteth every man that cometh into the world.[3]

These verses are quoted by Augustine as confirming what the Platonists had already suggested to him. And he supplements them with other scriptural statements, for example the words of

[1] Plotinus, *Enneads* v, 6. See J. M. Colleran, *Introduction to the Greatness of the Soul*, pp. 118–19. Compare *Soliloquies* i, 3 where Augustine describes God as 'Sun of my soul by whose illumination alone the intelligible truths can be perceived'.

[2] *Sermon* iv, 6.

[3] Quoted in *Confessions* vii, 9, 13.

Christ—'I am the light of the world. He that followeth me shall not walk in darkness but shall have the light of life'.[1]

Various attempts have been made to give clearer definition to Augustine's doctrine of divine illumination, although most of these founder on the rocks of certain undeniable and consistent principles of his thought. There is the pantheistic hypothesis, which annihilates the distinction between the Creator and his creation, between the One and the many. But Augustine makes it plain that such a fusion is a dangerous misconception. His description of the genesis of knowledge under the analogy of the imprinting of a seal upon wax[2] shows his conviction of the separate existence of the Creator. The seal remains a separate substance, although closely joined to the wax at the moment of impression. There is the equally untenable ontological explanation, particularly associated with the name of Malebranche.[3] This view identifies the intelligible world with God and declares that divine illumination is to be interpreted in terms of man looking directly upon God. But Augustine makes it clear that man enjoys at the best only a partial and incomplete vision of God, and the trend of his thought is much rather to suggest that it is in the ideas that man glimpses the divine than that man looks directly upon God, in whose radiance he sees the ideas. In this connection Augustine quotes the words of God to Moses—'Thou canst not see my face; for there shall no man see my face and live'.[4]

The explanation, which has proved most consistently tempting to interpreters throughout the centuries, declares that divine illumination operates in the manner of the abstractionism associated with Aristotle and St. Thomas Aquinas. On this view divine illumination is only another name for the active intellect (*intellectus agens*), and concept formation comes about by the light of the intellect playing upon sensibles and abstracting from them their intelligible forms. Boyer, who inclines to this

[1] *John* 8, 12. *The Literal Interpretation of Genesis* iv, 45.

[2] e.g. *The Trinity* xi, 3 and xiv, 21.

[3] Malebranche, *Recherche de la Vérité* and *Entretiens sur la Metaphysique et la Réligion.* For a detailed exposition of ontologism see Cayré, *op. cit.*, pp. 224–6. On Augustine's influence on Malebranche see *infra*, pp. 301–4.

[4] *Exodus* 33, 20.

view, puts it that 'God enlightens us by the very fact that our own intelligence enlightens us. Our intellect is nothing else than the divine Light tempered to the infirmity of our nature'.[1] This is to say that the light of the understanding, while remaining a gift of God, now operates in some independence from the divine source from which it came. The mind's activity becomes an active, synthetic one.

The abstractionist explanation of divine illumination, however, seeks to bring together the Platonic–Augustinian system with the Aristotelian–Thomist in just that area where their most outstanding differences lie. Abstraction of universal ideas from particulars by the power, or light, of the intellect gives to sense data an importance in the formation of ideas, which Augustine consistently denies them. As Gilson points out,[2] such a theory introduces into Augustinianism the conception of the soul acting on the body; we have already seen that Augustine consistently denies that this can happen. Truth must be sought only within the mind—'Do not go outside. It is in the inner man that truth dwells'.[3] Furthermore the abstractionist explanation minimises the dependence of man upon God. Augustine's view of the relationship of God and man is a theistic explanation, which combines the notion of human independence in respect of God with what Warfield calls 'a deeper and more significant dependence'.[4] Thus Augustine steers a middle course between pantheism, in which the creature becomes totally merged in the Creator and exercises no independent function of his own, and the deistic view, in which God is utterly remote and the creature has no access to divine support. Any interpretation of Augustine's illumination theory, which minimises the fundamental dependence of man on God and suggests that man learns in any other way than through an act of consultation with the interior

[1] C. Boyer, *L'Idée de la Vérité*, p. 206. St. Thomas Aquinas, *Summa Theologica* i, quaestio 85. For an exposition of St. Thomas' position see S. J. Curtis, *A Short History of Western Philosophy in the Middle Ages*, ch. 10, pp. 156–63.

[2] E. Gilson, *op. cit.*, p. 116.

[3] Augustine, *True Religion*, 72.

[4] B. B. Warfield, *Calvin and Augustine*, p. 397. Warfield talks of the pantheistic tendencies of Plotinus with which he contrasts Augustine's view of 'the creature set—with powers of his own over against God, the Creator'.

teacher, must fail to follow the basic intention of Augustine's mind.

Other attempts to explain the mechanism of divine illumination have been made, but none is fully satisfactory.[1] The conclusion is that Augustine was unable to give a sufficiently clear definition to his theory. Augustine's thought is not as rigorously and systematically defined as St. Thomas' was to be; his temper was less attuned to logical analysis and more tinged with the emotions of the mystic. Thus the light metaphor seems to have proved so immediately persuasive that it could at once be accepted on faith. Its rationale may be another mystery, which God has veiled from the minds of men, and for this reason Augustine may have chosen to devote his attention to working out the implications of the theory rather than to establish it on sufficiently strong intellectual foundations.

We may follow Gilson in supposing that Augustine was not in fact concerned to formulate a theory designed to account for concept formation; rather he was establishing a basis for testing the certainty of our judgements.[2] The light of God shining upon our thoughts illuminates them, and in so doing clearly demonstrates the truth. The illumination is the authority for the assertion that our thoughts are true, for it is in that illumination that we are able to evaluate our thoughts. On this view, the Augustinian theory of divine illumination and the Aristotelian theory of the active intellect are aimed at explaining different things.

Certainly the theory of illumination carries suggestions of considerable help to educators; the full implications of these will be followed up in a later chapter. Augustine declares that revelation is an essential prerequisite of all wisdom, and that this revelation comes in and through consultation with the divine teacher. Associated with this is the emphasis on the self-activity and moral purity of the learner as essential elements in the progress to knowledge.[3] By an act of will, the learner must disengage himself from preoccupation with goals of lesser worth

[1] F. Cayré, *op. cit.*, pp. 209–43.

[2] E. Gilson, *op. cit.*, p. 118: 'The Aristotelian active intellect produces concepts while Augustinian illumination produces truth.'

[3] e.g. *On True Religion* x, 20: 'So attend—diligently and uprightly, as far as you can. It is such people whom God helps.'

and deliberately interiorise his thought. In short Augustine's illumination theory drives home the responsibility of the learner and the importance of education. Whatever may be the inadequacies of its metaphysical super-structure, it provides in the hands of Augustine a sensitive interpretation of the activity of education and of the response of the human understanding to the challenge of the unknown.

SELF-KNOWLEDGE AND THE FUNCTION OF DOUBT

In examining Augustine's views on the nature of man, we drew attention to his confidence as to the reality and accuracy of the knowledge man has of himself. The importance of establishing the certainty of one's own existence lies in the fact that this knowledge is necessarily the foundation of all other knowledge. 'It is not possible,' Augustine says, 'for the soul to know anything, unless it knows itself.'[1] This certainty of the existence of the self takes its place with two other fixed points of reference which guide the process of knowing, namely truth and God. Doubt as to the certainty of his self-existence has the effect of closely enmeshing man in the toils of doubt at the very moment when he is 'on the threshold of faith'. It is the last resort of the sceptic to cast doubt on the reality of self-consciousness, and, if he can succeed in engaging a man in an interminable argument on this score, then the activity of self-education may be reduced to futility.

It has already been shown that the scepticism of the Academic philosophers, and of Carneades in particular, was an obstacle, which Augustine for his own peace of mind had to meet before he could advance in his understanding of the content of the Christian faith. Since scepticism is the first danger which threatens all intellectual enquiry, it is not surprising that Augustine devoted one of the recorded discussions at Cassiciacum to dealing with it; this was the dialogue, *Against the Academics*. Thirty-five years later in the *Enchiridion*, thinking of these early days, he commented:

> It was indeed essential at the very outset to remove this utter despair of reaching truth, which seems to be strengthened by the arguments of the Academics—they say that error can be

[1] *The Literal Interpretation of Genesis* vii, 28.

avoided only by entirely suspending belief—they strive by the most acute but most fallacious arguments to show that, even though a man's opinion should by chance be true, yet there is no certainty of its truth owing to the impossibility of distinguishing truth from falsehood.[1]

St. Augustine's temper, as his whole intellectual history shows, was not attuned to the mood of the sceptic. He admitted the possibility of human error, but was sure that this possibility must not drive man into the position of believing nothing at all. From his own experience he found ample evidence of the reality of error, but reacted violently against the question raised by the Academics as to 'whether a wise man ought to give his assent to anything, seeing that he may fall into error by assenting to falsehood; for all things are either unknown or uncertain'.[2]

The *Against the Academics* is in fact concerned to refute the suggestion that the senses are deceptive, and that there is no surer guide for man in his progress through life than the probable. Augustine declares his confidence in the existence of absolute truth and in the possibility of man attaining the higher objectives of education. It is in the *Soliloquies* that he first examines the really insidious doubt as to the existence of the conscious, thinking self. He confidently argues that the soul 'knows itself by a sort of inward presence, real and not imaginary'.[3] If man's thought is not confused and perverted by the quibbling of the professional sceptics, he enjoys an immediate certainty that he exists, that he lives and that he has an intellect. It is in fact by virtue of his possession and use of his intellect that he is assured of the certainty of his own existence. He knows that he thinks and from this he properly concludes that he exists.

The argument from the reality of thought to the existence of the thinking self recalls Descartes' 'I think; therefore I exist' (*cogito ergo sum*).[4] Although the principle does not occupy quite

[1] *Enchiridion* 22.

[2] *ibid.*

[3] *The Trinity* x, 16.

[4] The interesting question of the extent to which Descartes may have been influenced by Augustine in this matter is examined by G. Lewis, 'Augustinisme et Cartésianisme' in *Communications du Congrès International Augustinien*, pp. 1087–184. See also *infra*, pp. 296–8.

the central position in St. Augustine's thought, which it does in Descartes', nevertheless St. Augustine regards it as very important. Both in the *Soliloquies* and again in *The Free Will* he takes the reality of self-consciousness as the starting point in any attempt to establish other conclusions. Thus the second book of the *Soliloquies* centres on the attempt to demonstrate man's immortal nature. The argument is preceded by a series of questions designed to determine what can be taken for granted as a basis for further progress. The last exchange of question and answer is as follows:

Reason: Do you know that you think?
Augustine: I do.
Reason: Then it is true that you think?
Augustine: It is true.[1]

Similarly in *The Free Will* the investigation of the real question at issue is preceded by Augustine asking Evodius, 'Do you exist?'.[2] When Evodius answers in the affirmative, St. Augustine goes on to discover the implications of this with reference to man: To exist means to live, and to live is to have intelligence.[3] A stone merely exists; an animal both exists and lives; a man exists, lives and has intelligence. To admit that I exist is, therefore, to declare that I am a thinking being.

In *The Trinity*, as we have already noticed, there is a further exploration of the meaning and extent of the soul's self-knowledge.[4] It is concluded that we are immediately aware of the three functions of will, memory and understanding as making up the total activity of the mind. 'Who can doubt,' Augustine asks, 'that he wills, remembers and understands?'[5]

Augustine's argument is designed to emphasise the positive function of doubt as the starting point of all learning; doubt is in fact evidence of the ability to grow in understanding, and not the symptom of a fatal inability to learn. Man's habit of doubting is the proper consequence of his possession of a rational

[1] *Soliloquies* ii, 1. The language used here provides the closest parallel in Augustine to the language of Descartes: '*Cogitare te scis? Scio. Ergo verum est cogitare te? Verum.*'

[2] *The Free Will* ii, 7.

[3] *Esse, vivere, intelligere.*

[4] *The Trinity* x.

[5] *ibid.* x, 13.

mind; to be doubting is to be thinking. Augustine accepts doubt as the guarantee of man's ability to learn and indeed as a clear indication that he is positively using his power of thought to that end.

It is interesting to trace in Augustine's writings the growth of this reassuring conception of the role of doubt in learning. We find it first in *True Religion*, written just over a year after his return to North Africa. The doubter is bidden to take heart. At least he knows for certain that he doubts:

> If you do not grasp what I say and doubt whether it is true, at least make up your mind whether you have any doubt about your doubts. If it is certain that you do indeed have doubts, inquire where that certainty comes from.[1]

Then comes the flood of insight. When we doubt, it is because we are referring to the eternal verities within us so that we may make judgements. About the fact of doubt there can be no doubt:

> Everyone, who knows that he has doubts, knows with certainty something that is true, namely that he doubts. He is, therefore, certain about *a* truth. Thus everyone who doubts whether there be such a thing as *the* truth has at least *a* truth to set limit to his doubt.[2]

Writing about the same time, Augustine puts the question, 'Do you exist?', but immediately anticipates the hesitation which may arise in Evodius' mind, when faced with such a critical question:

> If you did not exist, then it would be impossible for you to be deceived.[3]

The thought is followed up in *The Trinity* and *The City of God.* The fact that a man makes a mistake in thinking is merely a reinforcement to the evidence that he exists. Nothing which does not exist can make a mistake. Then in *The City of God* comes the passage which yields the formula most closely asso-

[1] *True Religion* 73. For a more detailed exposition of the development of Augustine's conception of the function of doubt see E. Gilson, *op. cit.*, p. 21 and 54–5. Also W. Montgomery, *Aspects of Augustine's Life and Thought*, pp. 148–53.

[2] *ibid.*

[3] *The Free Will* ii, 7.

ciated with Augustine's positive view of doubt—'If I am deceived, then I exist' (*si fallor, sum*):

> I am most certain that I exist and that I know and delight in this. In respect of these truths, I am not at all afraid of the Academics who say, 'What if you are deceived?'. For, *if I am deceived, I exist*; he who does not exist cannot be deceived. And, if I am deceived, by this same token I exist. And, since I exist if I am deceived, how am I deceived in believing that I exist? For it is certain that I exist if I am deceived.[1]

St. Augustine's own experience as recounted in the *Confessions* had clearly shown him that doubt and error are the essential concomitants of thought. Doubt is evidence of the power to raise questions; owing to human frailty, error is an inevitable by-product of the exploratory activity of thought ranging over untrodden areas of experience. That error is identified as such when the intellectual exploration is continued is evidence of the power of the human reason to assess the adequacy of suggested answers and to distinguish between truth and falsehood. In further studying Augustine's method of teaching, we shall see that it is founded on the notion that man learns by raising doubts, i.e. by posing questions to himself, and by seeking and evaluating answers. We have already noted that Augustine sees self-knowledge as the first step in the growth of wisdom. In *The Trinity* he shows that in establishing the certainty of our own existence, nature and powers, we also establish the method of learning through questioning, which we shall have to employ throughout all the rest of our educational progress. Augustine's conclusions on this point may be represented schematically: (see diagram on next page.)

This is the educational significance of the assurance of the reality of the thinking self and of the effective power of the human understanding. It is an assurance founded on the positive and constructive nature of doubt, and even of error, and stressing the importance of critical judgement in the progress of the mind towards sure knowledge. In the phenomenon of doubt man identifies the method of learning, which is by raising questions,

[1] *The City of God* xi, 26. The critical words are as follows: '*Quid si falleris? Si enim fallor, sum. Nam qui non est, utique nec falli potest; ac per hoc sum si fallor.*'

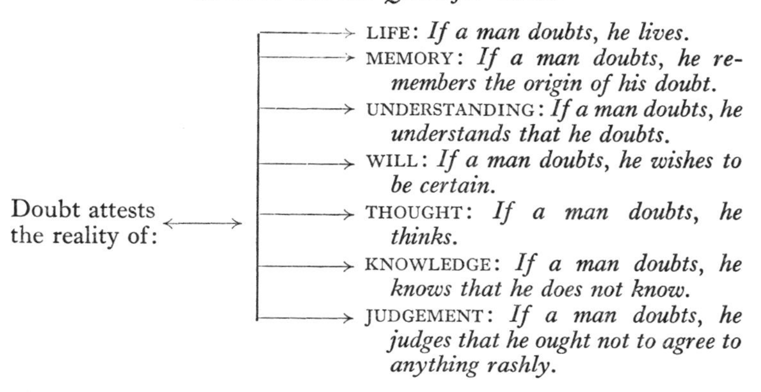

supplying answers and testing them by the critical intelligence. Therefore, by the sort of reaction he displays to the first faltering steps of the learner, the teacher may either give the learner confidence or destroy it. By his own reactions the teacher may show himself to be either an Academic, inhibiting further enquiry, or an Augustine confident about the possibility of knowledge. He may treat his pupil's first mistakes and early ineffectual self-questioning as symptomatic of a fatal inability to succeed in learning; alternatively he may regard them as the first stirrings of significant intellectual activity and progress. Thus at the critical juncture, when the learner flags or lapses into a mistake, the teacher's intervention and attitudes will either fortify his pupil's self-confidence, or allow doubt to lapse into the negative attitude of scepticism. If he does the former, he reveals himself as a true teacher; if the latter, he is guilty of serious professional misconduct. Thus the need to cultivate the self-questioning, critical attitude as the precondition of advance in knowledge is the message conveyed to the educator by Augustine's 'If anyone doubts, then he is thinking' and by his 'If I am deceived, then I exist'.

CONCLUSION

The life of self-education is seen by Augustine in terms of a progress which begins with the data of sense and ends with an understanding of absolute truth and the nature of God. Created by God and in His image, man possesses a measure of God's understanding and also of His freedom of will. Using his free will, man may either accept the rewarding labour of learning, or he may reject it for the life of idle amusement. With his rational intelligence he can launch out on the arduous task of learning with confidence in his inborn ability to reach the goal. Because it is only through the personal effort of his own will that he can learn, man is in a real sense his own teacher. Yet it is by the grace of God that knowledge is illuminated in his mind; therefore, he can advance in knowledge only to the extent that he enters into consultation with the interior teacher. Furthermore, since new knowledge can be added only to an existing framework, he must start his educational progress with some existing partial knowledge of the goal which he wishes to reach. Suggestions as to the reality of spiritual existence and of God come to him from observation of, and reflection on, his own nature, and his physical environment. In this way faith is brought into being, and by it the soul is sustained in its reaching out towards an understanding of reality.

Running through Augustine's theory of knowledge is the conviction that education must advance by an orderly progression from one step to the next. The sequence of these steps, as set out by Augustine in *The Greatness of the Soul*, may be used to summarise his theory of knowledge:[1]

1. *Animation* (*animatio*). The activity of the soul is directed towards the nutrition, growth and reproduction of the body. The vegetative stage.
2. *Sense Perception* (*sensus*). The soul 'directs itself exclusively to the senses', feels pleasures and pains and either welcomes or rejects what benefits or harms the body. This is the stage of habit formation, which man shares with the animals.
3. *Art* (*ars*). The activity of the soul is directed to understanding the natural world and the ways in which its materials are used by man to serve his needs. This is the stage of the arts and sciences.
4. *Goodness* (*virtus*). The soul begins to direct its attention towards itself. Thus it strives to gain its rightful mastery over physical nature. In so doing, it purifies itself from the dominance of false values and develops a more humane outlook—

[1] *The Greatness of the Soul* 70–79. Another closely parallel passage is in *Christian Education* ii, 9–11. See P. Alfaric, *L'Évolution Intellectuelle de St. Augustin*, pp. 471–5.

'it sets a high value on human society and wants nothing to happen to another which it does not want to happen to itself'.[1] In this way it is made fit to undertake successfully the labour of learning.

5. *Tranquillity* (*tranquillitas*). The tensions of the previous stage caused by the difficulty of resisting the pressures and enticements of the physical environment are overcome. Confidence and peace of mind are developed, and these are essential to disciplined thought and study: 'Corresponding to a lack of tranquillity in the presence of fear, there is a great lack of understanding; for tranquillity is absolutely necessary for the study of matters shrouded in mystery'. This is, therefore, the stage of self-purification, without which the mind would be dazzled and repelled by the vision of truth.
6. *Advance* (*ingressio*). Now that the mind is free from tension, the progress in learning begins.
7. *Contemplation* (*contemplatio*). The highest level of spiritual activity, in which the soul perceives its supreme good and rejoices in the knowledge of it.

According to this analysis, the necessary reorientation of man's thought from concentration on self-interest and sense experience to the area of spiritual existence occurs in the progress from the fourth to the fifth stages. Augustine notes that this change of direction from the outer to the inner is assisted by religion, which emerges at the third stage as a by-product of the wonder man experiences when he considers human achievements in the arts and sciences. A sense of religious awe, thus gained, assists in the purification of the soul in the fourth stage, and thus is a potent force in establishing an inner serenity, without which the soul cannot sufficiently concentrate on the quest for truth.

The implications of St. Augustine's theory of knowledge in the practice of teaching will be followed up in the ensuing chapters.

[1] *The Greatness of the Soul* 73. In stressing love of one's fellow man as an essential accompaniment of the life of wisdom, Augustine adds the social concern of Christianity to the philosophical detachment of neo-Platonism. Contrast Plotinus, *Enneads* iii, 5: 'The purification of the soul consists in leaving it to itself and not permitting it to have any dealings with others.'

5 The Art of the Teacher

Teachers offer themselves for imitation, and this is precisely what people call teaching.
On Music i, 6.

Instruction is completed by love.
The Practices of the Catholic Church, 56.

Our examination of St. Augustine's life and thought has already yielded evidence of his interest in the practice of teaching. In this chapter we shall review what he has to say and demonstrate about the teacher–pupil relationship and the general problems of method. Thereafter, we shall consider his analysis of the act of teaching and his views on the education of the Christian teacher.

There can be no doubt that Augustine regarded teaching as an art. We may recall that in several places he makes an important distinction between 'art' and 'imitation'; the former is soundly based on knowledge, the latter refers to the unthinking assimilation and repetition of techniques.[1] Since Augustine regards education as basically concerned with the acquisition of knowledge rather than with habituation, it would be anomalous if he were not to insist that the teacher's skill should be rooted in knowledge. We would expect to find that, in his own practice of teaching and in the advice he gives to intending teachers, he emphasises the need for the intelligent adaptation of means to ends and for sensitive and humane understanding. This is the way in which all the great teachers have interpreted their work, and it is by this standard that St. Augustine's attitude to the practice of teaching will be judged.

AUGUSTINE'S CREDENTIALS AS A TEACHER

Augustine's own experience of teaching was considerable. Up to the year of his conversion he practised teaching as a profession.

[1] *supra*, pp. 105–6.

At Tagaste he taught grammar for a year in a school, which he himself established. Later he taught in schools of rhetoric at Carthage and Rome. The reputation he acquired as a teacher of rhetoric speedily led to his appointment as a public orator and teacher of rhetoric at Milan. On his conversion to Christianity he laid down his secular teaching duties, but did not abandon the vocation of teaching. He clearly states in the *Confessions* that he was merely putting aside the work of formal instruction in the techniques of oratory in favour of a more challenging and significant teaching task.[1] In the months immediately following his conversion, this task was begun at a country house at Cassiciacum, near Milan, where Augustine spent some months discussing with a group of his friends and young pupils the implications of Christian involvement.

On his return to North Africa and his native Tagaste Augustine realised the need for the spread of education among Christians, both priests and laymen. Thus at Tagaste and later at Hippo he established communities, whose purpose was the preparation of well-educated Christian teachers for the North African church.[2] In a letter written at this time to a close friend, Nebridius, Augustine replies to an invitation from Nebridius to join him in Carthage for a time. The reply shows Augustine's strong feeling of responsibility towards his students at Tagaste:

> Shall I come to you? But there are some people who cannot come with me, and I am sure that it would be wrong to desert them. You can live agreeably with your own thoughts; but this is the condition at which they are still aiming.[3]

In regard to Augustine's attitude to teaching, it is also significant that of the two forms of monastic life open to him, the life of the solitaries and the community life of the cenobites, he chose the latter, realising that the opportunities for personal association and discussion, which the cenobitic life affords, was a greater stimulus to the pursuit of knowledge.

The range and quality of Augustine's teaching activity as a

[1] *Confessions* ix, 4–5.
[2] *supra*, pp. 23–4.
[3] *Letter* 10, 1.

priest and later as Bishop at Hippo are attested by the comments of his friends and contemporaries. It was at the monastery at Tagaste that Possidius, later to become a bishop of the North African Church, came under Augustine's influence. His *Life of St. Augustine*, written after Augustine's death, is his tribute to the influence of a great teacher. Throughout this work we are made aware of the affection and respect which Augustine inspired in those who came under his influence. Possidius reminds us of the amount of time Augustine gave to teaching, when we read in connection with his early years at Hippo that he 'taught both privately and publicly, both in his home and in the church'.[1] The warmth of Augustine's personality is stressed in one of Possidius' final comments to the effect that, although many were indebted to Augustine for instruction through his writings and letters, he made the greatest impression on those who had the privilege of hearing him preaching in his church and talking with his friends.[2]

Further tributes to Augustine's influence as a teacher are not hard to find. Nebridius pays tributes in letters to the stimulus gained from the correspondence he had with Augustine, whose letters recall the wisdom of the greatest teachers, Christ, Plato and Plotinus. They are 'pleasant to the ear because of their eloquence', but above all they are 'worth the labour of understanding because of the wisdom, which is in them'.[3]

At the end of *The Happy Life*, one of the early Cassiciacum dialogues, Trygetius acknowledges the stimulus he and others have received from the learning experiences they have had together under Augustine. This tribute comes in response to Augustine's spontaneous expression of the delight he himself has felt. His pupils have 'heaped gifts upon him' through the contributions they have made to the discussion. In this 'feast', to which he (Augustine) has invited them, he has been sumptuously fed by his own guests. The impression is that the discussion has been stimulating to all concerned, because all have been drawn into a fellowship of enquiring minds.[4]

[1] Possidius, *Life of Bishop Augustine*, in Migne, ***Patrilogia Latina***, vol. 32, cols. 33–66.

[2] *ibid.* 31.

[3] *Letter* 6.

[4] *The Happy Life* 36.

These and other references point to a teacher who has great respect for the personalities of his students. Throughout the dialogues of Cassiciacum there runs an atmosphere of expectancy and interest, such as is always associated with significant learning experiences. Where a member of the group is going off on the wrong track, or the discussion is losing pace, Augustine restores the situation tactfully and without offending the feelings of the younger members of the group. For example, at the end of the first day's discussion in *The Happy Life*, Licentius has been subjected to some good-humoured badinage in an attempt to make him commit himself to one or other of two alternative propositions. Augustine, the teacher, has also observed that some members of the group are puzzled by a reference to the Academic philosophers. Thus he feels it necessary to clarify the difficulties involved without too obviously publicising Licentius' failure to grasp the points at issue. The difficulties are cleared up and the lesson concluded without hurting the feelings of anyone:

> While we were thus making fun of him (Licentius) and, as it were, calling to him to swallow his own morsel, I noticed that the others were puzzled by the whole drift of the discussion. Being anxious to know what was the cause of all the laughter among us, they were looking at us with a serious expression. They looked like those who, when they were feasting among some very greedy and ravenous guests, shrink back from taking their own proper share due to an inability to relax, or out of shame. Because I was their host, I could not endure this and was troubled by this inequality and difference at my table. So I smiled to my mother. And she very willingly, as though she were ordering something they were short of to be brought from her pantry, said to me, 'Come, tell us again who are these Academics you are talking about and what they are driving at'. I then briefly and clearly described them so that no member of the group should go away without knowing. Whereupon she remarked, 'Those fellows you are talking about must be epileptics'. At the same time she got up to go away. So, seeing our conversation terminated, we all went off laughing and in the best of spirits.[1]

[1] *ibid.* 16. The Latin for epileptics is '*caducarii*', from the root 'cad-' meaning 'fall'. Like epileptics, the Academic philosophers have a

Thus also in Augustine's *Letters*, which often take the form of answers given to questions put to him by acquaintances, the tone is non-authoritarian. He offers suggestions for the consideration of the questioner, and encourages him to make his own personal assessment of them. There is always a willingness to spend sufficient time upon the question at issue to enable the learner to feel his own way forward to understanding. The patient labour expended by the teacher in guiding the learner towards the solution of a problem is justified by the new insights, which the method brings not only to the learner but also to the teacher. Thus, with reference to the need for a careful clearing of the ground as a necessary preliminary to the investigation of a difficult problem, Augustine says:

> I have preferred to travel the way on foot with weaker travellers rather than launch them through the freer air before they were sufficiently equipped with wings for the flight.[1]

With Rousseau in a later age, Augustine realises that in education one must 'hurry slowly'.

One of the first qualities of the successful teacher is that he should rate education as a human activity of the greatest significance. Education supplies 'nourishment' for the soul, as food does for the body, a thought which is expressed by Augustine's mother, Monica in one of her several interventions in the Cassiciacum dialogues: 'Ideas and thoughts are the nourishment of the mind, since it is through these that the mind gets to know things'. Augustine himself goes on to declare that souls which lack knowledge are 'full of vices and worthlessness'; the souls of the uneducated are 'filled with diseases which betray their malnutrition'.[2] Intellectual activity is, therefore, of absolute value, and the teacher's duty is to encourage it with all his skill. In so doing, he must remember that his pupils cannot

[1] *On Music* vi, 1.
[2] *The Happy Life* 8.

---

tendency to trip themselves up in their arguments and fall down. Monica's duties were concerned with the domestic arrangements. However, she is from time to time drawn into the discussion. Her brief contributions are marked by wit and good sense and treated with respect by the men.

be compelled to learn; they can only be influenced to learn by the teacher's own example, enthusiasm and love. Since intellectual enquiry, i.e. education, is an absolutely good thing, Augustine holds that there is no restriction to be placed on the range of such enquiry: 'Nothing is lost which we enquire into with serious purpose'.[1]

Looking upon teaching as a commission handed down from Christ himself, Augustine concludes that it is in teaching that man most significantly expresses his love of God and of his fellow man. It is every man's duty to see that his fellows are 'sound in body and soul';[2] as medicine (*medicina*) is supplied for their bodies, so teaching (*disciplina*) must be provided for their souls.[3] This does not imply that everyone must engage in teaching in its more formal sense. Augustine is aware that many of the most important lessons come informally by the force of example rather than by formal instruction. Formal lessons may be largely ineffective if there is a contradiction between a teacher's precept and practice:

> Whatever may be the grandeur of his style, the life of the teacher will count for more in winning the learner's obedience. The man who speaks wisely and eloquently but lives wickedly may, it is true, instruct many who are anxious to learn—but he would do good to very many more if he lived as he taught. There are many who seek an excuse for their own evil lives in comparing what their teachers teach with the way they behave. They say in their hearts, if not with their lips, 'Why do you not carry out what you ask me to do?' Thus they no longer listen attentively to a man who does not listen to himself and, in despising the instructor, they learn to despise the word that is taught.[4]

Augustine's writings reveal an awareness of the profession a responsibility of the teacher and of the conditions which promote or inhibit learning. In the words of one of his Sermons, the impulse to learn derives from an impression of 'the sweetness of truth', and the impulse to teach from 'the necessity of

[1] *On Music* vi, 23: '*Nihil deperit quod diligentius quaerimus*'.
[2] *The Practices of the Catholic Church* i, 56.
[3] *ibid.*
[4] *Christian Education* iv, 59–60.

love'.[1] Thus by precept and example St. Augustine suggests that mental stress in teacher or pupil is incompatible with effective education. We may recall that he saw the most crucial movement determining the success of education as the assumption of tranquillity of mind in place of tension: 'Tranquillity is absolutely necessary for the study of matters shrouded in mystery'.[2] St. Augustine well knew the temptation, which besets teachers, to be impatient with those who know less than themselves:

> There are many who learn calmly but who teach in an agitated manner. Although they have a patient teacher, they are harsh towards their pupils. We all know how calmly the Scriptures teach us. A man comes and reads the precepts of God, drinking them in peacefully from a peaceful source. Then he is approached by someone wanting to learn something from him. He storms and rages, accusing the learner of understanding too slowly. He throws the learner into confusion, so that he understands less well what the teacher himself had the opportunity of listening to in a calmer atmosphere.[3]

THE MOTIVATION OF LEARNING

Our study of Augustine's psychology has shown the importance he attaches to volition in human behaviour. What matters is that the will should be consistently directed towards objects that are worth loving. He sees all the movements of the universe, including the movements of the soul, as deriving their momentum from the divine love, by which everything was created and set in motion in the beginning. The curiosity, which impels the young child to reach out and grasp an object which he desires, is a manifestation of that same love which is behind every human aspiration, and which, if it is not misdirected, leads man to know God, who is the source of love.

Therefore, if the teacher is to succeed in stimulating his pupils to learn, his own behaviour must be motivated by love of

[1] *The Eight Questions of Dulcitius* 6.

[2] *The Greatness of the Soul* 73. Also *Christian Education* ii, 9–11. *Supra*, p. 137.

[3] *Sermon* 47, 9.

the subject he professes and of his students. Unless this condition is present, his students are unlikely to make the task in hand the object of their own personal devotion and effort; therefore, they are to learn less effectively than they otherwise would.

These thoughts are implicit in all that Augustine has to say on the subject of teaching method. For example, in *Christian Education* he lays down the two basic conditions of learning:

> Our hearer, or companion, should have an earnest desire to learn the truth and should have the capacity of mind to receive it in whatever form it may be communicated.[1]

St. Augustine argues that, if learning occurs only under the impulse of the desire to learn, there must always be a specific object of knowledge, which the learner desires to make his own. If a person desires to possess something, it is because he already believes that it really exists. But one cannot believe in the reality of something entirely outside the range of one's existing experience and knowledge. In other words, there can be no impulse to learn anything which is not already known in part:

> Unless we have some slight knowledge of a subject in our minds, we cannot be kindled with any enthusiasm to learn it.[2]

Therefore the teacher must begin with what the student already knows and give him a glimpse of what there is still to be known, and when this is done, the learner is said to 'fashion in his mind an imaginary form, by which he is fired with love'. This form in the imagination is composed of the materials of his existing experience. 'How does the learner form this image,' Augustine asks, 'unless he draws upon the things he already knows?'[3]

In the course of the same argument from *The Trinity* Augustine illustrates the point from the teaching of grammar

[1] *Christian Education* iv, 23.

[2] *The Trinity* x, 1. Also *ibid.*, 'What a man is completely ignorant of, he can by no means love—It is only something which is known which can be surely loved'. See *supra*, ch. 2, pp. 49–53 for the discussion of this point in relation to Augustine's emphasis on faith preceding understanding.

[3] *ibid.* x, 4.

and rhetoric, in which his own experience of teaching lay.[1] A student can become interested in rhetoric, only if he has had the opportunity to listen to orators and thus understand what rhetoric is and what it can achieve. Similarly a child will want to learn to read, only if he understands the relationship between spoken words and written symbols, and realises the practical advantages of understanding letters and words. When a person desires to know the meaning of a word, it is because he already knows that the word is a symbol of something other than itself. Added to the curiosity to know the meaning of the symbol is his awareness that the word is composed of familiar letters and syllables. Therefore his desire for understanding takes its start from what he already partially knows; he wishes to complete his knowledge:

> The more a thing is known and yet not fully known, the more the mind desires to know what remains to be known about it. If all a man knew was that a word was a spoken sound and did not know that it was the sign of something, he would seek nothing further—but because he knows it to be not only a spoken sound but also a sign, he wishes to understand it fully, and no sign is fully known unless we know what it is a sign of.[2]

By this and other arguments Augustine demonstrates his conviction that successful teaching depends upon the teacher adapting his material to the interests and experience of his pupils. Learning is a matter of progressively adding to and diversifying experience rather than of accumulating scraps of ill-digested and poorly integrated information. It is the insufficient attention given by teachers to the integration of knowledge which prompted A. N. Whitehead to condemn 'inert ideas', which he defined as 'ideas that are merely received into the mind without being utilised, or tested, or thrown into fresh combinations'.[3] The principle of coherency has been tested in the experience of the best teachers and supported from many different theoretical stand-points in the history of teaching. A

[1] *The Trinity* x, 1.
[2] *ibid.* x, 2.
[3] A. N. Whitehead, *Aims of Education and other Essays* (Benn, London, 1962), pp. 1–2.

conspicuous later example from the nineteenth century is the apperception doctrine of the German educator, Herbart, and the Herbartians; apperception, as opposed to simple perception, emphasises the unification or connectedness of knowledge, and defines the teacher's task in terms of 'widening the circle of thought'.[1]

We have already had occasion to observe that, in company with Descartes, Augustine regards the condition of doubt in positive terms as implying a desire to learn, i.e. a state of readiness for learning.[2] In *The Trinity* Augustine applies this optimistic belief to the practice of teaching. The statement, 'I do not know' (*nescio*), spoken by a student to a teacher, or spoken internally by the student to himself, signifies, 'I have as yet only a partial knowledge and I *desire* to know more fully'. This may well be a more promising beginning for learning than the apparently more positive 'I know' (*scio*), which may indicate nothing more than a complacent acceptance of untested and invalid assumptions. This was the unwarranted confidence of the slave boy in Plato's *Meno*, a confidence which Socrates had to break down by a preliminary questionnaire before the boy could realise his ignorance and therefore 'want' to learn.[3] Augustine is drawing upon his experience of teaching and learning, when he shows that a feeling of proper humility in the face of knowledge is a better beginning than the conviction that there is nothing further to be known. A man may be deceiving himself when he says 'I know this', but this is less likely when he says, 'I do not know it':

> The man who says, 'I know', and is speaking the truth, does not necessarily know what knowing means. But the man who says, 'I do not know', and is faithfully saying what he believes and knows that he is speaking the truth—that man at least knows what knowing is. This is because he is distinguishing the person who knows from the person who does not know

[1] e.g. in J. F. Herbart, *Lectures on Education*, trans. H. & E. Felkin (London, 1901), pp. 115–16. A further definition of apperception may be quoted from the Herbartian, C. de Garmo, *Essentials of Method* (Boston, 1899), p. 25: 'the process of giving significance to facts by relating them to more firmly established knowledge'. *Infra*, pp. 228–9.

[2] *supra*, pp. 130–4.

[3] Plato, *Meno*, 81C to 86B.

> when he accurately surveys himself and says, 'I do not know'. When he knows that this is true, how could he get this knowledge if he did not know what knowing is?[1]

Augustine's emphasis on the importance of the learner's volition and freely accepted purpose as the starting point of education has been tested and confirmed in modern experimental pedagogy. In developing his treatment of the conditions governing interest and attention, Augustine shows a good understanding of both the potentiality and the limitations of human nature. He understands that the desire to acquire a knowledge of some particular subject will carry the learner over serious obstacles; at the same time he notes that, if these obstacles are allowed to become too formidable, the learner's will to learn may be seriously affected. The desired knowledge must be possible of attainment, or the impetus will be lost. Thus the teacher must be careful to adapt what he teaches to the abilities and experience of his students and to the resources available to them:

> Those subjects are studied more eagerly when people do not despair of being able to grasp them. When a man has not the hope of being able to attain his end, he either loves the subject in a lukewarm manner or does not love it at all, however valuable he may see it to be.[2]

Once again Augustine illustrates the point from language learning: Everyone would acknowledge the value of learning all languages, but owing to the obvious difficulty of doing this, most people confine themselves to learning their own native tongue. Nevertheless, the value of knowing what words mean is attested by the curiosity aroused when a person is introduced to an unfamiliar word:

> Nobody is so lazy in respect of knowledge that, when he hears a strange word, he does not want to know what it means, and, if he can, he enquires about it and learns it.[3]

The value of the enquiring mind, that is the mind which is 'in love with knowledge', ranks very high among Augustine's

[1] *The Trinity* x, 3.
[2] *ibid.* x, 2.
[3] *ibid.*

values; it is the clearest reflection in the area of human life of the divine love, by which man was endowed with intellect and the will to understand the reasons of things.

THE TEACHER–PUPIL RELATIONSHIP

Two writings of Augustine are the richest sources of practical advice on teaching method, *Christian Education* and in particular *The Instruction of the Uninstructed*, both written in the three years following his consecration when he was preoccupied with the need to produce better educated leaders and teachers for the African Church. All the recommendations he makes in these two works derive their consistency from the commandment, which he sees as the basis of all personal relationships: 'Thou shalt love the Lord thy God and thy neighbour as thyself.' The same love, by which God has created man and instructs him, is the source of the human desire to learn, which it is the teacher's duty to inspire in his pupils. The personal relationship with God, which enables man to advance in understanding, and so live the good life, must be reflected in the association of teacher and pupil, since this association is designed to effect exactly the same purpose. Thus, in the instruction of his pupils the teacher must co-operate with the purposes and methods of God; his teaching must be founded on a personal relationship rendered productive by love. Indeed for Augustine teaching *is* interpersonal relationship in its most significant and expressive form. Good teaching is marked by mutual understanding and shared enthusiasm, in which the teacher must often take the initiative: 'There is no greater invitation to love than to anticipate in loving'.[1]

Augustine's thoughts about the practice of teaching derive from his emphasis on interpersonal relationships and reciprocal stimulation. Teaching in its inspirational and productive sense implies a common involvement of teacher and taught in tasks of mutual interest. If this mutual concern is absent, there remains only the boredom of 'repeating over and over again things, which are already thoroughly well known to the teacher and appropriate only for little children'.[2] On the other hand, when

[1] *The Instruction of the Uninstructed* 7.
[2] *ibid.* 17.

love is present, the familiar takes on the quality of novelty, and the teaching is raised from a pedestrian to an inspirational level, from mechanical repetition to the thrill of exploration and discovery. The following passage, which sensitively expresses the experience of intercommunication, comes from *The Instruction of the Uninstructed*:

> Let us then adapt ourselves to our pupils with a love which is at once the love of a brother, of a father and of a mother. When once we are linked to them in heart, the old familiar things will seem new to us. So great is the influence of a sympathetic mind that, when our pupils are affected by us as we speak and we by them as they learn, we dwell in each other and thus both they, as it were, speak within us what they hear, while we after a fashion learn in them what we teach.[1]

In such a situation the distinction between teacher and taught is largely obliterated; each is both teaching, and learning from, the other, since they are linked by a common purpose and in love with the same objectives. The extent to which this mutual sharing of experience is exemplified in the dialogues of Augustine has already been commented on and will be further developed later in this chapter.

As we have already seen, Augustine holds that, if love is to be effective in promoting learning, it must be specifically directed.[2] This implies that the teacher must be observant of individual needs and reactions and vary his teaching methods accordingly. His love must necessarily be expressed in different modes according to the maturity, cultural level and personal characteristics of the various persons constituting his audience. For example, if the Christian teacher is addressing an educated person, he must be careful not to bore or annoy him by pitching the level of his instruction too low:

> With such people we teachers must adopt a brief method. We must not lecture them boringly on things they already know. We must pass lightly over such matters, merely observing that we believe they already know this, that and the other thing. We should add that we are merely running over facts

[1] *ibid.*
[2] *supra*, pp. 54–5.

which must be brought to the attention of those who have received no instruction and do not know them. This should be done in such a way that the educated enquirer does not hear anything with which he is already familiar coming to him, as it were, from the mouth of a teacher.[1]

The most effective and persuasive teaching does not too obviously appear to be teaching in the formal, authoritarian sense too often associated with the schoolroom.

The importance of adaptation to individual differences in a spirit of Christian charity receives continuing attention in *The Instruction of the Uninstructed*:

> The same medicine is not to be applied to all, although to all the same love is due—Different people must necessarily affect the teacher in different ways—the teacher's talk should, as it were, wear an appearance expressive of the mind from which it issues; it should affect the hearer in different ways according as his frame of mind varies, just as his hearers too affect one another in various ways by their mere presence together.[2]

The analysis culminates in a sentence which crystallises much of the teacher's art and the nature of true discipline:

> With some love labours hard, with others it becomes weak. Some it strives to edify, to others it dreads to be a cause of offence. Before some it bows its head, before others it stands with head erect. To some it is gentle, to others stern, an enemy to none, a mother to all.[3]

Much of the advice given to teachers in *The Instruction of the Uninstructed* relates to the psychological influences which inhibit the pupil's response to the teacher's efforts. For example, when the pupil gives the appearance of being apathetic, it may be because he is suffering from 'a natural shyness' (*humana verecundia*) or unable to understand what is being said.[4] On the other hand his failure to respond may be due to the material of the lesson being already familiar to him. St.

[1] *The Instruction of the Uninstructed* 12.
[2] *ibid.* 23.
[3] *ibid.*
[4] *ibid.* 18.

Augustine concludes from all this that the teacher must carefully observe his pupils' reactions as the lesson goes along and adapt his method in accordance with his observations. The teacher must have regard, not merely to what he himself desires to teach but to what his pupils desire to learn.[1] In every way he must be sympathetic and subtle in his approach, as for example by employing 'gentle encouragement' (*blanda exhortatio*) and 'brotherly friendship' (*fraterna societas*) to combat self-consciousness.[2] He should do all he can to discover the reasons for his pupils' failures and then act in accordance with the diagnosis he has made.

In all the detailed practical advice, which St. Augustine gives to Christian teachers in *The Instruction of the Uninstructed* there is a sensitive appraisal of the psychological forces which affect the success of teaching. Among these he lays emphasis on the influence of the teacher's own attitudes to the work of teaching and to his pupils, because these attitudes quickly communicate themselves to his pupils. 'Our chief concern must be,' the declares, 'to see that we take pleasure in teaching; for the teacher is agreeable to his listeners to the extent that he takes pleasure in his work.'[3] Enthusiasm is infectious; by contrast a psychological barrier is set up when the teacher is compelled to teach when he would rather be doing something else. In such a situation the lesson is unlikely to stimulate the learner because 'we come to a work, which requires great calmness with minds already upset, lamenting that we are not allowed to observe the right order in our occupations that we want to observe, and that we cannot meet all the demands made upon us'. In consequence the lesson 'wells up from the arid soil of our dejection'.[4]

Some of the most interesting practical advice Augustine gives to the teacher is concerned with the use of language to communicate thought. In the next chapter we shall analyse the dialogue called *The Teacher*, which deals specifically with the problem of communication. In the meantime we should note Augustine's emphasis on lucidity as one of the first virtues and duties of the teacher. This is a question, to which Augustine devotes several sections of *Christian Education*.[5] He stresses the danger that clear communication may be inhibited by pedantry

[1] *ibid.* 51. [2] *ibid.* 18. [3] *ibid.* 4. [4] *ibid.* 14.
[5] *Christian Education* iv, 23–8.

on the teacher's part and interprets over-conformity to traditional standards of correct speech as a sign of weakness; absolute grammatical accuracy must not be allowed to outweigh every other consideration. Thus, for example, when the Christian teacher is instructing an African audience in the Latin tongue, he must not be too pedantically correct in the matter of vowel length, since African ears find it hard to distinguish between short and long vowels. Over-strict adherence to the rules of quantity would result in a pronunciation which would simply not be understood by a less sophisticated audience. Effective communication must be judged by its practical results:

> What is the value of purity of speech if it is not followed by understanding on the part of the listener? For there is no reason for speaking if those for whose benefit we speak do not understand what we are saying. Therefore, the teacher will avoid all words which do not teach.[1]

As a former teacher of grammar, Augustine realises the importance of attending to the accepted rules of accidence and syntax, but only provided the learner can understand the language of cultured people. On occasions the less generally accepted word should be used for reasons of clarity when that is the word which is understood. In one passage from *Christian Education* Augustine goes further and attributes to the vulgar idiom a directness and lack of ambiguity which cultured speech may sometimes lack.[2]

[1] *ibid.* iv, 24. See also *infra*, pp. 257–8. Augustine illustrates the African insensitivity to vowel length from the Latin word '*os*', which may mean 'bone' or 'mouth', according to whether the vowel is pronounced short or long. The teacher should not hesitate to use the barbarism '*ossum*' ('bone') instead of the more acceptable '*os*', since '*ossum*' is so clearly the singular of '*ossa*', and therefore indicates 'bone' ('*ŏs*') rather than 'mouth' ('*ōs*').

[2] *ibid.* iii, 7: 'It is often the case that the vulgar idiom is more useful in conveying the sense than the cultured speech of the educated. I would indeed use barbarisms in speech rather than speak better Latin and be found wanting in lucidity'. Again in *Expositions of the Psalms* 138, 20: 'Better that the teachers of grammar should blame us than that the people should not understand us'. H. I. Marrou, *St. Augustin et la Fin de la Culture Antique*, pp. 536–40, shows that Augustine himself rarely availed himself of the licence to offend against the rules of pure latinity.

Augustine's opposition to linguistic pedantry is frequently displayed.[1] Several times in the dialogues he expresses impatience when the course of the argument resolves itself into a wrangle over the meaning of words. 'Call it what you will,' he says at one such moment, 'for we must not make too much of a fuss about names when the thing itself is clear.'[2] So in a discussion of the difficulties of interpreting the Scriptures in *Christian Education*, Augustine makes a clear distinction between obscurities of style and mere departures from generally accepted rules of grammar. The solecisms and barbarisms, so reprobated by teachers of grammar and rhetoric, do not necessarily mean a failure of lucidity, but merely a deviation from the accepted standards of cultured speech and from the authority of the classical authors:

> A solecism is nothing else than the putting of words together according to a different rule from that which those of our predecessors who spoke with any authority followed—a barbarism is merely the pronouncing of a word in a different way from that in which those who spoke Latin before us pronounced it—Purity of speech is simply the preservation of the habits of speech established by the authority of those who have used the language in the past.[3]

The teacher must, therefore, value lucidity more highly than verbal ornament or pedantic purity of speech. In this regard Augustine distinguishes between the professional rhetorician (such as he himself had been before his conversion in Milan) and the teacher. For the former, eloquence consists in making people do what the speaker wants them to do. But the 'true eloquence' of the teacher on the other hand consists in 'making clear what was obscure'.[4]

When this is said, however, Augustine adds that to lucidity

[1] In *Christian Education* iv, 7 the distinction is made between lucidity and mere technical competence in grammar and rhetoric. It is the distinction between wisdom and mere eloquence. When a choice has to be made, then the former must be preferred: 'We must look out for the man who abounds in eloquent nonsense'.

[2] *On Music* i, 4: '*Non enim de nominibus laborandum est cum res aperta sit.*'

[3] *Christian Education* ii, 19.

[4] *ibid.* iv, 26.

(*perspicuitas*) must be added an attractive style of speech (*suavitas*). He commends Cicero for summing up the work of the teacher under three headings—teaching, giving pleasure and moving to right action.[1] All these three requirements are bound up together in the work of the best teachers. Therefore, although the primary purpose of the teacher is to make clear what was obscure, he will certainly lose the attention of his class, if he does not develop a pleasant and attractive style of speech:

> If there is no grace of manner, the fruits of the teaching come to only a few very keen students who want to know whatever is to be taught, however rough and unpolished the manner in which it is put.[2]

Augustine realises that an attractive delivery is even more telling when the audience is becoming weary. In other respects, he is very conscious of the danger of over-taxing his students' powers of concentration. Attention must flag, if the teacher attempts to hold it too long. But it can be temporarily revived by changing the method of teaching, and by allowing a time for relaxation between periods of concentrated work. At one point in the dialogue, *The Principle of Order*, Augustine brings the discussion to a close when the group is becoming fatigued. The particular interest of this episode lies not merely in the fact that he stops the lesson but in the tactful manner in which he does it. The argument has been based on the nature of the soul, which has been defined as 'immobile' (*immobilis*). However, the soul seems to be a passenger within the body, and the body undoubtedly moves around. Is not the soul, therefore, moved along with the body as the crew of a ship is moved when the ship moves? Is a horseman correctly described as moving when he is carried along by his horse? Vain attempts are being made to refine the concept of motion, when a servant appears from the house announcing dinner time. Augustine then breaks into the discussion as follows:

> I then said, 'This boy here is not asking us to give a definition of motion but displays the thing itself before our very

[1] Cicero, *Orator* 21.
[2] *Christian Education* iv, 26.

eyes. Come, then, let us go from here to another place for, unless I am badly mistaken, this would indeed be motion.' So they all laughed heartily and we went away.[1]

Augustine's conception of effective teaching in terms of mutual stimulation and informal communication has close affinities with other theories of learning and teaching based on very different philosophies. An interesting comparison may be made, for example, between Augustine's view of teaching as a mutual engagement of teacher and taught with the concept of 'communication' associated with the pragmatic theory of John Dewey in the twentieth century. For Dewey, communication means an interaction of persons exploring their 'shared interests and common concerns'. It is through communication in this dynamic sense that individuals enrich their common experience and develop their capacity for reflective thought. We may compare Dewey's words with St. Augustine's to show how the old and the new combine to shed light on the basic essentials of teaching:

> To be a recipient of a communication is to have an enlarged and changed experience. One shares in what another has thought and felt and . . . has his own attitudes modified. Nor is the one who communicates left unaffected. Try the experiment of communicating with fulness and accuracy some experience to another, especially if it be somewhat complicated, and you will find your own attitude towards your experience changing . . . communication is a process of sharing experience till it becomes a common possession. It modifies the disposition of both parties who partake in it.[2]

Is it not a common occurrence that, when we are showing to those who have never before seen them certain broad and beautiful vistas of towns or countryside, which we have been accustomed to pass by without pleasure due to their familiarity, our delight is renewed by their delight at the novelty of the scene? And the closer the friendship between us, the more strongly does this occur. For in proportion as we dwell

[1] *The Principle of Order* ii, 18.

[2] J. Dewey, *Democracy and Education,* (Macmillan, N.Y., 1929), pp. 6, 7, 11.

in them through the bond of love, so do things which were old become new to us also.[1]

THE ACTIVITY METHOD

Augustine's basic philosophical and psychological assumptions assign to the teacher a peripheral position in the process of learning. It is the learner himself who is central; he teaches himself in a direct encounter with the thing to be known. This view of the teacher as not being the cause of learning but as merely supplying the stimulus and perhaps the source materials marks one of the differences between the Platonic and Aristotelian systems. To the Aristotelian St. Thomas Aquinas the teacher is the cause of learning in as real a sense as the doctor is the cause of good health in his patient.[2] The Augustinian point of view, on the other hand, is one which has never lacked its supporters. In the twentieth century, for example, J. E. Adamson, writing in *The Individual and the Environment*, says:

> In the educative process itself there does not seem to be any room for the teacher—the whole business is between the individual and his worlds and the teacher is outside it, external to it.[3]

Augustine himself argues this point most thoroughly in *The Teacher*, which we shall study in the next chapter. In the meantime it should be noted that, on this view, teaching and learning are not set apart as two separate and distinct activities. When this distinction is made, the activity is often thought to be centred on the teacher and the learner comes to be seen as playing a subordinate and even passive role. In Augustine's

[1] *The Instruction of the Uninstructed* 17. In *Christian Education* i, 1, Augustine uses the parable of the loaves and the fishes to support his conviction that in the best teaching situation the teacher's knowledge is increased as well as his pupils'. As the food was increased in the act of distribution, so Augustine finds that the act of communicating his thought to others results in 'a marvellous increase of wealth' for himself.

[2] For further discussions of this point see pp. 206–7 and pp. 287–9.

[3] J. E. Adamson, *The Individual and his Environment*, (Longmans Green, London, 1921), p. 27.

view, on the other hand, the activities of teaching and learning come to be closely fused together and lose their distinguishing marks. The learner teaches himself, whether or not he is assisted by an external teacher. The activity of learning arises entirely of the learner's own volition in response to the presentation of some desired objective, and it continues so long as that objective proves attractive. Nothing which the teacher can do can produce learning, unless the learner voluntarily engages himself.

By this St. Augustine points to the difference between a method which involves the pupil in an activity of thought and one which does not necessarily do so. From his own experience of learning in school he understood the difference between the development of ideas and the rote memorising of words. On the one hand, there is the purposeful, exciting quest for knowledge; on the other hand the largely meaningless 'sing-song' of the schools. Augustine's own most significant learning was not gained from schoolmasters, but through the self-activity of thought. His real teachers were those who not merely talked to him through books (e.g. Aristotle, Cicero, Plato), but who also encouraged him to think critically about what they said. He makes it clear in the *Confessions* that he used the material gathered from these teachers as resource materials for the furtherance of his own intellectual quest; he accepted only what he discovered and verified by his own personal effort.

St. Augustine's teaching method is what is now called the method of 'activity', otherwise known as the 'direct' method, since it insists that the learner be directly engaged with the thing to be known. In his own teaching Augustine consistently demonstrates the method. In *The Instruction of the Uninstructed*, for example, he concludes his discussion of the principles of good teaching with the remark that the influence of examples of good teaching is greater than verbal expositions of theory:

> You would learn better by watching us and listening to us when actually engaged in the work itself than by reading what we write.[1]

Accordingly, he follows up his theoretical exposition by giving two examples of what he would himself say to people enquiring into the Christian faith. Again, in *Christian Education*

[1] *The Instruction of the Uninstructed* 23.

Augustine gives a theoretical exposition of some of the important principles of rhetoric. But he is careful to precede this by directing the attention of the learner to examples of effective rhetoric drawn from St. Paul and other Christian writers.[1] By commenting on interesting features of these passages he seeks to involve the learner directly in the subject, so that eventually he himself can withdraw, leaving the learner to continue the investigation on his own.

In other places Augustine stresses the principle of learning by self-activity, which he considers equally valid both on the lower and higher levels of learning. In *Christian Education*, for example, he illustrates the activity principle from learning to walk:

> It is as if a man wishing to give rules for walking should warn you not to lift the rear foot before you set down the other one and then should describe in careful detail the way you ought to move the hinges of the joints and knees. What he says is true and one cannot walk in any other way. But people find it easier to walk by executing these movements than to attend to them while they are going through them or to understand them when they are told about them.[2]

A favourite example of Augustine's is that of the child learning his mother tongue, an activity which demonstrates the direct method of language learning. In the preface to *Christian Education*, Augustine notes that 'every one of us learned his own language by hearing it constantly from his childhood', and adds that any subsequent language we have learned has been learned in the same way, that is 'by hearing it spoken'.[3] In a well-known passage from the *Confessions* he shows by careful observation of infant behaviour that the ability to speak arises from the felt need to communicate, and that skill is developed by practice:

[1] *Christian Education* iv, 9–21.

[2] *ibid.* ii, 55. Herbert Spencer was to take the same example to prove the same point in his essay on *Intellectual Education*: 'It has been well said concerning the art of speaking any tongue by drilling in the parts of speech and their functions that it is about as reasonable as prefacing the art of walking by a course of lessons on the bones and muscles and nerves of the legs—these technicalities are alike repulsive and needless'.

[3] *Chrisitan Educatian*. preface. 5

> It was not that older people taught me by showing me words arranged according to a fixed sequence of instruction in the way in which at a later date I learned my letters. Instead I sought to give expression to the feeling of my heart with the mind which you gave me, O God, with cries and with various sounds and movements of the limbs. I did this so that my will might be obeyed. Yet I was not able to express all I wanted to express or to communicate with all the people I wanted to talk to. So I went over the sounds in advance in my memory. When the older people called something by name and turned their bodies towards it in accordance with the word, I then perceived and grasped that the sound they were making, when they wanted to point a thing out, was its name. This was obvious from the movement of their bodies, which is as it were the natural language of all people and is expressed by their facial expression, by the glance of their eyes, the movement of their limbs and the tone of their voices. By these they indicate the feelings of their minds as they seek out, possess, reject or avoid things. And so little by little, by frequently hearing words placed in their appropriate positions in various sentences, I understood what they were the signs of, and, having in this way accustomed my mouth to these signs, I used them to express my desires.[1]

Augustine pursues the theme in a later chapter, where he remarks that in childhood he learned his own language in a pleasant manner 'by mere observation amid the caresses of my nurses, the jokes of smiling friends and the delights of those who played with me'. Amid such informal activity he learned 'to give birth to ideas'. He emphasises that the words, which he learned without clearly realising that he was learning at all, were learned 'not from teachers but from people talking'.[2]

The method, by which the young child learns his own native tongue without systematic instruction, seems to Augustine to exemplify the principle of all effective learning. By contrast he holds that the formal methods of the schools, in which theory is first expounded and opportunities for practice are later provided, is unsound. The young child learns to speak by un-

[1] *Confessions* i, 8, 13.
[2] *ibid.* i, 14, 23.

consciously imitating other people speaking; he discovers and formulates his own rules. The formal exposition of grammatical theory is appropriate at a later stage, but even then it is not absolutely necessary. In *Christian Education* Augustine makes this point with reference to the teaching of rhetoric to adults:

> Men who have a quick understanding and an enthusiastic temperament develop eloquence more easily by reading and listening to eloquent speakers than by following out the rules of eloquence.[1]

He notes that there are many orators who in fact have no first-hand acquaintance with the rules of rhetoric, and yet are more eloquent than many who have studied them. In public speaking natural endowment plays its part, and theory should be used to assist progress. But the indispensable element is the observation of orators in action:

> We know of no-one who is eloquent without having read and listened to the speeches and debates of eloquent men.[2]

The secondary place of theory is particularly stressed by Augustine, because he is thinking of adult learners. He wishes to allay the fears of those who imagine that, if they are to improve their ability to teach, they must, as it were, go back to school and learn innumerable rules. He gives it as the considered opinion of one experienced in the teaching and practice of rhetoric that theory can be dispensed with:

> It is not that I think rules are of no use, but I hold that, whatever use they have is to be learned elsewhere. If any good man should happen to have leisure for learning them, he is not to ask me to teach them either in this work or in any other.[3]

Since learning is a personal activity of thought, implying that questions are raised and answers formulated and evaluated by the learner himself, the teacher's duty is to stimulate questions

[1] *Christian Education* iv, 4.

[2] *ibid.* iv, 5.

[3] *ibid.* iv, 2. Augustine also acutely observes (*ibid.* iv, 4) that 'there is hardly anyone who can do both of these things, that is speak well and simultaneously think of the rules of speaking.'

and allow the learner to search for his own answers. Augustine recognises this method as equally appropriate and necessary on all levels of learning. The young child, learning his own language, thoughtfully analyses the speech and actions of the people around him and thus learns to express himself in speech. Similarly on the higher level of philosophical exploration the learner extends his knowledge by putting questions to himself. In a group situation, as at Cassiciacum, a question may be posed, or an answer formulated, by one member of the group; but no member learns anything, unless he repeats the question within his own mind and evaluates the suggested answer by the effort of his own judgement. In the last resort, only the unaided personal effort of each learner determines whether he learns anything or not. The point will be further analysed in our later discussion of *The Teacher*. In the meantime, the continuing internal exploration which runs through both the *Confessions* and *Soliloquies* of Augustine may be pointed to as excellent examples of the activity principle of learning. This activity may often be painful, as Augustine found in his own experience of wrestling with a complex problem:

> I almost made it and yet did not quite make it. However, I did not fall back into my original state, but as it were stood near to get my breath. And I tried again and I was almost there and now I could all but touch it and hold it. Yet I was not quite there. I did not touch it or hold it.[1]

And so the effort must continue until by self-activity the separate pieces are fitted together and the answer found.

GROUP LEARNING AT CASSICIACUM

The *Confessions* and the *Soliloquies* demonstrate the method of learning by private self-questioning, that is when the learner puts questions to himself without promptings from a teacher or other people. The Cassiciacum dialogues, apart from the *Soliloquies*, show the same method operating in a group situation. They follow the Socratic method of question and answer. In the hands of Socrates and Plato the dialogue became the only valid teaching method, since the aim of education,

[1] *Confessions* viii, 11, 25.

which they accepted, was to gain new personal insights into the world of reality rather than to memorise the insights of others. The Socratic method came to be regarded as synonymous with the dialectic method of definition, induction and critical analysis.[1] In the process of interaction characteristic of the Socratic method, both teacher and pupil are simultaneously learning and contributing to the systematic exploration of traditionally accepted assumptions. Behind the method lies the feeling that, in order to test a thought, it is a good thing to submit it to the critical attention of others. 'O Protagoras,' says the Socrates of the *Protagoras*, 'Do not think I engage in discussion with you for any other reason than to give thorough consideration to questions which puzzle me'.[2]

The Socratic method of Plato's dialogues in its essentials is faithfully reproduced in Augustine's Cassiciacum dialogues. Finaert, who studied Augustine as an orator, notes that in the dialogue form he found a medium suited both to his genius for discussion and his talent for rhetoric.[3] In taking over the form of the dialogue, Augustine was not merely copying an established and popular literary form but employing a form which admirably suited the teacher's true function, represented in Finaert's words by a need 'to address himself to a listener and to find out the listener's feelings'.[4] In the period of the Roman cultural decadence, in which Augustine himself lived, the dialogue, like other literary forms, had fallen from its high place as a teaching instrument par excellence into an instrument of barren display. An examination of Augustine's dialogues supports the judgement of R. A. Brown in the introduction to his edition of *The Happy Life*, that 'Augustine revitalised and adorned what had come down to him, instead of imitating a decadent genre'.[5]

Augustine's dialogues divide themselves into two groups. There are the dialogues of Cassiciacum—*Against the Academics*, *The Happy Life*, *The Principle of Order* and the *Soliloquies*.

[1] See R. A. Brown on 'The Dialogue as a Literary Form' in the introduction to his edition of *The Happy Life*.

[2] Plato, *Protagoras*, 348D.

[3] J. Finaert, *St. Augustin Rhéteur*, p. 44.

[4] *ibid.*

[5] R. A. Brown, *op. cit.*, p. 59.

These are followed by four other dialogues, written in Rome, or after his return to North Africa—*On Music*, *The Greatness of the Soul*, *The Free Will* and *The Teacher*. Of these two groups, the former is the more interesting for our study of the activity principle in teaching method. These dialogues are exploratory investigations rather than systematic expositions of a problem; their discursiveness and lively informality recall the Tusculan disputations of Cicero. With the exception of the *Soliloquies*, they are records of group learning experiences. They start with no fixed and final aim in view, but move on whithersoever the argument and the general will of the group direct them, and do not necessarily reach any very firm conclusions. By contrast, the later dialogues have a more formal structure. There is a more clearly marked line of demarcation between teacher and pupil, and there is only one respondent. In *The Greatness of the Soul* and *The Free Will* Augustine is the teacher and Evodius the respondent. *The Teacher* is a discussion between Augustine and his natural son, Adeodatus; *On Music* is between two anonymous persons identified as 'the teacher' (*magister*) and 'the pupil' (*discipulus*). These dialogues are more systematic expositions of topics, which the teacher has already carefully examined on his own account and wishes to open up to his pupil.

In the earlier dialogues, the philosophically sophisticated reader, anxious to find a systematic exposition of the topic indicated by the title, is disappointed. For the less sophisticated, however, the dialogues do stimulate thought on the problem in hand. Because they are exploratory rather than systematic, the argument seems sometimes to lose its direction, and at other times to resolve itself into an unprofitable dialectic. Since they are designed to teach the principles of effective thinking through trial and error rather than to reach firm conclusions, the reader must follow the path taken by the actual participants. At times this may try the patience of the sophisticated reader. But this is not the sort of reader for whom the dialogues are intended, as Augustine himself makes clear at the end of the first book of *The Principle of Order*. They are, he says, for the cultured person who, while not being a professional philosopher, has an interest in philosophy and has the will to probe beneath the surface of human problems.[1] In other words, the early dialogues

[1] *The Principle of Order* i, 31.

have a very clear pedagogical purpose. They are designed for those who, starting from the same position as the members of the Cassiciacum group, desire to follow the same course of training in philosophical thinking and thus to enjoy all the excitement of the chase. Augustine could have abbreviated the reporting; instead he enters into elaborate detail in the hope that the account of the whole course of the argument, including the false turnings and frustrated attempts, would stimulate the enquiring reader, as it had stimulated the group. Apart from Augustine himself, all the members of the Cassiciacum group were relatively unpractised in philosophical thinking. Alypius had been his pupil at Carthage three or four years earlier. Licentius and Trygetius were with Augustine for the purpose of receiving instruction in grammar and philosophy.[1]

In fact, Augustine recognises the pedagogical truth that the solution of a problem can come about only after a gradual and exploratory approach. Ready-made answers are no substitutes for conclusions won by the learner at the cost of hard personal effort and exertion. In the preliminary stages of the early Cassiciacum dialogues, the discussion lunges around rather wildly, before it achieves discipline and direction. The effect is to show that a teacher must give his students the opportunity to test and sharpen their powers of thought and self-expression in action, since this is the only way to achieve the disciplined concentration required for real progress. Thus Augustine himself listens to the fledgling attempts of his younger friends to wrestle with philosophical problems. But, when he feels that enough preliminary practice has been given, he intervenes to give direction and encourage a more concentrated attack:

> I do not want this discussion to go on for the mere pleasure of discussing. Let it be enough that up to this point we have had some preliminary play with our young people, in which philosophy appeared to be some sort of sport. Let us then be done with such childish ways. Our discussion is concerned with our human life, with morals and with the soul.[2]

[1] For analyses of the Cassiciacum situation see W. Montgomery, *Aspects of Augustine's Life and Thought*, p. 32 ff., and C. Boyer, *Christianisme et néo-Platonisme dans la Formation de St. Augustin*, pp. 135–67.

[2] *Against the Academics* ii, 22. Also *ibid.* i, 25.

The Cassiciacum dialogues are marked by the lively interaction of personalities. Each of them follows an easily recognisable and pedagogically sound pattern: By far the larger part of the dialogue consists of a long prelude, in which the implications of a definition, or definitions, are explored. At this stage, the teacher wisely allows the group members to take command of the discussion; hence the exuberance of the young learners sometimes causes them to take their eyes off the mark and become lost in side issues. These are the faults of immaturity, and a necessary part of the process of learning any skill. In the second half of the dialogues Augustine himself intervenes to give an uninterrupted exposition.[1] This intervention, which at an earlier stage would have been needless and authoritarian, is now desired and attentively listened to. The change of method from question and answer to continuous exposition takes place at the psychological moment when the group is ready for it. In the case of *Against the Academics*, Augustine's exposition comes as a result of a direct request from a member of the group. Augustine has proposed to put a question to Alypius, but the latter, being already exhausted by the previous effort, makes a counter suggestion:

> Instead of dealing with this matter by questioning, you may prefer to change the procedure into a continuous exposition.[2]

Augustine then goes on to make the following comment:

> I shall fall in with your wishes. After my long labours in the school of rhetoric I had thought I would be able to obtain lighter employment, that is to deal with the subject by questioning rather than by lecturing. Nevertheless we are a small group, and it will not be necessary for me to force my voice to the detriment of my health. So listen to my views in the form of a continuous exposition, as you request.[3]

In this stage the logic chopping and less concentrated

[1] The preludes are about twice as long as the expositions. H. I. Marrou, *St. Augustin et la Fin de la Culture Antique*, pp. 308–15, criticises their discursiveness and lack of philosophical exactitude while admitting their pedagogical purpose.

[2] *Against the Academics* iii, 14.

[3] *ibid.* iii, 15.

direction of the earlier question and answer give place to a frontal attack on the problem in hand. At the end the members express their gratitude and retire to turn over in their minds the thoughts, to which they have listened. Thus in *The Greatness of the Soul* Evodius declares that the discussion has prompted other questions, which he will want to raise on a later occasion when he has had the opportunity to turn them over in his mind.[1] At the conclusion of each of the dialogues the group members make it clear that they have been stimulated to continue the argument with others and internally with themselves. The closing words of *The Principle of Order* acknowledge this stimulus and express the confidence with which the students accept the notion of education as a continuing activity:

> With these words the discussion was brought to an end. It was after the evening torches had been brought in that we broke up our gathering, everyone of us being in a cheerful frame of mind and full of hope.[2]

Thus the dialogues of Cassiciacum, regarded as demonstrations of effective teaching and learning, reiterate the principle that a man learns only when he teaches himself. Learning necessarily consists of what Martin Buber, speaking of Plato's dialectic, calls 'a voiceless colloquy of the soul with itself'.[3] We have already cited the *Confessions* and the *Soliloquies* as exemplifying what Augustine refers to as an internal consultation with the teacher within us (*magister interior*). The *Soliloquies*, in which the participants are Augustine and Reason (*Ratio*), differ from the other dialogues in that the give-and-take of question and comment continues through to the end. But they resemble the other dialogues in that more than half the space is taken up with preliminary skirmishing and reconnoitring of the ground. At length Augustine reveals his state of readiness for more systematic instruction:

> *Augustine:* I observe that we have used a roundabout route following a lengthy chain of reasoning—what makes me anxious is that our talk has wandered

[1] *The Greatness of the Soul* 81.
[2] *The Principle of Order* ii, 54.
[3] Martin Buber, *Between Man and Man*, Fontana Library, p. 45.

> round in circles for such a long time, as if an ambush were being laid.

To which Reason replies:

> Our reasoning has not taken these circuitous routes in vain.[1]

Reason goes on to argue that the initial process of trial and error has prepared the ground for further advance and that at this stage Augustine must resist the temptation to accept propositions on the authority of others without submitting them to his own critical judgement. What is merely learned by heart is not learned at all. To this Augustine agrees:

> Perhaps you are right. I shall strive with all my might against this kind of sickness. Only let us begin the questioning and not be delayed by superfluities.[2]

And so the lesson proceeds with more pointed enquiry into the difficult question of personal immortality. Some progress is made; but even so education cannot be unduly rushed and further effort of thinking will be required before all the parts of the problems can be seen in relation to one another. Towards the end of the dialogue Augustine asks for a 'brief' explanation of an abstruse point, which lies beyond the immediate scope of the enquiry, but Reason, the teacher, will not attempt the impossible at this stage:

> You have had too little practice in philosophy to be able to see this. In all these circuitous arguments we have simply been exercising your powers so that you may become fit to see it.[3]

At the same time the teacher wisely does not discourage the pupil by summarily rejecting the question out of hand. A brief discussion of the problem ensues, in which certain questions are raised, which only serve to underline the full difficulty of the problem. But this is quickly brought to a close by Reason who declares that 'we shall speak of these things with greater care and subtlety later'.[4]

[1] *Soliloquies* ii, 25.

[2] *ibid.* ii, 26–7.

[3] *ibid.* ii, 24. Similar references are made to the sharpening of the mental powers in several other places, e.g. *The Teacher* 21; *The Principle of Order* i, 25 and ii, 17; *The Greatness of the Soul* 25.

[4] *Soliloquies* ii, 36.

The dialogues written after the departure from Cassiciacum are not so clearly marked with the personalities of the participants, and are therefore less spontaneous and informal.[1] Nevertheless, they are good examples of the art of Socratic questioning; in fact the respondent tends to reply in a more full-blooded manner than the characteristic 'yes' or 'no' of the respondents in the Socratic dialogues of Plato. Both Evodius in *The Greatness of the Soul* and *The Free Will*, and Augustine's son, Adeodatus, in *The Teacher*, defend the answers they themselves give, at times asking for clarification of the question put to them or expressing criticism of the teacher's views. Augustine, the teacher, deliberately encourages this attitude of sturdy independence. For instance, at one point in *The Greatness of the Soul* Evodius is tempted to set aside a definition, which Augustine has proposed, because he feels that Augustine himself does not accept it. However, Augustine corrects him with the words, 'Do not rely too much on authority, especially mine', and quotes the well-known advice of the poet Horace, '*sapere aude*', which may be rendered, 'Have the confidence to find your own knowledge'.[2]

Augustine is aware of the emotional hazards, to which the method of learning by critical examination of treasured assumptions is exposed. Hence the emphasis on self-knowledge as the first step in all learning. The following passage from the *Soliloquies*, well expresses the purpose of questioning as well as the difficulties which may be encountered. Augustine has caught himself out in an error of reasoning, and Reason encourages him:

> It is absurd to be ashamed (of your admission). It was for this very reason that we chose this method of discussion. There is no better way of seeking truth than by the method of question and answer. But hardly anyone can be found who is not ashamed of being proved wrong. So it nearly always happens that a good discussion is spoiled by some outburst of obstinacy with fraying of tempers, generally concealed but sometimes apparent. Our plan was to proceed peaceably and agreeably in our search for truth. I was to ask the questions and you

[1] i.e. *On Music, The Greatness of the Soul, The Free Will* and *The Teacher*.

[2] *The Greatness of the Soul* 41; Horace, *Epistles* i, 2, 40.

> were to answer. If you get yourself into difficulties, there is no need to be afraid to go back and try again.[1]

It is evidence of Augustine's sympathetic handling of the Cassiciacum group in the early dialogues that, although there is much good-humoured banter, there is very little evidence of 'fraying of tempers'. Augustine sustains the maximum of inter-communication within the group and therefore preserves the momentum of the learning and group cohesion. He seizes the moment of readiness for learning, but does not press the students to over-extend their present powers. In the preamble of *Against the Academics* Augustine notes that, after his young pupils, on his advice, had done some reading in the *Hortensius* of Cicero, they were 'not only ready for study, but eagerly desirous of it, even beyond what I had expected'. Therefore, Augustine seizes the moment to 'see what they are capable of at their age'.[2] The secretary is therefore summoned 'so that our discussions might not be carried off by the wind', and the seminar begins. How carefully Augustine assesses the readiness of his pupils and notes their progress is expressed in a report made by Augustine to Romanianus on the progress of his son, Licentius, a member of the Cassiciacum group:

> I must offer you my congratulations. Your son is beginning to be a philosopher. I am in fact holding him back so that he may first apply himself to the necessary preliminary studies and may be developed and strengthened for the work of philosophy.[3]

THE IMPORTANCE OF SPONTANEITY

The skill of the teacher largely consists in the ability to capture the moment when his students are 'in love with understanding', i.e. when they are ready and willing to enquire into some specific problem. The Cassiciacum dialogues show many examples of Augustine's awareness of spontaneity and interest as basic principles of education. The problems discussed in the dialogues arise from the interests of the group. If one question leads to

[1] *Soliloquies* ii, 14.
[2] *Against the Academics* i, 4.
[3] *ibid.* ii, 8.

others, it is because these other questions present themselves as necessary consequences of the first question. It is the purpose of the group, and not the teacher's arbitrary intervention, which determines the course of the discussions. For example, *Against the Academics* begins with an expressed interest in the question, 'What is happiness?' It is quickly found that happiness consists in the pursuit of truth. But does truth actually exist? The Academic philosophers, among others, have doubted it; thus the first question leads back to a more ultimate question, which in fact becomes the main theme of the larger part of the dialogue.

When the importance of spontaneity and interest is accepted, learning cannot be confined within the arbitrary confines of a school timetable or the walls of one particular school-room. The times of starting and ending the Cassiciacum dialogues were determined by the wishes of the participants, and the place by their inclinations and the state of the weather. The relative periods of time spent on philosophical argument, private reading, discussion of the poetry of Vergil and the management of Verecundus' farm, varied according to the urgency of the different tasks and the feelings of the group.[1] Thus for example the greater part of the second day of the discussion reported in *Against the Academics* was spent on duties about the farm. There was time for only a brief discussion, which was terminated by the coming of darkness:

> As darkness was preventing the secretary writing down the discussion and, as I saw a big problem rising ahead of us, I put off the discussion to another day. We had in fact begun the discussion when the sun was already declining in the west. Almost the whole day had been passed in organising our duties around the farm and in going over the first book of Vergil.[2]

But on a succeeding day the necessary routine tasks were rushed through, so that the discussion could be resumed:

> The day being bright and clear, we rose from our beds earlier than usual and spent only a little time with the farm-hands on

[1] *The Principle of Order* i, 26; *Against the Academics* i, 15 and ii, 10.
[2] *ibid.* ii, 10.

the tasks which had to be done. Then Alypius began the discussion—[1]

When the weather was fine, the discussion took place in the meadows surrounding the villa and under a favourite tree. 'The sun rose brightly', says Augustine at the beginning of the second part of *The Principle of Order*, 'The clear sky and a temperature, as inviting as it can ever be in winter in these parts, summoned us to go down into the meadow, where we often used to go informally.'[2] But on the previous day the sky had been overcast, and 'We set off for the baths—this place was suitable for our discussions and was familiar to us.'[3] If the day began badly but cleared, the discussion was begun in the baths and continued in the open air.

An outstanding example of the effect of spontaneous interest in touching off a significant learning experience is found in *The Principle of Order*, which explores the grounds for the assertion that the universe is subject to unvarying laws of cause and effect. However, the question was not proposed by Augustine or by any other member of the group; it arose from the need to find an answer to an apparently simple problem raised by their physical environment. The question confronted the group after they had retired to bed, but this did not prevent a discussion being initiated there and then.[4]

The circumstances were as follows: it was Augustine's habit, as he tells us, to lie awake for part of each night in private thought. One night his attention was attracted by the sound of the water which flowed along a channel behind the baths and just outside the dormitory, in which he and his pupils slept. Instead of the normal steady trickle of the water, the sound was alternately rising and falling, as though it were being intermittently blocked in its course. What was the cause of the

[1] *ibid.* Of the significance of the agricultural tasks see W. Montgomery, *op. cit.*, p. 37, who makes the point that they represented the responsibility properly assumed by Verecundus' temporary tenants to see to the necessary maintenance of the land and were in no sense part and parcel of 'a doctrinaire scheme of the philosophic simple life'.

[2] *The Principle of Order* ii, 1. See also *Against the Academics* ii, 14 and *The Happy Life* 23.

[3] *The Principle of Order* i, 25.

[4] *ibid.* i, 6–22.

phenomenon? Augustine was trying to think of an explanation, when Licentius stirred in his sleep to frighten off a mouse, which was troubling him. On being asked if he had noticed the irregularity of the sound, Licentius said that he had. Upon which Trygetius joined in from his bed to say that he also had been aware of it. Realising that they were awake, Augustine asked them what they thought was the reason for the irregularity in the sound of the water. At this time of night no one was using the baths. Licentius ventured the suggestion that temporary interruptions of the flow of the water were caused by the blockage of the channel by falling autumn leaves. Augustine himself could think of no better explanation, and praised the ingenuity of Licentius. After a moment of silence Licentius expressed surprise that this apparently insignificant phenomenon had attracted the curiosity of Augustine, so that they were all now searching for an answer to the problem. From this Licentius learns an important lesson about the movements of his own mind, namely that the curiosity, which leads to learning, is caused 'by some unusual event outside the normal pattern of cause and effect'.[1]

Licentius is, however, moved to register an objection to the terms of the statement. It seems to him that an event, which is 'outside' the usual pattern of cause and effect, is uncaused, i.e. has no cause. He can see that a cause may not be immediately obvious, but is convinced that 'nothing can happen without a cause'. Augustine's reaction is typical: he is delighted at such a display of independent thinking from Licentius on a matter of importance, which has not as yet been the subject of discussion:

> At this point I was buoyed up by a livelier expectation than I usually have when I ask them (my pupils) a question; the mind of the lad had conceived on the instant such an important idea, the question never up to this moment having been discussed between us. 'Well done, well done,' I said.[2]

But the teacher will not allow the pupil to rest on his laurels. He must justify his statement, and be made to reflect further on what he has said by defending it against Augustine's assault:

[1] *The Principle of Order* i, 8: '*Unde enim solet oboriri admiratio nisi res insolita praeter manifestum causarum ordinem?*'
[2] *ibid.*

I want you to defend your view for I am going to try to knock it down.[1]

After some badinage at the expense of Licentius, whose interest in poetry is represented as setting up a wall between himself and the pursuit of truth through philosophy, Augustine allows the conversation to lapse into silence. Thinking that Licentius' thoughts are again occupied with his favourite poetry, and in view of the fact that it is night time, Augustine does not think it advisable to force his pupil's attention. He is returning to his own private thoughts, when Licentius speaks again to show that his thoughts are still on the question that has been raised. He issues the invitation to Augustine to attack his statement that everything has a cause; on his part, he will do his best to defend it. Trygetius is asked for his opinion, and is inclined to favour the absolute rule of cause and effect. However, he is not sure of his ground and joins Licentius in desiring that the matter be discussed. The eagerness of the two boys to pursue the enquiry causes Augustine, the teacher, to experience 'a joy greater than ever I had dared hope for'.[2]

Thus the nocturnal enquiry is begun. Licentius shows that he appreciates the principle that nothing can be understood, which is not pursued by the personal effort of the learner, although the teacher may assist the process. 'Put your questions to me,' he says, 'Perhaps I may be able to explain this mysterious problem by myself and with your help.'[3]

Why is it, asks Augustine, that Licentius asserts that the water running through the baths in a channel does so by design? It is first of all because the channel has been constructed by men for the purpose of drinking and washing. So far design clearly operates. But what of the leaves which fell or were blown into the channel and so caused intermittent blockages until the water mounted up and flowed over them? How can such random movements of leaves be attributed to design? Are not such movements the result of pure chance? Licentius goes on to argue that the causes of the falling leaves can be found in such factors as the position of the trees over-hanging the water

[1] *ibid.*: '*Sed pervellem adesses huic sententiae, nam eam labefactare tentabo.*'

[2] *ibid.* i, 10.

[3] *ibid.* i, 11.

channels, the weight of the leaves combined with the speed of motion of the air and other contributory causes less easy to discern. The 'tormenting questioner' (as Augustine designates himself) may go on to ask why the trees were planted in the exact positions they occupy, or even to show that they were not planted by man but were self-sown. However, nothing can shake Licentius' conviction that everything in the universe has a cause. If we cannot discover all the chains of cause and effect, it is because our vision is limited. The onus is on the other side to display an example of an event without a cause.

Thus the discussion broadens out into an examination of the question of divine providence; the dormitory session continues enthusiastically until the dawn appears, and is resumed with only a short interval for refreshment.[1] The charm of the scene lies in the enthusiasm of Licentius, the good humour which pervades it, and the obvious delight experienced by the teacher, as he receives evidence of the intellectual enthusiasm and progress of the pupils. When Augustine, who professes himself 'an infant in philosophy', plays into Licentius' hands, Licentius 'jumps with joy on his bed'. At intervals throughout the discussion Augustine affectionately teases him for his addiction to poetry, and in particular for the labour he has been expending on the composition of a poem on Pyramus and Thisbe. When Trygetius, in spite of his initial diffidence, is spontaneously drawn into the discussion, Augustine experiences the joy of the teacher when he observes a demonstration of intellectual ability in a pupil after a period of apparent stagnation:

> I could not restrain my joy in seeing this young man, the son of a very dear friend, becoming my son also; and still more in seeing him growing and developing into a friend when I had despaired of being able to cultivate in him a taste even for the ordinary study of literature. Yet here he was plunging with all his will into the midst of philosophy, as if it were his own special field. While I was marvelling at all this in silence and was carried away with thankfulness, he called out to me . . .[2]

Thus the discussions at Cassiciacum demonstrate certain pedagogical principles, associated with what has now become

[1] *ibid.* i, 22.
[2] *ibid.* i, 16.

known as the 'activity method'. The problems raised are significant and timely, in that they arise from the experience of the students and are not arbitrarily imposed by the teacher. The challenge which initiates the learning is the result of 'some unusual event outside the usual pattern of cause and effect'. The learning originates in a problematic situation, and is motivated by the desire to understand it. The modern 'project' or 'activity' method expresses the conviction that learning can result only from a question spontaneously generated in the mind of the learner, or group of learners. Augustine's refusal to impose questions on his students or to give them his own ready-made answers is echoed in Dewey's questions:

> Is it the pupil's own problem or is it the teacher's or the textbook's problem, made a problem for the pupil only because he cannot—win the teacher's approval unless he deals with it?—Is it imposed from without and is the pupil's problem simply to meet the external requirements?[1]

The comparison with Dewey, who has contributed very much to the modern concept of activity in learning and whose views are founded on the modern experimentalist, scientific approach to knowledge, may be extended a little further at this point. Augustine's method as demonstrated in the nocturnal discussion encourages the setting up of hypotheses about the cause of the unusual sound of the water. But these are scrutinised intellectually and not subjected to the test of personal observation or experiment. No one goes to see for himself what is causing the unusual sound. Furthermore, although the question originates in sense experience, it is soon intellectualised and leads out into the realm of abstract speculation. For Augustine, of course, the important problems are purely intellectual ones; thus they are not what Dewey sees as real problems. In the latter's view, problems arise in experience and the process of enquiry towards their solution is carried along by the method of scientific experimentation, the progress of learning being closely related at all stages to the interaction of the thinking being with his environment. Furthermore, the validity of a suggested solution is determined by the extent to which it gives the learner a greater degree of control over his environment. Nevertheless,

[1] J. Dewey, *op. cit.*, p. 182.

Augustine's exploitation of curiosity and his emphasis on personal participation in a co-operative attack on a problem have certain obvious affinities with the modern progressive approach to teaching.

The scope given to the free curiosity of Augustine's pupils may again be illustrated by the description in *The Greatness of the Soul* of an occasion during the months at Cassiciacum, when Augustine was walking in the country with Licentius and Trygetius. One of the youths, having idly cut a worm in two pieces with a pointed stick he carried, observed with interest that the two parts of the worm wriggled off in different directions as if they were two animals instead of one:

> Amazed by the curious sight and eager for an explanation, the boys excitedly brought the two live pieces to where Alypius and I were sitting. We too, more than a little fascinated, observed the pieces running all over the tablet wherever they could.[1]

In this case the problem of the one apparently becoming two was experimentally explored. To test the complete independence of the two pieces in respect of one another, one piece was touched by the edge of the stick:

> . . . it turned itself towards the place of the pain, while the other, sensing nothing, went about its motions away from the first.[2]

This stimulated the question—'if the worm is cut up into more pieces, will these other pieces too continue to live separate existences?:

> To see how far this could go, we made the experiment of cutting the worm into a number of pieces. Then all the pieces began to move about, so that, if we had not done this to them and if the fresh wounds had not been visible, we might have supposed that each piece had been separately born and had been living its own independent life.

[1] *The Greatness of the Soul*, 62. This anecdote is introduced as a puzzling challenge to the doctrine of the indivisibility of the soul. *Supra*, pp. 67–8.

[2] *ibid.*

In this case too the question was one which was real and puzzling both for the boys and for the teacher. Using it in retrospect as a curious phenomenon bearing on the body–soul problem, to which he had never found a satisfactory answer, Augustine admits that, at the time when it was first brought to his attention by the boys and they looked to him for a solution to the problem, he had none to give them. The experimentation had left the problem of the indivisibility of the soul as puzzling as ever, and Augustine confesses with regret that he could only advise the boys to work hard on their studies, so that in the fullness of time they would be able to enquire into the matter with the hope of finding an explanation. Nevertheless, all present were stimulated to activity of thought on a problem of the deepest significance:

> If I wished to explain the talk I had with Alypius as the boys went away, when the two of us, each to the best of his ability, racked our brains, making guesses and finding new problems, we would have to devote many more words to this than we have given to the present discussion from its beginning with all its circumlocutions and digressions.[1]

CONCLUSION

Augustine's contribution to an understanding of the art of teaching displays a marked degree of consistency between his theory and practice. Out of his synthesis of Platonism and Christianity there emerges an ideal of teaching, which unites a respect for the intellect with a deep concern for the feelings and personality of the individual student in his charge. He interprets teaching in terms of encouragement and stimulation rather than of coercion and external, authoritarian control. Learning is generated and developed in intensity by personal exploration and discovery, the teacher providing the stimulus and some of the resource materials which the learner requires. Although the teacher's role becomes less dominant, his function remains important and makes considerable demands on professional skill. St. Augustine's practice of teaching is a logical application of his conviction that teaching is an art, which according to his definition is founded on knowledge and thought. Teaching

[1] *ibid.* 63.

cannot be successful in its outcomes, if it is regarded in terms of the mechanical application of techniques based on the imitation of others. The study of St. Augustine's demonstrations of teaching shows that teaching is nothing, unless it bears the stamp of the personality, enthusiasms and standards of a particular teacher.

Because Augustine holds that learning is motivated only by love of the thing to be learned, his teaching is free from the restrictive elements, which frequently frustrate the efforts of teachers working in schools. His basic duty of encouraging his students to learn is not distorted by time-tables, external examinations or prescribed syllabuses. Therefore, enthusiasm is well sustained, and there is always time for the fullest interaction of personalities.

In this activity of learning, understanding of the self proceeds *pari passu* with the development and enrichment of the intellect. We recall Augustine's twin objectives of knowledge—'God and my soul'—implying that a knowledge of the one cannot be attained without a knowledge of the other. The enlargement of knowledge requires a discipline of thought and of will; this can be achieved only by an increasing understanding and mastery of one's own nature. Therefore, Augustine sees teaching, whether it is conducted with or without the aid of an external teacher, as essentially a personalised situation. The learner may work in consultation with an external teacher; but he must always work in intimate personal consultation with himself and with the divine teacher within him.

An episode in *The Principle of Order* shows how a close teacher–pupil relationship can help a youth to grow in an understanding of himself.[1] The young Licentius had been the target of some badinage on account of his addiction to poetry, the suggestion being that the love story of Pyramus and Thisbe was of greater concern to him than the study of philosophy. Nevertheless, he had taken a full part in the discussion, and, in so doing, had concurrently been engaged in a serious reassessment of himself. In the morning after the nocturnal discussion reported above, he approached Augustine in private to seek reassurance as to Augustine's opinion of him, 'Tell me the truth', he says, 'What do you really think of me?' With great

[1] *The Principle of Order* i, 23.

affection Augustine gives him the reassurance he requires; whereupon Licentius tells him about his internal struggle to understand his own motives and thus to set himself in order. It appears that the previous night's discussion had satisfied him that philosophy was of greater value than poetic composition. His continuing self-analysis shows that he has discovered the inner freedom, which consists in reasserting the supreme value of moderation in all things, including poetry. Through his own thinking on the problem of design in the world he has in fact grown in a knowledge of himself. Now he can see meaning in things, which had previously puzzled him, including some aspects of his own behaviour; everything has worked together for good, because the lesson he has learned has maintained an intimate contact with his own personal problems and experience. Licentius confides this conclusion to Augustine in confidential tones:

> Dropping his voice and almost whispering in my ear, he said, 'What a curious combination of circumstances has brought me to understand that everything which happens to us comes about as a result of a beneficient design!'

Thus St. Augustine's versatile and sensitive approach to teaching presents a challenge to teachers, who, oppressed by the pressures and tensions associated with formal schooling, are tempted to lay aside their ideals in favour of administratively tidy procedures, which may well be out of harmony with the method by which human beings grow in a real understanding of themselves and their destiny.

6 The Problem of Verbal Communication

I agree with you that there is no possibility of our carrying on a conversation together unless, when we hear words, our minds are directed to the things of which the words are the signs. The Teacher, 22.

The person who teaches will avoid all words which do not teach. Christian Education iv, 24.

In the dialogue called *The Teacher* (*De Magistro*) Augustine gives the most sustained attention to the assumption commonly made by teachers that they are able to communicate knowledge to their students through the medium of words. Along with the dialogue, *On Music*, and the treatise, *On True Religion*, *The Teacher* was begun and completed in the period at Tagaste, between Augustine's return to North Africa in the autumn of A.D. 388 and his ordination at Hippo in A.D. 390. The reference in the *Reviews* summarises the theme of *The Teacher*:

> At the same time I wrote the book called *The Teacher*, in which the following proposition is enquired into and established, namely that there is no teacher who teaches man wisdom, except God, in accordance with what is written in the Gospel: 'One is your teacher, even Christ'. *The Teacher* begins with the following words: 'What do you think is our intention when we use speech?'[1]

The discussion on which *The Teacher* is based may have taken place in the monastic community, which Augustine established at Tagaste.[2] It would at least have been written there, since at the time Augustine was impressed with the urgent need to produce

[1] *Reviews* i, 12.
[2] *supra*, p. 23.

competent Christian teachers, both lay and cleric, to serve the North African Church. Later, in the earlier years of his episcopy he was to deal with the controversial issue of the Christian curriculum in his work, *On Christian Education* (*De Doctrina Christiana*) and to write a manual of hints to Christian teachers in *The Instruction of the Uninstructed* (*De Catechizandis Rudibus*). But in *The Teacher* he closely analyses the act of teaching in an attempt to define with some degree of precision both the scope and limitations of the teacher's task. By writing an account of a discussion on this theme with his son, Adeodatus, Augustine was no doubt clarifying his own thinking on the subject and hoping to encourage teachers, and teachers of teachers, to scrutinise critically their own ingrained assumptions and teaching practices.

It is uncertain whether *The Teacher* was published before or after Adeodatus' early death. If after his death, it was no doubt in part a tribute to the memory of a young man whose contributions to the argument in the dialogue justify Augustine's high regard for his intellect—'In wit he surpassed many learned men'.[1]

In its methodology the dialogue is a good example of the principles which it sets out to establish, namely that teaching reaches its proper goal only in the understanding of things and not in the memorisation, or manipulation, of words, and that the teacher's words are useless without the active involvement of the learner. Clearly Augustine himself had come to some conclusions about the nature of the teaching act and wished to communicate these to Adeodatus. However, he is reluctant to give a systematic exposition of his ideas, at least until Adeodatus has been stimulated to understand that a problem is in existence and would repay close investigation. In the first two thirds of the dialogue Augustine guides Adeodatus along the pathways of thought, over which he himself has passed. Each successive step in the argument must be established in both Adeodatus' and Augustine's minds with complete clarity before the argument can advance to the next step. Indeed it is an important part of Augustine's purpose to test his own conclusions by submitting them in open discussion to the criticism of Adeodatus' intellect. At one point in the dialogue Augustine admits that he has

[1] *Confessions* ix, 6, 14.

strengthened his own grasp of the principles at issue through 'teaching' them to Adeodatus:

> You have adequately recalled everything I would want you to recall. In fact I admit to you that these distinctions now seem much clearer to me than when we both set about digging them out of so many hiding places by the activity of enquiry and discussion.[1]

IS TEACHING POSSIBLE?

The Teacher begins by raising the question, 'What do you think is our purpose when we speak?' Adeodatus makes a cautious reply:

> As far as I can see, our purpose is either to teach or to learn.[2]

It appears that words are used with the intention of transmitting thoughts from the mind of one person to the mind of another. Teachers make the assumption that, in the act of teaching, the knowledge of the teacher passes to his students; the vocal activity of the teacher is presumed to be the cause of their learning. But it is noted that words are often employed by teachers, and also in the ordinary traffic of conversation, merely to stimulate someone to recall to mind something, which he already knows. In this case, the teacher is not 'teaching' in the ordinary sense of the word, but merely reminding his pupils of what they already understand. So it is with the silent language we employ in thinking; through its use we are either teaching ourselves something we did not know before, or we are reminding ourselves of what we already know. Therefore, the dialogue reaches the following conclusion:

> There are two reasons for speaking, either to teach or to remind other people or ourselves.[3]

[1] *The Teacher* 21.

[2] *ibid.* 1. '*—aut docere aut discere*'. The Latin conjunction used here for 'or' is '*aut*', which by contrast with the conjunction '*vel*' indicates two mutually contradictory propositions. At this stage Adeodatus makes a clear distinction between teaching and learning.

[3] *ibid.*

The process of inner speech, which constitutes thinking, is described in terms of the mental association of words and ideas:

> Even when we do not utter a sound, we are thinking words and therefore speaking within our minds. By this kind of speaking, we are merely calling something to mind, since the memory, in which the words are embedded, turns over the words, and so brings to mind the things themselves, of which the words are the signs.[1]

At the moment this definition is accepted. The two purposes of verbal communication seem to be satisfactorily defined in terms of generating new knowledge in the mind or recalling something already known, the recipient of the communication in either case being either another person or oneself. Of the use of words to recall to mind what has previously been learned, Augustine remarks that, although it is not what is ordinarily thought of as teaching, it is nevertheless an important function of teaching.

In the meantime it is necessary to establish the proposition that words are simply the signs, or symbols, of underlying realities, which are entirely different in their nature from their signs. In fact it is found to be easier to accept this proposition than it is to discover what exactly is the reality behind some of the most common words which we employ. A line from Vergil—'If it pleases the gods that nothing of such a great city should remain'[2] is used to establish the difficulty. Adeodatus falls victim to the tendency, which often renders teaching ineffective: he 'explains words by means of words, well-known words and signs by words and signs that are equally well-known'. He flounders when he is pressed to say what exactly is 'that one single thing', which is signified by certain words, and in particular by the word 'nothing'. 'Nothing' is a word, i.e. a sign, and therefore must be a sign of something; nevertheless, it appears to signify 'only what does not exist'.[3] It seems then that,

[1] *ibid.* 2.

[2] *ibid.* 3. Vergil, Aeneid, ii, 659: '*Si nihil ex tanta superis placet urbe relinqui.*' The reference is to the fall of Troy.

[3] After several vain attempts to find a definition of 'nothing', Augustine relieves the impasse by pointing to the absurdity of allowing 'nothing' to hold up the discussion.

if Adeodatus had been explaining the meaning of Vergil's line to a class of learners, he would in fact have communicated very little knowledge. His pupils would have learned merely that one word means the same thing as another word, but would not necessarily have grasped the ideas which the words signify, particularly if they had no previous acquaintance with the ideas associated with the words.

Augustine then asks Adeodatus whether in his opinion the meanings of words can be explained in any other way than by using words. To this Adeodatus mischievously remarks:

> First put your question to me without using words, and I shall reply in the same terms.[1]

Augustine readily accepts the challenge and proceeds to suggest a possible answer to his own question. Could we not teach the meaning of the word *paries* (wall) by pointing our finger at a wall without saying anything at all? Would we not in this case be teaching without using words? And what of the manual gestures of the deaf and the pantomime of actors?[2] These seem to be examples of teaching without the use of words, although in each case the communicant is still employing signs. Whether he explains the meaning of 'wall' by pointing to a wall, or employs the gestures used by the deaf when they wish to communicate, a sign is still being used; the pointing of a finger is itself a sign. Therefore, the attention of the learner is still being directed to signs rather than directly and exclusively to the realities which they symbolise. The signs, whether they are words or some other sort of gesture, seem to interpose a barrier between the learner and the things to be known.

Can anything be taught directly, that is entirely without the use of signs? It is suggested that there are actions, which the teacher could perform in front of the class, and in this way make a direct connection between the word and the idea for which it stands:

> What if I were to ask you what walking is and you were to get up and walk? Would you not be using the reality itself rather than words or any other signs to teach me?[3]

[1] *The Teacher* 5.
[2] On non-verbal gesture language see also *Christian Education* ii, 4.
[3] *The Teacher* 6.

It is agreed that this would be a more direct approach, another example of which would be the teacher, who wants to explain the meaning of a word, e.g. *saraballa* (helmet), and actually displays such a helmet before the eyes of his students. In so doing, he would be avoiding the dangerous assumption which teachers are prone to make, namely that, when they utter a word, their pupils will thereupon know the meaning of it, merely through hearing its sound. No 'lion' in fact comes out of the mouth of a speaker when the word 'lion' is uttered.[1] The distinction between the word and the thing (*res*) is further reinforced by posing the question, 'What is "man"?'.[2] If the answer, 'Man is a mortal, rational animal,' is given, the hearer has made the common assumption that he was being asked about the thing symbolised by the word, and not about the word itself. Strictly speaking, the question is ambiguous, and, before giving an answer, we should ask whether the query is about the thing or the word; if it is the latter, the correct answer would be, 'Man is a noun'.

In all attempts at making a direct connection between word and idea, the teacher must be careful to display before his class the precise thing, which the word expresses. For example, if he forgets that in teaching he must 'hurry slowly', he may speed up the pace of his walking before the class so that they wrongly take the meaning of *ambulo* (I walk) to be 'I hurry'. Thus, by avoiding as far as possible the use of signs to explain signs, we do not do away with the need for careful demonstration on the part of the teacher.

In all this we may see an interesting anticipation of the Direct Method applied to the teaching of languages and in particular to the teaching of Latin pioneered by W. H. D. Rouse at the Perse School, Cambridge earlier in the present century.[3] Rouse recommended that the beginner in Latin be taught the Latin words for the things which surround him in the class-room, such as *porta* (door), *fenestra* (window), *sella* (chair),

[1] *ibid.* 23: 'It is the sign and not the thing signified which comes out of a speaker's mouth.' See also *The Greatness of the Soul* 65, where Augustine asks Evodius, 'Does the sun come from you when you mention the sun?'

[2] *The Teacher* 24.

[3] See Rouse and Appleton, *Latin on the Direct Method* (1925) and W. H. S. Jones, *Via Nova* (1915).

creta (chalk), and that the instruction should take the form of question and answer in Latin to the exclusion of English. The four conjugations of the Latin verb are taught through the use of four verbs, which easily lend themselves to classroom activity: *ambulo* (I walk), *sedeo* (I sit), *surgo* (I stand up) and *revenio* (I return). The pupils learn the tenses of these verbs by observing the movements of the teacher, directly associating these movements with his spoken words and giving appropriate responses based on what they hear. *Ambulo* is the very verb, which Augustine uses to make his point.

The dialogue continues with the analysis of signs into their different classes. There are, for instance, signs which signify other signs, such as the verbal symbols 'word', 'name' and 'sign' itself. In the course of the discussion, we encounter St. Augustine's tendency to formulate rather fanciful derivations of words. *Verbum* (word), for example, is said to be derived from *verberare*, signifying something which 'strikes' the ear.[1] And we also meet examples of the sort of definitions beloved of the teachers of the traditional grammar; for example, 'a word is a meaningful sound uttered by the articulate voice'.[2] Adeodatus asserts that 'all nouns are words, but not all words are nouns'. However, when this statement is critically examined, it is found that, since words are by definition 'meaningful sounds', i.e. signifying something other than themselves, they are all in fact 'names' or 'nouns', both of which are represented in Latin by the word *nomen*. Augustine establishes the point by examples drawn from his favourite Christian and classical authors, St. Paul and Cicero. For example, in his denunciation of Verres Cicero declares that 'Verres caused the word *coram* to be deleted' from the records of a criminal trial; here clearly *coram* (in the presence of) performs the function of a noun, although it is commonly regarded as a preposition.[3] All this shows to what extent Augustine goes beyond the proliferation of formal classifications and definitions, so beloved of the traditional

[1] *The Teacher* 12.

[2] *ibid.* 9.

[3] J. M. Colleran in his edition of *The Teacher* (p. 229, n. 28) finds only two occurrences of *coram* in the Verrine Orations, the second occurrence being a repetition of the first; the ref. is to Verrines 2, 2, 101 and 104. In these places *coram* is used exactly in the manner in which Augustine describes it.

grammarians, and determines meaning in the light of the actual function which a word performs in a particular context. This is an important aspect of the total argument of *The Teacher*,[1] which aims at reinforcing the distinction between symbols and realities, thus focusing attention on the significance of meaning rather than words in a successful act of communication:

> We cannot carry on a conversation at all, unless at the sound of the words the mind is directed to the realities, of which the words are the signs.[2]

The child envisaged by Rousseau, who in answer to the question, 'What is the globe', replied that it is 'a round thing made of plaster',[3] was showing that he was thinking beyond the word to what the word symbolised for himself. That he misunderstood the question was due to a failure of communication on the part of the teacher, and not to stupidity, much less impertinence, on his own part. School-boy howlers, which tend to incur the wrath of teachers, are often unintentional and the result of the teacher's failing to make a close connection between the words he uses and the things they symbolise.

All this is intended to emphasise the distinction between ideas and the words, by which they are expressed. Words are merely instruments to be employed in the service of ideas; when words are so used for their own proper, if limited, purpose, then teaching occurs. A man may speak, in the sense that he mouths words; but unless these words represent meaningful ideas, he is not teaching, but merely engaging in a kind of verbal mimicry.

At any rate, it appears that in teaching, as it is commonly understood, there is no escape from the use of speech. This is to say that at least the greater part of the teacher's work can be carried out only by the use of verbal symbols, i.e. by an 'indirect' method; he cannot directly reveal to his pupils the realities of which he is speaking. Nevertheless, Augustine qualifies this with a statement, the full significance of which is not to appear until a later stage in the dialogue:

[1] *The Teacher* 19–20.

[2] *ibid.* 22.

[3] J. J. Rousseau, *Emile*, trans. B. Foxley (Everyman's Library), bk. 2, p. 74.

> Surely God and nature directly display and demonstrate to our sight the sun and the light, which permeates and covers everything, the moon and the other heavenly bodies, land and sea and the innumerable forms of life therein.[1]

Therefore, it appears that God shows himself to be the teacher *par excellence*, in that he makes no use of conventional symbols but shows the realities themselves.

The argument has led to a clear distinction between giving signs (whether verbal or otherwise) and teaching, while at the same time a very close connection has been established between the two, at least as far as the human teacher is concerned. It is generally assumed by teachers that the learner conceives in his mind the ideas that are in the mind of the teacher as a result of listening to the teacher's words. Are words then the cause of learning? Do they in some mysterious way carry with them ideas or judgements from the mind of the teacher to the mind of the learner?

It is Augustine's purpose to deny any suggestion of a direct casual connection between speaking and learning. If we know something already, then the presentation of the verbal symbol of it merely reminds us of what we already know. On the other hand, if we do not know a thing, the name of it cannot teach us what it is, since the word, or name, is merely a conventional symbol utterly unlike the thing symbolised. The word *caput* (head), for instance, is first merely a sound to the young child. It is only when he discovers its associated idea by frequent observation of its use that the sound becomes for him a symbol. This transformation of a sound into a symbol pregnant with meaning is not brought about by the presentation of the sign; rather it comes about 'in consequence of seeing the actual thing':

> After frequently hearing the word *caput* and marking the circumstances when it was said, I observed that it was the word for a thing which was already very well known to me from sight. Before I had made this discovery, this word was merely a sound to me. I learned that it was a sign, when I discovered what it was a sign of. I did this, as I said, not through signs, but by actually seeing the thing itself. So a

[1] *The Teacher* 32.

> sign is better learned, after the thing itself has been learned rather than the thing after the sign.[1]

Whereas teachers often seem to be acting on the assumption that to know the word is to know the thing signified, the opposite is in fact the case. The significance of the word comes to be known only after direct acquaintance with the thing itself.

To say that words do not teach is, therefore, as it appears, to infer that teachers cannot teach. They can merely remind their pupils about things which they have learned for themselves by direct experience of the things themselves, that is without the intervention of the teacher. If words cannot teach, then teachers cannot teach, at least not on the generally accepted assumption that teaching is the transmission of ideas directly from one mind to another. The short interval of time, which frequently elapses between the words of the teacher and the learning of the pupil, produces the mistaken belief that the talking is the cause of the learning, an example of the fallacy of *post hoc, ergo propter hoc*. The words of teachers are not the causes of ideas in the mind of the learner:

> We go astray when we talk about 'teachers', when there are really no teachers at all. The reason why we do talk in this way is that there is often no time lapse between the moment of speaking and the moment of learning.[2]

The conclusion is 'that we must not attribute to words more than is proper'.

Up to this point the discussion has reached a conclusion apparently damaging to the professional standing of teachers and pessimistic as to the possibility of educational effort. However, it would be strangely inconsistent with Augustine's optimism as to the possibility of man's attaining knowledge, if the argument merely led to this sceptical conclusion. Both learning and teaching are names which correspond to undeniable truths of human experience; therefore, it is simply a question of discovering what teaching and learning actually are, as distinct from what they are commonly supposed to be.

[1] *ibid.* 33: '. . . *Itaque magis signum re cognita quam signo dato ipsa res discitur*'.

[2] *ibid.* 46.

THE TRUE FUNCTION OF THE TEACHER

We shall find that the debate in *The Teacher* leads in the end to the conclusion that, although the teacher's function is more limited than is often supposed, it is still significant. Although the teacher cannot directly transmit knowledge to his pupils, he can stimulate them to learn for themselves, i.e. to teach themselves. The teacher can bring this about, only if he puts his pupils into direct contact with the things he wants them to know. In other words teaching is accomplished, not by talking but by demonstrating the things themselves;[1] correspondingly, learning comes about through the direct confrontation of the learner's mind with the objects of knowledge. In fact the human teacher must follow the method of God, the divine internal teacher, who, as we have already noted, displays to men 'the things themselves'. The words of the human, i.e. external, teacher serve merely to direct the learner's attention either to an object, which the teacher is showing, or to a mental image originating in previous personal experience and now stored in the pupil's memory. Unless the teacher can stimulate the learner to make his own examination and appraisal of what the teacher is pointing to, his words must remain mere sounds, signifying nothing.[2]

Thus far we have considered the function of the teacher in relation to scientific knowledge, defined by St. Augustine as 'the rational knowledge of temporal things'. There is, however, the higher level of knowledge, designated as 'wisdom' (*sapientia*)—'the intellectual knowledge of eternal things'.[3] Since knowledge can be gained only by the direct contact of the learner with the thing to be known, it follows that no human teacher can put the intelligible realities on display before his class, as he can do with material objects. In the area of spiritual truths, the teacher is deprived of what we have found to be the only method of

[1] *ibid.* 36: 'Through words we learn only words . . . the knowledge of words is completed only after the things they signify are understood.'

[2] *ibid.* 35. See also *Tracts on St. John's Gospel* 26, 7: 'What do people accomplish when they make pronouncements outside us? What do I accomplish when I speak? I merely convey a sound of words into your ears.'

[3] For the distinction between science and wisdom see *supra*, pp. 103–10.

teaching, viz., the method of showing; thus his function seems to be still further reduced. It may then be asked how exactly the learner comes to know the intelligible realities, if his teacher cannot show them to him.

At this point we must recall St. Augustine's explanation of the origin of the knowledge of absolute truth in terms of divine illumination, which postulates a direct vision of 'the eternal reasons', displayed internally 'in a sort of immaterial light of a unique kind'.[1] Although then it is true that the external teacher cannot display the eternal reasons to his pupils, nevertheless they are still taught them by the method of showing. Spiritual truths are displayed to the learner by the internal teacher, and the learner looks upon them 'directly in the inner light of truth, by which what we call the inner man is illuminated'.

Thus St. Augustine traces a clear analogy between the teaching which comes from God and the teaching given by man. In both cases, it is a matter of the teacher 'showing' to the learner the things he wants to know. In the case of the eternal verities, it is true that the external teacher cannot directly show them to his pupils, but through the skilful use of words he can still hope to stimulate them to look within themselves and so to attain a direct spiritual perception 'with the eye of the mind' (*oculo mentis*). By expressing in sensitive and appealing speech the ideas, which he himself has received by the effort of his own understanding, the teacher can rouse the learner to 'teach' himself; this in itself is a significant result of the teacher's efforts. However, if the learner does come to an understanding of truth, the cause of his learning is not to be found in the words of the teacher, but in the learner's own persistent effort of thought:

> If the person who listens to me sees these things for himself with his inward eye, he knows what I am talking about as a result of his own thought and not because he has listened to my words.[2]

Knowledge of spiritual truths comes about, therefore, by an act of direct spiritual scrutiny analogous to physical vision in the area of scientific knowledge. The analogy between the teaching

[1] *supra*, pp. 119–30. *The Teacher* 40.
[2] *ibid.*

of God and the teaching of man can, however, be pressed further: in both cases the initiative must come from the learner himself, who by the exercise of his free will must concentrate his mind upon the thing he wishes to understand; he must not only look, but also see. However, whereas the external teacher does nothing for his pupil, which the pupil could not achieve for himself without the help of a teacher, the divine internal teacher must confer illumination on the learner's mind by an act of grace. The human teacher is expendable, but the divine teacher is not; the man who searches for an understanding of the eternal reasons is taught 'by the realities themselves made manifest to him by God's revealing them to his inner self'.[1]

To return to the human teacher, his task is to kindle a desire for knowledge in his pupils' souls. To this end he makes use of words, but if he is aware that his pupils can learn only through their own mental activity, he will not talk too much. Realising that his own words may in fact get in the way of the learner's inner thought, the teacher will appreciate the value of the method of question and answer. By putting questions, the teacher makes it more certain that the learner thinks for himself. Through carefully planned sequences of questions the learner has complicated problems broken down for him into a series of simpler problems. Drawing on his own comprehensive knowledge, the teacher helps the student 'to bring the separate parts of the problem one by one into the light'.[2] In one of St. Augustine's favourite metaphors, the teacher acts as a guide along a road, which he himself has travelled and thoroughly explored. Later the student must learn to find his own direction and teach himself entirely by the use of his own resources.But Augustine emphasises that, even in the earlier stages of education, it is more correct to speak of the learner as 'a pupil of truth' than 'a pupil of a teacher'. The relationship of a pupil towards his teacher should always be that of a judge in confrontation with one who gives evidence rather than of an uncritical receiver of the teacher's words.[3] The learner 'must

[1] *ibid.*

[2] *ibid.* 40.

[3] *ibid.* 41: 'Inwardly he is a pupil of truth; outwardly he is the judge of a speaker or rather of what a speaker says' (*Intus est discipulus veritatis, foris iudex loquentis vel potius ipsius locutionis*).

look to the truth inside him, as far as he is able; this is the way in which he learns'.[1] The uncritical acceptance of the teacher's words without the personal effort of thought can result in nothing more than the 'scraps of information', which A. N. Whitehead sees as the characteristic and unprofitable result of much modern education. Augustine hammers home the point in the form of a pointed question: 'Who is so ridiculously inquisitive as to send his son to school to learn what the teacher thinks?'[2] Education consists in the progressive enlargement of the understanding; this is not achieved by memorising the words of another person but only by personal exploration of, and direct contact with, the things which the student desires to know.

The absurdity of the assumption that words are the carriers of knowledge, as germs are of disease, is further demonstrated in *The Teacher* by reference to the frequency of intentional and unintentional misrepresentation resulting from the use of words. Words do not necessarily reveal the mind of the speaker. There are, of course, deliberate liars, whose words do not express what they think or know. But equally serious are the unintentional failures of communication arising from faulty verbal expression and slips of the tongue. Therefore, Augustine advises the teacher to be careful and precise in the use of words. He must remember that a word may not be understood in exactly the same sense by all the members of his audience; thus where ambiguity is likely to arise, he must take great care to define his terms. To illustrate the point, Augustine takes the example of the Latin word *virtus* which can mean either 'physical strength' or 'goodness'. If the teacher makes the statement that certain animals are superior to man in *virtue*, he must be careful to show that he is using *virtus* in the former and not in the latter sense.[3]

The Teacher is brought to an end by Augustine pointing out to Adeodatus that the aim of the lesson he has been trying to teach and the method followed are mutually consistent. If Adeodatus has learned anything, it is because he has been prompted to think in response to the stimulus of his father's

[1] *ibid.* 45.
[2] *ibid.*
[3] *ibid.* 43.

questions. He has, in fact, consulted the 'inner teacher', or 'secret oracle' within him, and it is by the prompting of this divine 'word' alone that he has found the truth. To this proposition Adeodatus assents; he declares that he has learned three things: first, that words merely stimulate a man to learn; second, that very little of a person's thought may be expressed in the words he uses; third, that the authority for our judgements is the internal teacher (*magister interior*), who displays the eternal criteria by which judgement becomes possible. If Adeodatus can say that he 'knows for himself' these three propositions, it is because he has taught himself with the aid of the teacher within him.

WORDS AND REALITIES

Towards the end of his exposition in *The Teacher* Augustine expresses the desire to investigate the problem of verbal communication more thoroughly at a later time. Although he did not devote any other work entirely to the subject, frequent references throughout his writings show he retained his interest in it.[1] In the Cassiciacum dialogues the importance of the distinction between words and ideas emerges in brief, critical comments on the progress of the discussions, as when Evodius in *The Greatness of the Soul* remarks that he must waste no time on names 'when the thing itself (*res ipsa*) is clear'.[2] A little later St. Augustine reinforces the point by advising Evodius 'to take a livelier interest in things than in words'.[3] The distinction between words and ideas recurs at the beginning of *Christian Education*, and later in the same work Augustine advises the Christian teacher and student to get behind the words of the Scriptures to the thought. There are people who read the Scriptures, but do not really study them: 'they read to remember the words, but are careless about knowing the meaning'.[4]

In other places St. Augustine deals with the theme in a more sustained manner. For instance, in *The Trinity* he examines the

[1] See J. M. Colleran, *op. cit.*, p. 240, n. 84.

[2] *The Greatness of the Soul* 10.

[3] *ibid.* 11.

[4] *Christian Education* i, 2: 'All teaching is either about things or about signs'. Also *ibid.* iv, 7.

nature of the divine Word (the *Logos*);[1] this is the 'word', which is 'spoken by the teacher within us', and is to be distinguished from spoken words employed in communication between persons. The divine Word is so-called because of a certain superficial resemblance to speech. However, there is the essential difference that the inner 'word' is spiritual, while spoken words are physical in their nature.[2] Furthermore, the spoken word is merely the conventional symbol of an underlying reality, while the inner 'word' *directly* informs us of the truths of real existence; it does not re-present, or symbolise, spiritual realities in our minds, but actually *is* the truth itself. The eternal first principles are *immediately* presented to our thought in the divine Word; as Augustine puts it, 'the true knowledge is stored up *like a word* within us'. It is because this inner 'word' is spiritual that it cannot be taken from the mind of one person and transmitted to another, as physical words are transmitted. When we speak, 'we use a physical sign, so that by some sort of token passing through the senses, a similar thing may be brought into being in the mind of the hearer also'.[3] The spoken word flies out from the speaker, but the thought itself remains irrevocably enclosed within him. Thought is '*like*' inner speech, and all voluntary behaviour, whether expressed in speech or in any other way, is the outward manifestation of 'a word uttered within ourselves'.

Since the inner 'word'—'the word we speak in our hearts'—is a direct presentation of reality within the mind of the thinker, Augustine warns against the mistaken belief that this 'word' is couched in the verbal symbolism of any particular language. Each language has its own name to stand for a particular idea, but the idea itself is 'neither Greek nor Latin nor any other language'; it remains the same, whatever may be the language in which it is expressed in speech. Therefore, Augustine does not subscribe to the view that thinking *is* inner speech in the sense that we talk silently within ourselves in the words or idiom of a

[1] *The Trinity* ix, 12 and xv, 17–26.

[2] Thus in *The Greatness of the Soul* 65–7, Augustine distinguishes between the sound of a word and its meaning; the sound is the body of the word, i.e. its physical aspect; the meaning is the soul, or spiritual aspect.

[3] *The Trinity* ix, 12.

particular language. His conviction that words and ideas are entirely different in their nature leads him to the logical conclusion that thinking is one thing and speaking is another. The description of thought as 'inner speech' is therefore metaphorical, just as the term 'light' is metaphorically used in the doctrine of divine illumination as a description of the divine intervention.

The distinction between the inner 'word', spiritual in nature and therefore necessarily incommunicable, and the physical words, transmitted in speech or writing from one person to another, is the rationale behind Augustine's conviction that, whereas teachers can communicate words directly to their pupils, they cannot directly communicate thoughts. Augustine holds that, when a teacher talks of 'transmitting' knowledge from himself to his pupil, he is confusing thoughts with words, and therefore interpreting teaching as an external, mechanical process, when it is essentially an inner, spiritual activity. Whatever in fact occurs in the act of teaching, knowledge is not 'handed over' by the teacher. The learner, who 'grasps' the knowledge, which the teacher desires him to grasp, does not receive it from the teacher, as he would a physical object handed to him; what the learner does receive from the teacher is the teacher's words, which are merely symbolic, or at the most, suggestive of what the teacher is thinking 'internally'.[1]

Augustine was right in perceiving that teachers do not always keep the distinction between words and ideas clearly before their minds. The tendency to blur the distinction is the prime cause of the lack of relevance of schooling to the experience of the learner. The danger is particularly menacing in our modern secondary schools, where examination pressure tends to lay undue emphasis on rote learning at the expense of the time-consuming cultivation of genuine understanding. Augustine has, therefore, given strong support to a principle, which underlies modern progressive ideas on educational method, and which has turned the attention of the teacher away from second-hand knowledge and words to an engagement with meaningful

[1] In *The Trinity* xv, 17, Augustine states that the letters of the alphabet are signs of signs; they are 'the signs of words, just as words themselves are signs in our conversation of the things we are thinking about.' See also *The Trinity* ix, 12.

activities. The tendency for education to reduce itself to the manipulation of verbal formulae has been commented on by many thinkers, who see education in terms of the growth of understanding rather than the passing of examinations. In his essay on Intellectual Education Herbert Spencer, for example, criticised educational method in the spirit of St. Augustine:

> The rote system—made more of the forms and symbols than of the things symbolised. To repeat the words correctly was everything; to understand their meaning nothing; and thus the spirit was sacrificed to the letter—In proportion as there is attention to signs, there must be inattention to the things signified—as Montaigne long ago said: 'Savoir par coeur n'est pas savoir'.[1]

The same feeling underlies A. N. Whitehead's criticism of the education that is associated with 'inert ideas'; such an education 'is not only useless; it is, above all things, harmful'.[2] Similarly, John Dewey discussed the insidious tendency of words to be mistaken for ideas and so to corrupt genuine education:

> The importance of language in gaining knowledge is doubtless the chief cause of the common notion that knowledge may be passed directly from one to another. It almost seems as if all we have to do to convey an idea into the mind of another is to convey a sound into his ear.[3]

St. Augustine's discussion of the relationship between the verbal symbol and the underlying reality ('the thing itself') leads to the conclusion that words are purely conventional symbols, having no natural resemblance to the things they symbolise.[4] In *Christian Education* he states that 'men did not accept words as

[1] H. Spencer, *Education*, ch. 2 on Intellectual Education. J. J. Rousseau in *Emile*, bk. 2, p. 73, expresses the same view: 'In any study the symbols are of no value without the idea of the thing symbolised'.

[2] A. N. Whitehead, *Aims of Education*, (Ernest Benn, London, 1962), ch. 1, pp. 1–2.

[3] J. Dewey, *Democracy and Education*, (Macmillan, N.Y., 1929), ch. 2, p. 17.

[4] *On Music* vi, 24: 'Names are given by convention and not by nature' (placito, non natura, imponuntur). For similar sentiments see *Confessions* x, 20, 29; *Sermons* 288, 3; *The Instruction of the Uninstructed* 2, 3.

signs because they were already significant; on the contrary words are now significant, because men have come to an agreement about them'. However, in talking about the stylised gestures used in mime, he slightly modifies his rejection of any imitative function in the symbols used in communication:

> All men aim at a certain degree of likeness in their choice of signs, so that, as far as possible, the signs may resemble the things they signify.[1]

The controversy on the extent to which words are imitations of the things they represent is one aspect of the antithesis made by the Sophists between 'nature' and 'convention'. With reference to verbal symbols, the question is discussed in Plato's *Cratylus*, in which Cratylus himself maintains the view that there is for each thing a 'right name', which by its sound will suggest the thing which it depicts:

> A name is a vocal imitation of the thing which is imitated; the person who imitates with his voice is naming the thing he is imitating.[2]

On this view, when we find that the same idea is indicated by different combinations of sounds in different languages, it is merely that man has so far failed to find the exact combination of sounds, which 'naturally' represents the things itself. In the dialogue, the view of Cratylus is argued against the view of Hermogenes that the name of a thing is merely what we agree to call it. Cratylus' view as to the mimetic function of words foreshadows the modern gesture theory of the origin of human speech:

> Human speech arose out of a general unconscious pantomimic gesture language made by the limbs and features as a whole including tongue and lips, which became specialised gestures of the organs of articulation owing to the human hands and eyes being continually occupied with the use of tools.[3]

[1] *Christian Education* ii, 37–8.

[2] Plato, *Cratylus* 383. On the Cratylus see A. E. Taylor, *Plato*, ch. 5, pp. 75–89.

[3] R. A. Paget, *Human Speech* (1930). Paget's theory is called the oral gesture or tongue pantomime theory.

But Augustine holds that, except in the case of a few onomatopoetic words, we cannot learn about the thing symbolised by listening to the word which represents it. Hence we return to the point that words can do no more than merely remind the learner of something he already knows, or at the most stimulate him to enquire into their meaning.

The lesson impressed by St. Augustine is that in education the movement must be from clear ideas to the words, by which ideas are conveniently and conventionally designated. In the preface to *Christian Education* Augustine once again uses the familiar example of the child learning to speak his own language; he first perceives the objects around him, and then associates with these, and imitates, the words he hears spoken by other people; the 'human teacher'; therefore, does well to follow the natural or 'direct' method of learning:

> Everyone learned his own language by hearing it constantly from childhood; any other language we have learned has come to us in the same way, that is by hearing it spoken, or from a human teacher.[1]

Augustine goes on to cite the encounter of Philip and the eunuch on the Gaza road as a means of emphasising both the importance of the learner's own activity and also the significance, within its own proper limits, of the part played by the human teacher.[2] The eunuch did not enlist the help of an angel to instruct him in the meaning of the Scriptures, nor did God inwardly illuminate his mind without the initial stimulus of a human teacher. Also the essential conditions for a profitable learning experience were in existence: there was a person who believed that there was something of importance to know and who wished to know it; there was also a 'teacher' (Philip), that is one who already knew what the words of Scripture meant and was prepared to guide the enquiring eunuch to achieve his self-imposed purpose. In the terminology of modern educational psychology, the learner was in a state of 'learning readiness'. On the other hand, the teacher, having accurately defined his own role, was not to be satisfied with the learner's passive acceptance of the teacher's words as evidence of understanding and con-

[1] *Christian Education*, preface, 5.

[2] *Acts* 8, 26–39.

version. The pupil must learn for himself: 'If thou believest with all thine heart, thou mayest be baptised'. Stimulated by the words and encouragement of the teacher, the learner must carry on within himself the unspoken dialogue of thought about the realities, with which the teacher's words are associated.

The teacher's responsibility is, therefore, discharged when he has made clear the distinction between words and ideas and by his own example of effective thinking has given the learner encouragement and a sense of direction. By pointing out problems which his pupils may not yet have clearly recognised as problems, and raising questions about matters which are rooted in their own experience but which they have not yet seriously thought about, the teacher stimulates them to think for themselves. His task is essentially one of liberating the intelligence, which is precisely the pedagogical function, which Augustine attributes to the liberal arts, that is to lead the learner progressively 'through material objects to immaterial reality'.[1] By the self-questioning, which the teacher induces in the learner's mind, he opens out new prospects, reveals unsuspected depths and significance in familiar ideas and exposes the weaknesses of hitherto unquestioned assumptions. Thus the learner's mind is liberated, when it is afforded the opportunity and encouragement to perform its own rational activity. However, if the teacher fails to distinguish between words and thoughts, and offers his words as actual thoughts, which the learner should commit to memory, no such activity of reason occurs. Education centred on words rather than on realities eventuates in what St. Augustine calls 'a miserable slavery of the soul'.[2] If the teacher's words are accepted by the learner as informative rather than symbolic, as a substitute for, rather than as a stimulant to, thought, education becomes sterile and lacks the challenge of an ever-expanding development of the understanding.

CONCLUSION

We have examined St. Augustine's views on the nature and purpose of the act of teaching. He strongly opposes the notion that teaching, defined in terms of the activity of an external,

[1] *Reviews* i, 6.

[2] *Christian Education* iii, 9. Augustine quotes ii Corinthians, 3, 6: 'The letter killeth, but the spirit giveth life'.

human teacher, can be the cause of learning in another person. To see a causal relationship is an example of the common tendency to conclude that, because one event frequently follows after another, the one is the cause of the other. The teacher talks, so that the pupil may be stimulated to learn for himself; learning has its origin in an act of the learner's will and continues just as long as his will is focused on the immediate objective, which he holds before his mind. In other words, the learner is always his own teacher; when he enquires into his physical environment, he teaches himself by his own unaided resources, but when he seeks to understand the spiritual context of the universe—'the eternal reasons of things'—his enquiry reaches a successful outcome, only if in the last resort he is aided by the grace of the divine teacher within him, the *magister interior*. This teacher reveals to each man 'only as much as he is able to receive with reference to the condition of his will, which may be evil or good'.

The external human teacher, as it were the teacher in the classroom, must therefore remain on the periphery of the learning process; he must regard himself as expendable, and therefore encourage his pupils to think for themselves, so that they can continue to learn when the teacher takes his departure, as sooner or later he must do. Socrates' remark to the slave boy in Plato's *Meno*—'I like to hear you say what you think'[1]—is paralleled in many places by Augustine's delight in the revelation of some spontaneous and original effort of thought in his students at Cassiciacum. The teacher's task is not to transmit knowledge from his mind to his pupils, but rather to find out what his pupils already know and from this starting point to raise questions which arouse the desire to add to their existing knowledge. In this way, by encouraging the habit of self-questioning, he will be able to withdraw, in the confidence that the process, which he has initiated, will continue by its own momentum.

St. Augustine's arguments lead to the establishment of two propositions, which teachers must clearly understand:

First, teaching and talking are not the same thing; by teaching is meant an activity focused on the development of understanding, whereas speaking is merely 'giving signs', a function

[1] Plato, *Meno* 83.

ancillary to the function of thought. The teacher must 'give signs in order to teach' and not 'teach in order to give signs';[1] if he confuses teaching and talking, he is liable to ascribe an undue importance to his own talking, and in fact to act as though his own words were the end, and not the beginning, of education.

Second, teaching and learning are not two different activities but one single process, in which there is no clear distinction between teacher and taught. The learner is his own teacher, and, in the interaction of minds characteristic of all good teaching, the teacher himself learns as he teaches. In the classroom, teachers and students simultaneously 'teach themselves' or 'learn for themselves', which is to look at the same activity from two different standpoints. The whole purpose of the dialogue of *The Teacher* is to make this point. It begins with Adeodatus' clear separation of teaching and learning—'When we speak, our purpose is *either* to teach *or* to learn'[2]—and ends with his conviction that the two are indistinguishable—'I have learned that words simply stimulate a man to learn: I also know that, although a good deal of a speaker's thought appears to be communicated through his words, very little of it is actually expressed'.[3]

In his analysis of the act of instruction St. Augustine's emphasis is on the predominantly intellectual or speculative aspect of education, and this may appear far removed from the problems of universal education, as they face us in the present day. Nevertheless, his critique of the common assumptions of teachers has a universal relevance, his attitude being consistent with the views expressed by many later educational reformers, who have wished to liberate education from the shackles of formal, bookish studies and convert it to an exciting adventure of purposeful thought. For instance St. Augustine's exhortation to understand the Scriptures, and not merely to learn their words, is matched by Rousseau's characteristically explosive utterance: 'I hate books; they only teach us to talk about things we know nothing about'.[4] At Cassiciacum the reading of books

[1] *The Teacher* 30.
[2] *The Teacher* 1. See *supra*, p. 185, n. 2.
[3] *ibid*. 46.
[4] J. J. Rousseau, *Emile*, bk. 3, p. 147.

was purely recreative; the real educational task, was carried out in and through the interchange of ideas, words being used merely as stimulants to thinking.

St. Augustine's views on the methods of instruction are closely related to the Christian context. Therefore, Christ becomes the perfect example of the art of teaching, his mission being essentially to arouse men, and in particular the Jews, to an awareness of the important distinction between symbols and realities, so that they could move forward in their understanding of spiritual truth. For the Jews, as St. Augustine sees them, symbols had come to act as obstacles effectively shutting them off from genuine insight. Thus the great merit of Christ, the teacher, was that he 'used' verbal and other symbols for a purpose beyond themselves, that is 'to fix the thoughts of those who observed them on the worship of the one God'.[1] To set free the human intelligence through an encouragement to purposeful thinking, and so progressively to lead man to a more expansive knowledge of himself and his destiny sum up the purpose of Christ's teaching, as it should be the purpose of all teachers.

Finally, it is interesting to compare St. Augustine's denial that the teacher is the cause of learning with the view later expressed by St. Thomas Aquinas in his *Disputed Questions*, one of which is known as *The Teacher*.[2] St Thomas holds that learning comes about in one or the other of two different ways, each of which is a legitimate and effective way of learning. The first is the method of learning by discovery, the 'heuristic' method, which relies entirely on the learner's unaided activity; the second requires the services of a teacher, who, starting with a comprehensive knowledge of his subject matter, presents it systematically and logically to the learner. In this way, according to St. Thomas, the teacher 'aids the natural reason' and 'can truly be called a teacher inasmuch as he teaches truth and

[1] *Christian Education* iii, 10.

[2] Aquinas, *Quaestiones Disputatae*, vol. 1 (*De Veritate*), qu. 11. For a more comprehensive exposition of Aquinas, *The Teacher* see H. Johnston, *A Philosophy of Education*, ch. 7. Also S. J. Curtis, *Introduction to the Philosophy of Education*, pp. 92–4. A translation of *The Teacher* is to be found in Thomas Aquinas: *The Teacher and The Mind*, trans. J. V. McGlynn (Gateway Edition, Henry Regnery, Chicago, 1953). See also *infra*, pp. 288–9 and *supra*, p. 158.

enlightens the mind'. Thus to the question, 'Can a man learn for himself?' St. Thomas answers, 'Yes'; but to the question, 'Can a man teach himself?', he answers, 'No'. In other words, St. Thomas, unlike St. Augustine, makes a clear distinction between learning from a teacher and learning for oneself without a teacher's help. By 'teaching' St. Thomas means the action of one person on another; by 'discovery' he means the internal activity of self-instruction. Thus he has no objection to the teacher being described as the '*cause*' of his pupil's learning, although the teacher is merely the secondary instrumental cause of knowledge; in this respect the teacher is contrasted with God, who is the primary cause, and with the learner himself, who is the secondary principal cause. The teacher's secondary and instrumental function is truly causative, for the same good reason as the doctor is properly said to be the cause of health in his patient. The doctor co-operates with the patient's natural powers to this end; correspondingly the teacher's function is 'to cause knowledge in another through the activity of the learner's own natural reason'.

Both St. Augustine and St. Thomas agree in attributing to the teacher a significant part to play in education. Whether that part is to be defined in causal terms or not is a question which may make little practical difference to the actualities of the teaching situation, as both define it. Both agree that the teacher can merely assist the learner to learn; neither minimises the crucial role of the learner's own free will, since the effects desired by a teacher can always be thwarted by the conflicting intentions of the learner. St. Augustine's theory emphasises the ultimate importance of the activity of the involved learner and his absolute independence of the teacher; on the other hand, St. Thomas' view, marked as it is by his Aristotelian realism, makes greater concessions to commonsense by showing that the teacher is an indispensable, if temporary, participant in the ongoing process of every man's earthly education.

7 The Education of the Christian Teacher

As far as teaching is concerned, the function of eloquence is not to make people like what they dislike or to make them do what they do not want to do but to make clear what was obscure. Christian Education iv, 26.

If those who are called philosophers, especially the Platonists, have said anything which is true and in harmony with our faith, we should not shrink away from it, but appropriate it to our own use, as though we were taking it from people who were in unlawful possession of it.
Christian Education ii, 60.

Up to this point our examination of St. Augustine's contribution to the theory and practice of education has concentrated on the period between his conversion to Christianity in the autumn of A.D. 386 and his return to North Africa two years later. This was the period, in which his explanatory philosophical enquiry was appropriately cast in the dialogue form, and which ended with his ordination to the priesthood in A.D. 391. Commentators have noted, sometimes with ill-concealed surprise, that the dialogues of Cassiciacum make a general, rather than a specifically Christian, contribution to philosophy and education.[1] For a discussion of the problems of Christian Education we have to turn to the book, which was to have a considerable influence on the development of later medieval education, the *De Doctrina Christiana* (*Christian Education*), the writing of which was begun six years after St. Augustine's ordination and three years after his consecration as Bishop of Hippo.

[1] For discussions of this issue see W. Montgomery, *St. Augustine: Aspects of his Life and Thought*, pp. 47–50; C. Boyer, *Christianisme et néo-Platonisme dans la Formation de St. Augustin*, pp. 141–50. Boyer's critical examination of the view that Cassiciacum was an oasis of independent philosophy leads him to the conclusion that the dialogues give sufficient evidence of 'the intensity of Augustine's Christian life at Cassiacum'.

Christian Education consists of four books, of which the first two and part of the third were written in the year A.D. 397. For some unexplained reason the writing was suddenly interrupted and the work was not resumed and completed until the year A.D. 426, four years before St. Augustine's death.[1] In the relevant entry in his *Reviews*, written in the year A.D. 427, Augustine shows that the views on Christian education, which he had expressed in the earlier years of his episcopate, had stood the test of time. With only minor amendments he gives unqualified support to the arguments he had advanced thirty years before.[2]

When St. Augustine began to write his work on *Christian Education*, he had already had nine years' experience in North Africa as a teacher and teacher of teachers, during which he had realised the need for an educated priesthood, capable of entering into effective argument with cultivated pagans. *Christian Education*, along with *The Instruction of the Uninstructed*, written in A.D. 399, bears the marks of first-hand experience in the propagation of Christian doctrine in a world still aggressively pagan.

The content of *Christian Education* is summarised as follows:

1. *Preface:* a justification of the proposition that the Christian teacher should be adequately prepared for his task.
2. *Books 1 to 3:* An exposition of the rules governing the interpretation of the Scriptures—'the method of discovering what must be understood'.
3. *Book 4:* An exposition of the method of teaching the Scriptures, when they are understood—'the method of communicating what has been understood'.

St. Augustine identifies three necessary elements in the curriculum for the professional education of the Christian teacher: general education, specialised study of the subject matter he will teach and a study of the principles of teaching. In his general education, as Augustine sees it, the Christian teacher should be

[1] The work may have been laid aside due to his increasing preoccupation with the writing of the *Confessions*, which were begun in A.D. 397. The first part of *Christian Education* ends abruptly in the middle of the 25th of the 37 chapters which make up the 3rd book. See *Reviews* ii, 4.

[2] *Reviews, loc. cit.*

introduced to the culture common to all educated men in the Roman world of the time. His specialised study is in the content of the Scriptures; to interpret these with scholarly insight, he also requires training in the skills of literary interpretation, as practised by the teacher of literature (the *grammaticus*) in the Roman secular schools. A knowledge of the principles of teaching is necessary, if the Christian teacher is effectively to communicate the truths he has discovered.

St. Augustine anticipates the sceptical reaction which will be called forth by the suggestion that the Christian teacher requires the same quality and degree of preparation for his task as the secular teacher needs. In the preface to *Christian Education* Augustine argues that teaching cannot be successfully practised without training. He asks that Christians who underrate the need for the training of Christian teachers, on the ground that God himself will open their minds and loosen their tongues, should remember how much they themselves have learned from human teachers. He draws on numerous examples to show how God relies on human agents to assist the earnest searcher after truth.[1] Divinely inspired though the Scriptures are, they still require the application of sound rules of method for their correct interpretation.

In this connection, it is interesting to note that the indifference of many people to the suggestion that the Christian teacher should receive training in the skills of teaching was not eliminated in the thirty years which elapsed between the beginning of *Christian Education* and its conclusion. In the course of the fourth book, Augustine is again on the defensive: teacher training, that is training from human sources, is necessary and not to be despised. God assists the man who assists himself; it is as foolish to neglect the training of the Christian teacher on the grounds that the Holy Spirit will confer on him all the eloquence and lucidity he requires as it is to neglect prayer because 'Your Father knoweth what things ye have need of before ye ask him':

> The duty of a man to teach even the teachers does not cease when the Holy Spirit is given.[2]

[1] *Christian Education*, preface, 6–7.
[2] *ibid.* iv, 33. Matthew 6, 8.

THE MEANING OF CHRISTIAN SCHOLARSHIP

Augustine begins *Christian Education* with a discussion of the problems relating to the interpretation of the Scriptures. From this storehouse of wisdom the Christian teacher must learn to extract and interpret what has special or fundamental significance. By systematic and critical study he will build up for himself a comprehensive picture of divine truth out of what could remain an incomprehensible and ill-assorted mass. He must in fact bring to the study of Christian letters the same painstaking care and trained judgement, which the secular grammarian brings to the study of the literary documents of the classical culture. Both the secular grammarian and the Christian scholar and teacher are engaged in an identical interpretative task, although the content of their teaching is different.

The exposition of *Christian Education* opens with the distinction, now familiar to us, between words and things, symbols and realities. The study of records is the study of words, but words are merely symbolic and instrumental. Like any other student, the Christian must use signs as a means to an end, which lies beyond the signs. This end consists in the understanding of the realities, symbolised by the words. Thus a vital pedagogical principle is again enunciated:

> We should keep in mind that our examination of things should concentrate on what they are in themselves and not what other things they signify apart from themselves.[1]

In his communication with man through the Scriptures, God must necessarily employ words, i.e. verbal signs, and these must be correctly interpreted, if they are to inform the student and stimulate him to thought. Words do not convey an understanding of the realities they symbolise, unless the ideas with which they are conventionally associated have been made meaningful to the learner in his own experience. Therefore, the correct order of instruction is from 'realities' (*res*) to the signs, by which they are signified. Augustine acts in accordance with this principle by devoting the first book of *Christian Education* to a discussion of the various 'realities', with which the Christian teacher will have to deal when he interprets the Scriptures to his students. Thus the book provides a simplified statement of St.

[1] *Christian Education* i, 2.

Augustine's basic philosophy. The Christian teacher must know where he stands and what he believes, because this is the context within which he must interpret the Scriptures for himself and teach them to others.

The distinction between symbols and realities is repeated at the beginning of the second book, in which St. Augustine considers the method of interpreting the verbal signs by which God seeks to instruct the reader of the Scriptures:

> A sign is a thing which, quite apart from the actual impression it makes on the senses, causes something else associated with itself to come into the mind. Thus, when we see a footprint, we decide that an animal, whose footprint it is, has passed that way. When we see smoke, we know that there is a fire underneath. On hearing the voice of a living being, we think of the feeling in his mind.[1]

The examples quoted are what Augustine calls 'natural signs'; the association with the realities they signify are understood by the simple observation of cause and effect in the natural world. By comparison, words are 'conventional' signs, acting as symbols of realities which have no natural connection with the symbols; these are the signs with which the teacher and interpreter of Scripture are concerned. Words, spoken and written, are man's chief instruments for 'signifying the conceptions of their minds'.[2] Originally words were spoken signs, but their scope and influence have been greatly extended by man's invention of writing, through which the sounds of words are, as it were, made visible to the eye. The sin of discord, however, led different peoples to adopt different semantic systems, with the result that the Scriptures must be translated into a number of languages if they are to be universally understood.

St. Augustine emphasises that this necessity for translation is the cause of certain obvious difficulties encountered in the interpretation of the Scriptures and reinforces the need for the careful preparation of the Christian teacher before he makes the attempt to speak about the Scriptures to others. Because he is dealing with conventional, and not natural, signs, the multiplication of

[1] *ibid.* ii, 1.
[2] *ibid.* ii, 4.

translations of varying quality has led to divergent and even contradictory interpretations of the original text. Furthermore there are obscurities arising from the figurative language used by the writers of Scripture to enliven their exposition. By the use of such language signs become, as it were, twice removed from reality. But the difficulties encountered are not entirely man-made. Some obscurities of expression have been introduced by God Himself for the express purpose of challenging the intellectual powers of man. If the human intellect is to carry out its supreme rational task, it must be stimulated by difficult problems:—'The intellect pays slight attention to what is discovered without effort'.[1]

If the interpretation of the Scriptures by Christian teachers is to conform to acceptable standards of scholarship, it must be founded on the careful study of original sources. Therefore, Augustine maintains that the Christian teacher must have a thorough knowledge of both Greek and Hebrew.[2] The accuracy and general quality of translations vary, and, when they disagree in their rendering of a word or phrase, the Christian student must be able to consult the original sources of his texts. The translations of well-intentioned but unscholarly amateurs must be particularly scrutinised: 'In the early days of the faith every man who happened to get his hands on a Greek manuscript and thought he had even the smallest ability in the two languages, had the courage to translate it'. But, irrespective of the quality of different translations 'the examination of a number of texts often clarifies some rather obscure expressions'.[3] Therefore, the Christian teacher must be trained in the critical comparison of different translations. That a word is differently rendered in one Latin translation compared with another does not necessarily mean that one translator is wrong and another right; both may shed their own distinctive light on a thought through their choice of words by which to interpret it. Thus by comparing various translations with the original Greek or Hebrew, Christian students can receive fuller and more varied

[1] *ibid.* ii, 8. Also 'In some cases it is more pleasant to have knowledge communicated through figures of speech; what is difficult to search out gives greater pleasure when it is found'.

[2] *ibid.* ii, 16.

[3] *loc. cit.*

insights into Christian writ. In the manner of the Roman teacher of literature St. Augustine gives a number of examples to illustrate his point.[1]

If this comparative study of different renderings does not clarify the meaning of an unknown or ambiguous expression, then it should be stored in the memory, until it is encountered in other contexts or the student finds someone who can tell him what it means. Knowledge cannot be completed all at once but must advance by degrees:

> . . . we gradually come to know the meaning of unfamiliar words and idioms through the experience of reading or hearing them.[2]

In advocating the importance of careful Christian scholarship Augustine was asserting that the Christian teacher's concern is with the discovery and publication of truth and not with the verbal quibbling characteristic of the decadence of letters in the secular world of his day. The basic commitment of the Christian teacher to a body of religious truths must not result in textual interpretations, that are forced to conform to certain preconceived, or even fanciful, notions of the interpreter. When such distortions occur, it is because the interpreter fails to penetrate in thought behind the words to the idea. An unscholarly interpretation is certain to take away from the purity and persuasiveness of truth. However, it is in harmony with Augustine's educational theory, as we have already understood it, that he should warn the Christian student that accuracy and sensitivity of interpretation are not to be confused with the most literal interpretations of words. For this advice Augustine finds support in one of his favourite scriptural texts: 'The letter killeth, but the spirit giveth life'.[3] In his view it was just this failure to distinguish between words and meaning that was the cause of the Jews' constant misinterpretations of the actions of

[1] *ibid.* ii, 16–18. Among Latin translations Augustine recommends the Italia (otherwise Vetus Latina) as revised by the Church of Northern Italy in the fourth century prior to the Vulgate of St. Jerome. The most authoritative Greek version recommended is the Septuagint. See S. D. Salmond in vol. 9 of Marcus Dods, *The Works of Augustine*, p. 49, n. 1.

[2] *ibid.* ii, 21.

[3] *ibid.* iii, 9. *ii Corinthians* 3, 6.

Christ, as for instance His healing of the sick on the sabbath. Intellectual laziness in himself or his students is a weakness, against which the Christian teacher must always be on his guard, since it is a prime cause of error in the interpretation of God's word.

In his discussion of the particular problems involved in the interpretation of ambiguous metaphorical expressions Augustine draws widely on scriptural examples to illustrate his points. In all his work the Christian teacher must be guided by the 'truth of faith' (*veritas fidei*), and must reject as false an interpretation which contradicts the 'purity of life' (*honestas morum*), which faith enjoins on the believer. This is to say that the significance of particular expressions must not be determined in isolation from their total Christian context. Amid the endless variety of customs prevailing among men, Augustine finds it easy for the teacher to lapse into moral relativism, forgetting that God has given to man a body of clear and inviolable guides to conduct to help him in moments of perplexity. At the same time Augustine advises the Christian teacher to relate his interpretations of Scripture to the particular circumstances prevailing in the times and places, in which they were written. There is both an eternal and a temporal context, both of which must be taken into account if the Scriptures are to be accurately interpreted. Above all, the Christian teacher must not fall into the narrow-minded, provincial attitude, which consists in imagining that the customs of times and places other than his own are necessarily to be condemned:

> It frequently happens that a man will think nothing worthy of blame, except what the people of his own country and time are accustomed to condemn, and nothing worthy of praise, except what is sanctioned by the custom of his fellows.[1]

It is again consistent with St. Augustine's views on the motivation of all learning that he should insist that, in all his interpretation and exposition of the Scriptures, the teacher must be guided by the principle of Christian love. Starting from this basic educational principle, the Christian teacher is armed against over-hasty or false interpretations of scriptural texts, which might appear to be attributing evil to good men or even to

[1] *ibid.* iii, 15.

God Himself. Where the teacher finds such suggestions, he can be sure that the passages concerned are to be interpreted in a figurative or spiritual sense; for example:

> When our Lord says, 'He who loveth his life shall lose it', we are not to think that he is forbidding the prudence, by which a man ought to protect his own life. He is saying in a figurative sense, 'Let him lose his life'—that is, let him destroy and lose that perverted and unnatural use which he now makes of his life and through which his desires are fixed on temporal things.[1]

THE PROBLEM OF CONTENT IN THE GENERAL EDUCATION OF THE CHRISTIAN TEACHER

Augustine's discussion of curriculum content in relation to the general education of the Christian teacher focuses on the highly controversial question of the extent to which the liberal arts of the secular curriculum should be employed in Christian education. To what extent should the Christian tap the resources of the secular culture? Should he look upon the wisdom handed down from the pre-Christian past as superseded, and not merely supplemented, by the documents of Christian revelation, in which God has at last spoken out clearly and directly to man? The question had been acute from the earliest Christian times and had been rendered more controversial and acrimonious by the violent hostility of the pagan world to the Christian claims. From one point of view, the literature and thought of classical Greece and Rome were incompatible with the Christian spirit. Thinking on the question had thrown up conspicuous examples of the tendency to see human behaviour in terms of black and white, which has so often in the course of history prevented quick and reasonable compromise and aggravated prejudice sometimes to the point of bloodshed.

The question of whether the Christian, living in an environ-

[1] *ibid.* iii, 24. The point is repeated in *The Instruction of the Uninstructed* 50: 'Whenever a person finds in the Scriptures something which he cannot associate with the love of eternity, truth, holiness, or with the love of his neighbour, he should believe that what is said or done has a figurative significance; he should try to understand it in such a way as to associate it with this double love.'

ment impregnated by the classical culture, should, or could, cease to breathe the air, which surrounded him, had been vitiated by the failure to separate two propositions, which were at once logically distinct and yet intimately bound together. On the one hand, the Christian must reject the pagan spirit expressed in the pre-Christian classics; on the other hand, he must not abandon those elements, which were patently good and beautiful, nor cast aside what Marrou calls 'its scholarly, literary, scientific and philosophical techniques'.[1]

Should the Christian conclude that the falsehood of some elements in the secular culture vitiated the whole? The attitude of total rejection had been summed up in the scornful question of Tertullian—'What has Athens to do with Jerusalem?'.[2] This distracted attention from the admittedly difficult problems involved in the selective use of the liberal arts curriculum in Christian education. It also inhibited reasonable discussion of the underlying assumption that the wholesome medicine of truth may all be turned to poison, if a tincture of falsehood is mixed with it. It is the vexed question of censorship in its perennial form: through fear that elements of ugliness may exercise an unduly demoralising influence, aspects of truth are arbitrarily shut off from view. The educator, who starts with little faith in the discernment of the young, advocates, like Tertullian, the vigorous use of restrictive censorship. The humanist educator, who, like St. Augustine, rejoices in his pupils' constant revelation of their ability to distinguish between truth and falsehood, substitutes trust for repression and emphasises the fertilising value of truth, whatever its source, rather than the contaminating power of error.

Through the long controversy on this issue, from Tertullian in the second and third centuries A.D., through Clement and Origen to Basil and St. Jerome, who were contemporaries of Augustine, the less intransigent of Christian thinkers saw that the Christian must reach an accommodation with pagan culture.

[1] H. I. Marrou, *St. Augustine et la Fin de la Culture Antique*, p. 390.

[2] Compare Jerome, *Epistle* 22, 12: 'What communication can there be between light and darkness? What common ground between Christ and Belial? What has Horace to do with the Psalms? Or Vergil with the gospels? Or Cicero with the Apostle Paul?—We should not at one and the same time drink the cup of Christ and the cup of evil spirits.'

Even Tertullian himself was forced to the grudging admission that 'a knowledge of letters is requisite both for the business and commerce of life, and even for performing our devotion to God'.[1] The liberal view, strikingly summed up in Clement's words—'There is one river of Truth, but many streams fall into it on this side and that—I call him truly learned who brings everything to bear on the truth so that, gathering what is useful from geometry and music and philosophy itself, he guards the faith against assault'[2]—opened the way to a more rational approach to the problem of selection. The outstanding Christian apologists of the fourth and fifth centuries, Basil, St. John Chrysostom, Ambrose and Augustine himself, advocated a permissive approach to pagan culture. By the end of the fourth century, the Christian could approach the best of pagan literature and philosophy with a clearer conscience and therefore with a more acute discernment. To this clarification of thought on a controversial question, which had inhibited the development of an adequate Christian curriculum St. Augustine made an important contribution.

One of the most striking of Augustine's comments on the worth of pagan poetry is the passage in the *Confessions* where he rejects 'those idle vanities' of Vergil's *Aeneid*, on which he claims that he spent so much of a misguided youth.[3] But it is generally accepted that in the *Confessions* there is some exaggeration of the vices, into which St. Augustine threw himself. Therefore, the criticism of Vergil may be interpreted as a passing thrust made to strengthen the admonitory function of the *Confessions* rather than a view which St. Augustine consistently sustains.[4] In fact he frequently quotes from the works of Vergil, Cicero, and other classical authors. The curriculum at Cassiciacum, as we have seen, was divided between the discussion of fundamental problems of philosophy and the reading of the classical poets, in particular Vergil. In short, St. Augustine

[1] Tertullian, *De Corona* 8.

[2] Clement, *Stromata* i, 5 and 9.

[3] *Confessions* i, 13, 20–21.

[4] At times Augustine resorts to quotations from one pagan poet to support his criticisms of another, e.g. in *The City of God* i, 3 he quotes Horace, *Epistles* i, 2, 69, 'the new wine jar will long preserve its first tang' in support of the harmful and lasting influence of certain passages from Vergil on the young mind. *Infra*, pp. 293–4.

shows that he is well acquainted with the works of the classical poets and prose authors and that his conscience is not really troubled in this regard. He is convinced that, while secular learning contains a number of 'idle vanities', nevertheless it also contains elements that are of use and value to the Christian in his search for truth.

In the second book of *Christian Education*, St. Augustine examines the secular liberal arts curriculum to discover those elements in it, which could safely be incorporated in the Christian curriculum. In the first place, he cites scriptural authority in support of the view that the Christian should use what is valuable, whatever its source. For instance, he finds in Exodus that, by the express command of God, the Israelites on their departure from Egypt 'spoiled the Egyptians', taking with them 'jewels of silver and jewels of gold and raiment', which they had borrowed from the Egyptians.[1] The apparent immorality of such expropriation of the property of others suggests an allegorical meaning, and the passage is interpreted as a command to the Christian to help himself to what is valuable from the storehouses of pagan culture. This interpretation is, as Augustine maintains, further justified by the suggestion in the Acts of the Apostles that the outstanding success of Moses in leading the chosen people out of Egypt was due to the fact that he was 'learned in all the wisdom of the Egyptians and mighty in words and deeds'.[2] Augustine supports the point by citing examples of earlier Christian teachers who had followed Moses' example:

> We can see what a great load of gold and silver Cyprian, that most persuasive teacher and blessed martyr, brought with him from Egypt. And so also it was with Lactantius, Victorinus and Optatus.[3]

The episode of the Israelites coming up out of Egypt is cited again in the *Confessions*,[4] where Augustine remarks on the

[1] *Exodus* 3, 22 and 12, 35–6. *Christian Education* ii, 60. The analogy is also used by Origen, *Letter to Gregory*, Migne, *Patrilogia Graeca* ii, 87–9.

[2] *Acts* 7, 22.

[3] *Christian Education* ii, 61.

[4] *Confessions* vii, 9, 15.

danger that the valuable elements of the pagan culture may be turned to the service of pagan objectives instead of to the worship of the one true God. Granted, however, that the core of the Christian curriculum remains the study of the Scriptures, there is little danger of such a perversion of use.

While, therefore, the Christian must not allow himself to be turned aside by 'the false and superstitious fancies' of secular culture, he must recognise the essential truth of what is found in the best of pre-Christian literature and thought. For example, by the penetrating power of their intellectual vision, Plato, and others like him, gained some genuine insight into the nature of reality. Since God's providence was displayed in the universe before the period of Christian revelation, it was open to Plato to read and interpret the signs, or, as Augustine puts it, 'to dig truth out of the mines of God's providence, which is scattered about everywhere'.[1] It is because Plato was so successful in this effort that Augustine describes him as 'almost a Christian'.

The acknowledgement that God had not denied all knowledge of his nature to pre-Christian thinkers, that Christian literature did not enjoy a monopoly of truth, was a liberating force in Christian education. To concede these views was to make possible the further enlightenment of the pagan world through the pooling of its own culture with Christian revelation. St. Augustine's educational theory, as we have already discovered it in his earlier writings, is hostile to the assumption that the teacher has exclusive, or absolute, possession of the truth. Learning occurs by the learner's effort in adding to the understandings, which he already possesses; similarly the teacher must always be adding to his existing knowledge, which can never be complete, and he is helped to do this by the insights he receives from his pupils' reactions to his teaching. Thus in *Christian Education* St. Augustine insists that, if the Christian teacher is to enter into effective communication with the non-Christian, both must initially share in a body of common understandings. Therefore, the Christian curriculum must cultivate the skills of communication:

For the sake of the necessary things of this life we must not

[1] *Christian Education* ii, 60.

neglect those human institutions which enable us to carry on intercourse with people around us.[1]

As an outstanding example of the 'pure gold' to be found in pre-Christian thought, St. Augustine cites the Platonic exposition of the idea of immaterial existence, and takes the opportunity to refute the slander, spread by some of Plato's admirers, to the effect that Christ must have learned everything from Plato. Although in *Christian Education* Augustine gives his assent to the equally untenable opinion that Plato came under the influence of the writings of Jeremiah in consequence of a visit, which Plato was supposed to have made to Egypt at the time Jeremiah was there, he later refuted this view, showing that Plato had been born about a century after the time when Jeremiah prophesied.[2] In fact St. Augustine consistently expresses the view that classical philosophy and Christian revelation are two separate streams, which must now be allowed to mingle together to swell the irresistible flow of the one river of God's truth.

In this respect St. Augustine's views were not in advance of those of other liberal Christian thinkers. However, he made two original contributions, both of which harmonise with his general theory of education. The *first* has already been noticed: Augustine recognises that teaching is founded on intercommunication between teacher and taught. Therefore, he insists that an important reason for the Christian assimilating as much as he can of the secular culture is so that he can effectively propagate the faith. A holy ignorance of pagan learning would effectively close the door on any communication with pagans, and in particular with educated pagans. The *second* respect, in which St. Augustine supplements the views of other Christian thinkers, is as follows: He advocates that pagan learning should

[1] *ibid.* ii, 58.

[2] *ibid.* ii, 43. The refutation occurs in *The City of God* viii, 9, and in *Reviews* ii, 2. In *The City of God* Augustine also notes that about seventy years must have elapsed between Plato's death and the translation of the Old Testament into Greek in the Septuagint version; thus Plato could not even have read Jeremiah. Plato died in 347 B.C.; the oldest part of the Septuagint, namely the Pentateuch, dates from the early third century, B.C., and was probably completed by 200 B.C. See C. B. Bigg, *The Christian Platonists of Alexandria*, p. 28, n. 1.

be integrated with religious studies in a curriculum recognisably Christian in its direction; in this way he points to the idea of the Christian school. Even in the writings of the cultivated Basil or Jerome we are still in the presence of an obvious educational dichotomy. They speak, now as a secular *grammaticus*, and now as a Christian teacher; the two aspects of their nature are still imperfectly fused. The tension engendered by Jerome's uneasily divided loyalty to Cicero and to Christ was dramatically expressed in his famous dream, in which his Christian alter ego points an accusing finger at his Ciceronianism.[1] Marrou rightly says of Basil, whose writing is so liberal in its attitude to secular culture, that he still did not envisage 'an education specifically Christian, but only a Christian use of the traditional education'.[2] Until the rise of the monastic schools, Christian parents in general sent their children to the secular schools, supplementing their liberal education with religious instruction at home. The edict of Julian (A.D. 362), forbidding Christians to teach in schools, shows the extent to which Christian teachers were actually employed in these schools. Not all Christians, in the manner of Augustine on his conversion, abandoned their teaching appointments in the secular schools; at the time of the edict the two most highly reputed chairs of rhetoric were in fact occupied by Christians—Prohaeristius at Athens and Victorinus at Rome.[3]

In any analysis of the relationship of erudition and piety in the more liberal Christian teachers prior to Augustine, mention must be made of the integrated curriculum taught in the Catechetical schools, particularly at Alexandria. Clement's 'one river of truth' was adequately translated into teaching terms in the Christian school of higher education, over which he and his successor, Origen, presided with such distinction.[4] But the Catechetical schools touched only the fringe of the problem of Christian education. They affected only a few enthusiastic

[1] Jerome, *Epistle* 22, 13. Being brought before the judgement seat and asked what was his profession, he answered, 'I am a Christian', to which came the dreadful reply, 'Thou liest. Thou art no Christian but a Ciceronian. Where thy treasure is, there is thy heart also'.

[2] H. I. Marrou, *op. cit.*, p. 396. Also John-Baptist Reeves, *St. Augustine and Humanism, in Monument to St. Augustine*, p. 134.

[3] Marrou, *loc. cit.*, n. 4.

[4] Clement of Alexandria, A.D. 160–215. Origen, A.D. 185–254.

scholars at the tertiary stage, and were built upon an existing foundation of primary and secondary studies, obtained in the secular schools of the Empire and not in specifically Christian schools.

Thus in all the predecessors of Augustine there was a failure to understand that the circumstances of the time required the provision of Christian schools, in which from their earliest years Christian boys and girls should be exposed to a curriculum fusing the best of the liberal secular culture with Christian thought and revelation so as to lay the foundation of a new and distinctively Christian culture. Such a curriculum would represent a harmonious synthesis of the old and the new.

The real issue, which seems to our eyes to have been studiously avoided, was complicated by the genuine respect, felt both by Christian and pagan, for the liberal arts curriculum, which, having such a weight of tradition and authority behind it, was not to be lightly modified or reorientated to the demands of a new age. An analogous situation in modern times lay in unquestioning acceptance of the assumption that a curriculum concentrated on Latin and Greek language and literature represented the only path of true education, an assumption which was maintained long after the circumstances originally justifying it had passed away.

CRITERIA FOR THE SELECTION OF CURRICULUM CONTENT

In the second half of the second book of *Christian Education* Augustine critically reviews the secular curriculum with a view to selecting from it 'what is of use for the understanding of Holy Scripture'.[1] He expresses the view that the Christian should not spend his strength on the accumulation of vast funds of knowledge, when he is likely to use only certain elements of it. Undoubtedly in places St. Augustine gives the impression that he is too narrowly restricting the range of curriculum content for the Christian student. But in fact the general trend of his argument is that the Christian should be well informed in all the important branches of learning. We may see him as protesting against the mere accumulation of knowledge as an educational aim and stressing the aimlessness of curricula that

[1] *Christian Education* ii, 28.

are overcrowded and poorly integrated. St. Augustine is aware that there is much to learn, and from this he rightly concludes that curriculum content must be carefully scrutinised so that less essential elements may be rejected. His awareness of the need for economy in curriculum construction is shown, for example, by his repudiation of the formal study of rhetoric as a dominant element in the preparatory education of the Christian teacher. His equal appreciation of the need to give full attention to essential subjects is shown in his attitude to the science of dialectic (logical reasoning). Mastery of this science is basic to the successful interpretation of the Scriptures since 'it runs like a system of nerves through the whole structure'.[1]

In his analysis of the field of secular knowledge, Augustine makes certain distinctions, which give direction to the Christian curriculum planner, as for example between scientific knowledge and superstitious information and practices, among which he includes the worship of idols, astrological lore and such homely practices as the following:

> (for example) to go to bed if anyone should sneeze when you are putting on your slippers; to return home if you stumble when going somewhere; when your clothes are eaten by mice, to be more frightened at the prospect of coming misfortune than grieved by your present loss. Hence Cato's witty reply to a man who told him that mice had eaten his boots—'This is no portent; if on the other hand the boots had eaten the mice, that would indeed have boded no good'.[2]

The Christian student must gain an acquaintance with the heritage of the past as well as the institutions, which serve man's needs in the present. Among the latter St. Augustine makes a distinction between those that are 'superfluous' or 'luxurious' and those which are 'convenient and necessary'.[3] By superfluous human institutions, he means the fine arts—'pictures, statues and other works of this kind', including theatrical performances, dancing and story-telling. His rejection of the fine arts as necessary elements in the Christian curriculum is out of

[1] *ibid.* ii, 59. On the basic importance of logic in all liberal study see *supra*, pp. 114–15.
[2] *ibid.* ii, 31.
[3] *ibid.* ii, 38.

harmony with our modern appreciation of the need to educate the emotions as well as the intellect. But it should be noted that the exclusion does not entirely arise from an asceticism fearful of the seductive effects of the feelings; Augustine merely regards them as secondary to the main preoccupation of man, which is the pursuit of wisdom with the aid of the rational intelligence. Under the heading of convenient and necessary human institutions, Augustine mentions the arts of reading and writing, including the knowledge of shorthand, the important foreign languages, weights and measures, the coins in use among various peoples, distinctions of dress and ornament and so on. All such knowledge is useful, and there is, therefore, nothing wrong in seeking it, provided that the Christian remembers that it is of secondary importance compared with the study of the Scriptures.

The heritage of the past consists of the sciences and the arts, which are the fruits of careful investigations into the things that God created in the beginning. In this category Augustine includes history, natural science, the practical arts and the liberal arts of dialectic, rhetoric and number. Each of these subjects is admitted to the Christian curriculum, primarily for the contribution it can make to the elucidation of the Scriptures. For example, the knowledge of chronology, derived from the study of history, enables the Christian not only to clarify points of Scripture, which would otherwise remain obscure, but also to counter the fallacious arguments of unbelievers. With this knowledge the Christian can show that it is more likely that Plato should have been influenced by Jeremiah than that Christ should have been influenced by Plato, since Plato was nearer in time to Jeremiah than Christ was to Plato. Ignorance of the modes of reckoning time in the Greek manner by Olympiads, or in the Roman manner by consulships, has led to wrong conclusions as to the age of our Lord at the time of his death, and so on.

By Natural Science Augustine means Geography, Zoology, Botany, what we should call Geology or Mineralogy, and Astronomy:

> . . . all that has been written about the location of places and the nature of animals, trees, herbs, stones and other bodies.[1]

[1] *ibid.* ii, 45.

In relation to the natural sciences, St. Augustine again points to the danger of pseudo-scientific knowledge or superstitious lore becoming intermingled with observed fact. Scientific studies must be carefully limited, as he puts it, to the description of what has been instituted in the past by God, and must not be used, as the soothsayer does, in a vain attempt to determine what will be, or ought to be. The use of charms, for instance, in an attempt to affect the course of natural happenings, whether in medicine or agriculture, cannot be supported on the evidence of past observation. Augustine's awareness of the perversion of scientific truth in the service of superstition emerges most strongly in his evaluation of astronomy: The stars are no exception to the general rule that all creation moves according to the divine principle of order, but the study has become so entangled with superstitious lore that it is difficult for the student to approach it in an unprejudiced way. Inasmuch as astronomy is a science, it clearly enables man to predict the future movements of the heavenly bodies by inference from their past movements. But this well-founded scientific prediction is quite different from the astrologer's claim that a connection exists between the movements of stars and human destinies. Because of the dangers inherent in this unscientific lore St. Augustine feels that astrology is best left alone.

As to the practical arts, St. Augustine divides them into three categories:

1. Those which aim at the production of some physical object, such as a house, a bench or a dish: 'Something is made, which remains as the result of his work when the effort of the workman is over'.
2. Those in which 'man assists God in His operations', e.g. medicine, agriculture and navigation.
3. The arts of physical expression, e.g. dancing, racing and wrestling.[1]

Of all these Augustine remarks that the Christian student needs only a superficial knowledge. The purpose of studying them at all is not so that the Christian may practise them, but

[1] *ibid.* ii, 47.

so that 'he may not be wholly ignorant of what the Scripture means to convey, when it employs figures of speech derived from these arts'.[1]

From this outline of the content of the Christian curriculum, as St. Augustine sees it, it will be understood that he puts the study of the Scriptures, and the preparation of the Christian teacher to teach the Scriptures, at the centre of the curriculum and deploys other studies around this focal point. He holds that the liberal education of a Christian must draw its content from areas of the secular culture, including the study of human institutions and the physical sciences. However, the criterion he employs in making his selection of curriculum content is the extent to which the peripheral studies are likely to assist the Christian student in furthering the one purpose of his education, namely the understanding and teaching of the word of God.

Thus St. Augustine postulates a curriculum, which has an over-all unity and one clearly defined purpose. The study of the Scriptures is not merely one among a number of subjects of study; it is the central subject, which draws from the peripheral subjects the resources they can provide to guide the Christian along the pathway of self-education towards an understanding of spiritual reality.

It is interesting to compare St. Augustine's unified conception of the curriculum with later attempts to define what in modern times has been called by the Herbartians[2] 'the core of concentration'. St. Augustine's curriculum is diagramatically represented below in terms of a core of concentration and peripheral studies: (see diagram on next page.)

With this we may compare the core of concentration and subordinate studies as determined by Tuiskon Ziller, one of the German Herbartians, who proposed a core of Cultural Studies, consisting of a combination of history and literature:[3]

[1] *ibid.*

[2] The followers of the German educator, J. F. Herbart (1776–1841), whose description of learning in terms of apperception, or the unification of knowledge, stimulated attempts to structure the curriculum as an organic whole instead of an agglomeration of separate elements. *Supra*, p. 148.

[3] For Ziller's conception of the core of concentration see C. A. McMurry, *Elements of General Method*, 1892.

CORE OF CONCENTRATION ACCORDING TO ST. AUGUSTINE

(*Christian Education* ii, 40–58)

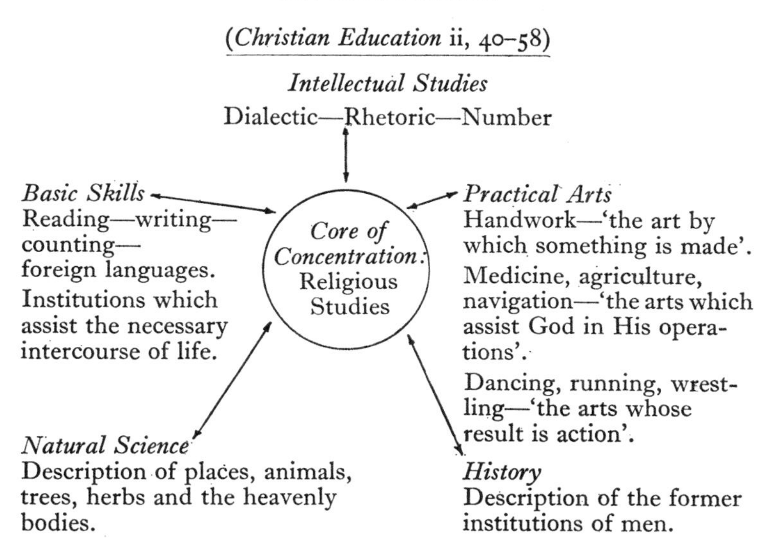

CORE OF CONCENTRATION ACCORDING TO ZILLER

(see De Garmo, *Herbart and the Herbartians*, ch. 4, pp. 113–23)

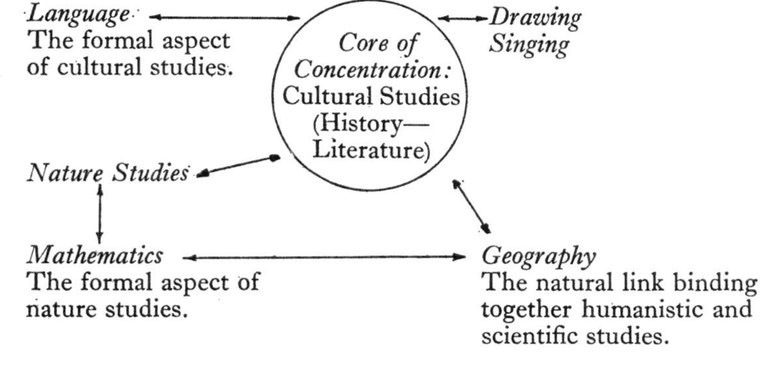

In both cases the peripheral studies are selected mainly for the contribution they make to the development of the core study. But they are also chosen for the extent to which they facilitate human communication and contribute to man's knowledge of the world he lives in. Hence in St. Augustine's curriculum the group of subjects headed Basic Skills have a clear application in scriptural study, but they also 'assist the necessary intercourse of life'. Dialectic and rhetoric are important to the Christian teacher in the propagation of religious truth; at the same time, they are justified for their general value in promoting human communication and understanding. So also the practical arts have their obvious utility, while at the same time an acquaintance with their principles and terminology enables the student to make sense of scriptural references to these arts. In this way each subject of study has its own importance and is developed according to its inner logic, while at the same time through the contribution it makes to the central core it plays its part in a unified course of study.[1]

St. Augustine's notion that the curriculum should be centred on the study of religious truth has been embedded in the philosophy of church schools throughout the centuries. But, whether it is argued that religious study, or some other subject or combination of subjects, should be the focal point of the curriculum, St. Augustine's theory of curriculum construction has a contribution to make in support of contemporary attempts to heal the fragmented condition of the curriculum of secondary education in particular, and to bring about a greater degree of integration of studies through what has come to be known as the core curriculum.

THE LIBERAL ARTS IN THE CHRISTIAN CURRICULUM

St. Augustine concludes his discussion of the content of the Christian curriculum with a reference to the liberal arts, which he regards as of basic educational significance. This is because they are founded on first principles, which were not created by man or established by convention, but are the product of the divine fiat. Thus the liberal arts justify their place in the Christian curriculum, only if they are used to lead the student from a preoccupation with particulars to an intellectual understanding of general principles.[2] This purpose of opening the learner's eyes to the reality of immaterial truth expresses the only objective of Christian education, as St. Augustine sees it.

[1] See *The Principle of Order* ii, 44: 'All the liberal studies are learned partly for practical use and partly for the understanding and contemplation of reality'.

[2] *Reviews* i, 6. Also *On Music* vi, 1.

The liberal arts assist this supreme educational purpose in a unique way because of the clear insights they yield into the thoughts of God, if they are taught in such a way as to liberate the intelligence. If, however, the teaching is narrowly utilitarian, the results will be unimpressive, as when the art of logic resolves itself into 'a love of wrangling and the childish vanity of trapping an adversary'.[1]

In his references to dialectic and rhetoric St. Augustine continually recalls that the purpose of education is the pursuit of truth, and warns that the pedantic adherence to rules and the mechanical application of techniques learned in the professional schools may result in a situation in which technical mastery may be regarded as more important than truth. In other words, the liberal arts are means, not ends; in Augustine's terminology they are properly to be classed among the things that are 'for use', rather than among the things that are 'for enjoyment'. The liberal arts are to be used as instrumental to the end that truth may be enjoyed. Thus the Christian student and teacher must beware of the idle vanity resulting from the clever manipulation of the techniques of the dialectician and rhetorician. As Augustine argues in *The Teacher*, the purpose of teaching and learning is not so that the teacher may have the opportunity to display his powers of speech, but that the learner may be stimulated to learn. Thus the Christian teacher will not confuse means with end; he will study the liberal arts in a spirit of humility, since they are powerful aids to lead him beyond his own self-glorification to an understanding of unchanging truth.

St. Augustine's own professional practice of the art of rhetoric had made him well aware both of its value as an instrument of instruction and of the dangers inherent in its misuse for the purposes of indoctrination. Remembering that all learning is brought about by the voluntary involvement of the learner in a labour of love, he sees the Christian teacher's task in terms of persuasion rather than of coercion. For this reason, Augustine maintains that the teacher must be 'eloquent' in the sense in which the word was employed by the best of Greek and Roman teachers. Thus in the last book of *Christian Education* Augustine devotes attention to the techniques of expressing thought with incision and yet with grace and pro-

[1] *Christian Education* ii, 48.

priety. However, his view of teaching as founded on the close personal relationship of teacher and taught leads him at the outset to deny that a teacher's eloquence is reducible to exact rules. Therefore, he warns the reader not to expect from him just another handbook of rhetoric. The aim of the teacher, and particularly of the Christian teacher, is to lead his pupils to an understanding of truth, which is quite different from the purpose of professional orators, whose business is primarily to charm their audience by the sound of their words and to arouse emotion rather than thought. The eloquence of the teacher must be set in a more significant frame of reference, and is therefore a more demanding accomplishment. In the first place, it is wrong to suppose that eloquence is displayed only in words; it speaks through the example of the teacher's life, through the graciousness of his personality and intellectual integrity, all of which exert a strong influence on the minds of his pupils. Therefore, however eloquent a teacher may be, 'his life has the greater influence in ensuring that his audience is receptive to his words':

> There is no shortage of those who base a defence of their own wicked lives on the behaviour of those who are set over them, and who are their teachers. Such people say in their hearts, or even go further and say with their lips, 'Why do you not practise what you teach?' The result is that they are not receptive to the teacher's words, because he does not listen to them himself, and, as they despise the teacher, so they also despise what he teaches them.[1]

Therefore, Augustine sets a higher value on the teacher's integrity of character than on his mastery of the techniques of instruction. He argues that the Christian teacher will speak with a simple and persuasive eloquence, merely because he is talking about what is for him of real and priceless value. His exposition must necessarily be eloquent, because his thought is controlling his words and not vice versa:

> . . . he thinks that a thing is well said in proportion as it is true in fact and that a teacher should govern his words and not let the words govern him.[2]

[1] *ibid.* iv, 60.
[2] *ibid.* iv, 61.

Thus St. Augustine holds that content and method are two intimately associated aspects of teaching. What precisely is taught is determined not only by the words which the teacher employs, but by his traits of personality and general attitudes to life and to knowledge; by these he either reinforces or weakens, emphasises or distorts, the effects of his words. Therefore, Augustine maintains that eloquence, in the proper sense of the word, cannot exist in isolation from goodness and truth. The essential integrity of the Christian teacher, arising from his firm grasp of truth, endows him with a natural eloquence. Hence true eloquence, as contrasted with the sophisticated rhetoric of the secular orator, is capable of a simple definition:

> To speak eloquently and also wisely is simply to bring words to bear on truths, which ought to be listened to.[1]

Here Augustine is echoing the sentiments of such masters of eloquence as Cicero and Quintilian, both of whom deny the terms 'orator' and 'eloquence' to those whose words are not strongly reinforced by substance, and in whom the gift of speech (*oratio*) is not supplemented by rational argument (*ratio*).[2] The manner of living of the good and wise teacher is 'an eloquent sermon in itself'; on the other hand, the rogue who 'abounds in eloquent nonsense' charms his pupils with what is not worth listening to and may win their unthinking acquiescence for what is false. Such teaching is socially dangerous, a fact in support of which Augustine quotes the words of Cicero:

> Although wisdom without eloquence is of little service to states, yet eloquence without wisdom is frequently a positive injury and is never of service.[3]

Augustine recognises that the Christian teacher needs to have some training in the techniques of exposition, but this is to be done through the study of examples of good teaching rather than

[1] *ibid.*

[2] Quintilian, *The Education of an Orator* xii, 1, follows the elder Cato in his definition of an orator as 'a good man skilled in speaking' (*vir bonus dicendi peritus*).

[3] Cicero, *Concerning Rhetorical Invention* i, 1, quoted in *Christian Education* iv, 7. Augustine also quotes Cicero, *Orator* 21: 'Wisdom is the foundation of eloquence'.

by memorising rules.[1] Since there are people who eloquently expound falsehood, there must also be those who spring to the defence of truth with a confidence reinforced by training in the art of teaching. Truth cannot afford 'to take its stand unarmed against falsehood'.[2] Therefore, the art of rhetoric is not to be despised by the Christian teacher and student because of the immoral uses to which it is often put. In itself rhetoric is amoral, and may be utilised with equal effect to press the claims of truth and falsehood. As evil men realise the influence of rhetoric in the cause of falsehood, so teachers must realise that the art of speech is a force in support of truth, which will not win if it has to overcome the handicap of a teacher who is 'sluggish, frigid and sleepy'.[3]

Thus St. Augustine believes in the cultivation of Christian eloquence, while also, as we have noted, minimising the need for formal instruction in rhetoric as a basic requirement in the education of the Christian teacher. In this respect he makes a radical change of emphasis, relegating to a relatively subordinate place a discipline, which in the view of his time was an essential element in general culture and the climax of Roman schooling. In this respect Marrou notes Augustine's modernity,[4] in that he puts his trust in native ability, enthusiasm and the natural strength and eloquence of truth rather than in rules of method. In the mind of the teacher content must be the prime consideration, while methods of presentation must remain supplementary. Thus Augustine declares that it is not enough to analyse intellectually the stylistic characteristics of a great teacher in order to appreciate his real worth. In his opinion the power of a teacher is something to be felt rather than dissected, and so to be freely and imaginatively imitated rather than slavishly copied. 'To describe its beauty and show how it inspires the intelligent reader—this is impossible to communicate to anyone who does not himself feel it', says St. Augustine,

[1] *Christian Education* iv, 1: 'If a man wants to speak not only with wisdom but with eloquence also, I would send him to read and listen to eloquent men and give him practice in imitating them rather than advise him to spend his time with the teachers of rhetoric'.

[2] *Christian Education* iv, 3.

[3] *ibid.*

[4] H. I. Marrou, *op. cit.*, pp. 516–17.

in analysing a passage of simple eloquence from the Prophet Amos. And again of the same passage:

> An intelligent reader is instructed more by reading it with feeling than by subjecting it to careful analysis.[1]

This emphasis on sensitivity as well as on intellectual analysis is characteristic of Augustine's view of teaching and learning. He sees that the art of the teacher is not capable of exact definition or scientific measurement, because it necessarily involves a meeting of minds, and is, therefore, a spiritual function. So the virtue of a teacher lies not primarily in his words but in the thoughts, of which his words are merely symbolic. As the creative act is not confined by rules but makes its own rules, so the style of the teacher is not something superimposed or engrafted on his thought and personality; his style, or method, is the natural and unselfconscious expression of thought by an individual personality. So it follows that:

> The rules, which are laid down in the art of oratory, could not have been observed, noted down and reduced to system, if they had not first had their birth in the genius of orators.[2]

To Augustine, of course, the Christian teacher is the teacher *par excellence*, since his teaching is most closely aligned with truth. Therefore, by maintaining that the Christian teacher is not to be bound by exact rules of method, Augustine is saying that the act of teaching in its highest reaches is an act of spiritual intercommunication and creative power analogous to the original work of the Creator Himself. As we saw in our discussion of *The Art of the Teacher*, both the external teacher (i.e. man and the internal teacher (i.e. God) merely stimulate the learner to discover knowledge for himself, but cannot, or do not, force it into him.[3] Thus in the last resort good teaching depends more upon art than technique, which is why, as Augustine says in *Christian Education*, he refused to write a text book of rhetoric. He is addressing himself to the Christian teacher, who will not seek to win general applause for his public performances, but who will simply teach. Thus he rejects the pretensions of the

[1] *Christian Education* iv, 21.
[2] *ibid.*
[3] *supra*, pp. 194–6.

rhetorical schools, in which he himself once practised with such conspicuous success.[1] It is enough that the Christian teacher should have the inborn ability to teach and be guided by the advice of one who has himself practised with success. By so doing, he will avoid many pitfalls, while the truth, which he has to expound, will lead him by its inner dynamism to the most effective means of expression.

The tendency of all the advice given by St. Augustine on rhetoric is to caution the Christian teacher against over-concentration on the stylistic mannerisms characteristic of the Roman cultural decadence, in which, as M. L. Clarke says, 'The cultivation of the art of words for its own sake was apt to lead to neglect of words as a means of conveying meaning'.[2] With particular reference to the art of teaching, St. Augustine's chapters in *Christian Education* on 'the means of communicating what has been understood' stress the special temptations and dangers to which teachers and teachers of teachers are exposed. Frequently their instruction remains on the merely verbal level, and thus fails to inspire the learner with significant purposes. St. Augustine's repeated warnings to the Christian teacher to beware of verbalism recall Quintilian's criticism of people who feel it impossible to write elegantly, except on the condition that what is written requires an interpreter.[3]

SUMMARY AND EVALUATION

In evaluating St. Augustine's *Christian Education*, we must take into account the purpose it was designed to fulfil. It was an attempt to define in general terms the course of preparatory studies for the Christian teacher. It came into being in response to the urgent need for well-educated Christians, who would be capable of entering into effective discussion with the cultured pagans; therefore, it is not primarily directed to the problems of Christian education in schools. The shortage of Christian

[1] *Christian Education* iv, 14: 'All these things, when taught by teachers, are reckoned of great value. Large prices are paid for them and they are put up for sale with great advertisement (*magna iactatione venduntur*)'.

[2] M. L. Clarke, *Rhetoric at Rome*, p. 159.

[3] Quintilian, *op. cit.* viii, 2, 21.

teachers in the province of North Africa and elsewhere required the provision of a handbook, which would give guidance to the mature adult, whether lay or cleric, when he spoke for the faith. St. Augustine's work is, therefore, specifically directed to those who have the time and the opportunity to acquire only some general instruction in the difficult problems involved in Christian teaching. It is meant to meet a particular emergency rather than to supply a blue-print for a comprehensive and graduated curriculum of Christian education from childhood to maturity.

Thus the value of *Christian Education* consists rather in the general principles it suggests than in the detailed recommendations it makes on the Christian curriculum and Christian schools. Circumstances had not laid upon Augustine, as they had on Jerome, the responsibility for the education of some Christian children, or for the planning of a curriculum for a particular Christian school.[1] The course of preparatory education suggested by St. Augustine closely resembles the time-hallowed curriculum of the Roman grammar schools. But there is the difference that the two traditional aspects of grammar, namely 'the knowledge of correct speech' (*recte loquendi scientia*) and 'the explanation of the authors' (*poetarum enarratio*) are based on the study of scriptural, as well as of secular, texts. In this way Augustine suggests by implication a Christian grammar school, in which the best of classical thought is fused with Christian doctrine to produce a liberally educated Christian. Like Quintilian's orator, such a man will be able to play an influential part in the world of men, because he has at his command the faculty of reason (*ratio*) as well as the faculty of speech (*oratio*) and supplements a good supply of words (*copia verborum*) with an equally abundant supply of true ideas (*copia rerum*).[2]

Therefore, although in *Christian Education* St. Augustine gives a definitive statement of the ideal of Christian education and scholarship, there is substance in Marrou's criticism that

[1] In *Epistles* 107 and 128, Jerome sets out a curriculum for two girls, Paula and Pactula. In *Against Rufinus* ii, 8, he describes the curriculum followed by boys who were taught in the monastery he established at Bethlehem.

[2] Cicero, *De Oratore* 3, 31, 125: '*Rerum copia verborum copiam gignit*'.

Augustine neglects the institutional aspect of the problem of Christian culture.[1] No doubt this is because he became immersed in the administration of an important and restless see, where his energies were increasingly diverted by the time-consuming necessity to defend the faith against the assaults of heresy. Augustine had, therefore, perforce to leave the problems of the Christian school to be solved in a later age.

The Christian school grew slowly and painfully out of the relentless pressure of events. The increasing paralysis of secular culture under the barbarian invasions compelled the monastic institutions, which owed a good deal to the inspiration of Augustine's seminaries at Tagaste and Hippo, to make their own provision for the educational needs of a darkened world. In a few large centres in the East, from as early as the second half of the second century, catechetical schools dedicated to higher studies had come into being. But neither East nor West was quick to evolve Christian elementary and secondary schools. A hundred years after the publication of Augustine's *Christian Education* there were probably still no Christian schools in Africa.[2] An abortive attempt by Cassiodorus at Rome about A.D. 534 to set up such a school in imitation of the catechetical schools at Nisibis and Alexandria was followed by the short-lived monastic school of Cassiodorus at Vivarium in Calabria. For the first permanent schools of Christian learning in the West we must, therefore, look further still, to the monasteries of the seventh century in Ireland and the Bishops' schools, which sprang up in consequence of the mission to England of the monk, Augustine, sent by Gregory the Great in A.D. 597.[3]

In conclusion, the main reason for the importance and influence of St. Augustine's *Christian Education* lies in its declaration of the essential worth of the best of pre-Christian thought. His statement that 'every good and true Christian should understand that, wherever he may find truth, it is his Lord's' has deserved its reputation as 'the watchword of

[1] H. I. Marrou, *op. cit.*, p. 400.

[2] H. I. Marrou, *op. cit.*, p. 401.

[3] P. de Labriolle, *History and Literature of Christianity from Tertullian to Boethius*, p. 506 ff. W. Boyd, *History of Western Education*, 6th ed., 1952, pp. 107–13.

Christian humanism'.[1] St. Augustine firmly declared that revelation had given a clearer sense of direction to the Christian student, but had not absolved him from engaging in the labour of learning. For the Christian, as for the non-Christian, concentration of purpose and a well-trained judgement are the necessary conditions of all learning, and these can come in their fullest measure only after long effort. But to the adult Christian, whose education was neglected in his youth, St. Augustine gives a word of hope. Sincerity, strength of mind and a natural aptitude for learning and teaching may compensate for the lack of formal education. At any rate, the Christian's efforts must not be paralysed by this lack; he is to move forward confidently upon the journey of his self-education in preparation for the task which lies before him, drawing upon all available resources, both Christian and secular, which may help him on the way.

[1] D. W. Robertson, translator's introduction, p. xiii, *Christian Education* ii, 28.

8 The Developing Concept of the Liberal Arts

Study of the liberal arts, provided of course that it is moderate and kept within bounds, makes its students more alert, more persevering and better equipped to embrace truth. The result is that they desire truth more enthusiastically, pursue it with greater constancy and in the end rest in it more satisfyingly. This, Licentius, is what I call the happy life.

The Principle of Order i, 24.

Standing out from the dead level of mediocrity associated with the Roman cultural decadence, St. Augustine exercised a considerable influence on the development of the medieval curriculum of the liberal arts. An assessment of his contribution to the practice of education must include an appraisal of his work in refining and transmitting to the future the conception of a curriculum of general education preparatory to higher professional study and founded on the study of the liberal arts.

ORIGINS OF THE ENCYCLOPEDIA

The concept of the 'encyclopedia', or 'circle' of liberal studies appropriate to the general education of a free man, emerged in Greek educational theory and was given greater precision by the Romans. Plato's elementary curriculum was founded on the traditional branches of gymnastic and music, while his curriculum for the higher education of his Guardians included arithmetic, geometry and astronomy, harmonics (the theory of music) and the beginnings of dialectic.[1] Our knowledge of Aristotle's curriculum is incomplete, but it is probable that it closely followed Plato's, except that Aristotle may have given stronger emphasis to natural science over mathematical studies.

[1] Plato, *Republic* ii, 376; iii, 403 and vii, 521–36.

The practical bias of the Roman character at first resisted the supposedly softening influence of Greek liberal study. The curriculum devised by Cato the Censor to counteract the Greek influence, of which he strongly disapproved, included ethics, rhetoric, medicine, military science, husbandry and law, a catalogue which includes only one subject from the Greek liberal curriculum, i.e. rhetoric, which appealed to the Roman mind on grounds of its practical utility. However, the advancing tide of Greek culture could not be held back by such as Cato; thus at the beginning of the last century of the pre-Christian era we have Marcus Terentius Varro's lost work, *The Nine Books of Disciplines*, in which there is strong evidence to suggest that he dealt with the subjects of the Greek liberal curriculum with the addition of medicine and architecture.[1]

Cicero, a contemporary of Varro, made a distinction between preparatory education (*puerilis institutio*) and higher education (*politior humanitas*), and sub-divided preparatory education into two areas: the arts of communication, i.e. grammar, rhetoric and dialectic, and the theoretical disciplines of arithmetic, geometry, astronomy and music.[2] A century later Quintilian added history, law and philosophy to Cicero's list of the seven arts, and described this course as the 'encyclopedia' (ἐγκύκλιος παιδεία).[3] Other lists of the liberal arts from the late Republic and early Empire show differences of detail as well as a tendency to add to the original Greek circle of disciplines. For example, Marius Victorinus, the orator, whose translations of the Platonic books were studied by St. Augustine, mentions grammar, poetic and rhetoric, music, astronomy, law and philosophy.[4]

Therefore, in the first three centuries of the Christian era the number of the liberal arts was not yet crystallised as seven either in the Latin world of the West or in the Hellenistic East. Philo of Alexandria, who was contemporaneous with Christ,

[1] For evidence on the constituent elements in Varro's *Nine Books of Disciplines* see T. Davidson, *Aristotle and Ancient Educational Ideals*, p. 242; H. I. Marrou, *St. Augustin et la Fin de la Culture Antique*, p. 226, n. 4; H. Parker, *The Seven Liberal Arts*, in *English Historical Review*, vol. 5, 1890, pp. 417–61.

[2] Cicero i, 187; ii, 1; iii, 12. H. I. Marrou, *op. cit.*, p. 108, n. 5.

[3] Quintilian, *The Education of an Orator* i, 10, 1; x, 1, 31–4 (History); xii, 3 (Law); x, i, 35–6 (Philosophy).

[4] H. I. Marrou, *loc. cit.*

lists six arts—grammar, rhetoric, dialectic, arithmetic, geometry, music.[1] The younger Seneca enumerates five liberal studies (*liberalia studia*), namely grammar, music, geometry, arithmetic and astronomy. But he also speaks of medicine as a liberal art, and subdivides philosophy into rational, natural and moral; rational philosophy is further broken down into dialectic and rhetoric. Thus he classifies two of the liberal arts under the higher study of philosophy.[2] Among the Greeks, Sextus Empiricius in his treatise, *Contra Mathematicos*, repeats the list of Seneca, adding dialectic to the arts, and again dividing philosophy into the three branches of logic, physics and ethics.[3]

In the third century of the Christian era catalogues of the liberal arts, described as 'circles of studies' (*ἐγκύκλια μαθήματα*) or 'preparatory studies' (*προπαιδεύματα*) are given by Origen (A.D. 185–224), Porphyry (A.D. 233–*c*.301) and later by Lactantius (A.D. *c*.250–335). All mention grammar and rhetoric; Porphyry alone includes dialectic, but calls it philosophy. All three list geometry, music and astronomy, while Porphyry alone adds arithmetic. Therefore, only Porphyry mentions all of the seven arts of the medieval curriculum.[4] By the time of Martianus Capella, whose *Marriage of Philology and Mercury* was written probably in the fourth or early fifth century, the number seven seems to be more firmly established. Capella's work deals with the recognised catalogue of the seven liberal arts, excluding Varro's medicine and architecture, in spite of the fact that Capella acknowledges a debt to Varro, by whose 'learning and industry' he claims that he was 'assisted'.[5]

To sum up, from the last century of the Republic Roman schools were acquainted with the notion of 'liberal education' (*liberalis eruditio*), that is a curriculum which laid the groundwork for higher education. Yet there was no firm agreement as to the exact number of the arts. In general, liberal education carried on the tradition of an education worthy of a free man

[1] T. Davidson, *op. cit.*, p. 243.

[2] L. Annaeus Seneca, *Moral Epistles* 88, 3–14.

[3] H. I. Marrou, *op. cit.*, p. 216. T. Davidson, *op. cit.*, pp. 243–4.

[4] Porphyry, *Lives of the Philosophers*; Lactantius, *Divinae Institutiones* 3, 25 ff.

[5] Martianus Capella, *Marriage of Philology and Mercury* iv, quoted P. R. Cole, *Later Roman Education in Ausonius, Capella and the Theodosian Code*, p. 25.

(*eruditio libero digna*), maintaining the clear distinction, established by Plato, between the liberal or intellectual arts and the servile or mechanical arts.[1] In an examination of the content of liberal education the younger Seneca makes the point:

> I exclude from the liberal studies wrestlers and all the skill that is concerned with oil and dust. Otherwise I would be admitting perfumers, cooks and other people who apply their wits to our pleasures—None of these teach virtue.[2]

It should be noted that the conception of a 'circle of studies', as used for instance by Quintilian, did not signify a curriculum inclusive of all available knowledge. Rather it meant a 'well-rounded' course of study. The Greek metaphor of the wheel had reference rather to the shape, which was the most satisfying of shapes, than to the more modern notion of all-inclusiveness.[3] This carefully selected course of study was the birthright of the free man and the basis of knowledge necessary for the advance to higher study. Isocrates expresses this preparatory function in terms of 'an exercise of the soul and a preparation for philosophy', and this is echoed by Cicero in a fragment of his lost *Hortensius*, with which Augustine was familiar, and by the younger Seneca who asks:

> Why do we educate our sons in the liberal studies? These studies do not confer virtue, but they prepare the mind for the reception of virtue.[4]

AUGUSTINE'S CATALOGUES OF THE LIBERAL ARTS

Augustine's views on the composition of the curriculum of the liberal arts are derived from references more or less extended in five of his works:—*The Principle of Order*, *The Greatness of the*

[1] Plato, *Republic* vii, 522b and following.

[2] L. Annaeus Seneca, *Epistles* 88, 18.

[3] Marrou, *History of Education in Antiquity*, trans. Lamb, p. 406, n. 3 and *op. cit.*, pp. 228–9, finds no evidence until Byzantine Greek that the term 'ἐγκύκλιος' was used in the inclusive sense. Vitruvius i, 1, 7, strongly suggests the meaning 'well-rounded' when he talks of 'encyclic learning' (*encyclios disciplina*) as being like a single body composed of a number of limbs.

[4] Isocrates, *Antidosis* 266. Cicero, *Hortensius*, fragment 23.

Soul, the *Confessions*, *Christian Education* and the *Reviews*.

In *The Principle of Order* the reference to the liberal arts arises in the context of a discussion aimed at establishing the universality of the principle of order in the universe.[1] It is held that the liberal arts demonstrate in a very clear manner the existence of fundamental order in a universe, whose obvious imperfections and shifting standards might seem to the superficial observer to demonstrate the opposite conclusion. It follows that, if man is to perceive law and order in the world, he must expand his understanding according to what Augustine calls 'the right order of instruction' (*ordo eruditionis*). The correct sequence is discovered by following through the course of the enlargement of human understanding and experience in the course of history, a theory which has affinities with the modern recapitulatory theory of human development.[2] Thus St. Augustine catalogues the arts in the order in which they have appeared in the course of the development of the human race. He finds that, in the first place, there arose successively the three arts designed to facilitate man's communication with himself in thought and with his fellows in spoken and written language: grammar, dialectic and rhetoric. These were followed by music, geometry and astronomy, arising from human enquiry into the mathematical principles expressed in the harmonies of music, the proportions of beautiful shapes and the orderly movements of the stars in their courses.[3]

In *The Greatness of the Soul* St. Augustine describes the seven steps, which the individual soul must take in its educational progress from primitive beginnings to the source of divine wisdom. Again it is made clear that the development of the individual must run parallel to the development of the race. The earlier, primitive preoccupations with the basic physical pro-

[1] *The Principle of Order* ii, 35–48 and ii, 13–14.

[2] *ibid.* ii, 46. The development of Augustine's notion of a historical order of studies from a fragment of Cicero's *Hortensius* is noted by P. Alfaric, *L'Évolution Intellectuelle de St. Augustin*, p. 448, n. 2. See also Augustine, *Letter* 33, 2. Cultural epochs have been used to determine the presentation of curriculum content by the German Herbartians, such as T. Ziller and W. Rein. For Ziller's views, see C. De Garmo, *Herbart and the Herbartians*, ch. 3, on Ziller's Theory of the Historical Stages of Culture.

[3] *The Principle of Order* ii, 14.

cesses and the unsophisticated delight in sensual pleasures lead on to the level of 'art'.[1] At this stage man's accumulated experience results in the development of arts, crafts and the great diversity of social institutions. In the long catalogue of human achievements, recorded by St. Augustine at this point, the liberal arts appear functionally defined rather than named. Grammar in its liberal sense is introduced along with elements from the fine arts:

> The invention of so many signs in letters, words, and gestures, in sounds of all kinds, painting and statues, the languages of so many peoples, their many institutions, some new and some revived, so many books and records of every sort for the preservation of memory.

Mention of grammar is followed by reference to 'the power of reasoning and thinking' (dialectic), 'eloquence' (rhetoric), 'the discipline of counting' (arithmetic), 'the art of modulation' (music), 'the subtlety of measuring' (geometry) and 'conjecturing about the past and future from the present' (astrology).

In the *Confessions* reference to the liberal arts occurs in the fourth book, where St. Augustine recalls that at the age of twenty he read for himself 'all the books of what are called the liberal arts', to which he refers in the following terms:[2]

—the art of speaking (grammar and rhetoric)
—the art of discussion (dialectic)
—the dimensions of shapes (geometry)
—music
—numbers

In *Christian Education* the liberal arts are discussed at length, as we have noted in the previous chapter.[3] The necessity for the study of grammar by the Christian student and teacher is emphasised throughout, although the subject is rarely referred to by name. The more systematic discussion of the content of the Christian curriculum begins with history, natural science, the mechanical arts, and passes on to the liberal arts, defined as 'those which relate to the intellectual understanding'. This leads St. Augustine to discuss in succession dialectic, rhetoric

[1] *The Greatness of the Soul* 72. *Supra*, p. 136.
[2] *Confessions* iv, 30.
[3] *Christian Education* ii, 45–56; *supra*, p. 230 ff.

and the discipline of number. Music and geometry are indirectly referred to as practical applications of the laws of number:

> Whether numbers are considered in themselves or as applied to the laws of figures or sounds or other motions, they have fixed laws, which were not made by man but which the ingenuity of clever men has brought to light.[1]

In the *Reviews* Augustine states that, while living in Milan, he 'tried' to write treatises on the liberal arts, his aim being to show how through these the understanding might be led 'by a series of sure and certain steps' to a conception of spiritual existence.[2] In the same place he reports that he had completed six books on the art of music and a work on grammar, but that the latter had subsequently been lost; he adds that the same fate had overtaken the beginnings of the treatises he had intended to write on dialectic, rhetoric, geometry, arithmetic and philosophy.

Of these several catalogues of the liberal arts the most complete are those from *The Principle of Order*, *The Greatness of the Soul* and the *Reviews*. For purposes of comparison the lists derived from these works are set out as follows:

The Principle of Order	*The Greatness of the Soul*	*The Reviews*
Grammar	Grammar	Grammar
Dialectic	Dialectic	Dialectic
Rhetoric	Rhetoric	Rhetoric
—	Number	Arithmetic
Music	Music	Music
Geometry	Geometry	Geometry
Astrology	Astrology	—
Philosophy	—	Philosophy

[1] *ibid.* ii, 56.

[2] *Reviews* i, 6. In *Letter* 101, 3 Augustine states that he was interrupted in this project by 'the burden of ecclesiastical duties laid upon me'. The work *On Music* survives. The work *On Grammar*, included in Migne, *Patrilogia Latina*, vol. 32, pp. 1385–408, may not be authentic. By comparison with *On Music*, it is a pedestrian work; H. I. Marrou, *St. Augustin et la Fin de la Culture Antique*, pp. 570–76, surveying the evidence for the authenticity of the work, *On Grammar*, concludes that it is probably an abridgement of St. Augustine's original work to serve as a school text-book. This is supported by Cassiodorus' remark that in his time there existed an abridged work on grammar, whose author was Augustine. Cassiodorus, *Institutions* 2, 1.

In the first two of these catalogues St. Augustine presents the liberal arts in the sequence of the later medieval trivium and quadrivium. In his 'right order of studies' (*ordo eruditionis*) grammar, dialectic and rhetoric (the later trivium) precede and are in fact necessary preliminary steps to the discovery of music, geometry, arithmetic and astrology (the later quadrivium). In assessing the extent to which Augustine saw the arts in these two categories or successive stages, the order in which they are mentioned in the *Reviews* carries weight. Grammar and music receive prior mention, for the reason that in the first place Augustine wishes to remark that he had in fact written treatises on both of them, whereas he had made only abortive attempts to write on the other arts. The list of 'five other disciplines' is then set out in the following order: dialectic, rhetoric, geometry, arithmetic, philosophy. Once again in this list the arts of communication precede the theoretical studies and the list culminates in the discipline of philosophy.

It is to be noted that in all these lists there are seven arts, although St. Augustine never actually mentions the number seven. It is reasonable to conclude, as Marrou does, that by Augustine's time the number seven had become fairly well established as the number of the liberal arts.[1] However, that the catalogue of the arts was not as definitely established as it was later to be is supported by the variations in the constituent elements of the three lists noted above and by St. Augustine's fluid terminology in referring to the various arts. It is only in the passage from the *Reviews* that he refers to arithmetic by that name; elsewhere it is called 'the discipline of numbering' (*numerandi disciplina*), 'the discipline of number' (*numeri disciplina*) or simply 'number'. In *The Greatness of the Soul* the names of the arts are not mentioned, but each is indicated by a circumlocution, such as 'the art of modulation' (music) and 'the subtlety of measuring' (geometry). In *The Principle of Order* arithmetic is not referred to as a separate discipline, although it is made clear that number is the basis of all the other theoretical studies:

In all these disciplines reason found everything reducible to

[1] H. I. Marrou, *op. cit.*, p. 192, n. 5. Also p. 220, n. 2.

> numbers—in the objects of sense, reason recognised the shadows or traces of numbers.[1]

Two features of these lists require further comment: a) the inclusion of philosophy in *The Principle of Order* and the *Reviews*, and b) the exclusion of astrology from the *Reviews*.

The term 'philosophy', as most frequently employed by St. Augustine, refers less to a particular subject of study than to the spirit which permeates all liberal study. Philosophy is 'a love of and desire for wisdom', which 'looks to the attainment of happiness'.[2] Nevertheless, in other places philosophy is regarded as the higher discipline, to which all that comes before is a prelude. Its purpose then is to enable the learner, who through the study of the liberal arts has learned to think in terms of universals rather than particulars, to fuse together all that he has previously learned in a concentrated exploration of ultimate reality.

This is the sense in which the term 'philosophy' is used in the catalogues of arts, which we are considering. In *The Principle of Order* Augustine sees philosophy as the search for answers to the more difficult problems relating to the nature of reality and of good and evil. He declares that such an enquiry should not be entered upon, until the student has a 'double knowledge' (*duplex scientia*),[3] consisting of a) the knowledge of good disputation (dialectic) and b) the knowledge of the power of numbers (arithmetic). Starting from the observation of numerical phenomena, arithmetic raises questions relating to the nature of unity; then philosophy takes over, places the concept of unity in a wider context and thus renders it more meaningful. In so doing, philosophy poses the 'double question', which we have already noted in an earlier chapter:

> Through philosophy the learner discovers the nature of unity but in a deeper and more divine sense. Philosophy asks a double question—on the one hand about the soul and on the other hand about God.[4]

[1] *The Principle of Order* ii, 43.
[2] *The Practices of the Catholic Church* i, 21.
[3] *The Principle of Order* ii, 47. Plato also was wary of introducing philosophy into the curriculum too soon. *Republic* vii, 539.
[4] *The Principle of Order* ii, 47; *supra*, p. 48.

In this sense philosophy is a unifying study of a higher order compared with the other liberal arts, and dependent for its success upon an intellectual maturity to which each of the arts makes its necessary contribution, if the proper order of studies is followed. Thus we should ask why St. Augustine includes it in a catalogue of studies, which are essentially of a preparatory nature. The possibility has been suggested that he had in mind two grades of philosophy, a higher and a lower: the higher philosophy would be the outcome of the course of liberal study, while the lower philosophy would play its part along with arithmetic, music, geometry and perhaps astronomy as a preparatory study. This elementary philosophy would introduce the learner to the kinds of problems, which form the content of philosophy on the higher level, and to the philosophical method. It would then form a training ground for a better directed attack upon the two fundamental questions of philosophy concerning the nature of the soul and God. This assumption of two levels of philosophy could be supported by reference to the teaching situation at Cassiciacum, where the students were obviously being encouraged to try themselves out on philosophical thinking. By his comments St. Augustine makes it clear that his students are merely engaging in warming-up exercises in preparation for more serious efforts at a later time. He also rejoices openly at the signs they give of progress towards a genuine philosophical grasp of difficult problems. However, Marrou cannot find any persuasive evidence that St. Augustine clearly distinguished between a preparatory stage of philosophical limbering up and more mature study.[1] There is no doubt that St. Augustine saw the whole course of education as one continuous movement from the spontaneous learning of childhood through the more persistent and self-conscious enquiry of later years to the goal of divine illumination. Thus in the absence of a clear statement from St. Augustine that by philosophy as a seventh subject in his catalogue of the arts he meant merely a preliminary study, we would be unwise to assume that he intended this. His inclusion of philosophy should rather be taken as an expression of his conviction that it is central to any course of liberal education. It is the culmination of

[1] H. I. Marrou, *op. cit.*, pp. 193–4.

education, but in a real sense it must permeate the whole of education.[1] Therefore the teacher must be ready, as St. Augustine himself was at Cassiciacum, to seize the moment when philosophical questions arise in his students' minds and to encourage at least a tentative exploration of them. It is the task of philosophy, as St. Augustine sees it, to guide the whole course of education and give it meaning and purpose.

When St. Augustine includes the study of the movements of the heavenly bodies in his catalogue of the liberal arts, he refers to it as '*astrologia*' and not '*astronomia*'. He appears to use '*astrologia*' with reference both to the science and the pseudo-science, which claims to foretell the future from the stars. In this respect St. Augustine was conforming to the normal usage of his time. The term '*astrologia*' preceded '*astronomia*', and denoted a study, which contained a mixture of both scientific and superstitious elements.[2]

Where Augustine speaks of 'astrology', he is careful to exclude the superstitious elements—'the lying divinations and impious ravings of the astrologers'.[3] He expresses a deep suspicion of a study, in which scientific fact was so thoroughly intermingled with superstitious imaginings.[4] In its scientific aspect he commends the subject as displaying to the sight the regularly recurring rhythms in the movement of the stars and thus in a particularly dramatic way pointing to the controlling principle of number in the universe. Thus the study is both a stimulus to rational enquiry and a standing temptation to abandon reason for superstition—'a demonstration (of truth) to religious minds and a great torment to the merely curious'.[5] Great care is required to see that its true claims are disentangled from its misleading associations and assumptions. Augustine's worry on this score originated in the experiences of his period with the Manichaeans, when he had attached himself to the 'mathe-

[1] P. Alfaric, *op. cit.*, p. 445, n. 3.

[2] Lewis and Short, *Latin Dictionary*, cite Jerome (died A.D. 420) as showing the first clear example of '*astrologia*' with reference to the pseudo-science alone, and the younger Seneca as the first authority for the use of the word '*astronomia*'.

[3] *Confessions* vii, 8: '*Iam etiam mathematicorum fallaces divinationes et impia deliramenta reieceram.*'

[4] e.g. *Christian Education* ii, 32–6. *Against the Academics* i, 19.

[5] *The Principle of Order* ii, 42.

maticians' (i.e. astrologers) so closely that he was oblivious to the warnings of his friends.[1]

St. Augustine's continuing suspicion of the irrational and irreligious tendencies of astrology no doubt accounts for its absence from the list quoted in the *Reviews*, which were written at the end of his life. There Augustine lists the arts, on which he had intended to write treatises, and makes no mention of astrology. On the other hand, the significance of the science of 'the movements of the stars' (*astrorum motus*) and the fact that the subject was deeply embedded in the liberal arts curriculum forbade him entirely to exclude it from his earlier lists.

In the fifth book of the *Confessions* St. Augustine expresses his debt to philosophers, whose writing on astronomy had helped to free him from the errors of the Manichaean astrology:

> They foretold eclipses of the sun and moon many years before they happened and predicted the exact day and hour and said whether the eclipses would be partial or total. Their calculations did not fail. . . . They wrote down the laws they had discovered and their treatises are read to this day.[2]

In contrast to this he sets the Manichaean teaching which contradicted the conclusions which he had himself reached 'by calculation and observation'.[3] These and other references do not support Marrou's contention that Augustine omitted astronomy from his list of the arts in the *Reviews*, merely because he was deficient in a knowledge of the subject.[4] Its omission from the list of treatises mentioned in the *Reviews* is sufficiently accounted for by the suspicions he repeatedly expresses when he mentions the subject. His observation of the effect of the study on ignorant, as well as more sophisticated, minds had clearly rendered it distasteful to him. In the light of this uneasiness about a subject so intimately associated with pagan superstition, it is reasonable to suppose that, when at the

[1] *Confessions* iv, 3, 4.
[2] *ibid.* v, 3, 4.
[3] *ibid.* v, 3, 6.
[4] H. I. Marrou, *op. cit.*, pp. 249–51.

end of his life he wished to establish philosophy in a catalogue, which was already being identified with the number seven, he would have chosen to exclude astronomy rather than any other of the arts.

Augustine's contribution to the concept of the seven liberal arts, which were to have such a notable future in the medieval and later humanist curricula, may be evaluated as follows: He paved the way for the best of medieval and humanist teaching, first by reasserting the significant, and indeed indispensable, part played by the liberal arts in the movement of the human soul towards the source of truth; in the second place he insisted that philosophical enquiry, directed to apprehending the eternal reasons of things, must grow out of the soil of human thought. While not compromising on the essential superiority of eternal things over temporal things, of the divine over the human, he asserted the significance of human interest and endeavour. In this way he purged the Christian conscience of its uneasy feelings in regard to secular knowledge and by his sympathetic treatment of the liberal arts opened the way to a broader Christian humanism.

Furthermore, St. Augustine contributed to the acceptance of seven as the number of the liberal arts and to the determination of the component elements in the catalogue. In particular, he eliminated from the list of the arts the accretions which had gathered about them since Varro added medicine and architecture to the Greek encyclopedia. More or less directly he suggested the distinction of the arts into two groups of three and four respectively, a distinction which was later crystallised in the medieval trivium and quadrivium; in so doing, he recalled a distinction originally made by Cicero but later forgotten.[1] In general, he reasserted the contribution of the best of Roman educational thought as represented by Cicero and Varro,[2] and handed it on reinforced by Christian insight to the medieval and modern world. In all this St. Augustine effectively paved the way for the definitive catalogue of the arts and for the final establishment of the number seven in the writings of Boethius

[1] *Supra*, p. 242.

[2] On the extent of Varro's influence on Augustine, see H. Parker, *op. cit.*, p. 432. Augustine frequently cites Varro with approval, e.g. *The City of God* vi, 2–6; *The Principle of Order* ii, 54 etc.

and Cassiodorus in the sixth century and of Isidore of Seville in the early seventh century.[1]

Finally, St. Augustine's inclusion of philosophy in the catalogue of the arts did not result in the abandonment of astronomy, which was already too deeply entrenched. Nevertheless his criticisms and warnings about its dangers may have been influential in purging it of its superstitious elements and promoting the advance of the science of astronomy. On the other hand, his inclusion of philosophy was valuable for its assertion that all liberal educational effort is essentially philosophical; the purpose of education is the integration of all aspects of human experience and interest into a unified and essentially spiritual conception of reality. In this way St. Augustine laid the groundwork for the emergence in the medieval curriculum of theology as the culmination of liberal study, to which philosophy itself was to be preparatory.

CONTENT AND METHOD: GRAMMAR

In his references to the practice of teaching St. Augustine shows a special interest in grammar, dialectic, rhetoric and music, his interest in the first three being rooted in his own experience of teaching in the years preceding his conversion. The interest of the grammarian would naturally extend to the subject of music, which was very closely associated with poetry in the Graeco–Roman culture. We shall now briefly examine St. Augustine's views on content and teaching method in relation to each of these liberal arts.

St. Augustine's view of grammar includes the two traditionally interconnected strands described by Quintilian and others: the knowledge of correct speech (*recte loquendi scientia*) and the explanation of the poets (*poetarum enarratio*).[2] The

[1] S. J. Curtis, *A Short History of Western Philosophy in the Middle Ages*, pp. 32–3 and p. 32, n. 1. Boethius first used the term '*quadrivium*'. Boethius and Cassiodorus finally determined the number seven as the number of the liberal arts. Isidore of Seville (A.D. 570–636) refined the distinction between '*trivium*' and '*quadrivium*' in his Etymologies.

[2] Quintilian i, 4, 2. Also Sergius in Keil, *Grammatici Latini* iv, p. 1485, lines 15–16: 'The art of grammar has consisted of the understanding of the poets and of the method of writing and speaking

latter was the end, to which grammar, in the narrower sense of accidence and syntax, was the means. But in the best teachers of grammar the two components were intimately associated, as can be seen in the following list of the six aspects of grammar as set down by a grammarian of the second century A.D., Dionysius Thrax:

1. The accurate reading of texts with due regard to prosody.
2. Explanation of poetic figures of speech.
3. Exposition of rare words and subject matter.
4. Etymology.
5. Statement of regular grammatical forms.
6. 'The criticism of poetry, which is the noblest part of all.'[1]

St. Augustine defines grammar in its narrower sense as 'the art which guards and controls human utterance'.[2] Its function is to determine the rules governing the inflection of words and to secure consistency in syntactical usage. In so doing, the grammarian leans on the authority of the past, and thus may be regarded as the custodian of the linguistic tradition. For example, the grammarian supports his contention that a syllable should be short on the grounds that 'our predecessors, whose books still survive, and are open to grammarians, have used it as a short, and not as a long, syllable'.[3]

Attention has already been drawn to the account given in *The Principle of Order* and in *Christian Education* of the development of grammar from the invention of significant sounds to the invention of letters—'the signs of sounds made by the articulate voice with which we speak'.[4] This represents the first stage in

[1] Dionysius Thrax, born *c.* 166 B.C. J. E. Sandys, *History of Classical Scholarship*, pp. 7–8.

[2] *Soliloquies* ii, 19: '*Est autem grammatica vocis articulatae custos et moderatrix disciplina.*'

[3] *On Music* ii, 1. The grammarian is '*custos historiae*'. Also *Christian Education* ii, 19: 'What is purity of speech other than the preservation of the custom of language established by the authority of those who spoke in ancient times?'

[4] *The Principle of Order* ii, 12.

correctly.' For an exhaustive treatment of Augustine's views on grammar see G. Bellissima, 'Sant' Agostino Grammatico' in *Congrès International Augustinien, Communications*, p. 35.

the development of the art of grammar. It is followed by a period of consolidation, when the grammarian analyses the accepted usages of speech and writing, classifies words into the various parts of speech and formulates rules of correct speech. He distinguishes, for example, between vowels, semi-vowels and mutes, observes the clear distinction between long and short vowels and thereafter insists that speakers conform to established practice.[1] When this stage has been reached, the art of grammar has come into being.

But so far, grammar is still considered in its narrower aspect of 'the knowledge of correct speech'. The invention of letters, brought about by the need to be heard and understood at a distance, leads on to the literary aspect of grammar. Thus grammar enlarges its scope, opening out into the interpretation and criticism of literature.[2] Since St. Augustine's basic concern is, as we have seen, with the elucidation and evaluation of ideas rather than with the manipulation of words, we would expect to find his interest focused on the teaching of grammar in the broader sense. As to grammar in the narrower sense of accidence and syntax, St. Augustine's knowledge conforms to the accepted theory of his time; for instance, he recognises the usual eight parts of speech,[3] and defines the pronoun in a form of words closely corresponding to the definition given in the first century A.D. by the grammarian Probus and by Charisius in the fourth century:

> A pronoun is a part of speech, which, when put in place of a noun, represents the same sense, although not so completely.[4]

In figures of speech, collectively known as 'tropes' St. Augustine also makes the traditional division into eleven types.[5] In *Christian Education*, while making his usual protestation that he is not to give a formal lesson, he discusses some of the figures of speech, which should be known by the Christian teacher in his

[1] *ibid.* ii, 35.

[2] *ibid.* ii, 37.

[3] *ibid.* ii, 36. The parts of speech are noun, pronoun, verb, adverb, participle, conjunction, preposition, interjection.

[4] *The Teacher* 13.

[5] Allegory, enigma, parable, metaphor, catachresis, irony, antiphrasis, synecdoche, hyperbole, climax, antithesis.

work.[1] He notices for example that metaphor is often used unwittingly in ordinary conversation, as when we say, 'May you flourish' (*floreas*). In *The Trinity* he discusses the meaning of St. Paul's, 'We now see through a glass in an enigma but then face to face': he notes that the kind of trope called an 'allegory' is further sub-divided, and that one of these categories is the 'enigma'. An allegory is 'a trope wherein one thing is understood from another';[2] on the other hand, an enigma contains an underlying meaning, which need not be immediately obvious, and is, therefore, 'an obscure allegory'. Thus by his use of the term 'enigma' St. Paul meant 'an image or likeness, but one which was obscure and difficult to see through'. The figure of climax is illustrated in *Christian Education*, as we have already seen, by two examples from St. Paul, 'our greatest orator'.[3] Again in *The City of God* antitheses are described as 'among the most elegant ornaments of speech'; the sentence which follows enables us to glimpse the style of the grammarian's lecture:

> Antitheses might be called 'oppositions', or to speak more accurately 'contrapositions'. But this latter term is not in common use among us, although Latin, and indeed the language of all nations, employ the same ornaments of style.[4]

In several places St. Augustine makes incidental reference to barbarisms and solecisms, that is departures from generally accepted grammatical usage. In this connection we have had occasion to remark on his aversion to linguistic pedantry and insistence that the function of words is to express clear, unambiguous meaning. Thus the Christian teacher must speak in the language of the people he is addressing if he is to be understood, and this may involve some violation of the accepted standards of cultured speech.[5] In answer to the Donatist grammarian, Cresconius, who has reproved Augustine for using the term '*Donatistae*' (Donatists) instead of '*Donatiani*', which

[1] *Christian Education* iii, 40.

[2] *The Trinity* xv, 15: '*Quid est allegoria nisi tropus ubi ex alio aliud intelligitur?*'

[3] *Christian Education* iv, 11. *Infra*, pp. 264–5.

[4] *The City of God* xi, 18. Also *The Principle of Order* i, 18.

[5] For examples of this viewpoint see *Christian Education* ii, 19 and iii, 7. Also *Expositions of the Psalms* 138, 20; *Sermon* 37, 14. *Supra*, pp. 154–5.

would more properly derive from the name '*Donatus*', Augustine states his view with particular reference to the duty of the Christian grammarian:

> The less time we have to spend on rules governing the derivation of words, the more clearly is what we say understood. Our major purpose consists, not in the exposition of the rules of speech but in the demonstration of truth.[1]

He goes on to defend his use of the form '*Donatistae*' on the grounds that he is following the authority of 'custom', i.e. of commonly accepted usage. This he distinguishes from 'the authority of our predecessors' (*auctoritas veterum*), upon which Cresconius is basing his case. In other places Augustine pokes gentle fun at the linguistic puritans and supports the claims of contemporary usage against those of past standards. 'It is better,' he says in the course of an explanation of a Psalm, 'that the grammarians should reprove us than that the people should not understand us.'[2] And again in a Sermon he pulls himself up after using the grammatically correct form of the present subjunctive of the verb '*nare*' (to swim), and substitutes the form known in popular usage. He follows with the comment:

> Provided that everybody is being instructed, let the grammarians have no fears.[3]

On the higher level of literary interpretation St. Augustine gives a number of demonstrations of the grammarian's teaching method, applied both to secular and sacred literature. We have already noticed the episode in *The Teacher*, in which St. Augustine wishes to show the difficulty in establishing the meaning of even the commonest words and by question and answer seeks from Adeodatus an adequate definition of each successive word throughout a line of Vergil.[4] Each word is carefully analysed in the manner of the well-known grammatical commentaries of Servius and others. St. Augustine's work, *Expo-*

[1] *Against Cresconius* ii, 2. There are two alternative readings here—'*expositione sermonis*' or '*expolitione sermonis*'—that is either 'the exposition of the rules of speech' or 'the polishing up or refinement of the rules of speech'.

[2] *Expositions of the Psalms* 138, 20.

[3] *Sermon* 37, 14.

[4] *The Teacher* 3–4. *Supra*, pp. 186–7.

sitions of the Psalms (*Enarrationes in Psalmos*) applies to the scriptural writings the method of the secular grammarian's explanation of the texts. As an example of this transference of grammatical method to the Christian context, we draw a few sentences from *The Trinity*, where St. Augustine is explaining St. Paul's famous sentence, 'Now we see through a glass darkly, but then face to face'. The argument focuses on two possible readings of the word, which is rendered in English 'glass', i.e. 'mirror':

> If we ask what this 'glass' is and of what sort it is, then surely the thought confronts us that in a glass nothing is seen but an image. Therefore what we have tried to do is to be able to see our Creator through this image, that is through ourselves—'We see through a glass', St. Paul has said; that is we see by means of a glass (*speculum*) and not from a watch-tower (*specula*). This ambiguity does not exist in the Greek language, from which the epistles of the Apostle were translated into Latin. In Greek 'glass', in which we see the images of things, and 'watch-towers', from the height of which we command a more sweeping view, are pronounced quite differently. It is obvious that the Apostle, in using the word '*speculantes*' in respect to the glory of the Lord, meant it to come from '*speculum*' and not from '*specula*'.[1]

Further glimpses of the grammarian in action can be gleaned from other places in St. Augustine's writings. For example, from the *Discourses on the Heptateuch*, in the section on the book of Leviticus, there is a discussion of ambiguous expressions, a comparison of corresponding expressions in Greek and Latin, an analysis of certain syntactical peculiarities and an explanation of figures of speech.[2] As would be expected in the writings of one who had himself practised as a teacher of grammar, St. Augustine allows himself briefly to slip into the style of the grammarian on slight provocation; for instance, in the *Soliloquies* he gives a short exposition of the idea of the comparative degree:

> One thing may be compared with several things and may be

[1] *The Trinity* xv, 14.

[2] *Discourses on the Heptateuch* iii, Concerning Leviticus ii, 9.

both greater and smaller at the same time. So it happens that nothing in itself is either greater or smaller. These words apply when comparisons are made.[1]

CONTENT AND METHOD: DIALECTIC AND RHETORIC

Turning to the arts of dialectic and rhetoric, we find St. Augustine highly critical of the methods and objectives of the secular schools, the focus of his criticism being that the subjects are not necessarily used in the service of truth. In the hands of people concerned only with technical virtuosity, dialectic and rhetoric are simply instruments of public entertainment, aiming at victory in debate without regard to the truth of what is taught. But when they are employed for an educative purpose, i.e. to reinforce the effects of teaching, their function is to clarify truth. In his argument with the Donatist grammarian, Cresconius, St. Augustine remarks, 'That man is rightly called eloquent, who speaks not merely fluently and with style but also with truth';[2] and he follows this with the statement that nobody can properly be called a dialectician 'unless he conducts his discussion not merely with subtlety but with due regard to truth' (*non solum subtiliter sed veraciter*).[3] The conclusion is that neither the rhetorician nor the dialectician can be absolved from responsibility for the moral effects of his profession on the grounds that the arts themselves are morally neutral. Augustine admits that dialectic is the art which 'teaches how conclusions follow from premises, that is either true conclusions from true premises or false conclusions from false premises'.[4] But in the practice of any art more is involved than merely a knowledge of the laws of argument. In fact St. Augustine holds that, as soon as the dialectician or rhetorician stands up to practise his profession, he becomes a teacher, which is to say that he

[1] *Soliloquies* ii, 8.

[2] *Against Cresconius* i, 16. The point is again well made in *Christian Education*: '(The Christian teacher) would prefer to give pleasure by reason of his content rather than by his words (rebus quam verbis). He would consider that a thing is well said only if it is true in fact and that a teacher should control his words and not let his words control him.'

[3] *loc. cit.*

[4] *op. cit.* i, 25.

assumes a moral responsibility for everything he says and does. In Augustine's opinion, the effect produced by a teacher can never be neutral; he necessarily makes his pupils either better or worse than they were before; he leads them either towards or away from the truth. For this reason St. Augustine holds that the teacher of falsehood is in fact a contradiction, that is when 'teaching' is defined in responsible professional terms. Hence Augustine also reminds Cresconius that the whole purpose of dialectic is 'to separate truth from falsehood'.[1] From this it follows that, when dialecticians neglect the critical scrutiny of premises, they are engaging in a futile and dangerous exercise far removed from the profession of the teacher:

> By cunning questions they trap unwary people into agreeing with them, and either laugh at them when they are deceived by an obvious lie or persuade them to accept a concealed lie, which they themselves usually believe to be the truth.[2]

On the other hand, the dialectician who realises his professional responsibility is 'a genuine master of discussion', that is one who makes a distinction between truth and falsehood'. St. Augustine elaborates the task of the dialectician-teacher as follows:

> It is to lead people from what they know to what they do not know, or are unwilling to believe. He shows all the other conclusions that follow from what they already understand or accept on faith. The effect on such people is that, starting from one truth which they already accept, they are compelled to give their assent to other truths, which they had previously rejected. Thus they begin by dismissing a true idea as false, but, when they find that it is in harmony with something which they already accept as true, they make a clear distinction between this true idea and what is false.[3]

St. Augustine offers us few sustained demonstrations of the theoretical exposition of logic. His emphasis is always on practice rather than theory, and he was writing largely for those who

[1] *op. cit.* i, 19.
[2] *loc. cit.*
[3] *loc. cit.*

were unlikely to have a sophisticated knowledge of formal logic.[1] Among the incidental demonstrations of the logical method to be derived from his writings, we have in *Against the Academics* a discussion of disjunctive propositions as a basis for argument and a starting point for learning.[2] Again in *The Greatness of the Soul* St. Augustine interrupts the argument to give Evodius a simple lesson on the laws of logical reasoning;[3] the disputants are trying without success to reach a satisfactory definition of 'sensation'. To give better direction, Augustine reminds Evodius of the character of a good definition:

> A definition contains neither less nor more than what it has undertaken to explain. Otherwise it is a bad definition.

Taking the example of the proposition, 'Man is a mortal animal' Augustine goes on to show how its validity can be tested by reversing it to see whether the converse is true. 'A mortal animal is a man' is not necessarily true; from this it must be concluded that the original definition is a faulty starting point for deduction for the reason that it includes too much, i.e. animals as well as men. To improve the definition, we would have to narrow its scope by adding the term 'rational':—'Man is a rational, mortal animal'. Conversely, a definition may exclude too much, as if it were said that 'All men are grammarians'. The reverse proposition—'All grammarians are men'—is true, but again the fact that the proposition is not reversible reveals an inherent defect in it. Augustine goes on to show that a definition is still more defective, when one proposition is only partially true and the converse clearly false, and worse still when both the proposition and its converse are false. St. Augustine concludes the lesson by advising Evodius to keep in mind the principles of definition, which he has just learned, there being many other principles which Augustine will teach him at another time. In the meantime what has been learned is immediately used to resolve the difficulty which prompted the lesson.

We have had several opportunities to observe St. Augustine's love of a hierarchical arrangement of his materials, involving a

[1] Marrou, *op. cit.*, pp. 244–5, comments on the elementary and untechnical nature of Augustine's references to dialectic.

[2] *Against the Academics* iii, 23.

[3] *The Greatness of the Soul* 47–58.

clear distinction between means and ends. Ends are superior to means; things 'for use' are inferior to things to be enjoyed for their own sake. Hence St. Augustine ranks dialectic as superior to either grammar or rhetoric, the dialectician being concerned with ideas, i.e. with realities, and the grammarian and rhetorician with words, i.e. the symbols of realities and the instruments employed by the teacher to stimulate his pupils to search for the realities. Hence it is the dialectician who speaks when Augustine advises his students to stop arguing over the name to be given to a thing when the idea itself is clear.[1] To impede the progress of learning by wrangling over terminology is in fact to allow grammar, which should be secondary and instrumental, to take a position of precedence over dialectic, 'the discipline of disciplines'.

Thus Augustine sees dialectic as the subject which enables man to achieve the higher purpose of education, since it gives him the power to penetrate in thought beyond physical phenomena, among which the words of the grammarian and the rhetorician are included, to truth itself. Thus dialectic is the method both of teaching and of learning, the two being regarded by St. Augustine as essentially the same activity:

> This discipline of disciplines, called dialectic, teaches us how to teach and how to learn. In it reason puts itself on display, reveals itself for what it is, shows what are its aims and its powers. Dialectic knows how to know; it alone has not only the desire but the power to produce knowledgeable people.[2]

The dialectical method of instruction is of course the method of question and answer, which may take the form of an interchange between a teacher and a pupil, but which must eventually be sustained as an inner dialogue in the mind of the pupil himself. In his *Soliloquies*, which in themselves demonstrate the method of dialectic, St. Augustine remarks that 'there is no better way to truth'.[3]

[1] e.g. *On Music* i, 1 and i, 4. *The Greatness of the Soul* 10. *The Soul and its Origin* iv, 20.

[2] *The Principle of Order* ii, 38. The latin is terse and vigorous: 'Haec (ars dialectica) docet docere; haec docet discere; in hac se ipsa ratio demonstrat atque aperit quae sit, quid velit, quid valeat. Scit scire; sola scientes facere non solum vult sed etiam potest.'

[3] *Soliloquies* ii, 14.

In dealing with St. Augustine's treatment of the liberal arts in the curriculum of Christian education, we have already discussed his attitude to the art of rhetoric:[1] Eloquence is an essential characteristic of the well-educated man, but it is the natural mode of expression of a well-stocked mind rather than the product of art. In this St. Augustine follows Cicero's well-known statement that 'An abundance of content gives birth to an abundance of words'.[2] When employed as an instrument of instruction, eloquence goes hand in hand with truth, which finds its own convincing manner of expression and does not need to be propped up by the tricks of the secular orator's trade.

Such demonstrations of the teaching of rhetoric as we have from St. Augustine are found principally in his *Christian Education* and take the form of commentaries on selected passages of Christian eloquence, principally from the epistles of St. Paul.[3] St. Augustine sees St. Paul as the outstanding Christian example of the strong bond of union between eloquence and truth. He is 'our great orator',[4] whose exposition was 'accompanied by eloquence because it was produced naturally', i.e. without any straining after-effect. In this connection St. Augustine warns the Christian teacher against the attempt to disentangle style from content, since the two are inseparable. When wisdom self-consciously aims at eloquence, content must necessarily take second place to style; then the means come to be confused with, and more highly valued than, the end.[5]

Using a number of specimens of Christian eloquence from the Prophets and St. Paul, St. Augustine demonstrates the intimate bond of connection between content and style, which is the mark of all really significant speech. He expresses his admiration of the quality of Christian eloquence in the following words:

[1] *Supra*, pp. 231–6.

[2] Cicero, *De Oratore* iii, 31, 125: 'Rerum copia verborum copiam gignit.'

[3] e.g. in *Christian Education* Augustine discusses and illustrates the rhetorical qualities of the styles of St. Paul and the Prophet Amos (iv, 7–21); of St. Paul (iv, 39–40); of Ambrose and Cyprian (iv, 45–50).

[4] *Christian Education* iv, 15.

[5] *ibid.* iv, 21: 'Wisdom does not direct its attention to eloquence, but eloquence stems from wisdom, as long as wisdom remains with it.'

The subject matter being talked about is such that the words employed seem not so much to be sought out by the speaker as to be, as it were, spontaneously linked to the subject matter itself. It is as if you were to imagine wisdom emerging from its home, which is the heart of the wise man, and eloquence following after it without being summoned, just like an inseparable attendant.[1]

One of the examples of Christian eloquence chosen by St. Augustine is the well-known sentence of St. Paul:

> We glory in tribulations also, knowing that tribulation worketh patience; and patience, experience; and experience, hope; and hope maketh not ashamed, because the love of God is shed abroad in our hearts by the Holy Ghost which is given unto us.[2]

With reference to this passage St. Augustine gives an exposition in the manner of the Christian *grammaticus*, noting that, although St. Paul had no formal training in rhetoric, he achieves the rhetorical figure of climax by the natural sincerity and upward movement of his thought. The successive terms follow the crescendo of his ideas from 'tribulation' through 'patience' and 'experience' to the sublime pinnacle of 'hope'. The triumphant movement is also emphasised by the succession of short statements, or clauses, which are followed by a 'period', i.e. a rounded sentence, whose clauses 'are suspended on the speaker's voice until the whole is completed by the last clause'.

When St. Augustine mentions the traditional concepts and terminology of the rhetoric schools, he is of course on familiar ground.[3] The influence of Cicero is naturally very prominent; for example, St. Augustine quotes Cicero's three-fold definition of the orator's duty—'To teach, to give pleasure and to persuade'[4] and his well-known classification of the three styles of rhetoric: the subdued style (*submisse loqui*), the moderate style

[1] *ibid.* iv, 10. Compare Cicero, *Orator* 21: 'Wisdom is the foundation of eloquence, as it is of all other things.'

[2] *Christian Education* iv, 11; *Romans* 5, 3–5.

[3] e.g. *The Principle of Order* ii, 40. *Christian Education* iv, 11–13.

[4] *Christian Education* iv, 27. Cicero, *Orator* 21.

(*moderate loqui*) and the grand style (*granditer loqui*).[1] Augustine observes that in the curriculum of Christian education rhetoric must ordinarily be employed in the subdued style for the purpose of assisting the serious student in his intellectual enquiry. But, when the occasion demands, the rhetorician-teacher must rouse his audience to an awareness of their own moral peril. 'What more could the ears of reasonable men desire in this utterance?', St. Augustine asks in the course of his examination of a passage from the Prophet Amos: 'In the first place, with what a resounding impact the denunciation beats against what we may call the sleeping senses so as to rouse them to wakefulness'.[2] St. Augustine well understands that rhetoric is a useful tool in the hands of responsible teachers for the purpose of arousing the unthinking majority to action for their own safety. His psychological insight tells him that many men are moved to action by emotion as much as, if not more than, by pure reason; in consequence, the Christian orator, while being a man of cultivated intelligence with a developed social conscience, must also be aware of the psychological forces which influence behaviour. Thus in *The Principle of Order* St. Augustine makes the following comment on the more utilitarian function of rhetoric:

> Foolish men, in pursuit of what they rightly regard as good, useful and honourable, often follow their senses and habits rather than the purest evidence of truth, which only the exceptional mind beholds. Thus it is necessary that men be not only instructed but also deeply moved. Hence reason gave the name of rhetoric to the subject which aims at bringing this about; it is a subject characterised more by necessity than integrity, whose lap is filled with seductive enticements, which she distributes to the people, so that they may be led to what is to their own advantage.[3]

[1] *Christian Education* iv, 34–58. Cicero, *Orator* 29 is quoted by Augustine in *Christian Education* iv, 34: 'That man will be eloquent who can speak of small things in the subdued style, of modest things in the moderate style and of great things in the grand style.'

[2] Amos, 6, 1–6. The passage begins, 'Woe unto them that are at ease in Zion, and trust in the mountains of Samaria, who are heads and chiefs of the people, entering with pomp into the house of Israel'. *Christian Education* iv, 17.

[3] *The Principle of Order* ii, 38.

In the light of St. Augustine's stress on content rather than method, on ideas rather than words, it is not surprising that we find in his writings no reference to the artificial '*controversiae*' and '*suasoriae*', which played such an important part in the exercises of the secular rhetoric schools of the Empire.[1] This rhetoric of display with its highly coloured declamations and fantastic themes makes the point of the elder Seneca's well-known criticism of the higher education of the Roman decadence —'All the great Roman orators, who can be compared with the glories of Greece, or even be preferred to them, lived in the days of Cicero; since then things have gone from bad to worse'.[2] Thus St. Augustine, who in Milan had withdrawn from the business of professional rhetoric, went back to Cicero, the fountain-head of Roman rhetoric, and suggested that it was only with St. Paul that rhetoric resumed its rightful place as the servant of truth and the natural flowering of a sensitive and cultured mind. Eloquence, employed as an instrument of instruction, should effortlessly spring to the aid of a teacher when he has something to say and help him to say it with accuracy and effect.

CONTENT AND METHOD: MUSIC

The character of music, regarded as a liberal art in the classical encyclopedia, has already been mentioned.[3] It was a purely theoretical study of numerical relationships, the student's aim being to transcend particular examples of number and to reach out to an understanding of absolute number in its spiritual purity.[4] As Marrou puts it, music as a liberal art is 'a mathemati-

[1] e.g. The *Controversiae* and *Suasoriae* of the elder Seneca. The '*controversia*' dealt with a disputed point of law in relation to some imaginary and often highly coloured situation; in the '*suasoria*' the student was required to declaim on a question of conscience involved in some fictitious or historical episode.

[2] Seneca, preface to *Controversiae*. Quintilian, *op. cit.* ii, 10, 7–8, protests against declamation as an end in itself, stigmatising such exercises as 'theatrical ostentation or insane raving'.

[3] *Supra*, p. 117.

[4] In *Letter* 101, 3, Augustine defines the liberal purpose of music as follows: 'The influence of numbers is more easily studied in sounds than in any other kind of movement; this study reaches out towards the higher secret places of truth, along what we may refer to as pathways marked off in successive steps; along these paths wisdom pleasantly reveals herself.'

cal science exactly as arithmetic or geometry is',[1] and this is the form in which it appears in the sixth book of St. Augustine's treatise, *On Music*. When he makes reference to the aesthetic appreciation of musical sounds or to executive skill in music, these are regarded as superficial aspects of a discipline which is basically intellectual and therefore liberal.

While marking St. Augustine's emphasis on the purely theoretical aspect of musical study, we should record that in places he does reveal his own understanding and enjoyment of music as an aesthetic experience. The most notable passage is that in the tenth Book of the *Confessions*, where he describes the emotional impact made upon him on hearing the liturgy of the Church sung. He admits somewhat grudgingly that there is satisfaction to be found in the words of God to man when they are sung 'with a sweet and accomplished voice'.[2] He feels that the holy words raise the hearts of the listeners 'more religiously and fervently into a flame of devotion'. But there is always the danger that the music may lull the intellectual faculties to sleep, so that the mind ceases to carry out its essential duty of penetrating beyond the sweet sounds, in which the words are clothed, to the sense. Nevertheless, he approves of the custom of chanting in church, on the ground that it is capable of raising minds less capable of purely intellectual effort to a state of religious feeling.

Again, in a Letter addressed to Marcellinus, Augustine speaks of God as

> ordering all events in His providence until the beauty of the completed course of time, the component parts of which are the dispensations adapted to each successive age, shall be finished like the grand melody of some unspeakably skilful master of song.[3]

But, as Marrou points out, Augustine never employs the term '*musica*' in the sense familiar to modern ears.[4] Music in the executive and emotive sense is described by the verb '*cantare*' (to sing), '*cantus*' (a song), and so on. In Augustine's

[1] H. I. Marrou, *op. cit.*, p. 197.
[2] *Confessions* x, 33, 49.
[3] *Letter* 138, 5. Also *Expositions of the Psalms* 32, 8.
[4] H. I. Marrou, *op. cit.*, p. 198, n. 4.

view, aesthetic experience in itself is productive of physical pleasure, but on that account can distract the recipient from the higher and more significant effort of thought. Hence the music, which takes its place in the catalogue of the liberal arts, must be purely intellectual in its appeal. If it is to 'lead out the understanding' from the phenomenal world to the world of unchanging reality, the study must concentrate on the mathematical basis of rhythm and harmony.

It is for this reason that the metrical analysis extending through the first five books of the treatise, *On Music*, opens out into the metaphysical exploration of absolute number in the sixth and last book. This triumphant climax to the prosaic catalogues of metrical feet in the earlier books is foreshadowed at the opening of the first book, which begins with a questionnaire leading to a definition of the term 'music'. In the first place, a definition, which probably originated in Varro, to the effect that music is 'the knowledge of good measurement' (*scientia bene modulandi*), is carefully scrutinised.[1] 'Measurement' (or 'modulation') signifies 'a certain skill in movement' (*movendi quaedam peritia*).[2] This skill consists in the preservation of 'measure' or 'proportion' (*modus*) as between the different parts of a movement. Hence rhythms and harmonies, satisfying to the ears, are formed 'by a fixed arrangement of quantities' (*certa dimensione temporum*). St. Augustine remarks that this mathematical basis of music is recognised in the Latin word for rhythm, i.e. '*numerus*' (number). The rhythmical phrases of the poet are matched by the 'measures' (modulations) of the musician.

In the first book of *On Music*, attention is focused on the word 'knowledge'.[3] Music, considered as a liberal art, that is as a means of education, must be securely established on a basis of theoretical knowledge. St. Augustine notes that the nightingale 'modulates' her voice with great effect in the springtime and that her song is both rhythmical and sweet. But since she performs by instinct, that is without knowledge, she cannot be said to be skilled in the liberal art of music; she merely demonstrates

[1] C. J. Perl, 'Augustinus und die Musik' in *Actes du Congrès International Augustinien*, p. 447. H. I. Marrou, *op. cit.*, p. 199, n. 3.

[2] *On Music* i, 3.

[3] *ibid.* i, 4–6.

a flair for imitation. By the same criterion Augustine denies the title of musician to those who merely play on instruments. Their effects are achieved by imitation, a relatively unthinking process, combined with a certain manual or vocal dexterity:

> All those who take their cue from sense perception, commit to memory the pleasure they get from sensation, and, calling upon a certain flair for imitation, move their bodies in reaction to that pleasure, do not possess knowledge, no matter what degree of skill and learning they appear to bring to bear upon the many things they do. Such people do possess knowledge, only if they grasp with the purity and strength of the intellect the thing itself, which they claim to be demonstrating.[1]

We have already dwelt on the distinction Augustine makes between art and imitation.[2] An art has its foundations well sunk in the intellectual comprehension of general principles. On the other hand, technical skill may be merely the product of imitation and practice, and is therefore rooted in sense impression, habit and physical endowment. Thus in St. Augustine's view technical or executive competence is not an essential characteristic of the student of music.

The argument is fundamental to St. Augustine's view of music as a liberal art, and should be taken a little further at this point. By his criterion the musical performer may, or may not, deserve the title of musician. Indeed the time and effort he has expended on the development of technique is likely to have distracted him from the intellectual exploration of musical theory. To determine the qualifications of a musician, we would therefore have to ask him to put down his instrument and answer questions, which reach back into the realms of philosophy and metaphysics. In St. Augustine's opinion the musician need not be able to perform music; it is sufficient that he should have grasped with the intellect the eternal principles, which find their expression in the harmonies and rhythms of music.

St. Augustine reinforces the point by comparing the musician with the physician or the artisan. A man may know all that artisans ought to know or more, but may lack the physical

[1] *ibid.* i, 8.

[2] *supra*, pp. 105–6.

endowment necessary for success in practice. For example due to lack of physical co-ordination he may not be able 'to strike the same point repeatedly with an axe'.[1] Nevertheless, he should be held in greater honour, because he has a theoretical grasp of the principles involved. Similarly, the physician is, properly speaking, the man who 'knows' the principles and function of medicine. Thus the most learned physician may be less competent in the technical skill of surgery than one who has less basic medical knowledge. The successful surgeon may have developed merely 'a practical healing technique residing in his hands', while the physician on the other hand would have much deeper understandings, enabling him to see the relationships between various medical techniques within a broader context of knowledge. On this view the surgeon, like the popular singer who earns the extravagant applause of the crowd, may be merely 'skilful' and not necessarily 'wise'.[2]

To illustrate St. Augustine's conception of the teaching of music as a liberal art, designed to develop the power of abstract thought on first principles, we choose an example drawn from the second book of *On Music*.[3] At this point a catalogue of twenty-eight metrical feet has been set out, and St. Augustine goes on to establish by question and answer the principles which determine which metrical feet can be properly associated together to form larger rhythmical units. The argument starts with the 'self-evident' truth, which we have already encountered in our study of St. Augustine's theory of knowledge, namely that equality is superior to inequality. Nevertheless, a line of verse composed of the same foot reiterated would be wearisome. Thus another truth is established, namely that the satisfaction we derive from our perception of all the aspects of the created universe is founded on the impression of unity in diversity:

> What can be more pleasing to the ears than when they are moved by variety, while not being cheated of equality?[4]

[1] *On Music* i, 9.

[2] The distinction was long recognised in practice through the combination of barber and surgeon in the same person.

[3] *On Music* ii, 16–19.

[4] *On Music* ii, 16: '*Quid est enim auribus potest iucundius esse quam cum et varietate mulcentur nec aequalitate fraudantur?*' Compare T. P. Nunn's thesis in his *Education: Its Data and First Principles*, 3rd ed.

Thus St. Augustine appears to argue that the inequality, which lends interest to a line of verse, is a defect, but one which serves to highlight by contrast the essential equality, which lies behind the diversity and binds the whole into a satisfying unity.[1]

From the principle of unity in diversity it is tentatively concluded that the poet can associate together metrical feet, which are of the same total duration but differ in the composition of their elements. Thus the following metrical feet, namely the amphibrach (∪ – ∪), dactyl (– ∪ ∪), anapaest (∪ ∪ –) and sponde (– –), are of the same duration, since they each contain four 'times' (*tempora*).[2] Therefore, it should be possible to bring any of these together in a line of verse. But it is then observed that the amphibrach is not in fact used by poets in conjunction with any of the other feet. Why is this?

Thus the teaching moves on to encompass the notion of a metrical foot as divided into a rising cadence and a falling cadence. These two 'parts' of a foot, more familiarly represented by the Greek terms '*arsis*' and '*thesis*' appear in their Latin

[1] This unsophisticated explanation of the function of imperfection in the world recurs in *The Principle of Order* ii, 12–13: The executioner, himself a sordid figure, is necessary to the continuance of order in a well governed state; similarly the faults of style in a speech or poem may be deliberately introduced to heighten the general impression of the purple passages—'Take these (barbarisms) away from poems and we miss some very pleasant seasonings ... By including in a speech a number of passages that are subdued and present an unpolished appearance, the woodland pastures and places of charm stand out in clearer relief. If there are only unpolished passages, the elements of beauty do not catch the eye; they do not hold sway over what we may call their own territory and possessions; by the brightness of their own illumination their effect is reduced and the whole speech confused.'

[2] The reader should be aware that the metrical movement of classical verse was determined by the recurrence of long (–) and short (∪) syllables in regular sequences; also that the long syllable was regarded as approximately twice the length of the short syllable.

1945, p. 18: 'The artist strives to express through his materials a single scheme in which the elements, however diverse in nature, have each its place, not accidental or irrelevant, but necessary and meaningful. He succeeds in so far as he can impose upon them this "unity in diversity".'

equivalents of '*levatio*' and '*positio*'.[1] In clapping the hands to beat out the rhythm of a metrical foot, we first raise one hand and then bring it down on the other. The raising of the hand then represents the '*levatio*' of the foot, and the falling of the hand represents the '*positio*'. Applying this concept to the various metrical feet listed, St. Augustine notes that there are those in which the rising note occupies the same duration of time as the falling note, as for example the pyrric (∪ ∪), sponde (– –) and dactyl (– ∪ ∪). But there are other feet, in which the durations of the rise and fall are not equal. Proportions of one to two are observed in the iamb (∪ –), of three to two in the bacchius (∪ – –) and of three to four in the epitrite (∪ – – –). It is observed, however, that in all these cases of inequality of duration as between the two parts of the foot, the inequality is not of a pronounced degree. In each case the rising note is extended or diminished by only one beat (*tempus*) as compared with the falling note.[2]

But the amphibrach stands in contrast to all the other feet in respect of its degree of inner inequality, the duration of the rising note being to the duration of the falling note in the proportion of one to three. Therefore, while the amphibrach can be used in association only with feet of equal total duration (i.e. 4 beats), it nevertheless cannot be used in conjunction with other 4-time rhythms (i.e. the dactyl, anapaest or sponde), since it radically differs from these in the relative durations of its arsis and thesis.

Returning then to the principle that the satisfaction derived from musical rhythms depends upon an overall equality in the duration of measures accompanied by some moderate degree of inner inequality, the argument shows that in its internal structure the amphibrach departs too far from the principle of equality and in this respect is not matched by any other foot:

> These feet are most satisfying, whose two parts have a relationship of equality in respect of each other. Next comes

[1] The Greek terms originally referred to the putting down and raising of the foot in marching. Gildersleeve and Lodge, *Latin Grammar*, p. 455, note that 'The Roman grammarians, misunderstanding the Greek, applied the terms to the lowering and raising of the voice and thus reversed the significations'.

[2] *On Music* ii, 18.

> the proportion of one to two, of two to three and of three to four. But the proportion of one to three has no internal consistency. We do not count three after one but come to three through two, which comes between. Here is the reason why the amphibrach must be excluded from the association we have been discussing.[1]

This may be taken as a typical example of St. Augustine's approach to the teaching and study of music considered as a liberal art. The lesson is marked, as is his teaching in general, not by authoritative pronouncement but by the continual encouragement to thought on general principles, the whole of the work *On Music* being in the form of question and answer. The lesson on the amphibrach becomes the means of demonstrating and reinforcing principles of wide reference, such as that the equal is superior to the unequal, while at the same time harmony, or order, is interpreted in terms of diversity existing within a framework of uniformity. In this way the teacher of music uses his subject matter to develop his students' understanding of first principles, this being the aim of all liberal education.

CONCLUSION

Augustine's conception of content and method in liberal education rests on an explicit contrast between the theoretical and the practical, an outlook which has come under the sharp criticism of some modern educational theorists, such as John Dewey, the pragmatist, who regards the distinction between applied and pure knowledge as artificial and misleading. He associates the distinction with a society in which 'all useful work was performed by slaves'.[2] In criticism of the Platonic and Augustinian interpretation of the term 'art', Dewey says with some exaggeration:

> The very word 'art' may become associated not with the specific transformation of things making them more significant for the mind but with the stimulation of eccentric

[1] *ibid.* ii, 19.

[2] J. Dewey, *Democracy and Education*, (Macmillan, N.Y., 1929), p. 268.

fancy—The separation and mutual contempt of the 'practical' man and the man of theory and culture—are indications of this situation.[1]

To the extent that St. Augustine suggests that practice is simply incidental to theory, that theory does not necessarily originate in practical experiment and is not continually enriched. by practical application, the criticism has validity. His introduction of the example of the physician, who knows the principles of surgery, but cannot operate, suggests useless knowledge, and admittedly does not help his case. Furthermore, in *True Religion* Augustine unequivocably states that an art is characterised 'not by experiencing but by reasoning'.[2] Here he is contrasting the popular view that an art consists in imitation and habituation with the serious intellectual and educative connotation of the term. In his view an art consists in the practice of purely intellectual activity aimed at the progressive expansion of knowledge in the non-scientific, i.e. metaphysical, sense.

We may grant that a gap set between theory and practice can lead to a degree of educational unreality. But the following points may be made in mitigation of the rigour of St. Augustine's position. The ever-present danger in academic studies that they lapse into a meaningless verbalism divorced from real significance is not a feature of the practical teaching situations we have met in Augustine's writings.[3] Furthermore Augustine does not expressly forbid the practice or enjoyment of the practical arts at any stage of education; he merely reminds us that studies which are to be classed as liberal must develop a strong intellectual content. With reference to music in particular, the generally accepted temper of his time must be

[1] *ibid.*, p. 159.

[2] *True Religion* 54: '*non experiendo sed ratiocinando*'. See J. M. Colleran, *The Greatness of the Soul and the Teacher*, note on 'art', p. 203, n. 45.

[3] Nevertheless the reality of the danger may be illustrated from the writings of St. Augustine himself, as Finaert reminds us: 'Alas! Augustine delights in subtle discussions and distinctions. He loves to dwell on words and draw from them conclusions startling by their gravity. One often reproaches him for this.' As teacher, Augustine protests against the preoccupation with words; as dialectician, he enjoys the game of weaving nice but unreal verbal distinctions.

appreciated. There was the ascetic tendency characteristic of the early Christian period; also in Roman society the practice of music was in the hands of professionals, the profession itself being held in poor regard. St. Augustine himself mentions musical instrument playing in the same breath as 'rope dancing and other such spectacles'.[1] Again, in *On Music*, he declares that if we are to grant that every flute and lyre player possesses a 'knowledge' of music, then 'nothing would be more worthless or debased'.[2] Instrumentalists and singers are dismissed as mere players, entertainers or actors (*histriones*), having no real musical knowledge but merely administering sensual pleasure to the ear of the unthinking populace.[3] On this view music was just another technique which the entertainer might add to his repertoire to increase his sales appeal.

Finally, an important factor preventing the closing of the gap between theory and practice was the Greek and Roman failure to make a clear distinction between the mechanical and fine arts. Therefore, all arts involving the practice of physical skills tended to be classed as illiberal. Criticism of this standpoint is justified, but it is a criticism of the whole climate of ancient opinion, which linked education, as Dewey says, 'with notions of leisure, purely contemplative knowledge and a spiritual activity not involving the active use of bodily organs'.[4]

St. Augustine's definition of liberal education may seem limited in the context of the responsibilities of education in modern times. But it constitutes a standing reminder to educators in all ages that the cultivation of intellect is neglected only at the risk of the moral and cultural decadence apparent in the world of his time. Through the stimulus of his own personality and thought the teacher of the liberal arts must release his students' minds from petty preoccupations and distorting prejudices and open their understanding to those aspects of life which are true and unchanging.

[1] *Letter* 9, 3.
[2] *On Music* i, 7.
[3] *ibid.* i, 11.
[4] J. Dewey, *op. cit.*, p. 358.

9 The Educational Influence of St. Augustine

Toutefois, dans la philosophie de saint Augustin et au milieu même des contradictions ou des confusions qui les informent, que de riches et solides données. Disciple de l'antiquité, Augustin a fecondé avec une puissance extraordinaire le champ de la psychologie, avançant par ses analyses des idées et des passions cette connaissance de soi-même, qui est la condition de toute connaissance.

J. F. Nourisson, La Philosophie de St. Augustin, vol. 2, p. 457.

The rich resources of St. Augustine's educational thought have been repeatedly scrutinised and vigorously reinterpreted in relation to the needs and dilemmas of the centuries which have passed since his death. The limits of the present work will permit only a cursory review of those thinkers and periods, which have been most generously inspired by the spirit of St. Augustine. We shall start with the recovery of Europe from the age of darkness following the barbarian onslaughts, a recovery symbolised by the crowning of the Emperor Charlemagne by the Pope in A.D. 800. In conclusion we shall briefly review some characteristic and influential twentieth-century theories of education; in so doing we shall show that St. Augustine's educational assumptions have something to say to a century, whose restlessness of soul and uncertain standards recall the spiritual bewilderment, which motivated St. Augustine's self-education and formed his educational opinions.

THE PRE-THOMIST PERIOD

In the period from his death to the restoration of the works of Aristotle to the West in the twelfth century St. Augustine was the dominating force in the development of thought. He was the channel through which Greek philosophy, and in particular Platonism, flowed through the dark ages and into the medieval world. The influence of his political thinking, in particular through his *The City of God*, upon the unification of Europe under Charlemagne was considerable. In his life of Charlemagne Einhard says:

> While dining he (Charlemagne) used to listen to a musical entertainment or to a reader. There used to be read to him histories and stories of the deeds of men of old times. He also used to take special pleasure in the books of St. Augustine, in particular in those which are called *The City of God*.[1]

With the possible exception of Boethius (A.D. *c.*480–524) and until the arrival upon the scene of John the Scot in the ninth century, there was no great original thinker apart from St. Augustine. The uncertainty of the times directed the attention of men of ability and thought into supplying the more practical and immediate needs of a ravaged Europe. More characteristic of the centuries which followed the barbarian victories were Gregory the Great and St. Benedict, men devoted to action rather than thought. When at last the political chaos was dissolved in the Carolingian renaissance and men could turn again to philosophy, the thought of St. Augustine was a starting point and continuing inspiration.

Boethius, basically an Aristotelian rather than a Platonist, nevertheless owed much to the influence of St. Augustine. In his *Consolation of Philosophy* he discusses St. Augustine's adaptation of Plato's theory of reminiscence, while his description of happiness (*beatitudo*) in terms of the peace, for which the restless soul of man craves, is strongly influenced by St. Augustine.[2] Similarly, the less contemplative and more practical thinkers of the dark ages, such as Cassiodorus, Isidore of Seville, the Venerable Bede and Alcuin of York, repeatedly cite St. Augustine as the source of inspiration for their educational ideals. In his work *On the Arts and Disciplines of Liberal Letters*,

[1] Quoted by J. F. Nourisson, *La Philosophie de St. Augustin*, vol. 2, p. 157.

[2] On Boethius see D. J. B. Hawkins, *A Sketch of Medieval Philosophy*, pp. 17–21; G. Leff, *Medieval Thought from St. Augustine to Ockham*, pp. 46–50.

which recalls the manner of Martianus Capella, Cassiodorus made an exhaustive compilation of the liberal arts, which he had come to know and love in the school of his master, Boethius. This became the standard guide and text book, determining the development of the curriculum in the monastic schools.[1] Cassiodorus' master, Boethius, had been the first to use the term '*quadrivium*' of the four arts of arithmetic, geometry, music and astronomy; Cassiodorus himself went on to use the term '*trivium*' in reference to the studies of grammar, rhetoric and dialectic. This formulation, which owed much to St. Augustine, was to exercise a profound influence on the curriculum for a thousand years.[2]

Both Boethius and Cassiodorus drew heavily on St. Augustine's work on *Christian Education*, which was also influential on Isidore, who became Archbishop of Seville and was revered in the later middle ages as the fifth doctor of the Church in company with Jerome, Ambrose, Augustine and Gregory the Great.[3] Isidore's *Origins* or *Etymologies*, which was to be used as a school text book until the thirteenth century, is a compilation of natural, philosophical and theological knowledge. His thinking on the seven liberal arts was influenced by St. Augustine, as was also his famous Books of Sentences, in which he follows St. Augustine's arguments in defending the spirituality of the soul. In his treatise, *On Divine Predestination and Grace*, Isidore commends St. Augustine for his synthesis of philosophy and religion: 'What else do we mean by the treatment of philosophy', he asks, 'other than the exposition of the rules of true religion?'.[4]

From Isidore St. Augustine's thought flowed on through the Venerable Bede (A.D. *c*.672–735), the father of the Carolingian renaissance and the first great English historian and man of letters. In his *On the Nature of Things*, modelled on Isidore's *Origins*, Bede accepts Augustine's views on the preparatory function of the liberal arts. Egbert, a pupil of Bede, became

[1] In support of secular learning in the Christian curriculum Cassiodorus quotes the same scriptural authority used by St. Augustine: 'Ye shall spoil the Egyptians.' Cassiodorus, *Institutions* 28; *Exodus* 3, 22 and 12, 35.

[2] M. de Wulf, *History of Medieval Philosophy*, vol. 1, p. 114.

[3] *ibid.*, pp. 115–16.

[4] Migne, *Patrilogia Latina*, vol. 81, col. 103.

Archbishop of York, where, inspired by the ideas of his teacher, he set up a school of which he became the first master. Egbert was succeeded as master of the school by Alcuin, who was later invited by Charlemagne to become the first master of his Palace school at Aachen.[1] In this way the ideas of Augustine on the content of the Christian curriculum became strongly influential in the great educational revival inspired by the liberal views of Charlemagne.

Alcuin, a leading figure in the Carolingian educational reforms, was primarily a schoolmaster and compiler of text books. Both at York and Aachen he based his curriculum on the study of the seven liberal arts, expressing the view that the house of knowledge cannot be perfectly built 'unless it is raised up on these seven columns or steps'.[2] The characteristic features of St. Augustine's educational thought permeate his writing. For example he approved the policy of using the best of pre-Christian thought in the service of Christian education.[3] The psychological ideas expressed in his book on the soul (*De Animae Ratione*) are those of St. Augustine, in particular his account of the relation of soul and body and of the nature of sensation. Augustine also inspired Alcuin's definition of man as 'soul and flesh' (*anima et caro*), his statement of the aims of education in terms of an enquiry into God and the soul,[4] and his description of the trinity of will, memory and understanding.[5] Alcuin frequently cites Augustine directly, and in one place gives a resumé of St. Augustine's well-known discussion of the right order of study (*ordo eruditionis*) in *The Principle of Order*.[6]

The thread of Augustine's influence, springing from the Celtic culture of Bede through his pupils, may be traced still

[1] On Alcuin see M. Roger, *L'Enseignement des Lettres Classiques d'Ausone à Alcuin*, p. 320 and 437–48; J. de Ghellinck, *Le Mouvement Théologique du xiie Siècle*, pp. 93–4.

[2] Alcuin, *De Grammatica* quoted de Wulf, *op. cit.*, p. 117.

[3] Alcuin, *Epistle* 307.

[4] de Wulf, *op. cit.*, p. 117.

[5] J. F. Nourisson, *op. cit.*, p. 158.

[6] de Ghellinck, *op. cit.*, p. 94, n. 2. Alcuin freely acknowledges his debt to Augustine in the preambles to his treatises, e.g. the *De Dialectica* in Migne, *Patrologia Latina*, vol. 101, col. 952 and the *De Grammatica*, Migne, *op. cit.*, col. 854. On the 'ordo eruditionis' see *supra*, p. 245.

further through a notable pupil of Alcuin, Rhaban Maur (A.D. ?776–?836). Rhaban Maur came under the influence of Alcuin in his later years when he had retired to found a school at the Abbey of St. Martin of Tours. Maur, who carried on the encyclopedic tradition of Cassiodorus and Isidore, carried Alcuin's ideas from France into Germany and is commonly regarded as the founder of German education, the first '*praeceptor Germaniae*'. He frequently makes direct references to St. Augustine, and in his book, *On the Education of the Clergy*, he quotes verbatim whole passages from Augustine's *Christian Education*.[1] He is strongly in support of the philosophy of Plato and recommends the study of this philosophy from other sources, but particularly from St. Augustine.

Up to the beginning of the thirteenth century St. Augustine was the authority most frequently cited in philosophical and theological disputes; he was particularly influential in maintaining a living contact between philosophy and religion, reason and faith. His conviction that there should be no essential contradiction between philosophical insight and revelation, inspired the thought of John the Scot, otherwise known as Scotus Erigena, (A.D. 800–870), the first original thinker of medieval times.

John the Scot was probably born in Ireland and certainly educated in an Irish monastery. He rose to occupy a prominent position at the court of Charles the Bald, where he appears to have been Head of the palace school.[2] He began his scholarly career as a translator of Cassiodorus, Boethius, Isidore and Augustine. A new direction was given to his thought when he learned Greek and began to translate the Greek fathers. Through the writings of Dionysius the Areopagite, generally known as the pseudo-Dionysius, he came under the influence of the neo-Platonic philosophy. Fundamentally thereafter he remained a neo-Platonist and developed the Plotinian conception of an impersonal One, from which all things emanate and to which they will in the end return.

Three elements drawn from St. Augustine were of great

[1] de Ghellinck, *op. cit.*, p. 94, 2.

[2] S. J. Curtis, *Short History of Western Philosophy in the Middle Ages*, (Macdonald, London, 1959), pp. 35–6; de Wulf, *op. cit.*, pp. 121–2.

importance in the thought of John the Scot: In the first place, he considered that philosophy and religion are not two separate studies, but one. The study of philosophy is simply 'the exposition of the principles of true religion, through which God, the supreme and principal cause of all things, is worshipped in a spirit of humility and investigated in a rational manner'.[1] Therefore, he concluded, 'true philosophy is true religion and conversely true religion is true philosophy'.

In the second place John the Scot followed Augustine's principle that faith must precede understanding; if reason contradicts faith, then faith has been insecurely grounded and insight defective. St. Augustine's commendation of Evodius in *The Greatness of the Soul*—'You do right in asking for nothing more than reason teaches'—is paralleled in a statement from John the Scot:

> Authority proceeds from reason, but reason never proceeds from authority. For all authority which is not approved by true reason, is seen to be weak.[2]

Thirdly, in his account of the structure of reality in his work, *Concerning the Division of Nature*, John the Scot accepted St. Augustine's doctrine of the seminal seeds, the primordial causes of all created things. He describes these seeds as 'the species or forms, in which the unchanging reasons of everything which had to be made, were lodged'.[3]

After John the Scot two hundred years elapsed before any further original contributions were made to thought. In the works of St. Anselm (1033–1109) and of Abelard (1079–1142) the universals controversy reached its most acute phase.[4] This issue was in itself a product of the continuing attention given to St. Augustine's writings, in which the Platonic theory of the separate existence of universal ideas was presented with the

[1] Scotus Erigena, *On Divine Predestination and Grace* i, 1, quoted in Nourisson, *op. cit.*, p. 161.

[2] Scotus Erigena, *On the Division of Nature* i, 69; de Wulf, *op. cit.*, p. 124; Augustine, *The Greatness of the Soul* 7.

[3] de Wulf, *op. cit.*, p. 126.

[4] For an account of the universals controversy see M. H. Carré, *Realists and Nominalists*; also S. J. Curtis, *op. cit.*, pp. 48–69. The controversy had made its first appearance in Remi of Auxerre (A.D. 841–908).

modification that the ideas exist in the mind of God.[1] In this controversy Anselm followed St. Augustine, while Abelard opposed Platonic realism (i.e. the real existence of the universal ideas), and moved towards a position of moderate realism. Thus Abelard associated himself with the Aristotelian conviction that universal ideas are formed by abstraction from particulars.

Anselm's writings bear a very clear impress of the mind of St. Augustine. His famous ontological argument for the existence of God is rooted in St. Augustine's hierarchical conception of existence.[2] Anselm also followed St. Augustine in declaring that learning must start with faith: 'Faith seeking understanding' (*fides intellectum quaerens*) is Anselm's equivalent for St. Augustine's 'Believe in order that you may understand'. Anselm makes the point in the preface to his *Proslogion*:

> I do not seek to understand so that I may believe, but I believe so that I may understand.[3]

The point is repeated in one of his letters:

> The Christian must advance to understanding through faith, not through understanding to faith. Nor must he retreat from faith, if he has no power to understand.[4]

Other echoes of St. Augustine are heard in the course of Anselm's psychological analyses and theory of knowledge. For example, he finds suggestions as to the nature of the Trinity in the triad of memory, understanding and will,[5] uses language reminiscent of St. Augustine's theory of divine illumination[6] and follows St. Augustine in describing the soul as a separate substance and asserting its unitary nature.

Abelard represents a turning point in the development of thought. The increasing interest in the philosophy of Aristotle aroused by the commentaries of Arabian thinkers[7] led him to move away from the pure Augustinian metaphysics. Nevertheless, in his enthusiasm for enquiry by the method of question

[1] *supra*, p. 110.

[2] On Anselm see de Wulf, *op. cit.*, pp. 160–69.

[3] Anselm, *Proslogion* 1.

[4] Migne, *Patrilogia Latina*, vol. 158, col. 1193.

[5] Anselm, *Monologion* 33.

[6] Anselm, *Proslogion* 14.

[7] Alkindi (A.D. 800–873); Avicenna (A.D. 980–1037); Averroes (1126–1198).

and answer Abelard is a true descendant of St. Augustine. It is from Augustine that he drew the text which carried him through a life of controversy beginning with the challenge to his master, William of Champeaux, and which inspired the method adopted in his own school at Melun near Paris—'*Quaerite disputando*' (Enquire by disputing).[1] Close study of the text of Abelard has shown that, in spite of Abelard's independence of mind, there are many echoes of St. Augustine.[2] Thus, although Abelard moved away from St. Augustine in adopting an abstractionist explanation of the origin of knowledge in the human mind, he followed St. Augustine in seeing the cognitive activity of the mind as self-generated and directed outwards by the will to the objects of sense perception.[3]

In Abelard's disciple, Peter Lombard (1100–1160), and in Hugh of St. Victor (1096–1141) the influence of Augustine is seen in a purer form playing on minds less boldly original and controversial than Abelard's. Hugh's mystical temper caused him to make some distinction between theology and philosophy. However, de Wulf notes that the extent of this separation has often been exaggerated, and in support of this quotes Hugh's striking sentence—'Learn everything and afterwards you will see that nothing is superfluous'[4]—which may itself be an echo of Augustine's 'Nothing is lost which we search out with some diligence' (*Nil deperit quod diligentius quaerimus*). In fact his spiritual kinship with St. Augustine is so close that he has been called a second Augustine'.[5] Although tinged with the Aristotelianism of Abelard, he nevertheless follows Augustine very closely in his account of the soul. Thus he conceives of the powers of willing, remembering and understanding, not as distinct and separate faculties, but as various aspects of the vital activity of the indivisible soul.

Finally, the *Sentences* of Peter Lombard, so highly regarded in the Middle Ages as a school text book, are a collection of quotations, at least 80 per cent of which are drawn from St.

[1] S. J. Curtis, *op. cit.*, pp. 55–6.
[2] E. Portalié, *Augustinianisme, Dictionnaire de Théologie Catholique*, vol. 1, col. 2503.
[3] M. H. Carré, *op. cit.*, pp. 55–6.
[4] Hugh of St. Victor, *Didascalion* vi, 3; de Wulf, *op. cit.*, p. 211.
[5] J. F. Nourisson, *op. cit.*, p. 164. Also E. Portalié, *op. cit.*, col. 2503.

Augustine. The Augustinian influence on him is so pronounced that with good reason Portalié describes the book as a synthesis of Augustinian theories'.[1]

ST. AUGUSTINE AND ST. THOMAS AQUINAS

The rediscovery of Aristotle by the West provided the stimulus for the transformation of thought which reached its impressive climax in the Aristotelian–Christian system of St. Thomas Aquinas (1225–74). In the twelfth century Abelard had had access to only a few of the logical works of Aristotle; in the thirteenth century, owing to the appearance of Latin translations of the Arabian versions of Aristotle, the whole corpus of his logical works, including the Physics and Metaphysics, was made available to Western scholars.

This revolution of thought resulted in an injection of Aristotelianism into the stream of Augustinian thought. In a number of ways the Aristotelian philosophy is different from Platonism. The strength of Aristotle and St. Thomas lay in the complexity and wholeness of their systems; by contrast, Augustinianism lent itself to the free movement of contemplation rather than to the more disciplined effort of system building. There is an obvious contrast between the succinct reasoning of St. Thomas, and the often diffuse and undisciplined argument of St. Augustine. Undoubtedly the time, in which St. Thomas lived, was ripe for a new orientation of thought, giving a fresh vitality to the old, without supplanting it entirely. This was the task which the genius of St. Thomas performed for the thirteenth century. While he was moved to reject certain views long associated with St. Augustine, St. Thomas frequently cites him and always with high regard.

Following the teaching of the Arabian, Averroes, who had expressed the conviction that in matters of theology reason is inoperative, St. Thomas clearly demarcated the separate areas of faith and reason. The subject matter of faith is known through revelation, and it seemed to St. Thomas that this is an entirely different method of knowing from the method of reason, which must take its start from experience and demonstration. Thus St. Thomas' theory of knowledge is founded on the belief that all rational understanding originates in sense perception. He insists

[1] E. Portalié, *ibid.*

that in this life universal ideas are discoverable only in particulars, that is in the area of temporal existence, and not in a world of the spirit transcending the sensible world. Since experience is the starting point of all learning, it becomes the function of the mind, through what St. Thomas terms 'the active intellect' (*intellectus agens*), to abstract the universal idea from the particular example. Thus in St. Thomas' epistemology learning becomes a continuous progression from particulars to general ideas, whereas in Platonism and Augustinianism sense perception as the basis for understanding can carry the learner only part of the way forward; a time must come when he must, as it were, close his eyes and indulge in pure thinking, in which sense data are of no assistance.

It is evident that St. Thomas's inductive approach to learning, which emphasises the real significance of sense data, would cause him to repudiate St. Augustine's conviction that the body cannot in any circumstances act upon the soul. For St. Thomas, physical causes play a real and indeed indispensable part in cognition. Nevertheless, he does not think of learning in purely mechanical terms.[1] He agrees with St. Augustine that material things cannot impress themselves on the soul, because they are of a different and inferior nature. Nevertheless they do present themselves as data, from which the mind through the active intellect abstracts the intelligible forms. In St. Thomas's terminology the sensible forms, presented to the possible intellect, are actualised (i.e. rendered intelligible) by the illumination of the active intellect. For example, it is the active intellect which distinguishes between the qualities of a particular horse and those which are common to all horses, and so 'actualises' the general idea of 'horse'. Through the process of abstraction of the general from the particular man organises his experience and so renders it meaningful.[2]

[1] S. J. Curtis, *op. cit.*, p. 140, points out that St. Thomas' account of learning in terms of the abstraction of universals from particulars does not mean that St. Thomas falls into subjective idealism any more than into materialism.

[2] St. Thomas, *Summa Theologica*, 1a, q. 85, a.1: 'This is to abstract the universal form from the particular or the intelligible species from the images; that is to consider the nature of the species without considering the individual principles which are represented by the image.'

Thus, while from St. Augustine's standpoint understanding is a purely spiritual act assisted by a direct communication from God, the interior teacher, St. Thomas sees God as always acting through intermediate agents. The bread, which man requires to nourish his body, reaches him only by way of the farmer and the baker, and so it is with all the other materials man needs to satisfy his physical wants. St. Thomas uses the same principle to explain the origin of human knowledge: Knowledge is not directly shown to man in the manner of the Augustinian divine illumination, but always comes into being through the activity of the human intellect working upon the raw materials, which God has lavishly supplied in the sensible world. Clearly this is a doctrine which attributes a greater responsibility and scope to the human mind, and consequently in the words of Leff supplies 'a more precise mechanism of the way in which the essence of things was grasped'.[1] Indeed the main concern of both Augustinians and Thomists in the thirteenth century was to give a more exact account of the origin of our general ideas. St. Thomas holds that, although these general ideas, i.e. universals, are most real in themselves, nevertheless particular things are most real to man in his present life bounded by space and time. Therefore, while on the one hand the individual can be known only in terms of the universal, i.e. as a recognisable member of a class, the particular is the only avenue through which the mind can approach the universal.

Thus, in the opinion of St. Thomas, man's physical environment, including his own body, is raised to a position of significance, which Augustine denies it. The point may be made by comparing the Augustinian and Thomist interpretations of individuality. For St. Thomas an oak tree or a man comes into being through the reception of form by inert matter. The form of a horse is essentially the same for all members of the species; therefore, the principle of individuality rests in the particular matter, which has been invested with form. In Augustine, on the other hand, the immaterial form is the principle of individuality; it is this which differentiates this horse from all other horses, or Socrates from all other men. To think otherwise would be for Augustine a serious encroachment on the self-determination and

[1] G. Leff, *op. cit.*, pp. 233–4.

unique quality of the immaterial soul. St. Thomas's account of human individuality certainly sees it as dependent more on man's temporal than on his eternal part, an attribute of body rather than of soul.

In all this St. Thomas was expressing his faith in the efficacy of secondary, or instrumental, causes, whereas for St. Augustine only primary, or principal, causes were real causes. This difference of emphasis was brought out in the comparison, made in an earlier chapter, between St. Augustine's and St. Thomas's views on the nature of teaching and learning.[1] Both held that learning was essentially a matter of the self-activity of the learner, whose volition in the last resort determines the success or failure of all teaching, and who may, or may not, be assisted by a teacher. However, as St. Augustine saw it, the teacher cannot in any proper sense be described as the cause of his pupil's learning; on the other hand, St. Thomas held that, when the teacher does intervene to give systematic instruction, he is actually the cause of learning, in that he effectively directs a process, which St. Thomas described as the actualisation of the learner's active potentiality for knowledge. In the beginning this is merely a potentiality, which can be actualised only gradually and under the stimulus of the physical environment, in which teachers are included. Therefore, although the learner is a self-activating organism, he must at all points rely on help supplied externally from his environment. Thus St. Thomas held that man cannot entirely teach himself, but must rely on the help of teachers for systematic instruction. He concluded that for some purposes teaching becomes 'a more perfect way of acquiring knowledge' than the more diffuse and unsystematic way of self-education:

> The teacher, who has the whole of knowledge, can more expeditiously lead to knowledge than a man can be led by himself. For the teacher knows the principles of knowledge in some connection.[2]

While establishing the work of the teacher as the cause of his pupil's learning, St. Thomas did not make the mistake of con-

[1] *supra*, pp. 206–7. St. Thomas, *Quaestiones Disputatae de Veritate* xi.

[2] St. Thomas, *op. cit.*

cluding that St. Augustine minimised the importance of the teacher's task:

> In establishing that God alone teaches, St. Augustine in his treatise, *Concerning the Teacher*, does not intend to deny that man teaches externally, but only to establish that it is God alone who teaches internally.[1]

The attraction of St. Thomas' views on teaching and learning lies in the fact that they harmonise more closely with the commonsense view that learning begins with particulars and advances by a continuous exploratory movement without any need for a transition from learning through sense perception to the method of pure thought. This is what is implied by the notion of learning in terms of the actualisation of potentialities. At every stage the learner is stimulated to further progress by the knowledge he has already gained; he is involved in the present tendencies of his learning rather than in a vision of a distant, ultimate goal embraced by faith. Thus the Augustinian 'faith before reason' is transmuted into St. Thomas' 'nothing is willed unless it is known'.[2]

Enough has been said to show that Thomism is not a complete departure from the authority of St. Augustine but rather an attempt to bring Augustinian theory more into line with observation and experience. In a well-known passage from the *Summa Theologica* St. Thomas represents his task as finding a middle way between the two extremes of exaggerated Platonic realism on the one hand and the materialistic sensationalism characteristic of the Greek, Democritus, on the other.[3] He feels that in Aristotle we find a way of reconciling the claims of sensation and of thought. Experience suggests that sensation does take the initiative in the cognitive process; it is equally clear that thought is different from mere sensation. By his notion of the active intellect, which renders sense data meaningful and enlarges the bounds of meaning far beyond the restricted purview of particular sense impressions, St. Thomas supplied an essential link missing in St. Augustine. In the words of Carré, St. Thomas' respect for St. Augustine is shown by his

[1] *ibid.*
[2] *ibid.*
[3] St. Thomas, *Summa Theologica* i, q. 84, art. 6.

policy of 'adapting the Platonism of the great Church Father so as to avoid conflict with his own position'.[1] Portalié puts it that, far from posing as adversaries of St. Augustine, as they were accused of doing, the Thomists 'put themselves to his school and, while modifying certain theories, introduced and absorbed in their system all the theology of the doctor of Hippo'.[2]

In spite of the rebirth of Aristotle and the genius of St. Thomas, the thirteenth century did not abandon St. Augustine. Many of the Franciscans followed Augustine rather than Aquinas. Of particular interest is the continuing impact of the Augustinian theory of divine illumination, which passed through the middle ages in the form of the *scintilla* (spark). St. Bonaventure, a Franciscan and contemporary of St. Thomas, used the term *scintilla* in his *Journey of the Mind to God* to describe the ultimate stage in knowledge, which consists in the ecstatic union of the soul with God.[3] Similarly Eckhart (1260–1329), whose temper is more mystical, sees the divine 'spark' as the image of God within man. Although dimmed by sin, the spark cannot be wholly extinguished; when fanned into a bright flame, it becomes the light, by which man achieves union with God. In analysing the image of God within the soul, Eckhart also follows Augustine's account of the trinity of memory, will and understanding, which he superimposes on the Platonic trinity of sensuous, spirited and rational elements in the human soul. Although Eckhart was the first to identify the spark with the active intellect of the Thomists, he later rejected this view and saw it as something set over and above the powers of the soul in the manner of St. Augustine's 'immaterial light of a unique kind', in which unchanging truth is seen.

RENAISSANCE AND REFORMATION

In the later thirteenth century a reaction in favour of St. Augustine set in, when Thomism came under the attack of Roger Bacon, Duns Scotus and William of Ockham. Scotus for example followed Augustine in opposition to St. Thomas in exalting the superiority of the will over the intellect. Continuing

[1] M. H. Carré, *op. cit.*, pp. 90–93.
[2] E. Portalié, *op. cit.*, col. 2514.
[3] S. J. Curtis, *op. cit.*, p. 207.

the universals controversy, William of Ockham (1290–1350) challenged St. Thomas' theory of the active intellect and declared that 'there is no universal actually existing outside the mind'.[1] The movement away from abstractionism became so strong that in the fifteenth century, as Curtis notes, the adherents of St. Thomas were being referred to as 'the ancients', and those of Ockham as 'the moderns'. Thus the way was paved for the return of St. Augustine, whose mode of thinking was more congenial to the less coldly intellectual Renaissance mind. Nourisson sums up the position in the early sixteenth century by saying that the philosophy of St. Augustine became the most powerful ally of Platonism, invading all the schools and making such notable converts as Cardinal Sadoleto and Pope Leo X.[2] The Renaissance scholar and man of affairs, Castiglione (1478–1529), declared that the education of his courtier must be incomplete, unless it included some experience of the thought of Plato and St. Augustine.[3]

Noteworthy also was the influence of St. Augustine on the art and literature of the early Renaissance. Boccaccio presented Petrarch with a copy of Augustine's *Expositions of the Psalms*, and in a letter Petrarch thanked the donor for 'a magnificent and outstanding gift'.[4] But most striking is the influence of Augustine on the mind of Dante (1265–1321), an influence which has been carefully studied by E. K. Rand in his *Founders of the Middle Ages*.

Rand finds a natural affinity between the minds of Dante and Augustine, based on their common aspirations towards goodness and beauty and their mutual sense of the mystery of existence. Dante's references to Augustine, which are not frequent but always significant, reveal a particular knowledge of *The City of God* and *The Greatness of the Soul*. *The City of God*, in conjunction with the prophetic and mystical utterances of Vergil in the *Aeneid* and also in the 4th *Eclogue*, in which Vergil was supposed to prophesy the coming of the Messiah, provided the support for Dante's inspired belief in the renewed mission of

[1] *ibid.*, p. 234.
[2] M. de Wulf, *op. cit.*, pp. 467–9.
[3] W. Boyd, *History of Western Education*, (Black, London, 6th ed., 1954), p. 215.
[4] Petrarch, *Epistles* 2.

Rome. Dante saw the earthly city as being allied to, but not identified with, or controlled by, the heavenly city. By this he expressed his conviction that the secular state, withdrawn from the jurisdiction of the Church, should of its own free will support the aspirations of man towards a knowledge of the divine purpose.[1] In this advocacy of a reconstructed relationship of church and state St. Augustine's influence was considerable.

Dante furthermore found support in St. Augustine's *The Greatness of the Soul* for his view of the educational progress of the human soul in terms of a series of stages from preoccupation with sense data to a knowledge of immaterial reality.[2] Dante advises Can Grande in a letter to turn to this treatise, if he wishes to illuminate the mystical meaning of the 1st Canto of the Paradisio.[3] The ladder imagery of the soul's progress from an earth-bound condition to the pinnacle of its ascent, where it loses itself in the divine mystery, was also found by Dante in Augustine's *Confessions*. This is made clear in the Convivio, where Dante uses the *Confessions* as an outstanding example of the propriety of self-analysis.[4] He observes that Augustine's purpose was to assist the progress of man 'through the way of learning'; hence it was quite appropriate that in the *Confessions* Augustine should describe his own adventurous spiritual progress. To teach by reference to a particular example is the most effective method:

> Thus in the *Confessions* Augustine begins to talk about himself, so that through the progress of his own life, which is from the good to the better and from the better to the best, he may give an example and a lesson which cannot receive its true support by itself.

Dante's reverence for St. Augustine as an inspired teacher is

[1] G. Leff, *op. cit.*, pp. 302–3. For an analysis of Dante's interpretation of *The City of God* see E. Gilson, *Dante et la Philosophie*, (J. Vrin, Paris, 1939), pp. 200–204 and 218–19.

[2] *The Greatness of the Soul* 70–79. The passage is analysed *supra*, pp. 136–7.

[3] E. K. Rand, *Founders of the Middle Ages*, p. 259. Dante, *Epistle* 10, 28. John-Baptist Reeves, St. Augustine and Humanism, in *Monument to St. Augustine*, p. 150.

[4] Dante, *Convivio* i, 2, 14.

recognised when he places him in the highest heaven along with St. Francis and St. Benedict, whereas St. Thomas is on a lower level.[1] This distinction reflects the Renaissance appreciation of the more intuitive and imaginative aspects of human awareness. The ultimate measure of a teacher's greatness for Dante lay in the element of wonder, which marks his teaching, and in the extent to which intellectual rigour is leavened by intuition and a continuing sense of mystery.

The Renaissance humanist teachers of the two centuries following Dante show evidence of Augustine's influence in their educational theory and practice. In his work, *Concerning Studies and Letters*, Bruni recommends St. Augustine along with St. Jerome and Lactantius to the special attention of Christian students on the grounds that they are 'great theologians and profoundly versed in literature'.[2] Vergio uses St. Augustine's account of his own education in the *Confessions* as the text for his book, *On the Education of Children*.[3] Guarino is acquainted with St. Augustine's *On Music*, which he describes rather narrowly as 'a tract on scansion'.[4] Elsewhere he advises students entering upon a course of independent reading to apply themselves to books which deal with a wide range of subjects, recommending as outstanding examples Pliny's *Natural History* and Augustine's *The City of God*.

> —so valuable for the light it throws upon the historic rites and ceremonies and the religious beliefs of the ancient world.[5]

In commending the attitude to classical literature of the most liberal Christian thought, Aeneas Sylvius stresses the importance of the early impressions made on the growing mind. To support his point he uses a quotation from Horace, which Augustine himself uses in the same context, to the effect that the wine jar preserves for long the tang of the wine, with which it was first

[1] Dante, *Paradisio*, canto 32, 35. Also canto 10, 82 ff. E. K. Rand, *op. cit.*, p. 258.

[2] L. Bruni, *Concerning Studies and Letters* in W. H. Woodward, *Vittorino da Feltre and other Humanist Educators*, pp. 124–5.

[3] W. H. Woodward, *ibid.*

[4] *ibid.*, p. 165.

[5] *ibid.*, p. 173.

filled.[1] Ambrogio, reporting on a visit to the library of the great humanist schoolmaster, Vittorino da Feltre, mentions that he found there among other books 'a treatise of St. Augustine, *On Music*, and the *Categories*, which are ascribed to St. Augustine'.[2]

These references among others establish the influence of St. Augustine's Christian humanism as a powerful force influencing the development of the theory and practice of Renaissance education. He was also strongly influential on the minds of the Reformers. Martin Luther assessed the effect of St. Augustine on himself as follows:

> Among the Fathers Augustine has most certainly the first place—He pleases me more than all the others. He has taught a pure doctrine and submitted his treatises with Christian humility to the Holy Scripture.[3]

And again, in a comment recorded by a friend, Luther expressed his admiration for St. Augustine with a fine enthusiasm —'I did not merely read Augustine; I devoured him'.[4]

John Calvin (1509–69) drew his teaching on predestination directly from St. Augustine, as also the doctrine of divine illumination and the notion of the interior teacher: 'It is Christ, the interior teacher,' he says, 'who will teach us. It is He who causes men to give us external signs in order that, turning inwardly towards Him, we may receive His lessons.'[5] The architects of the Reformation turned to Augustine in appreciation of his emphasis on the part reason plays in the perfect fulfilment of faith, as well as for his teaching on predestination, grace and free will. Thus the Protestant theologian, Warfield, has summed up the Reformation as 'a revival of Augustinianism', which he defines

[1] Aeneas Sylvius, *Concerning the Education of Children* in W. H. Woodward, *op. cit.*, p. 150; Horace, *Epistles* i, 2, 70; Augustine uses the quotation in *The City of God* i, 3. *Supra*, p. 219, n. 4.

[2] W. H. Woodward, *op. cit.*, p. 70. The reference is to the *Categoriae Decem*, wrongly attributed to Augustine and printed in Migne, *Patrilogia Latina*, vol. 32, cols. 1419–40.

[3] J. F. Nourisson, *op. cit.*, p. 177.

[4] L. Cristiani, 'Luther et St. Augustin', in *Communications du Congrès International Augustinien*, p. 1031: '*Augustinum vorabam, non legebam.*'

[5] J. Calvin, *Institutes* iv, 14. See 'Calvin et St. Augustin' in *Communications, op. cit.*, p. 1043.

as 'the thetical expression of religion in its purity'. As we have seen, the two conceptions of prevenient grace and the freedom of the human will held together rather uneasily in St. Augustine's mind;[1] it was simply his inability to fuse them which prevented some humanist thinkers, such as Erasmus of Rotterdam, from supporting the Reformation.

SIXTEENTH- AND SEVENTEENTH-CENTURY FRENCH THOUGHT

The trend of thought in sixteenth- and seventeenth-century France, a period distinguished by the genius of René Descartes (1596–1650), was to establish ethics on a basis, which would satisfy reason and also harmonise with Christian teaching. The period was marked by an easy alliance of faith and reason, which explains the popularity of St. Augustine, whose thought provides the key to the intellectual strivings of the time: 'Everyone in France,' says Remsberg, 'was an Augustinian in some respect.'[2]

St. Augustine's impact was of special significance in that the period was marked by noteworthy contributions to the theory and practice of education. Michel de Montaigne (1533–92), who expressed enlightened views on education in his *Essays On Pedantry* and *On the Upbringing of Children*, reminds us of the Augustine of the *Confessions* in the account he gives of his intellectual and spiritual development. Both passed through scepticism and periods of attachment to various philosophies before reaching a condition of spiritual equilibrium; both had great faith in the human reason combined with a just appreciation of its limitations. Like St. Augustine, Montaigne stressed the educational significance of doubt in preference to the uncritical acceptance of statements on authority. A passage from *The City of God*, for instance, is used by him to justify his own mature scepticism: as long as faith remains firm, we may properly entertain doubts about matters, which have not been presented to the senses, demonstrated to the reason or revealed in the Scriptures. Montaigne comments as follows:

I follow St. Augustine's opinion that a man does better to

[1] *supra*, pp. 56–61.

[2] R. E. Remsberg, *Wisdom and Science at Port Royal and the Oratory: A Study of Augustinianism*, (Antioch Press, Ohio, 1940), p. 27.

bend towards doubt than incline towards certainty in matters of difficult trial and dangerous belief.[1]

Montaigne's essays on education show St. Augustine's influence in the distinction between science and wisdom—'*scientia*' and '*sapientia*'. Neither Montaigne nor Augustine despises scientific knowledge, but both recognise that education has a broader purpose than the acquisition of a knowledge of the physical environment; when education remains on the level of purely physical interest, it serves only a limited purpose. Similarly Montaigne repeatedly deplores the over-preoccupation with purely verbal learning and the assumption that knowledge is, as it were, grafted on to the learner by an external teacher. 'We work only to fill the memory,' he says, 'and we leave the understanding blank.' Like Augustine, he sums up the higher objectives of education under the term 'philosophy'. The teacher must ask not 'How much Greek or Latin does a boy know?', but rather, 'Has he grown better and wiser?'. Education's supreme task is to cultivate a knowledge of how to live the good life,[2] and to this end the learner must develop the habit of self-scrutiny. The trend of all these educational opinions, including Montaigne's double use of the term 'philosophy' with reference to a subject of study and also to a method of enquiry permeating the whole curriculum, follows the spirit of Augustine very closely.

Passing on to Descartes, we recall the striking resemblance between the Cartesian, '*cogito ergo sum*' (I think and therefore I exist) and Augustine's '*si fallor, sum*' (if I fall into error, I exist).[3] There is no convincing evidence that Descartes was familiar with St. Augustine's argument. Although the statements bear a resemblance to each other, detailed scrutiny reveals a characteristic difference in the two approaches. St. Augustine's theory of knowledge starts with the certainty that he exists:—'Do you know that you exist? I do know.' From this he concludes that he is alive, remembers, understands, wills,

[1] Montaigne, *Essais* iii, 11, p. 334; Augustine, *The City of God* xix, 18; N. Abercrombie, *op. cit.*, p. 44.

[2] F. Strowski, *Montaigne*, p. 246; S. J. Curtis and M. E. A. Boultwood, *Short History of Educational Ideas*, (University Tutorial Press, London, 1953), p. 138.

[3] *supra*, pp. 131–3.

thinks, knows and judges.[1] It is the certainty of self-existence which gives the assurance of all the rest. Descartes, on the other hand, finds his first ground of confidence in the indubitable fact that he is a thinking being (*res cogitans*).[2]

Nevertheless, to both Augustine and Descartes the question mark of doubt was a necessary starting point for learning. Both Abercrombie and Gilson point out that, since both Augustine and Descartes stand in the idealist philosophical tradition, they must be expected to reach conclusions bearing a family likeness to each other.[3] Therefore, it is not necessary to postulate a direct influence of Augustine upon Descartes in this respect. However, as we have already remarked, the temper of the time was Augustinian rather than Aristotelian, and this undoubtedly resulted in at least an indirect impact of the mind of St. Augustine upon Descartes. Descartes, for instance, stresses the essential inadequacy of sense data to furnish a knowledge of reality, and the danger that over-preoccupation with sense may inhibit the more significant activity of interior thinking and learning.[4] In his *Discourse on Method* he insists that the difficulty in grasping truth is not that it is too remote from the human mind but that people find difficulty in 'raising their minds above the things of sense':

> They are so accustomed to considering nothing except what they can imagine—a mode of thinking restricted to material things—that whatever cannot be represented by images seems to them not intelligible.[5]

All this is evidence of an identity of stand-point between the two thinkers. It is clear that many of his contemporaries saw Descartes as 'a celebrated modern disciple of St. Augustine' and

[1] Augustine, *Soliloquies* ii, 1; *The Trinity* x, 13; *The Free Will* ii, 7.

[2] Descartes, *Meditations* ii in N. K. Smith, *Descartes' Philosophical Writings*, p. 206. Descartes asks: 'What am I? A thinking being, that is, surely a doubting being, an understanding being.'

[3] N. Abercrombie, *St. Augustine and French Classical Thought*, p. 90. J. F. Nourisson, *op. cit.*, p. 226. E. Gilson, *Studies on the Role of Medieval Thought in the Formation of the Cartesian System.*

[4] Descartes castigates the scholastic principle— '*nihil in intellectu quod non prius in sensu*' ('there is nothing in the understanding which is not first in sense perception').

[5] Descartes, *Discours* iv in N. K. Smith, *loc. cit.*

his writings as 'a sort of popular exposition of Augustinianism adapted to a new age'.[1] Mersenne, a close friend of Descartes, remarked that in his view no argument advanced by Descartes would contradict the views of St. Augustine:

> The more a man will be well read in the teaching of St. Augustine, the more will he be disposed to embrace the philosophy of Monsieur Descartes.[2]

There is no doubt that the unison of Augustine and Descartes was of great advantage to the common cause, in that it served to win the favour of the theologians for Descartes, and in this way to give a new impetus and wider diffusion to the thought of St. Augustine.

A brief reference may be made at this point to a less rewarding aspect of St. Augustine's influence on the educational beliefs and practices of seventeenth-century France. The Jansenist community of Port Royal[3] was one of the two teaching orders which sprang up in the seventeenth century in opposition to the Jesuit Order; the other was the Order of the Oratory of Jesus, founded in 1611 primarily for the purpose of educating priests, although it later extended its activities to the education of young nobles. Both the Port Royalists and the Oratorians came under the influence of the Cartesian philosophy and clashed with the Jesuits on points of theological doctrine. The educational theory and practice of the Port Royal schools was moulded by Jansen, afterwards Bishop of Ypres and the author of a notable heresy. In his *Augustinus*, published in 1638, two years after his death, he defended the doctrines of grace and predestination, which had already been condemned in connection with the heretical teaching of John Calvin. According to Jansen, following St. Augustine, a man's free will avails him nothing when it comes to the question of whether or not he will be saved. God's grace is given gratuitously and not in return for any merit on the part of the recipient.

Thus the educational practice at Port Royal was considerably affected by the bleak facts of original sin, predestination and

[1] J. F. Nourisson, *op. cit.*, p. 207.

[2] *ibid.*, p. 213.

[3] For the Port Royalists see H. C. Barnard, *The Little Schools of Port Royal*, (Cambridge University Press, 1913).

grace not sufficient for all but granted to some and denied to others in an apparently capricious manner. This is an aspect of St. Augustine's thought which least influenced his own educational practice and is an unpromising beginning for any educational effort.[1] In the Port Royal schools the child was seen as exposed to the assaults of the devil intent upon besmirching the new-found purity attained by the child at baptism when his original sin was washed away. As the duty of the physician is to prevent the invasion of the body by disease-carrying germs, so the educator must stand continual guard over the soul of the child to prevent the entry of the devil. If the child can be kept in a state of innocence until fortified by reason, then all may be well. It is clear that such a punitive doctrine would effectively paralyse any genuine educational effort.[2] Fortunately the contradictions inherent in the Port Royal attitude to education rendered their educational practice superior to their theory. As time passed, the Jansenist influence receded; there was a liberalisation of curriculum and method, and less compunction was felt in allowing children to study the works of classical literature. The resulting union of Christian piety and liberal interests was much closer to the spirit of St. Augustine's ideals.

After Descartes, the three greatest representatives of French thought in the seventeenth century, namely Bossuet (1627–1704), Fénelon (1651–1715) and Malebranche (1638–1715), were considerably influenced by the views of St. Augustine. His close association with the intellectual life of the time is exempli-

[1] J. Burnaby, *Amor Dei*, ch. 8, pp. 223–4 shows 'how easily St. Augustine's psychology of grace could be perverted', and uses Jansenism to exemplify the point. In Jansenism pleasure moves the will to action, but it is a force alien to the nature of the will itself; therefore, pleasure becomes an unpleasant necessity. However, St. Augustine's thought, rightly interpreted, is that the love of the soul for the desired object is of the very nature of the will; love is, as we have seen, 'the weight of the soul'.

[2] In this connection note the reply given by the confessor of the Port Royal community to Jacqueline, sister of Pascal, who had sought his advice on the extent to which she should indulge her talent for poetic composition: 'This is a talent, of which God will not demand an account from you, since humility and silence constitute the lot of your sex—you ought to hate this talent and the others, which are perhaps the reason why the world holds you back; for it wishes to reap what it has sown.' R. E. Remsberg, *op. cit.*, p. 67.

fied by Bossuet, who has been described both as 'the soul of the age' and 'the living incarnation of St. Augustine'.[1] The thinking of all three tended to a synthesis of the ideas of St. Augustine and Descartes. Both Bossuet and Fénelon clearly reflect St. Augustine's ideas on the nature of the soul and its relationship with the body, on divine illumination and the problem of grace and free will. The very title of Bossuet's treatise, *On the Knowledge of God and of Oneself*, recalls St. Augustine's two primary objects of knowledge: 'God and my soul'. His definition of the soul as 'an intelligent substance born to live in a body and be intimately united with it' recalls St. Augustine's 'a substance participating in reason and adapted to ruling the body'.[2] Similarly Fénelon, in his treatise *On the Existence of God* and *Letters on Various Subjects connected with Metaphysics and Religion*, reproduces St. Augustine's emphasis on the absolute dominion of the spiritual over the physical, and follows his account of sensation in terms of the soul using the body. In other aspects of his psychological analysis, Fénelon echoes the language of St. Augustine, for example in his description of memory:

> My brain is like a cabinet of pictures, which are moved and arranged at the will of the master of the house—All these images present themselves and withdraw themselves, as I please, without becoming at all confused. I call them and they come. I send them away and they conceal themselves, I know not where. They gather together or separate from one another according to my desire.[3]

Both Bossuet and Fénelon follow St. Augustine in his account of divine illumination and the interior teacher. For example, Fénelon speaks of 'those unchanging ideas, which we carry within us' and of 'the interior teacher, who causes us to be silent, speak, believe, doubt, confess our errors, confirm our judgements, and whose voice is heard from the one end of the universe to the other'.[4] Similarly Bossuet aligns himself with St.

[1] The latter by J. F. Nourisson, *op. cit.*, p. 250.

[2] Augustine, *The Greatness of the Soul* 22: '*Substantia quaedam rationis particeps, regendo corpori accommodata.*'

[3] Fénelon, *Treatise on the Existence of God* i, 2.

[4] J. F. Nourisson, *op. cit.*, pp. 243–4; Fénelon, *loc. cit.*

Augustine rather than Plato, in declaring that the universal ideas have no existence independently of the mind of God; they are 'either of God or rather God himself'.[1]

Bossuet and Fénelon wrestle with the difficult facts of free will, predestination and grace, and both follow St. Augustine in emphasising the freedom of the human will. Fénelon sees this freedom as a self-evident truth and calls on St. Augustine as witness of this:

> Every man in his right senses who consults with himself and listens to himself carries within himself an unconquerable confidence in favour of this freedom—Here, says St. Augustine, is a truth, for the illumination of which man does not need to plumb the reasonings given in books. Nature cries out this fact to us. It is imprinted within our hearts by the liberality of Nature.[2]

Correspondingly, Bossuet concludes that the two propositions of the perfect foreknowledge of God and the freedom of man's will are 'like two ends of a chain, although one cannot see the middle part by which the chain is rendered complete'.[3] Like St. Augustine, he feels that the secret of the connection between the two ends may be forever hidden from man, but he never doubts that the connection actually exists. This faith, which emphasises the responsibility of the individual for his own choices, provides the ground of optimism as to the educability of man and the efficacy of teaching. Fortunately it was this profitable and human optimism rather than the bleakness of Jansenism which exerted the major influence on the educational thinking of seventeenth-century France.

Nicholas Malebranche, sometimes known as France's second metaphysician and a lover of the contemplative life, joined the Oratorians in 1660 at the age of 22. His philosophy, linked with the development of Cartesian rationalism and with the Jansenism of the Oratory and Port Royal, was much concerned with the body–soul problem, in which he followed and elaborated the

[1] Bossuet, *On the Knowledge of God,* quoted by J. F. Nourisson, *op. cit.*, p. 255.

[2] Fénelon, *Letters on Metaphysics* 2; J. F. Nourisson, *op. cit.*, p. 254.

[3] Bossuet, *Treatise on the Free Will* 4.

occasionalist explanation of Arnold Geulincx (1625–69).[1] Geulincx had concluded that in view of the different natures of body and mind there could be no possibility of direct interaction between the two. Yet experience constantly suggests that the mind does respond to the promptings of the body and vice versa. Malebranche, agreeing with Geulincx, saw the solution of the dilemma in terms of a continual intervention of God in the stream of experience. Mind and body are indirectly linked through God, who becomes the one cause of the movements both of the body and of the mind. This divine intervention explains the correspondence of mental and physical events.

Malebranche expresses his debt to St. Augustine for helping him to find this explanation of a puzzling problem:

> The infinite distance, which exists between God and the mind of man does not prevent man being united immediately and in some very intimate way to God—It is through this union that man receives his life, his light and all his joy. St. Augustine speaks to us in a thousand places in his works of this union as being the most natural and most necessary to the mind.[2]

Through such reasoning Malebranche reached the ontological conclusion that man sees truth in God, i.e., that man is able to look directly on God and in Him has an immediate intuition of truth. We have already discussed this interpretation of St. Augustine's doctrine of divine illumination and shown that it is at variance with Augustine's repeated assertion that man cannot look upon God directly. Malebranche recognised that he was stretching St. Augustine at this point, but thought that Augustine had recoiled from the intuitionist explanation because he imagined it to be perilously near pantheism, which identifies God with His creatures. Malebranche argued that the mystical union of the soul with God does not necessarily carry with it the

[1] On Geulincx and occasionalism see R. A. Tsanoff, *The Great Philosophers*, (Harper, N.Y., 1953), pp. 305–6. Tsanoff defines occasionalism as follows: 'On the occasion of certain bodily changes God causes my mind to have certain ideas and on the occasion of certain ideas in my mind He causes certain actions to be performed. This is the doctrine of occasional causes or occasionalism.'

[2] Malebranche, preface to *De la Recherche de la Vérité*; J. F. Nourisson, *op. cit.*, pp. 227–8.

notion of the identity of the Creator and the creature. In the Preface to this *Recherche de la Vérité*, Malebranche acknowledges his debt to Augustine for his account of the nature of the universal ideas or eternal reasons of things. But he concludes that Augustine's principles necessarily suggest the conclusion that 'it is in God that we see corporeal things'.[1]

In the same work Malebranche follows St. Augustine in talking of 'the light of truth which lighteneth all the world'.[2] Again, in establishing the distinction between soul and body, he refers the reader to specific passages in Augustine's treatises on *The Trinity* and *The Greatness of the Soul*, as well as to the *Meditations* of Descartes.[3] His account of memory and imagination follows closely the famous passage in the tenth book of the *Confessions*, which we examined in an earlier chapter.[4] Furthermore he quotes with approval St. Augustine's conception of the principle of divine order as basic to all moral theory:

> The eternal law, says St. Augustine, is that everything exists in perfect order—*ut omnia sint ordinatissima*.[5]

The influence of Malebranche's reinterpretation of Augustine in these respects was considerable. Augustine became controversial, and this brought into being, in France and beyond, a large number of admirers and disciples of his ideas. Through the writings of Malebranche Augustinianism penetrated into all the religious orders, including the Benedictines and Jesuits, and spread abroad to Italy and England. This widespread respect was summed up by Michel-Ange Fardella of Sicily in the preface of a work designed to support the spirituality of the soul against the materialists: to defend St. Augustine, he declared, is to defend truth:

> As I pondered over the excellent and admirable books of the Bishop of Hippo, it became perfectly clear to me that no

[1] Malebranche, *ibid.*: '*Je soutiens que suivant les principes de St. Augustin on est obligé de dire que c'est en Dieu qu 'on voit les corps.*' *Supra* p. 127.

[2] Malebranche, *op. cit.* iii, 2, 6.

[3] *ibid.* i, 10.

[4] *ibid.* ii, 1, 5. *Supra*, pp. 88–96.

[5] Malebranche, *Réflexions sur la Prémotion Physique,* quoted by J. F. Nourisson, *op. cit.*, p. 232.

other Christian and philosopher has more correctly or thoroughly examined the affections of the human mind than the most clear-sighted Augustine. Looking at the understanding soul not from the outside but as it were within its deepest recesses, he has shown that it is immaterial and eternal—and he has established this by the strongest arguments.[1]

ST. AUGUSTINE AND THE MODERN WORLD

The intellectual activity of seventeenth-century France presents the last clearly defined example of the impact of St. Augustine on the thinking of an age. The fine harmony of faith and reason then achieved was followed by the extreme emphasis on reason characteristic of the Age of Enlightenment. To find the more subtle traces of St. Augustine in the nineteenth and twentieth centuries would require a philosophical and theological analysis beyond the specifically educational purpose of this book. Our modern world does not so obviously display the influence of Augustine in its modes of thought and educational outlook; in fact it might appear to have turned away from the path he mapped out and to look upon education in the practical terms of science rather than the idealistic framework of wisdom. Nevertheless, the vitality of St. Augustine's thought is such that its influence can be traced in more or less devious and subtle ways. It breaks through at moments when the achievements of scientific knowledge seem less than sufficient to lead man to the happy life, which Augustine defined in terms of wisdom and love. This continuing influence of the Augustinian reaction to life has been traced along very many paths by the contributors to the *Monument to St. Augustine*, published in 1930 on the fifteenth centenary of his death, and to the International Augustinian Congress held in 1954 to mark the sixteenth centenary of his birth.[2]

The most representative philosophies of modern times, beginning with the early-nineteenth-century positivism of Auguste Comte (1798–1857), are characterised by their rejection

[1] J. F. Nourisson, *op. cit.*, pp. 236–7.

[2] *Monument to St. Augustine* (London, Sheed and Ward, 1930). *Actes et Communications du Congrès International Augustinien* (Paris, Études Augustiniennes, 1954).

of absolute standards and fixed ends. They tend to focus attention on St. Augustine's 'rational knowledge of temporal things', excluding the supposedly untenable notion of more significant understandings reached by the way of purely interior thought.

Of these relativist philosophies the most educationally influential has been pragmatism. This philosophy is closely identified with the educational thinking of the American, John Dewey (1859–1952), the father of modern progressive education, the year of whose birth coincided with the publication of three landmarks in the progress of modern scientific realism: Charles Darwin's *Origin of Species*, Karl Marx' *Critique of Political Economy* and Herbert Spencer's essay, *What Knowledge is of Most Worth?* Pragmatism exalts the scientific method to a position of dominance in all human enquiry, makes light of the distinction between the theoretical (*sapientia*) and the practical (*scientia*), and rejects absolute truths, described by Dewey as 'general answers supposed to have a universal meaning that covers and dominates all particulars'; by the pragmatic test absolutes are found to be useless: 'They do not assist enquiry; they close it.'[1] In rejecting final ends as the aim of education, pragmatism interprets learning in terms, which apply equally to the lowest as well as the highest forms of organic life; learning occurs only through a continual interaction with the social and physical environment:

> Education is that reconstruction or reorganisation of experience, which adds to the meaning of experience and which increases the ability to direct the course of subsequent experience.[2]

Pragmatism is a philosophy which professes to come down to earth in a search for more realistic and useful answers to the problems posed by an age of rapid social change.

However, the pragmatic emphasis has not gone without its critics, who have reasserted the importance of the education of the intellect and the spirit, and the significance of long-term

[1] J. Dewey, *Reconstruction in Philosophy*, (Mentor Books, N.Y., 1950), ch. 8, p. 149.

[2] J. Dewey, *Democracy and Education*, (Macmillan, N.Y., 1929), ch. 6, pp. 89–90.

objectives and eternal truths. 'In the absence of a clear ideal,' says R. M. Hutchins, one of the most outspoken critics of pragmatism, 'and one that is attainable through education, the pedagogical problem is insoluble.'[1] This points back in the direction of St. Augustine.

Thus in the melting pot of present-day educational thinking, there are two distinct trends at work, a progressive and a conservative. On the one hand, there are those, who, with William James, profess to find 'a sense of joyous adventure' in participating in a world 'not certain to be saved—growing not integrally but piecemeal by the contribution of its several parts', a world 'fundamentally pluralistic and irrational';[2] or who, like Bertrand Russell, see scientific knowledge as the sum total of all knowledge, and thought in terms of 'clarifying the fundamental ideas of the sciences and synthesising the different sciences into a single comprehensive view of that fragment of the world that science has succeeded in exploring'.[3] On the other hand, there are those whom William James classed as of a more 'tender-minded' disposition, who proclaim the truth of his admission that 'our esteem for facts has not neutralised in us all religiousness'.[4] Their educational thinking focuses on the tried and tested wisdom of the past, and they regard this wisdom as the essential knowledge, which man must come to possess if he is to live the good life. These 'essentialists' proclaim that, in times of rapid change and successive crises, there is a particularly strong need for what Augustine called 'the eternal lights of the virtues'. By contrast with the pragmatists' joyous acceptance of the uncertainty of the present, the essentialists stress man's need for the solid support of the slowly gathered store of wisdom, which is man's heritage, at least from his human past, if not from God. One of the earliest statements of this viewpoint in reaction against the Deweyan experimentalist approach to education was voiced in the mid-thirties by the American, W. C. Bagley, in *Education and Emergent Man:*

[1] R. M. Hutchins, *Some Observations on American Education*, (Cambridge University Press, 1956), p. 31.

[2] Wm. James, *Pragmatism*, (Longmans Green, N.Y., 1907), pp. 290–91.

[3] B. Russell, *Sceptical Essays, Philosophy in the 20th Century*, (Unwin Books, London, 1960), p. 54.

[4] Wm. James, *op. cit.*, pp. 14–15.

It is the most conservative functions of education that are most significant in a period of profound change—the very time to avoid chaos in schools is when something akin to chaos characterises the social environment. The very time to emphasise in the schools the values that are relatively certain and stable is when the social environment is full of uncertainty and when standards are crumbling.[1]

Almost twenty years later, Sir Richard Livingstone in post-war England diagnosed the ills of our century in terms of 'intellectual and spiritual disorder' and 'a creeping paralysis of moral standards'.[2] We have seen that St. Augustine judged his own age of decadence and crisis in similar terms, holding that human progress cannot rest on any view of truth as hypothetical or uncertain, but must be based on the continual interpretation of the situations of life in the light of eternal truth. One of the most recent contributions to the philosophy of education, P. H. Phenix' *Education and the Common Good*, published in 1961, has made yet another defence of the Augustinian against the pragmatic, experimentalist standpoint: 'Truth is not something that is fashioned in response to human wants. It is not created but discovered. Truth is what is so, whether or not anyone wills it.'[3] Previously in his *Philosophy of Education* (1958) he had also clearly expressed St. Augustine's basic principle of education: 'Love constitutes a basic criterion for the educative process'.[4]

This last statement points to the notion that men grow as persons in their understanding of the realities of existence in and through the enrichment of personal relationships. This significant aspect of Augustinianism has come to the fore in the

[1] W. C. Bagley, *Education and Emergent Man*, (Nelson, N.Y., 1935), pp. 154–5.

[2] R. Livingstone, *Education and the Spirit of the Age*, (Oxford University Press, 1952), p. 22.

[3] P. H. Phenix, *Education and the Common Good*, (Harper, N.Y., 1961), p. 35. Contrast the pragmatic view of truth from J. Dewey, *Reconstruction in Philosophy*, p. 129: 'The hypothesis that works is the true one; and truth is an abstract noun applied to the collection of cases, actual, foreseen and desired, that receive confirmation in their works and consequences.'

[4] P. H. Phenix, *Philosophy of Education* (Holt, Rinehardt & Winston, N.Y., 1958), pp. 207–8.

work of the Christian existentialists, among them Soren Kierkegaard in the nineteenth century, Nicholas Berdyaev, the Catholic Gabriel Marcel and the Protestant Martin Buber in the twentieth.[1]

Kierkegaard's thought expressed a revolt against the objective trends and system building, associated with Thomism but also characteristic of Descartes, which reached its climax in the dialectic of Hegel. From such trends, which postulate an observer standing outside the process and examining it critically from an impersonal stand-point, there can come only the empirical knowledge associated with the scientist. The Christian existentialist condemns such an approach as essentially soulless and therefore insufficient; it neglects the most significant approach to knowledge, which comes through involvement in personal relationship rather than through scientific method and cold facts. Thus Kierkegaard states that Descartes' '*cogito ergo sum*' (I think and therefore I exist) reverses the knowledge process which ought to read '*Sum ergo cogito*' (I exist and therefore I think). This is, as we have already shown, the precise difference between Descartes' and St. Augustine's formulations of a superficially similar viewpoint on the foundations of certainty.[2] Augustine asserts that the guarantee of one's personal existence lies in the assurance that we 'live and will and think', that is that we are personally involved in reality. In this respect, therefore, the existentialists reflect very clearly the interiority characteristic of Augustine's approach to knowledge.[3] With St. Augustine too they declare that man cannot be known by scientific examination alone, which must fall short of explaining his existence in its full depth and significance.

Thus the existentialist, or personalist, philosophy of such acknowledged Christians as Kierkegaard reasserts the Augustinian principle that there is not one way of knowing but two.

[1] On the existentialist (something known as 'personalist') philosophers, see F. C. Coppleston, *Contemporary Philosophy*, (Burns and Oates, London, 1956), chs. ix–xii. Also S. J. Curtis, *Introduction to the Philosophy of Education*, (University Tutorial Press, London, 1958), pp. 81–9.

[2] *supra*, pp. 131–3 and 296–8.

[3] Thus F. C. Coppleston, *op. cit.*, p. 130, says of Marcel, as it can equally be said of Augustine, that 'his philosophy is the expression of, or rather that it is part and parcel of, his own spiritual itinerary'.

There is the objective way characteristic of science and applicable to the causes and effects of the physical world. But there is also the more significant and revealing way of knowing, that is the inward way characterised by the intimate and personal involvement of a spiritual being with a spiritual object of knowledge. It is the distinction between the standpoint of the impartial, uninvolved spectator on the one hand and the actor or participant on the other. Coppleston puts the existentialist viewpoint in words very reminiscent of St. Augustine:

> The problem considered by the philosopher presents itself to him as one which arises out of his own personal existence as an individual human being, who freely shapes his destiny but who seeks clarification in order to be able to do so.[1]

Thus the Christian existentialists see the true meaning of existence in terms of personal relationship, and declare that the truth of relationship must always elude the methods of the scientist. As St. Augustine finds the explanation of life in terms of a close and dynamic relationship between the two primary objects of knowledge—'God and my soul'—so Gabriel Marcel and Martin Buber find it in the living relationship of persons, which finds its warranty and explanation in the love of God for man.[2] Buber expresses this truth of relationship in terms of the primary word 'I-Thou', and is in the closest harmony with the spirit of St. Augustine when he talks of human relationship as 'the real simile of the relationship with God', and declares that 'the extended lines of relations meet in the eternal Thou'.[3]

It is basic to St. Augustine's view of human nature that in this life man is earth-bound, and yet in a real sense capable of initiating and directing his search for the spiritual realities, which explain the conflicting phenomena and restlessness of the physical environment. Man is a citizen of both an earthly and a heavenly city, which is to say that he is both independent of, and dependent on, the support of a power outside himself and the world of physical existence. Education, which on any view

[1] F. C. Coppleston, *op. cit.*, p. 129.

[2] See M. V. C. Jeffreys, *Mystery of Man*, (Pitman, London, 1957), p. 29.

[3] Martin Buber, *I and Thou*, (Scribner, N.Y., 2nd ed., 1958), pp. 103 and 75.

should lead man to a knowledge of himself, must recognise this dual aspect of man. M. V. C. Jeffreys, a notable contributor to a religiously orientated approach to education, expresses the Augustinian view, when he stresses the two elements of dependence and independence, which coexist in man's nature: Man is 'a creature who needs redemption'; he has to learn 'how to expose himself to grace', and he can do this only through the deliberate and unprejudiced self-analysis which St. Augustine himself practised.[1] Like Augustine, Jeffreys sees love as the focal point of human self-sufficiency: 'Since persons grow as persons by loving and being loved', therefore man needs above all the experience of divine love playing on him.[2] Jeffreys therefore shares St. Augustine's conviction that an unbiased examination of the personal leads to a reality, which transcends the temporal conditions of human life and in which alone the contradictory elements in human nature can be perfectly reconciled. This is to repeat St. Augustine's two stages of knowledge: first a knowledge of the self and then a knowledge of God.

In the educational thinking characteristic of such religiously orientated twentieth-century thinkers as M. V. C. Jeffreys there is a reappraisal of the doctrine of man's original sin. The heat of the Pelagian controversy had led St. Augustine to talk of human nature as essentially depraved, an attitude, which, as we have already noted, sits uneasily with the educational optimism of his earlier writings. In fact the more rigorous interpretations of this doctrine have done educational harm, as for example in John Calvin's description of infancy as 'a seed bed of sin' and therefore 'odious and abominable to God'.[3]

Modern reinterpretations of the doctrine of original sin are less rigorous, but do not minimise its fundamental importance as a basic fact of human nature. It is felt that, along with a proper optimism as to the heights to which man can rise in his own strength, there must go an equal appreciation of man's weakened nature and his need of the support of his Creator. If this be so, then an important function of education is to lead the student to a just appreciation of his condition and his need. Jeffreys makes a clear distinction between a sense of sin and a sense of guilt; the

[1] M. V. C. Jeffreys, *Glaucon*, (Pitman, London, 1950), p. 21.
[2] *ibid.*, p. 19.
[3] J. Calvin, *Institutes* ii, 1, 8.

latter is associated with Jansenism and is educationally disastrous; the former is the beginning of man's salvation:

> Guilt is a morbid condition, which psychology can help to resolve; but man remains in sin so long as he indulges the illusion of self-sufficiency, for the sense of sin is essentially the recognition of that conflict in man as a creature at odds with himself.[1]

The reassertion of man's fallen nature and his need for redemption through love has been briefly but expressively put in an appendix to his book, *Freedom in the Educative Society*, by the late Sir Fred Clarke, who had a great admiration for St. Augustine's views on education. Clarke noted that years of experience and reflection had served only to confirm his view that 'of all the needs of democracy some abiding sense of the reality of original sin may yet prove to be the greatest'. Clarke's professed aim in his educational thinking was one with which Augustine would surely have agreed, namely 'to reach a philosophy of education that will cover all the facts as we now understand them'. Such a realistic objective brought Clarke, as it did St. Augustine, to the conclusion that the issue of original sin is crucial:

> The idea, so far from being an outmoded theological invention, has been found to be a necessary one forced upon us by reflection upon our own humanity and upon our efforts to live this life as befits human beings.[2]

The most important contribution, which the philosophy of education may make to our modern age of doubt and crisis, may be found in a renewed attempt to bring man to an understanding of his true nature. What is required for this may be a new synthesis of the old and the new, as St. Augustine himself brought together old ways of thinking with the new Christian insight. A good example of the possibilities of such a synthesis is to be found in the writings of William James (1842–1910), the American philosopher and psychologist, one of the early advocates of pragmatism and yet one who retained and expressed

[1] M. V. C. Jeffreys, *op. cit.*, pp. 22–3.

[2] F. Clarke, *Freedom in the Educative Society*, (University of London Press, 1947), p. 97.

in his writings, a genuine religious feeling. We have already recalled his statement that 'our esteem for facts has not neutralised in us all religiousness'.[1] While distinguishing between the 'tough-minded' (i.e. pragmatic) outlook and the 'tender-minded' (i.e. idealistic) outlook, James demonstrated in his own personality and writings the truth of his assertion that the two outlooks are always commingled in different proportions in every person. In his *Pragmatism* (1907), James applied the pragmatic test to the hypothesis that God exists, and concluded that 'whatever the residual difficulties may be, experience shows that it certainly does work'.[2] His much earlier essay, *The Will to Believe* (1897) is a declaration of the inadequacy, in relation to the most important issues of human life, of the coldly scientific attitude of absolute suspension of belief until there is sufficient evidence to satisfy the reason. Situations of real life often demand that we commit ourselves to a belief without waiting until we are absolutely sure of its grounds. Consequently, James described his essay as 'An Essay in justification of faith, a defence of our right to adopt a believing attitude in religious matters, in spite of the fact that our merely logical intellect may not have been coerced'.[3] He holds that 'in truths dependent on our personal action, faith based on desire is certainly a lawful and possibly an indispensable thing'.[4] This notion of faith as the precondition upon which the attainment of certain truths, including religious truths, becomes possible, is a compelling modern restatement of St. Augustine's principle that faith must precede understanding. 'Faith in a fact can help create the fact'[5] is James' equivalent of St. Augustine's, 'You must believe in order that you may understand'. Thus St. Augustine's commitment to a religious explanation of life is by no means a dead letter, even among our modern scientific thinkers. Once again, to adopt the terminology of William James, the hypothesis that God exists and that the knowledge of Him is an important objective of education is still a 'live hypo-

[1] *Supra*, p. 306.

[2] Wm. James, *Pragmatism*, p. 299.

[3] Wm. James, *The Will to Believe*, (Longmans Green, N.Y., 1905), pp. 1–2.

[4] Wm. James, *op. cit.*, p. 25.

[5] Wm. James, *loc. cit.* Also *op. cit.*, p. 62: 'Believe that life is worth living, and your belief will create the fact.'

thesis',[1] defined as 'one which appeals as a real possibility to him to whom it is proposed'.

In these ways the lines of communication between St. Augustine and the modern world, with its educational problems of unprecedented magnitude, are real and meaningful. Maurice Blondel, writing on the fifteenth centenary of Augustine's death portrays the irresistibility and continuing flow of his thought under the metaphor of 'a great living stream' which 'still preserves its own name, its freshness, its impetuosity, its seminal virtues, its dynamic fertilising energy'.[2] If this is so, then every new plumbing of its depths must bring up fresh examples of its timeless quality or (if one prefers it) its modernity. One particular example of this may be used to illustrate the point: It has been noted by John-Baptist Reeves, writing on the same occasion as Maurice Blondel, that St. Augustine's penetrating self-analysis in the *Confessions* 'has anticipated our modern civilisation even so far as to provide us with his own psychoanalysis, upon which he built a whole philosophy'.[3]

In spite of this, twentieth-century writers on education have been guilty of some neglect of St. Augustine's thought. Few modern text books on the theory of education give him more than a passing mention. Thus, for example, J. S. Brubacher's *A History of the Problems of Education* (2nd edition, 1966) has eight references to St. Thomas and only one brief reference to St. Augustine. Theorists, who start from a religious ground, both Protestant and Catholic, deal more thoroughly with the influence of St. Thomas than with St. Augustine: The Catholic, Jacques Maritain, in *Education at the Crossroads* (1943) makes mention of St. Thomas but not of St. Augustine; the Protestant, J. D. Butler, in his *Four Philosophies and their Practice in Education and Religion* (1957) indulges in a thorough analysis of St. Thomas but has only five passing references to St. Augustine. The general neglect of the resources of St. Augustine is doubtless due, in part at least, to the more dramatic impact and greater tidiness of St. Thomas' system, a fact which originally contributed to the adoption of St. Thomas rather than St.

[1] Wm. James, *op. cit.*, pp. 2–3.

[2] M. Blondel, 'Latent Resources of Augustinianism', in *Monument to St. Augustine*, pp. 320–21.

[3] John-Baptist Reeves, *St. Augustine and Humanism*, *op. cit.*, p. 137.

Augustine as the architect of the doctrinal system of the Roman Catholic Church.

FINAL ASSESSMENT

The study of an educational thinker, who lived at a period so remote from our atomic age, is doubly justified, if he not only sheds light on the times he lived in, but also transcends their confines to make a contribution of enduring significance. The study of St. Augustine's theory is rewarding on both these grounds. It is rooted in the educational experiences of his own personal life, and also in the dilemmas and controversies of the times he lived in; out of this total, dynamic context he draws lessons that are of permanent relevance to educators. The whole tendency of his life and thought is a testimony to the value of intellectual education in the life of man. His picture of education as a laborious journey of the soul, inspired by love and hope, is unique in the literature of education. So also the spiritual serenity (*beatitudo*), which emerges as the supremely significant quality of the educated person, is an eloquent statement of the ideal of human culture in any age. Its effect is greatly heightened, because it is based on penetrating reflection on the hard-won lessons of the author's living experience.

St. Augustine emphasises that education reaches its climax, when the individual learner commits himself to a value system. Commitment does not imply the easy, unthinking acceptance of the statements of authority; it is the culmination of a long and laborious effort of the will in searching and finding. St. Augustine's own intellectual and spiritual growth can be cited as an excellent example of the student and teacher, who has established his own beliefs by a personal effort of rational enquiry and who for that reason desires to encourage a similar effort in his pupils. Thus, although St. Augustine's educational suggestions have most appeal to those who stress the centrality of supernatural religion, it can be said that in his thinking about education there is no evidence of the closed mind nor any lack of encouragement to critical thought. Life will not be 'happy' (*beata*), until by his own effort the individual person learns to love what ought to be loved and shun the unlovely. It is not surprising that such a basic truth of Augustinianism slips out into the light in some of our most notable twentieth-century contributions to education theory, even when St. Augustine himself is not cited as the source. For example, Sir T. Percy Nunn's educational classic, *Education: Its Data and First Principles*, contains the following: 'It is an ancient and profound truth that education should teach men to love and to hate the right things.'[1]

St. Augustine's advice to educators derives its realism from his perceptive understanding of human nature. Nourisson, whose analysis of St. Augustine, written a century ago, is still one of the most sensitive, attributes the permanency of St. Augustine's thought to this psychological understanding:

> The thought of St. Augustine is constantly nourished at the living source of psychology. Thus, when everything is taken into account, the Bishop of Hippo is an eminent philosopher because he remains a psychologist of the first rank.[2]

This clear insight into the human condition enabled St. Augustine to reconcile the apparent contradictions inherent in human nature and so make the purposeful forward movement of education possible. He recognised that man must always be subject to authority, while at the same time he must necessarily always be free. St. Augustine was sensitive to the important distinction between liberty and licence, and represented the discipline of learning as the supreme example of liberty directed with concentrated effort to the highest ends.

Finally, St. Augustine presents a high ideal of teaching as a task of basic human significance. The teacher 'offers himself for imitation',[3] and therefore must openly display in himself those qualities, which his pupils must develop, if they are to become successful students. Among these qualities is a love of knowledge and of mankind, combined with intellectual enthusiasm and integrity. In other words the teacher must be a philosopher, if he is to be able to lead others to an enjoyment of the good life.

If it seems strange to modern ears that teachers should be

[1] T. P. Nunn, *Education: Its Data and First Principles*, (Arnold, London, 3rd ed. 1945; first published, 1920), p. 184.

[2] J. F. Nourisson, *La Philosophie de St. Augustin*, p. 453.

[3] *On Music* i, 6.

philosophers, it is because we have ceased to define education in comprehensive terms but have narrowed it down to subject specialisms, pedagogical techniques and examination grind. Failure to sustain a liberal approach to education robs education of the spontaneous enthusiasm characteristic of the seminars at Cassiciacum or the Socratic dialogues of Plato. It is this constriction of the process of education, which inspired A. N. Whitehead's criticism of modern education: 'In schools of antiquity philosophers aspired to impart wisdom; in modern colleges our humbler aim is to teach subjects'.[1] A similar impression of inadequacy led T. P. Nunn to deplore 'the weakening of individuality, the chilling of enthusiasm, the disillusion, that so often attends the progress of a boy through a school'.[2] St. Augustine is a great teacher, because he sets the general function of the teacher above his specialised task. He owes his allegiance, as all great teachers have done, not to a subject but to truth; he educates not for examinations but for the simple joy and advantage of understanding the reasons of things. To a world, which is always inclined to undervalue the teacher's contribution to society, St. Augustine says that education is an absolutely good thing and of supreme value; by contrast ignorance is always bad: 'To do evil is simply to stray away from education'.[3] It follows that anyone who properly claims the title of 'teacher' must be a good man, since nobody can profess what is supremely good and at the same time be evil in his heart. Therefore, to talk of an evil teacher is to indulge in a contradiction in terms:

> Do not look for an evil teacher. If a man is evil, he is not a teacher. If he is a teacher, he is not evil.[4]

This is the high conception of teaching, which St. Augustine presents as a guide-post to the modern world groping for moral direction amid social change and technological invention. Our age requires more urgently than ever the services of teachers

[1] A. N. Whitehead, *The Aims of Education and other Essays*, (Ernest Benn, London, 1962), ch. 3, p. 45.

[2] T. P. Nunn, *op. cit.*, p. 247.

[3] *The Free Will* i, 2: '*Male facere nihil est nisi a disciplina deviare.*'

[4] *ibid.* i, 3: '*Quapropter desine velle investigare nescio quem malum doctorem. Si enim malus est, doctor non est; si doctor est, malus non est.*'

possessed of that broad, well integrated knowledge, which St. Augustine called 'wisdom' or 'philosophy', and which clearly proclaims the supreme value of the trained intelligence of man:

> Far be it that we should believe without receiving or asking for a reason. For we should not even be capable of belief, unless we possessed rational minds.[1]

[1] *Letter* 120, 3.

Conspectus

Life and Selected Writings of St. Augustine

The dating of the events in the life of St. Augustine follows P. Courcelle, *Recherches sur les Confessions de St. Augustin* (1950) and V. J. Bourke, *Augustine's Quest for Wisdom* (1944). The chronology of the writings of St. Augustine follows H. Marrou, *St. Augustin et Augustinisme* (1956) and V. J. Bourke, *op. cit.*

The 'P.L.' references are to volumes of Migne, *Patrilogia Latina*, vols. 32–47 of which are devoted to the writings of St. Augustine. Reference is also made to Possidius' *Life of St. Augustine* in P.L. 32, pp. 33–6.

A.D.	CHILDHOOD AND YOUTH (*Tagaste—Madaura—Carthage*)
354	Born at Tagaste.
?365–369	Studied Grammar at Madaura (*Confessions* ii, 3, 5)
369–370	Spent a year in idleness at Tagaste (*Confessions* ii, 3, 6)
370–373	Studied Rhetoric at Carthage (*Confessions* ii, 3, 5)
373	Conversion to philosophy through reading Cicero's *Hortensius* (*Confessions* iii, 4, 7: *Soliloquies* i, 17: *The Happy Life*, 4)
	Enrolled as an auditor in the sect of the Manichaeans (*Confessions* iii, 6, 10)
	SECULAR TEACHER (*Carthage—Rome—Milan*)
373–374	Taught Grammar at Tagaste (*Confessions* iv, 4, 7)
374–383	Taught Rhetoric at Carthage (*Confessions* v, 7, 13)
	Wrote *On the Fair and the Fitting* (*De Pulchro et Apto*) (*Confessions* iv, 13, 20). This book was lost.
383	Introduced to the Manichaean Bishop Faustus (*Confessions* v, 3, 3)
383–384	Taught Rhetoric at Rome (*Confessions* v, 8, 14)
	Abandoned Manichaeism (*Confessions* v, 14, 25)
384 (autumn)	Appointed public teacher of Rhetoric at Milan (*Confessions* v, 13, 23)
	THE END OF THE BEGINNING (*Milan—Cassiciacum—Rome—Carthage*)

385–386	Conversion to platonism through reading the 'books of the Platonists' (*Confessions* vii, 9, 13)
386	Became a catechumen in the Catholic church (*Confessions* v, 14, 25)
386 (autumn)	Conversion to christianity in the garden at Milan (*Confessions* viii, 8–12)
	Resigned his appointment as public teacher of Rhetoric (*Confessions* ix, 2, 4)
	Retired to Cassiciacum with a group of friends (*Confessions* ix, 3, 5)
	Against the Academics (*Contra Academicos*) P.L. 32.
	The Happy Life (*De Beata Vita*) P.L. 32.
	The Principle of Order (*De Ordine*) P.L. 32.
387	*The Soliloquies* (*Soliloquia*) P.L. 32.
387 (March)	Returned to Milan (*Confessions* ix, 6, 14)
	The Immortality of the Soul (*De Immortalitate Animae*) P.L. 32.
387 (lent)	Baptised by Bishop Ambrose (*Confessions* ix, 6, 14)
387–389	*On Music* (*De Musica*) P.L. 32.
387 (spring)	Left Milan for Rome (*Confessions* ix, 8, 17)
388	*The Greatness of the Soul* (*De Quantitate Animae*) P.L. 32.
388–390	*The Practices of the Catholic Church and The Practices of the Manichaeans* (*De Moribus Ecclesiae Catholicae et De Moribus Manichaeorum*) P.L. 32.
388 (autumn)	Returned to North Africa (*Letter* 126, 7)
	Set up a community at Tagaste (*Letter* 126, 7. *Possidius*, 4)
388–395	*The Free Will* (*De Libero Arbitrio*) P.L. 32.
388	*On Genesis against the Manichaeans* (*De Genesi contra Manichaeos*) P.L. 34.
389	Death of Adeodatus (*Confessions* ix, 6, 14)
?389	*The Teacher* (*De Magistro*) P.L. 32.
390	*True Religion* (*De Vera Religione*) P.L. 34.
388–395	*83 Various Questions* (*De Diversis Quaestionibus Lxxxiii*) P.L. 40.
	THE PRIEST
391	Ordained Priest at Hippo (*Letter* 126, 7)
	Set up a monastic community at Hippo (*Letter* 126, 7)
392	*Against the Manichaean Conception of Two Souls* (*Contra Manichaeos de Duabus Animabus*) P.L. 42.
394	*The Sermon of our Lord on the Mount* (*De Sermone Domini in Monte*) P.L. 35.
	BISHOP OF HIPPO
395–396	Coadjutor Bishop of Hippo (*Sermon* 339, 3)
396	Succeeded Bishop Valerius as Bishop of Hippo (*Letter* 31)

	The Christian Struggle (*De Agone Christiano*) P.L. 40.
397	*Christian Education* (*De Doctrina Christiana*) (in part) P.L. 34.
	Against the Letter of the Manichaean (*Contra Epistolam Manichaei*) P.L. 42.
	Seven Various Questions in reply to Simplicianus (*De Diversis Quaestionibus VII ad Simplicianum*) P.L. 40.
397–401	*The Confessions* (*Confessiones*) P.L. 32.
397–398	*Against Faustus the Manichaean* (*Contra Faustum Manichaeum*) P.L. 43.
399	*The Instruction of the Uninstructed* (*De Catechizandis Rudibus*) P.L. 40.
399–416	*The Trinity* (*De Trinitate*) P.L. 42.
401–414	*The Literal Interpretation of Genesis* (*De Genesi ad Litteram*) P.L. 34.
400–402	*Against the Letter of Petilian* (*Contra Litteras Petiliani*) P.L. 43.
405–406	*Against Cresconius the Donatist Grammarian* (*Contra Cresconium Grammaticum Partis Donati*) P.L. 43.
405	*On the Nature of the Good* (*De Natura Boni*) P.L. 42.
413–427	*The City of God* (*De Civitate Dei*) P.L. 41.
414	*The Excellence of Widowhood* (*De Bono Viduitatis*) P.L. 40.
415	*Letter* 166 to Jerome, On the Origin of the Soul. P.L. 33.
416–417	*Tracts on St. John's Gospel* (*In Joannis Evangelium Tractatus*) P.L. 35.
418	Visited Caesarea in Mauretania (*Letters* 190–193)
	On the Grace of Christ and Original Sin (*De Gratia Christi et Peccato Originali*) P.L. 44.
419	*The Soul and its Origin* (*De Anima et eius Origine*) P.L. 44.
	Discourses on the Heptateuch (*Locutiones in Heptateuchum*) P.L. 34.
420	*Against the Two Letters of the Pelagians* (*Contra Duas Epistolas Pelagianorum*) P.L. 44.
421	*Against Julian, Defender of the Pelagian Heresy* (*Contra Julianum Haeresis Pelagianae Defensorem*) P.L. 44.
	Enchiridion P.L. 40.
422	*The Eight Questions of Dulcitius* (*De Octo Dulcitii Quaestionibus*) P.L. 40.
425	*Grace and Free Will* (*De Gratia et Libero Arbitrio*) P.L. 44.

426	Named his Successor to the See of Hippo (*Letter* 213)
426–427	*Christian Education* (*De Doctrina Christiana*) (completed) P.L. 34.
	Reviews (*Retractationes*) P.L. 32.
428–429	*The Predestination of Saints* (*De Praedestinatione Sanctorum*) P.L. 44.
430 (May)	Hippo besieged by the Vandals (*Possidius* 29)
(August)	Death of St. Augustine (*Possidius* 31)
386–430	*Letters* (*Epistulae*) P.L. 33. (270 in number chronologically arranged by the Benedictine editors in four books: book 1, A.D. 386–395; book 2, A.D. 396–410; book 3, A.D. 411–430; book 4, undated letters.
391–430	*Sermons* (*Sermones*) (arranged in groups according to topics) P.L. 38 & 39.
391–430	*Expositions of the Psalms* (*Enarrationes in Psalmos*) P.L. 36 & 37.

Note: The probably spurious treatises *On Grammar* (*De Grammatica*), *Principles of Dialectic* (*Principia Dialectica*) and *Principles of Rhetoric* (*Principia Rhetorices*) are printed in the Appendix to vol. 32 of Migne's *Patrilogia Latina*, cols. 1383 ff.

Bibliography

I. THE WRITINGS OF ST. AUGUSTINE

(a) *The Latin Text*. The works of St. Augustine are printed in Migne's *Patrilogia Latina*, 1841–2, of which 16 volumes (32–47) are devoted to St. Augustine.

The distribution of the works in Migne is set out below. Only works mentioned in this book are noted. Reference is made to the volume of Migne and to the column in which the text begins:

VOLUME	TITLE OF WORK
Vol. 32	*Retractationes* (583)
	Confessiones (659)
	Soliloquia (869)
	Contra Academicos (905)
	De Beata Vita (959)
	De Ordine (977)
	De Immortalitate Animae (1021)
	De Quantitate Animae (1035)
	De Musica (1081)
	De Magistro (1193)
	De Libero Arbitrio (1221)
	De Moribus Ecclesiae Catholicae et De Moribus Manichaeorum (1310)
	APPENDIX
	De Grammatica (1383)
	Principia Dialectica (1409)
	Principia Rhetorices (1439)
Vol. 33	*Epistolae* (62)
Vol. 34	*De Doctrina Christiana* (15)
	De Vera Religione (121)
	De Genesi contra Manichaeos (173)
	De Genesi ad Litteram, liber imperfectus (219)
	De Genesi ad Litteram (245)
	Locutiones in Heptateuchum (485)
Vol. 35	*Quaestiones Evangelicae* including
	In Ioannis Evangelium Tractatus (1379)
	De Sermone Domini in Monte (1229)

Vols. 36 & 37 *Enarrationes in Psalmos*
Vols. 38 & 39 *Sermones*
Vol. 40 *De Diversis Quaestionibus LXXXIII* (11)
De Diversis Quaestionibus VII ad Simplicianum (101)
De Octo Dulcitii Quaestionibus (147)
Contra Epistulam Manichaei (173)
Enchiridion (231)
De Agone Christiano (289)
De Catechizandis Rudibus (309)
De Bono Viduitatis (429)
Vol. 41 *De Civitate Dei*
Vol. 42 Controversial Writings against the Jews, Manichaeans, Priscillianists and Arians including
De Duabus Animabus contra Manichaeos (93)
Contra Faustum Manichaeum (207)
De Natura Boni (551)
De Trinitate (819)
Vol. 43 Controversial Writings against the Donatists including
Contra Litteras Petiliani (245)
Contra Cresconium Grammaticum (445)
Vols. 44 & 45 Controversial Writings against the Pelagians including
De Anima et eius Origine (475)
Contra Duas Epistolas Pelagianorum (550)
De Gratia Christi et de Peccato Originali (559)
Contra Julianum (641)
De Gratia et Libero Arbitrio (881)
De Praedestinatione Sanctorum (959)
Vol. 46 *Indices*
Vol. 47 *Supplementum*

(b) *Translations*

Deferrari, Roy D. (ed.), *The Authentic Writings of the Fathers of the Church* (Catholic University of America Press, Washington, D.C.):
Vol. 2 includes *Christian Instruction*, *The Christian Combat*.
Vol. 4 includes *The Immortality of the Soul*, *The Magnitude of the Soul*, *On Music*.
Vol. 5 includes *The Happy Life*, *Answer to Skeptics*, *Soliloquies*, *The Principle of Order*.
Vols. 8, 14, 24 *The City of God*.
Vols. 12, 18, 20, 30, 32 *Letters*.
Vol. 16 includes *The Excellence of Widowhood*, *The Eight Questions of Dulcitius*.

Vol. 21 *Confessions.*
Vol. 35 *Against Julian.*
Vol. 45 *The Trinity.*
Vol. 56 *The Way of Life of the Catholic Church and of the Manichaeans.*
(the series continues)

Dods, Marcus (ed.), *The Works of Aurelius Augustine* (Clark, Edinburgh, 1872–1883) including
Vols. 1, 2 *The City of God.*
Vols. 6, 13 *Letters* (selected)
Vol. 7 *The Trinity.*
Vol. 9 includes *On Christian Doctrine*, *The Enchiridion of Augustine*, *On the Catechising of the Uninstructed.*

Library of Christian Classics (S.C.M. Press, London):
Vol. 6 *Augustine: Earlier Writings*, ed. J. H. S. Burleigh (1953) includes
The Soliloquies, *The Teacher*, *On Free Will*, *Of True Religion*, *The Nature of the Good*, *To Simplician—On Various Questions, book* 1.
Vol. 7 *Augustine: Confessions and Enchiridion*, ed. A. C. Outler.
Vol. 8 *Augustine: Later Works*, ed. J. Burnaby (1955) including *The Trinity*, books 8–15.

Brown, R. A., *De Beata Vita* (*The Happy Life*), (Patristic Studies, Catholic University of America Press, Washington, D.C., 1944).

Christopher, J. P., *St. Augustine: The First Catechetical Instruction* (*De Catechizandis Rudibus*) (The Newman Bookshop, Westminster, Maryland, 1946). Translated and annotated.

Colleran, J. M., *The Greatness of the Soul and The Teacher* (Newman Press, Westminster, Maryland, 1950).

Healey, J., *The City of God* (Dent, London, 1903).

Hudleston, R., *The Confessions of St. Augustine*, the revised translation of Sir Tobie Matthew (Collins, Fontana Books, London, 1957).

Jolivet, R., de Labriolle, P., Thonnard, E. J., *Dialogues Philosophiques*, with preface by E. Gilson (Desclée de Brouwer, Paris, 1955):
Against the Academics, *The Happy Life*, *The Principle of Order*, *The Soliloquies*, *The Immortality of the Soul*, *The Greatness of the Soul*, *The Teacher*, *The Free Will*, *On Music* (book 6).

Price, Kingsley, *Education and Philosophical Thought* (Allyn and Bacon, Boston, 1962). Ch. 4 contains intro. and selections from *The Principle of Order* and *The Teacher.*

Oates, W. J., *Basic Writings of St. Augustine* (Random House, N.Y., 1948):

Vol. 1 includes *Confessions, Soliloquies, The Immortality of the Soul, The Morals of the Catholic Church, Concerning the Teacher.*

Vol. 2 *The City of God, On the Trinity* (excerpts).

Paolucci, H. (ed.), *The Political Writings of St. Augustine* (Henry Regnery, Chicago, 1962). Selections from *The City of God* and other writings.

Pryzywara, E., *An Augustine Synthesis* (Harper Torchbooks, N.Y., 1958), Excerpts from St. Augustine grouped under topics.

Robertson, D. W., *Christian Education*, with introduction (Liberal Arts Press, N.Y., 1958).

Sheed, F. J., *The Confessions* (Sheed and Ward, London, 1945).

Tourscher, F. E., *The Philosophy of Teaching*, a translation of St. Augustine's *De Magistro* (Villanova College, Pennsylvania, 1924).

Watts, W., *Confessions*, 2 vols. (Loeb Classical Library, Heinemann, London, 1919).

2. BOOKS ON ST. AUGUSTINE

Abercrombie, N., *St. Augustine and French Classical Thought* (Clarendon Press, Oxford, 1906).

Actes et Communications du Congrès International Augustinien (Études Augustiniennes, Paris, 1954).

Alfaric, Prosper, *L'Evolution intellectuale de St. Augustin*, vol. 1, *Du Manichéisme au Néoplatonisme* (Nourry, Paris, 1918).

Bardy, G., *St. Augustin, L'Homme et l'Oeuvre* (de Brouwer, Paris, 1948).

Battenhouse, R. W., *A Companion to the Study of St. Augustine* (Oxford, 1955).

Bertrand, L. M., *Saint Augustine* (Appleton, N.Y., 1914).

Bourke, V. J., *Augustine's Quest for Wisdom: Life and Philosophy of the Bishop of Hippo* (Bruce, Milwaukee, 1945).

Boyer, C., *Christianisme et néo-Platonisme dans la Formation de St. Augustin* (Catholic Book Agency, Rome, 1953).

Boyer, C., *L'Idée de Verité dans la Philosophie de St. Augustin* (Beauchesne, Paris, 1921).

Burnaby, J., *Amor Dei: A Study of the Religion of St. Augustine* (Hodder and Stoughton, London, 1938).

Cayré, F., *Initiation à la Philosophie de St. Augustin* (de Brouwer, Paris, 1947).

Combès, G., *St. Augustin et la Culture Classique* (Plon, Paris, 1927).

Courcelle, P., *Recherches sur les Confessions de St. Augustin* (de Boccard, Paris, 1950).

Cunningham, W., *St. Augustine and his Place in the History of Christian Thought* (Hulsean Lectures, 1886).

Finaert, J., *St. Augustin Rhéteur* (Société d'Edition 'Les Belles Lettres', Paris, 1939).
Finaert, J., *L'Evolution Littéraire de St. Augustin* (Société d'Edition 'Les Belles Lettres', Paris, 1939).
Gallacher, D. A., *Saint Augustine and Christian Humanism in Some Philosophers on Education*, pp. 46–66 (Marquette University Press, Milwaukee, Wisconsin, 1956).
Gilson, E., *Introduction à l'Etude de St. Augustin* (J. Vrin, Paris, 3rd ed., 1949).
Gilson, E., *The Christian Philosophy of St. Augustine*, trans. L. E. M. Lynch (Gollancz, London, 1961).
Grandgeorge, L., *St. Augustin et le Néoplatonisme* (Leroux, Paris, 1896).
Henry, P., *La Vision d'Ostie* (J. Vrin, Paris, 1938).
Henry, P., *St. Augustine on Personality* (St. Augustine Lecture Series, 1959, Macmillan, N.Y., 1960).
Marrou, H. I., *St. Augustin et la Fin de la Culture Antique* (de Boccard, Paris, 4th ed., 1958).
McCabe, J., *St. Augustine and his Age* (Putnam, London, 1903).
Montgomery, W., *St. Augustine: Aspect of his Life and Thought* (Hodder and Stoughton, London, 1914).
Monument to St. Augustine (Sheed and Ward, London, 1930). Essays on various aspects of St. Augustine's thought by prominent Augustinian scholars.
Nourisson, J. F., *La Philosophie de St. Augustin*, 2 vols. (Libraire Académique, Paris, 1865).
O'Meara, J. J., *The Young Augustine: The Growth of St. Augustine's Mind up to his Conversion* (Longmans Green, London, 1954).
Ottley, R. L., *Studies in the Confessions of St. Augustine* (London, 1919).
Pope, H., *St. Augustine of Hippo* (London, 1937).
Portalié, E., Article on St. Augustine in *Dictionnaire de Théologie Catholique*, vol. 1, cols. 2268–472; and on Augustinianism, *op. cit.*, cols. 2501–61 (Paris, 4th ed., 1931).
Rand, E. K., *Founders of the Middle Ages*, ch. 8 on St. Augustine and Dante (Harvard, 1929).
Tolley, W. P. T., *The Idea of God in the Philosophy of St. Augustine* (N.Y., 1930).
Warfield, B. B., *Calvin and Augustine* (Presbyterian and Reformed Publishing Co., Philadelphia, 1956).
Warfield, B. B., Article on Augustine in *Encyclopedia of Religion and Ethics*, vol. 2, pp. 219–24 (Clarke, Edinburgh, 1909).
West, Rebecca, *St. Augustine* (Nelson, London, 1933).

3. BOOKS ON THE CLASSICAL, PATRISTIC AND MEDIEVAL PERIODS

Abelson, P., *The Seven Liberal Arts: A Study in Medieval Culture* (Columbia University, N.Y., 1906).

Armstrong, A. H., *An Introduction to Ancient Philosophy* (Methuen, London, 2nd ed., 1949).
Armstrong, A. H., *Plotinus* (Methuen, London, 1953).
Beare, J., *Greek Theories of Elementary Cognition* (Oxford, 1906).
Bigg, C. B., *The Christian Platonists of Alexandria* (Oxford, 1913).
Burch, G. B., *Early Medieval Philosophy* (Columbia University, N.Y., 1951).
Carré, M. H., *Realists and Nominalists* (Oxford, 1946).
Clark, D. L., *Rhetoric in Graeco-Roman Education* (Oxford, 1957).
Clarke, M. L., *Rhetoric at Rome: A Historical Survey* (Cohen and West, London, 1953).
Cochrane, C. N., *Christianity and Classical Culture* (Oxford, 1940).
Cole, P. R., *Later Roman Education in Ausonius, Capella and the Theodosian Code* (Columbia University Teachers' College Contributions to Education, no. 27, N.Y., 1909).
Coppleston, F. C., *Medieval Philosophy* (Methuen, London, 1952).
Coulton, G. G., *Studies in Medieval Thought* (Nelson, London, 1946).
Curtis, S. J., *A Short History of Western Philosophy in the Middle Ages* (Macdonald, London, 1959).
Davidson, T., *Aristotle and Ancient Educational Ideals* (Heinemann, Great Educators Series, London, 1900).
Dill, S., *Roman Society in the Last Century of the Western Empire* (Macmillan, London, 2nd ed., 1899).
Drane, A. T., *Christian Schools and Scholars* (Burns and Oates, London, 1881).
Duchesne, L., *The Early History of the Christian Church*, 3 vols. (Murray, London, 1910).
Frend, W. H. C., *The Donatist Church* (Oxford, 1952).
Ghellinck, J. de, *Le Mouvement Théologique du xii*e *Siècle* (de Brouwer, Paris, 1948).
Gilson, E., *L'Esprit de la Philosophie Médiévale* (J. Vrin, Paris, 2nd ed., 1948).
Gilson, E., *Etudes sur le Rôle de la Pensée médiévale dans la Formation du Système Cartésien* (J. Vrin, Paris, 1930).
Gilson, E., *La Philosophie au Moyen Age de Scot Erigène à G. d'Occam* (Payot, Paris, 1930).
Gilson, E., *La Philosophie au Moyen Age des Origines Patristiques à la Fin du xiv*e *Siècle* (Payot, Paris, 2nd ed., 1944).
Gilson, E., *Reason and Revelation in the Middle Ages* (Scribner, N.Y., 1939).
Haarhoff, T., *Schools of Gaul: A Study of Pagan and Christian Education in the Last Century of the Western Empire* (Oxford, 1920).
Hawkins, D. J. B., *A Sketch of Medieval Philosophy* (Sheed and Ward, London, 1947).
Henry, P., *Plotin et l'Occident* (Louvain, 1934), ch. 3 on St. Augustine the Convert.
Ker, W. P., *The Dark Ages* (Mentor Books, N.Y., 1958; first published 1904).

Labriolle, P. de, *History and Literature of Christianity from Tertullian to Boethius* (Kegan Paul, London, 1924).
Leff, G., *Medieval Thought from St. Augustine to Ockham* (Pelican Book, 1958).
Marrou, H. I., *History of Education in Antiquity*, trans. G. Lamb (Sheed and Ward, London, 1956).
Monceaux, P., *Histoire Littéraire de l'Afrique Chrétienne*, 7 vols. (Paris, 1901–23).
Monroe, P., *Source Book of the History of Education*, Greek and Roman Period (Macmillan, N.Y., 1921).
Parker, H., Article on the Seven Liberal Arts in *English Historical Review*, vol. 5, pp. 417–61, 1890.
Pickman, E. N., *The Mind of Latin Christendom*, vol. 1, (A.D. 375–496) (Oxford University Press, 1937).
Roger, M., *L'Enseignement des Lettres Classiques d'Ausone à Alcuin* (Paris, 1905).
Spicer, E. E., *Aristotle's Conception of the Soul* (University of London Press, London, 1934).
Steenberghen, F. van, *The Philosophical Movement in the 13th Century* (Nelson, London, 1955).
Whittaker, T., *The Neo-Platonists: A Study in the History of Hellenism* (Cambridge, 1928).
Wicksteed, P. H., *The Reactions between Dogma and Philosophy* (The Hibbert Lecture, 1916), Williams and Norgate, London, 1920.
Wulf, M. de, *History of Medieval Philosophy, vol. 1, from the beginnings to the end of the 12th century*, trans. E. C. Messenger (Nelson, London, 1951).
Wulf, M. de, *An Introduction to Scholastic Philosophy Medieval and Modern*, trans. P. Coffey (Dover Publications, N.Y., 1956, first published 1903).

Index of Persons

Index of Topics